THE IRISH TIMES
BOOK
of the
YEAR
2007

EDITED BY
PETER MURTAGH

Gill & Macmillan

Gill & Macmillan Ltd
Hume Avenue
Park West
Dublin 12
with associated companies throughout the world
www.gillmacmillan.ie

© 2007 *The Irish Times*
978 0 7171 4 2606
Design by Identikit Design Consultants, Dublin
Print origination by Carole Lynch
Index compiled by Helen Litton
Printed by Butler & Tanner, Somerset

The paper used in this book is made from the wood pulp
of managed forests. For every tree felled, at least one tree
is planted, thereby renewing natural resources.

A catalogue record is available for this book
from the British Library.

1   3   5   4   2

Contents

Introduction

One of the final pieces in *The Irish Times Book of the Year 2006* concerned Bertie Ahern and his interview with RTÉ's Bryan Dobson in which, doe-eyed and Diana-like, the Taoiseach sought to win over the public to his version of events surrounding the various financial 'dig-outs' he received from businessmen while Minister for Finance in the mid-1990s.

A full 12 months later, the Taoiseach was still pleading his case . . . but now it was before the Mahon tribunal and the forensic cross-examination of Senior Counsel Des O'Neill. As a consequence, the closing pages of this year's *Book of the Year* are also dominated by Mr Ahern and his intriguing way with money.

The common factor is not just the Taoiseach and money. Miriam Lord's razor sharp political eye and wicked way with words grace this year's *Book of the Year*, as she did last year's, on this and several other subjects, not least the 2007 General Election which Mr Ahern and his party won handsomely.

Also bookending the 2007 edition is the matter of civil partnerships for gay people. A closely argued call for complete marital rights between gay people, written by Declan Kiberd in October 2006, is complemented by a personal celebration by one mother, writer Mary Russell, on the occasion in September 2007 of her daughter's gay civil partnership ceremony. As a debating issue and point of political and social friction, equality of treatment for gay people across all aspects of life has emerged in Ireland over the past 12 months and seems unlikely to go away.

It's been an eventful year (name one that wasn't). Pádraig Nally, the Mayo farmer who shot and killed a Traveller, running from his property after an apparent attempted break-in, walked free in December, acquitted by a jury of all charges following a re-trial. Kathy Sheridan tried to make sense of it all . . . a task she also undertook in July during the trial of Joe O'Reilly for the murder of his wife, Rachel.

Global warming started to penetrate the public consciousness, due in part to the film *An Inconvenient Truth*, narrated by Al Gore, and the rolling series of UN climate change reports, compiled by, among many other scientists, a climatologist from NUI Maynooth. This growing awareness is reflected in the fact that the Green Party now has two seats at the Cabinet table.

The whole country was numbed when two parents in Wexford murdered their children before taking their own lives, an episode they planned with almost detached, clinical precision. Again journalists – and others – tried to make sense of it.

Horror of a different kind unfolded at Virginia Tech in the US, a tragedy analysed by Denis Staunton, who later in the year wrote a chilling eyewitness account of an execution. Here in Ireland, gun crime showed little sign of diminishing, an aspect of modern life that kept crime correspondent Conor Lally busy.

Other great issues of the year were pondered by Fintan O'Toole, Breda O'Brien, John Waters and other *Irish Times* writers. Ruadhán Mac Cormaic concluded his Douglas Gageby Fellowship on migration with a fine and penetrating analysis of the changes and challenges facing Irish society.

Wit and laughter were provided not only by Miss Lord, but in large measure also by Róisín Ingle, Frank McNally, Newton Emerson, Hilary Fannin and Kilian Doyle. They've been joined of late by Ross O'Carroll-Kelly.

Abroad, our eyes on the world were those of Lara Marlowe, Denis Staunton, Paddy Agnew, Daniel McLaughlin, Clifford Coonan and Nicholas Birch.

And sport, as always, provided a heady mixture of excitement, drama, triumph and despair. Drama and triumph for Pádraig Harrington at the British Open (watched by Philip Reid); triumph for all-Ireland victors Kilkenny and Kerry (celebrated by Seán Moran and Tom Humphries); the unexpected and spirited performance of the Irish team at the Cricket World Cup, which was reported upon by Richard Gillis.

Gerry Thornley was in Croke Park for the Ireland-England game, a performance – by players and audience alike – that, as he noted, could not have been dreamt of better. And Cyril Byrne's majestic photograph of Paul O'Connell reaching high in the lineout spoke its own 1,000 words.

These events, and many more, feature on the pages that follow. They are but a small selection of what appears in our newspaper six days a week – many more hundreds of thousands of words than is possible to assemble for a compendium intended as an annual keepsake of some of the best writing in the newspaper.

As in previous years, the selection is mine and therefore displays predictable flaws – subjectivity and the consequences of difficult choices. My thanks to colleagues who made suggestions; to those who helped me dig out the material, especially willing hands on the picture desk and in engravers who helped with the photographs; and to all at Gill & Macmillan, especially Aoife O'Kelly, and my long-suffering and indulgent editor, Emma Farrell.

Peter Murtagh
The Irish Times
Tara Street
Dublin
September 2007

Journalists and Photographers

Paddy Agnew is Rome Correspondent.

John Banville is an author, former Literary Editor of *The Irish Times* and regular book reviewer for the newspaper.

Tony Bates is the founder–director of Headstrong, the national centre for youth mental health.

Eileen Battersby is Literary Correspondent.

Nicholas Birch is a correspondent based in Istanbul.

John Butler writes the Modern Moment column in the *Irish Times* Magazine.

Alan Clarke is the illustrator who has brought Ross O'Carroll-Kelly to life . . .

Donald Clarke is Film Critic and a feature writer.

Tony Clayton-Lea is a rock journalist.

Joe Cleary lectures in English at NUI Maynooth. His essay about the cultural achievement of The Pogues is in his latest book, *Outrageous Fortune: Capital and Culture in Modern Ireland* (published by Field Day), which looks at literature, theatre, film and music; drawing connections between capital, culture and criticism in modern Ireland.

Tom Clonan is *Irish Times* Security Analyst.

Marc Coleman was Economics Editor until July 2007 when he left to pursue a career elsewhere.

Stephen Collins is Political Editor.

Clifford Coonan is Beijing Correspondent.

Paul Cullen is Consumer Affairs Correspondent.

Deaglán de Bréadún is a political correspondent and colour writer.

Michael Dervan is Music Critic.

Kilian Doyle writes Emissions, a column loosely pegged to cars and driving, which appears in the Motors supplement on Wednesdays.

Keith Duggan is a sports writer.

Aidan Dunne is Art Critic.

Newton Emerson is a political satirist from Northern Ireland.

Kieran Fagan is a freelance journalist and former member of staff.

Hilary Fannin is *Irish Times* TV critic.

Seán Flynn is Education Editor.

Quentin Fottrell is a freelance writer.

Richard Gillis is Cricket Correspondent.

Miroslawa Gorecka was a student at Drogheda Grammar School and is now studying medicine at NUI Galway.

Peter Hanan is a caricaturist who draws the illustration for the Saturday Profile in Weekend Review.

Alison Healy is an *Irish Times* reporter.

Shane Hegarty is an *Irish Times* journalist and columnist.

Kitty Holland is an *Irish Times* reporter.

Kate Holmquist is a feature writer.

Ann Marie Hourihane is an *Irish Times* columnist.

Tom Humphries is chief sports feature writer and writes a weekly column, Locker Room, for Monday's sports supplement.

Róisín Ingle is a columnist and feature writer. Her column appears weekly in the *Irish Times* Magazine.

Dan Keenan is Northern News Editor.

Declan Kiberd is a professor at University College Dublin's school of English and drama and is chair of Anglo-Irish literature and drama. He is an essayist, book reviewer and regular contributor to different sections of *The Irish Times*.

Conor Lally is Crime Correspondent.

Landlord's Life, which has ceased, was written by a landlord who preferred to remain anonymous . . .

Karlin Lillington is a technology writer.

Miriam Lord is an *Irish Times* journalist specialising in political colour writing.

Ruadhán Mac Cormaic is Migration Correspondent. He was the 2007 Douglas Gageby Fellow and wrote a series of reports on the effects of migration on Ireland and the new communities that have set up home here. His series may be read in its entirety at www.ireland.com/focus/gageby. The fellowship is granted annually (on application to the Editor and following interview) to a journalist at the beginning of his/her career and is funded by the *Irish Times* Trust, proprietor of the newspaper. It is named in honour of former editor Douglas Gageby.

Frank McDonald is Environment Editor.

Patsy McGarry is Religious Affairs Correspondent.

Frank McNally writes An Irishman's Diary.

Denise McNamara is a journalist based in Galway.

David McNeill is Tokyo Correspondent.

Deirdre McQuillan is Fashion Editor.

Brendan McWilliams is a meteorologist and author of Weather Eye, a daily column on the Bulletin Page.

Lara Marlowe is Paris Correspondent of *The Irish Times* and also reports regularly from the Middle East.

John Moran is a sub-editor with *The Irish Times*.

Seán Moran is GAA Correspondent.

Gerry Moriarty is Northern Editor.

Orna Mulcahy is Property Editor.

Maurice Neligan is a cardiac surgeon who writes Heartbeat, a weekly column in the Health Supplement.

Breda O'Brien is an *Irish Times* correspondent.

Carl O'Brien is Social Affairs Correspondent.

Ross O'Carroll-Kelly is the alter ego of writer and satirist Paul Howard.

Fionnuala O'Connor is a freelance journalist based in Northern Ireland.

Barry O'Halloran is a business journalist.

Hugh Oram is a freelance writer and expert on the history of Irish newspapers.

Fintan O'Toole is an *Irish Times* columnist and commentator.

Michael Parsons is a reporter based in Kilkenny.

Jane Powers writes on gardening for the *Irish Times* Magazine.

Philip Reid is Golf Correspondent.

Mary Russell is a freelance journalist who specialises in travel writing.

Kathy Sheridan is a feature writer.

Lorna Siggins is Marine Correspondent and Western Correspondent.

Denis Staunton is Washington Correspondent of *The Irish Times*.

Gerry Thornley is Rugby Correspondent.

Orla Tinsley is an aspiring writer.

Martyn Turner's cartoons appear on the Opinion page.

John Waters is an *Irish Times* columnist.

Johnny Watterson is a sports reporter.

Noel Whelan is a barrister, political analyst and columnist in Saturday's *Irish Times*.

Photographers whose work features in this year's edition include *Irish Times* photographers Cyril Byrne, Alan Betson, Dara Mac Dónaill, Matt Kavanagh, Brenda Fitzsimons, Eric Luke, Frank Miller, Matt Kavanagh, Bryan O'Brien and David Sleator. Kate Geraghty is on secondment to *The Irish Times* from the *Sydney Morning Herald*, where her place has been taken by Bryan O'Brien.

The Irish Times Book of the Year 2007 also features the work of freelance photographers or photographers attached to Irish and international photo agencies, including: Tom Conachy; Niall Carson/Press Association; Domnick Walsh/Eye Focus; Cathal Noonan/Inpho; Win McNamee/Getty Images; the Collins agency; Stephen Hird/Reuters; RTÉ; Mickey Smith; Daragh Mac Sweeney/Provision; Julian Herbert/Getty Images; Fergal Shanahan; James Flynn/APX; Fennells agency; Akintunde Akinleye/Reuters; Guang Niu/Getty Images; Agusti Torres; Ray McManus/Sportsfile; Gareth Bentley; Eamonn Farrell/Photocall Ireland; You

Sung-Ho/Reuters; Morgan Treacy/Inpho; Pat Murphy/ Sportsfile; Garrett White/Collins Court Pictures; Deirdre Rooney; Paul Faith/Press Association; Brian Farrell; Kevin Lamarque/Reuters; Joe O'Shaughnessy; Andrew Redington/Getty Images; Dylan Vaughan; Aidan Crawley; Brendan Moran/Sportsfile; Gary O'Neill; Robbie Reynolds; Phil Noble/Reuters; Martin Rickett/Press Association; Aaron Pierce; Charles McQuillan/Pacemaker; Damien Guerchois; Dave Martin/Associated Press; Don MacMonagle; Eamonn Keogh; Michael Mac Sweeney/Provision; Mark Stedman/Photocall Ireland; Inpho/Press Sport; Christian Sinibaldi; and Cathal McNaughton/Press Association.

MONDAY, 2 OCTOBER 2006

An Apology Is Not Enough

Editorial

What a breathtaking exposition of the culture of Fianna Fáil we have witnessed in recent days. Taoiseach Bertie Ahern received some €50,000 in payments from 12 businessmen friends while he was minister for finance in 1993 and 1994. The purpose to which they were put is his own business. The whip-around, we were led to believe, was mostly in cash.

It subsequently turns out that the biggest of those payments – €5,000 – was drawn on a company cheque from NCB. And to cap it all, Mr Ahern, acting as the private man rather than the holder of the third-highest office in government, is the recipient of another whip-around – £8,000 sterling – from friends in Manchester for being the guest speaker at a function or, maybe, not speaking at all.

And current Minister for Finance Brian Cowen, who is purported to be Mr Ahern's chosen successor, says that it is 'not incorrect'. What beggars belief is that senior ministers like Mr Cowen, Dermot Ahern, Mary Hanafin, Séamus Brennan and Micheál Martin see nothing wrong in this whole episode at all. The incredulity experienced by the public at large that Fianna Fáil has learned nothing from the past 10 years of tribunals is palpable. The country is convulsed by the revelations.

Students from grade three in Sutton Park, Dublin, under a weeping ash tree during a tour of the Botanic Gardens, Glasnevin, to celebrate National Tree Day. Photograph: Alan Betson.

Seán Murphy (14) from Waterford, who is ranked third in Ireland, hits the waves during the Irish and British kitesurfing championships, which were held at Banna, Co. Kerry. Photograph: Domnick Walsh/Eye Focus.

The Taoiseach has not just let himself down, compromised the highest political office in the land, but also stunned those people outside of Fianna Fáil who had come to believe in him. He has been a good Taoiseach over the last nine years; warts and all, he has won the affection of the public; he has done significant service for this State in negotiating the Belfast Agreement, social partnership between employers and trade unions, the development of the economy and, for the first time in our history, the achievement of full employment. He has served this State well at home and abroad. Nobody wants to have his head on a plate.

But the public at large, especially those loyal Fianna Fáil people who have had to swallow more than they deserve in recent years, want accountability and standards in public life. Mr Ahern is a million miles away from where they – never mind the Progressive Democrats – want their leader to be. In an article in an English newspaper, the *News of the World*, yesterday, the Taoiseach wrote: 'I am happy to answer them [the Opposition and the PDs, presumably] because I have done nothing wrong. In the law, in ethics and in relation to tax.'

What Mr Ahern did, as minister for finance, is wrong. It may not have been outside the law at the time but it is morally wrong and ethically wrong. There is an important principle involved. There can be no separation between the private and the public actions of an individual when one is a public office-holder. There can be no whip-arounds from businessmen to sustain a personal lifestyle. And it is the failure of the Taoiseach, his Ministers and his advisers to grasp this principle that could lead to his downfall tomorrow. What he did was wrong and he must say so. An apology is not enough.

TUESDAY, 10 OCTOBER 2006

Why Gay Marriage is a Good Idea

Declan Kiberd

Every day the papers are filled with news of celebrity couples trying to undo their marriage bonds. Now we read of a lesbian pair who seek the ratification of the married state. Has anything changed since the essayist Michel de Montaigne (1533-1592) compared marriage to a cage, with the birds inside seeking to get out, while those outside try desperately to get in?

Last week Dr Katherine Zappone asked the High Court to recognise her Canadian marriage to Dr Ann Louise Gilligan. They have been living together, caring for each other in sickness and health, for 25 years. They married legally in Canada in 2003. If that certificate cannot be recognised here, they contend, they should have the right to marry under Irish law.

There will be many more cases made by same-sex couples, male as well as female. The issues raised are complex and challenging.

Fifteen years ago, a former colleague of mine in a Californian university died suddenly. He happened to have been gay and to have lived for many decades with the same partner. The couple had entertained my wife and me to dinner on many occasions, displaying their ultra-modern apartment with obvious pride.

When my colleague passed on, his partner got embroiled in an acrimonious legal battle. Having been in what was tantamount to a family relationship, he contended that he had the right to stay on in their rent-controlled flat. The judge in Santa Barbara threw out the case, but up in San Francisco or down in Los Angeles, my friend would have won with little difficulty. Those cities by the early 1990s had 'domestic partnerships laws', by which straight and gay couples in long-standing relationships might qualify for pension, housing and insurance rights.

If you think such laws are a recipe for endless litigation, you are quite right. But it's inevitable. Ever since the 1960s, more and more people have lived in stable relationships outside of traditional marriage – in Ireland now well over one in five children is born out of wedlock.

In the US today, courts are filled with claimants in cities that recognise 'domestic partnerships'. Such claimants have to prove financial interdependence and shared living over a significant period, as Drs Zappone and Gilligan who lived together and jointly shared properties have done.

The American cases have often proved tricky to adjudicate, especially when the relationship has been a gay couple. Surviving kith and kin often make a protracted claim against their dead relative's estate, while the inheritance lawyers clean up. Hence the proposal that states recognise same-sex marriage.

The proposal has been opposed, of course, but often on spurious grounds. Conservative columnists, with no sense of self irony, portray the attempt to found a gay family as an attack on traditional family values. The idea has also been laughed to scorn by 'radical' elements within the gay community, elements which like to see themselves as locked into a perpetual war with the repressive institutions of bourgeois society.

A country like ours, which decriminalised homosexuality in the 1990s with no great rancour, should be open to this change. After all, our very Constitution enshrines the family unit as the basis of this society. It is now more than 15 years since a float bearing members of the Gay and Lesbian Network was cheered down O'Connell Street in the St Patrick's Day Parade.

For Drs Zappone and Gilligan, the benefits of a formalised marriage are just the same as those for heterosexual people: they make a lifelong vow of commitment in full view of family and friends.

Once we accept that homosexual relationships are on the same level as heterosexual ones, then the same social responsibility can be expected of gay persons in the conduct of their lives.

It was the furtive, clandestine and ultimately illegal nature of gay sex which often in the past militated against the development of stable relationships. After Aids, most people want not just safety but the stability that goes with it. Far from deploring gay marriage, traditionalists should applaud the idea.

Once gay weddings are legal, partners could buy houses and plan for a future as a couple in the community. They will find an outlet for familial instincts which in the past led some desperate souls, for the sake of appearances, into ill-advised marriages with members of the opposite sex. Teenagers, on finding themselves gay, will have ready role models; and the barriers of hurt that can separate them from their own families will be broken down.

Marriage has many pains, joked Dr Johnson, but the single life has fewer pleasures. Gay marriage is a good idea – but has the community, gay as well as straight, got the imagination to go through with it?

SATURDAY, 14 OCTOBER 2006

Farewell to D'Olier Street

Hugh Oram

The handful of reporters who made up *The Irish Times* in 1882 had barely occupied their new premises when they were plunged into one of the great news scandals of the day – the Invincibles set upon and stabbed to death Lord Frederick Cavendish in the Phoenix Park.

This weekend, 124 years on, the bulk of a staff now numbering 500 will be moving 300 metres from those same but expanded premises to the new Irish Times Building in Tara Street.

Over the weekend of 18 and 19 March 1882, the paper had taken possession of a former upholsterer's shop at No 31 Westmoreland Street. Over the years it would eventually occupy about half of the triangle framed by Westmoreland Street, Fleet Street and D'Olier Street. It is a ramshackle, chaotic building with a maze of dark corridors and recesses which, until June 2002, echoed at night to the deep rumble of presses and the roar of departing dispatch vans.

Since then the printing has been consigned to Citywest and now the editorial and commercial departments abandon the many colourful ghosts and rich history of what has become known as the Old Lady of D'Olier Street.

The Irish Times was launched on 9 March 1859, by Captain (later Major) Laurence Knox. He took over vacant premises at No 4 Lower Abbey Street, almost beside the present-day Veritas bookshop, to launch the paper as a conservative thrice-weekly publication; it was a revival of *The Irish Times* that had been published between 1823 and 1825.

Early success meant that within 14 weeks the paper went daily, but, curiously, another newspaper launched by Knox at the same time, the *Saturday Herald*, was short-lived.

The new *Irish Times* was a modest enough affair and all the production work was done at the premises. Typesetting was a manual task and the printing press could produce 5,000 sheets an hour, printed on one side only. In those days, pages were uncut, so better-off readers got their butler to cut the newspaper for breakfast-time reading.

Major Knox died aged 37 in 1873 and *The Irish Times* was bought for £35,000 by Sir John Arnott, the founder of Arnotts department store, a Scot who had come initially to Cork to make his fortune. The paper was then making a handsome profit of £7,000 a year.

Arnott quickly expanded the paper. He launched the *Weekly Irish Times*, published at the end of the week as a compendium of the week's

Irish Times sub-editor John Moran (centre) leading a symbolic 'knock down' in the paper's newsroom to mark the final day of the newspaper in D'Olier Street, Dublin, before its move to new premises in nearby Tara Street. Knock downs are performed traditionally by printers, usually to mark important moments in their craft such as a retirement, during which the departing printer is banged out of the building by colleagues striking pieces of metal on table tops. The practice harks back to the so-called hot metal era when newspaper pages were made from molten lead, a feat now achieved by computers. Pictured with Moran are (seated left) Déaglán de Bréadún, Father (shop steward) of the paper's National Union of Journalists chapel (branch); Geraldine Kennedy (seated right), Irish Times *editor; and (also seated) Liam Ryan, chief sub-editor; (rear standing, left to right) Liam McAuley, letters editor; Joe Culley, sports sub-editor; Shay Kelly, picture desk secretary; Rachel Burroughs, finance department secretary and Dominic Coyle, deputy business editor. Photograph: Cyril Byrne.*

news and with lots of features, the equivalent then of the current Saturday *Magazine*. In those days, all the daily papers published this type of weekly edition.

Depots were opened, in Rathmines and at the old Parsons bookshop at Baggot Street Bridge. The paper also took over the adjacent premises in Lower Abbey Street, at No 3.

But even this wasn't enough, and so in 1882 *The Irish Times* moved into Westmoreland Street, while retaining the Lower Abbey Street premises for more than 30 years. In 1895, the paper acquired No 11 D'Olier Street, and so for the first time the building occupied by the paper ran right through the block. No 31 Westmoreland Street was the front, public office, an extraordinarily magnificent place, designed to impress customers as they placed their small ads.

The counters were gleaming mahogany and J.J. Simington, the paper's general manager, took exceptional care to preserve them. Heaven help a front-office staffer who wrote something on the counters without protecting it with layers of paper. Simington was a remarkable man who had joined the paper in 1878 as a 16-year-old and went on to work in the company for a further 65 years.

Staff longevity was common; a man called Stoddart was the financial editor years ago and remained in the job until he was 92, when he dropped dead at work. He simply couldn't afford to retire.

Simington himself was succeeded as general manager by G.J.C. Tynan O'Mahony, usually known as 'Pussy' because allegedly he once drank the milk left out for the works cat. He was the father of comedian Dave Allen and another *Irish Times* journalist of note, Peter.

Behind the front office, a grandiose staircase swept up into the offices proper of the newspaper, including the rather rudimentary editorial offices.

As *The Irish Times* expanded its occupation of the site, so too did the tangle of corridors and warren of offices grow ever more complicated.

In 1907, when John Healy was appointed editor, the paper, for the first time, had someone who had less than a shadowy existence in charge of editorial.

In 1916, *The Irish Times* was luckily out of the direct line of fire from the events in Sackville Street, now O'Connell Street. If it had stayed in Lower Abbey Street, it could have been put out of business. In addition to extensive reporting coverage of the Rising and deeply hostile editorials, the paper also published the *Sinn Féin Rebellion Handbook* a year later, still a remarkably vivid source for historians.

Technologically the paper also moved on. It was the first in Ireland to install banks of Linotype machines, which mechanised the business of typesetting. But *The Irish Times* was still hand-setting some of its type until well into the Second World War, the Emergency.

The 1930s saw an extraordinary collection of editorial talent assembled in Westmoreland Street.

Robert Maire Smyllie, usually known simply as Bertie, had been appointed editor; as assistant editor, one of his innovations had been An Irishman's Diary, begun in 1927.

A very big man, yet surprisingly agile, when he came in to work he showed a remarkable turn of speed dodging through the hangers-on and supplicants who lay in wait for his mid-afternoon arrival in the front office.

Upstairs in the newsroom, reporters and editorial writers included Lionel Fleming, later a distinguished BBC correspondent, the Hon. Patrick Campbell (later Lord Glenavy), who was said to have developed his stutter especially for his humorous appearances on BBC television, and Edward MacSweeney, later known as Maxwell Sweeney at RTÉ.

When Smyllie had filed his copy for the evening, out came his favourite bottle of brandy, while his deputy, Alec Newman, later himself editor, whipped out his bottle of Power's. These days, newspaper newsrooms are remarkably sober places, but then, a permanent aroma of intoxication pervaded the place. So too did the stench of stale cigarette smoke.

Much of the business of the paper was done in adjoining pubs. Smyllie held court in the Palace Bar, still extant just across the other side of Westmoreland Street. Also popular was the now vanished Pearl Bar – the site is now included in the Westin Hotel. And *The Irish Times* even had its own social club in Middle Abbey Street and later in two dingy rooms on the fourth floor opposite the Fleet Street works entrance. Strictly for after-hours drinking.

An extraordinary air of anarchic and bohemian eccentricity prevailed. Smyllie used to sing decidedly blue lyrics while working. (In the 1970s and 1980s the newsroom would echo to Eugene McEldowney's republican ballads.) And Smyllie could read proofs using one hand while playing dominoes with the other.

He was a stickler for grammar and style. 'The only commencement in this life is at Trinity

College,' he was wont to thunder. The stylebook was enormous, Latin dictionaries abounded and war was waged on the split infinitive.

The paper also diversified for the first time, running a servants' registry office called Mrs Synnott's, billed as being 'under the charge of Matron', where people could hire domestic staff.

The 'characters' were by no means the preserve of editorial. Bill ('Windy') Coyne, a porter in the front office, was batman during the First World War to the then managing director, Sir Lauriston Arnott. He kept a union flag in the basement – in those days, *The Irish Times* was still a diehard unionist newspaper.

On one occasion, a young staffer of nationalist leanings made a derogatory remark to Coyne, who retorted: 'You are disgracing my king's flag. Step outside for a bout of fisticuffs.'

A number of old codgers with vague association with the paper actually lived on the premises unofficially, without anyone apparently noticing. One of the best known, 'Twitchy' Doyle, an elderly journalist with a perpetually dripping nose, had given the manuscript of his life's work, an ending to Dickens's unfinished Edwin Drood novel, to Smyllie, who had promptly lost it.

Wilfred Brambell, an assistant to the editor of the *Irish Field*, then part of the company, would later win acting fame in the BBC series *Steptoe and Son*.

Somehow, the paper kept going during the Emergency, much reduced in size and heavily censored. For VE day in May 1945, Smyllie thwarted the censors with a front page decorated with a series of photographs forming a 'V for Victory'. He had railed constantly against wartime censorship.

But change in the paper was slow coming. The first woman reporter to cover news was Barbara Dickson, appointed in 1939, but it would be another 30 years before there was a serious influx of female talent.

Gerry Mulvey, 86 last month, joined the paper in 1947 and became news editor, then deputy editor. Together with Cathal O'Shannon, he is one of the few survivors from that era. Many brilliant people from that post-war period, such as Brian Inglis and Bruce Williamson, are long passed on.

Cathal O'Shannon, who joined the paper in 1948, when it ran to a maximum of eight pages, remembers that the only entrance then was through the grand front office in Westmoreland Street. The Fleet Street works entrance and the D'Olier Street 'Front Office' didn't come until much later.

In the reporters' room, a central desk was flanked by several phones on the wall, while it was part of the job spec of junior reporters to keep the coal fires going. A hydraulic system was used to take copy from the subs' room down to the linotypes in the case room for setting.

The Irish Times printed weekly results of chess matches, and on one occasion the results of a competition that had been held 10 years previously turned up in the paper. The copy had been stuck in the hydraulic system for a decade.

Reporters got an allowance of 3 shillings and 6 pence a day for lunch or dinner and 3 shillings a week for tram or bus fares. None had a car, so for a country marking, free rail tickets were supplied by CIÉ.

Those were the days of the long, liquid lunch and when professional organisations held their annual dinners, dress was usually formal and *Irish Times* reporters covering them had to wear evening dress. Now, newspaper life is far more sober, perhaps a little less congenial and a lot more competitive.

O'Shannon remembers one of the sub-editors indulging in some four-letter invective as the demure Church of Ireland correspondent walked in with his weekly copy. 'Do excuse him, he's our arts correspondent!' was the excuse.

He vividly recalls the strange scents that infused the place, old newsprint mixed with the smell of lead from the foundry where the metal plates for the press were made. 'It was such a distinctive smell – it stays with you for ever. It was also very noisy, from all the linotypes, and when the great press started printing at 1 a.m., the whole building shook.' These days printing is totally separated from editorial so newspaper offices are remarkably quiet.

In September 1951 disaster struck when fire swept through the offices just after a new printing press had been installed, causing much damage. That's why *The Irish Times* has so little photographic or other archival material from before that date. After the fire, much rebuilding had to be done on the Fleet Street side and new facilities were added, including a canteen.

The *Dublin Evening Mail*, in Parliament Street, came to the rescue, and for a while *The Irish Times* was produced in its offices. Nine years later, in 1960, *The Irish Times* bought the *Mail* in a vain attempt to save it, but it closed in 1962. Another casualty of this time was the tabloid *Sunday Review*. Started in 1957, it lasted until 1963; it was too much ahead of its time.

In the 1960s and into the 1970s the modernising influence of its new editor, Douglas Gageby, transformed the paper, turning a small, conservative newspaper with a 30,000 circulation into something much more substantial and liberal, the voice of the Catholic middle class.

News editor Donal Foley had a remarkable ability for discovering female writing talent and many women journalists began to make their mark, including Maeve Binchy, Mary Maher, Christina Murphy, Renagh Holohan, Eileen O'Brien, Geraldine Kennedy and the irrepressible Nell McCafferty.

Young reporters such as Conor O'Clery, Kevin Myers, Henry Kelly, Fergus Pyle – later editor – Michael Viney, James Downey, Dermot Mullane and John Horgan cut their teeth, and political coverage was transformed by Michael McInerney, John Healy, and later Dick Walsh. Coverage of the arts, business and sports was allowed to flourish, the latter under the sway of Paul McWeeney.

In 1974 The Irish Times Trust was established in a bid to safeguard the editorial independence of the paper from predatory press barons. The old shareholders sold their stakes in the company to a trust of public figures that would monitor the paper's implementation of a charter upholding basic commitments to political impartiality and pluralism in Irish society.

Although a break from the past, the new structure would be dominated still for many years by the company chairman and chief executive, Major Thomas Bleakely McDowell, who moved seamlessly from one era to the next. His fine oak-panelled office with a blazing fire fronted on D'Olier Street; known as 'The Bunker', it was one of the great company secrets.

The front public office in Westmoreland Street remained untouched until 1976. Thereafter, that part of the site was occupied by the headquarters of the Educational Building Society. The focus of the Irish Times site shifted to Fleet Street and D'Olier Street, while the clock that was outside the old front office was eventually re-erected in D'Olier Street.

The next big revolution at the paper came in the summer of 1986, when the old rotary letter-press machine used for printing the paper was replaced by a brand new web offset press. For the first time, *The Irish Times* could print colour. The first full colour advertisement in *The Irish Times* was for Brown Thomas on 18 August 1986.

That year saw the final retirement of Douglas Gageby, whose two spells as editor spanned Fergus Pyle's and the appointment of Conor Brady as editor, the first Catholic to hold the job.

Typesetting had started to be computerised from 1978 and another revolution was under way: instead of typing out their copy which was then typeset by compositors, journalists now input their own copy into the computer system, 'single key-stroking'.

The new form of production and printing also meant that Brady, ably assisted by his deputy, Pat

O'Hara, was able to dramatically expand the pagination of the paper and the number and regularity of supplements, now a daily feature. Pasting up pages evolved into all-electronic page creation and design.

There has always been a strong sense of family, often literally, throughout *The Irish Times*, from the caseroom to the newsroom. The caseroom, where the linotype operators set the newspaper in hot metal before the introduction of computers, was always a hotbed of activity and friendly, if occasionally combustible, banter between journalists and printers. The overseers and managers who ruled over this frequently frenetic kingdom had to be men of strong individuality such as Mick Costello, Jim Cooke, Pat Ruane and Paddy O'Leary. The latter was renowned for his mantra,

'Don't worry, God is good', most often used when the production world was crashing around his ears.

In recent years the technical and production leaps the newspaper made were driven by innovative individuals such as former director of technology Séamus McCague and former managing director Louis O'Neill.

The installation of that new press began a 20-year revolution in the way in which the newspaper is produced. Half way through that 20-year period, in 1994, *The Irish Times* became the online pioneer in newspaper publishing in these islands, when it launched its own website. Today, the printed and web versions of the paper co-exist side by side and who knows what changes the internet may bring in future?

Republic of Ireland football manager Steve Staunton celebrating Kevin Kilbane's goal at the European Championship qualifier against the Czech Republic at Lansdowne Road, Dublin, on 11 October 2006. The game finished 1-1. Photograph: Cathal Noonan/Inpho.

And then, four years ago this month, in October 2002, Geraldine Kennedy was appointed editor, the first female editor of a national daily newspaper in Ireland. Remarkably, the commercial operation of the paper was then also under the control of a woman, managing director Maeve Donovan.

Now the newspaper moves to the silent, smoke-free, largely sober confines of a gleaming new office – all has changed, changed utterly.

SATURDAY, 14 OCTOBER 2006

A Family Affair

John Banville

Memoir: The son of John Profumo gives his perspective on the most famous transgression of the 1960s.

Anyone looking in this book for juicy and heretofore unguessed-at secrets of the Profumo Affair will be disappointed. True, the author does offer much arcane and interesting information, of a general nature. For instance, we are told Donald Duck's middle name, and that friction welding was invented, along with much else, in 1963. Otherwise, though, the book is exactly what its subtitle says it is, a family memoir. David Profumo's jaunty and entirely unrevisionist account of the Affair, 'perennially the little black dress of scandals', as he wittily writes, represents no more than an episode, albeit a fraught one, in the saga of the Profumo family.

Profumo is the son of the man whose liaison with the call-girl Christine Keeler contributed to – some would say brought about – the fall of Harold Macmillan's government in, yes, 1963, that *annus mirabilis*. He is a loving and loyal son, and his portrait of his parents – his mother, the actress Valerie Hobson, occupies as large a part in the narrative as does her peccant husband – shows them to have been, with one notable lapse, an unexceptional, well-heeled and well-placed Tory couple, remarkable only in the depth of their devotion to each other, which survived infidelity, lies and public disgrace, and which ended only with their deaths.

The Profumos had their origins in Sardinia, and made their money in the perfume trade, as the name implies, though profumo, as David of that ilk gleefully admits, may also be a pejorative term, as in, one supposes, stinker. The third Baron Profumo had settled in London in the 1880s and started a highly successful insurance company, and his son, the fourth baron, became a barrister. John Profumo, the fourth baron's boy, was born at the family home in Basil Street, near Harrods, in 1915. His mother was from Edinburgh. 'She was an actress and a dancer,' David Profumo writes, 'and they were introduced by [the baron's] younger brother Charlie, the chancer, black sheep, and stage-door Johnny of the family.' Showbiz, then, was in the blood.

Valerie Hobson, the woman John Profumo was to marry, was from a naval family originally from Co. Waterford. Stage-struck at an early age, she was not yet 11 when she entered RADA to study acting and dancing, and by the time she was 15 she had played her first part onstage – like Humphrey Bogart, her career began with the immortal line 'Who's for tennis?' – and was offered film work at Shepperton Studios. In London she was spotted one day by Oscar Hammerstein II, who gave her a part in the chorus of his musical ball at the Savoy, which was showing in the city. Next came an invitation to Hollywood, and on the eve of her 17th birthday she signed a contract with Universal Studios.

Although she played in a number of films, including *Bride of Frankenstein*, real Hollywood success eluded her, and she returned to London, where she continued plugging away at her career. Her most memorable film part was that of the grown-up Estella in David Lean's masterpiece, *Great Expectations*. Valerie by then was possessed of a wonderfully fine-skinned, pale and somewhat glacial beauty; as Lean assured her, 'You are exactly right for the part. Estella is a woman without a heart, dead, unable to feel.' However cool she may have looked, though, Valerie Hobson did have a heart, and a tender and feeling one, at that, and John Profumo, rascal though he may have been, loved her for it.

Was a time when every schoolboy knew and sniggered over the details of the Profumo scandal, but the generations march on, so for the children here are the facts, such as they are. Profumo, a middle-ranking politician in Macmillan's government – he was secretary of state for war, which did not even give him a seat at the Cabinet table – had a brief dalliance with the 19-year-old, gorgeous, but already somewhat debauched Keeler, whom he met one weekend at Cliveden, the great house in Berkshire owned by Bill Astor, son of Nancy, the first woman MP to sit at Westminster.

Cliveden already had a reputation for power-mongering, dubious social mixing and general low-jinks. Early in the century the Cliveden Set, including Lloyd George, Shaw, Charlie Chaplin and FD Roosevelt, was a highly influential clique, though in the late 1930s the Set was accused of wanting to appease Hitler. By the 1960s the place had become distinctly louche, with, as Philip Larkin would write in another context, 'a cast of crooks and tarts'.

At the beginning of July 1962 the secretary of state for war and his wife were invited to Cliveden for the weekend. Living in a cottage on the estate – later, after a mysterious death there, Spring Cottage was exorcised, the priest who performed the rite describing it as one of the most evil places he had ever visited – was Stephen Ward, an osteopath and amateur pimp, who that weekend had a bevy of girls staying, including Christine Keeler. As Profumo wrote in his submission to Lord Denning, who was preparing the official report on the frightful vista of the Profumo scandal,

All the girls were very young, and very pretty, and very common, and I remember that subsequently my sister, Lady Balfour of Inchrye, who was there with her husband a week or so before, had said that she and her husband were absolutely scandalized that Bill [Astor] should allow this man Ward to go up to the pool [at the main house] with all these common tarts.

In fact, Profumo had already met Keeler at a nightclub in London, and had remembered her. Keen to see her again, he consulted Astor, who in turn advised him to consult Ward. From such casual beginnings come the great disasters.

The Profumo Affair was very mild, compared with, for example, our own dear scandals of recent years, but at the time it caused an uproar – described by our own, as they say, Patrick Skene Catling, so David Profumo tells us, as 'the western world's favourite twentieth-century bedtime story'.

Keeler was notoriously talkative, especially to the press, and it was not long before rumours of her liaison with Profumo began to circulate. Eventually the *Sunday Pictorial* bought her story for £1,000, an appreciable sum in those days, and Profumo was interviewed by various representatives of the great and the good, including the director-general of MI5, Roger Hollis. Profumo, probably more afraid of his wife than of his prime minister, stoutly denied having had a sexual affair with Keeler. He was not believed, but his word was accepted, as is often the case when the Establishment comes unwillingly up against awkward truths.

Indeed, Profumo might have got away with his peccadillo had it not been for the fact that among Stephen Ward's circle was Captain Yevgeny Ivanov, the assistant naval attaché – in other words, a spook – at the Soviet embassy in London. Ivanov was a party animal, whose nickname was 'The Playboy of the Eastern World'. He and Ward had been introduced over lunch at the Garrick Club by, of all people, the editor of the *Daily Telegraph*,

Stephen Coote, whom Ward had treated for lumbago. Ivanov was also highly appreciative of the charms of Christine Keeler. Naturally, when the story broke of Profumo's doings with the same young woman, the accusation was that he had been sharing her favours with a Soviet spy – the joke going the rounds was that the Red had been not under the bed but in it.

The Ivanov connection, tenuous though it had been, was disastrous for Profumo. Harold Wilson's Labour opposition went in for the kill, led by George Wigg, one of Wilson's heavy gang, who later became paymaster general and then Lord Wigg – it was the righteous Lord who in 1976 was charged with kerb-crawling, accosting women and disturbing the peace; as David Profumo remarks, 'I just thought I would mention it.'

Though Profumo continued for a long time to lie to his political masters and to threaten newspapers with libel writs, the story would not go away, nor the allegations abate. The man would simply have to go. And go he did, resigning in June 1963, a year after meeting Keeler, and not long afterwards Macmillan's government went too. Tory rage knew no bounds.

Profumo had always been viewed with distrust and even distaste by the knights of the shires – his nickname in some quarters of clubland was 'The Head Waiter' – although there were one or two dissenting voices, such as that of one eccentric Tory MP who suggested in the House of Commons that given Christine Keeler's youth and beauty, Profumo should be congratulated rather than reviled for his success with her. But the general reaction was one of outrage and wounded piety.

David Profumo wisely refrains from speculating too deeply on what effect the scandal had on his mother. He reports one wag remarking on 'How Green Was My Valerie', but it is likely that she had a fair idea all along that Jack the Lad was a bit of a boyo. There is no doubt that she suffered a great deal of pain, but she bore the disgrace and public contumely with dignity, patience and fortitude. She loved her husband and knew that he was fundamentally a decent man, as he showed himself to be by devoting the rest of his working life to charity, becoming a volunteer at Toynbee Hall, which cared for the poor and the lost in London's East End. His duties there included taking in washing and working in the kitchens, and sometimes dancing with old ladies during tea parties.

Describing his father's long struggle to redeem himself and be reaccepted by the Tory Establishment – eventually Queen Elizabeth would sit him on her right hand at a dinner party – David Profumo relates that oft-repeated but splendid anecdote told by John Aubrey of Edward de Vere: 'This Earle of Oxford, making of his low obeisance to Queen Elizabeth, happened to let a Fart, at which he was so abashed and ashamed that he went to Travell, 7 yeares. On his returne the Queen welcomed him home, and sayd, "My Lord, I had Forgott the Fart."' Profumo's sins were never to be forgotten, but he was forgiven, more or less. Not the least of the tributes to this sinning but not wicked man is his son's lively, funny, stylish and unfailingly fond memoir. Any errant father would be glad of such a forgiving son.

And Donald Duck's middle name? Fauntleroy.

SATURDAY, 21 OCTOBER 2006

When We Roamed the Earth

Present Tense, by Shane Hegarty

In the Belarusian city of Pripyat, abandoned after the Chernobyl disaster 20 years ago, nature has reclaimed its territory. Wolves roam the streets; lynx, elk and bears stalk the motorways; plants widen the cracks of the concrete buildings. The forest has eaten up avenues and smothered entire tower blocks.

If you have wondered how long the remnants of mankind would survive if we were to somehow suddenly and totally disappear from the earth, Pripyat has proven a chastening model of just how unsentimental Mother Nature is. According to an analogy, if the entire life of the universe could be compressed into a year, mankind would only have walked in the door six minutes ago. On that scale, were we to disappear tomorrow, almost all trace would be gone in about the time it takes for the cosmos to have lunch.

A recent *New Scientist* article went into the disconcerting detail, explaining that in a short space of time a future intelligent species, or passing alien, would have to look very hard to find any evidence of our having been here at all. The *London Times* followed up by putting humanity's destiny into apocalyptically snazzy poster form – a cut-out-and-keep timeline of our species' futility.

If Homo sapiens vanished overnight, most of the man-made pollutants, though not all, would disappear within weeks. While light pollution currently means that nowhere in Germany, for instance, is truly dark, electricity generators would quickly whirr down.

Meanwhile, animals would steadily move back into the urban landscape. Fish stocks would eventually return to full levels, as happened during the Second World War, the last time mankind stepped back from large-scale fishing. And, thanks to interbreeding, dogs would return to a hardier state. As one expert asks in *New Scientist*: 'If man disappears tomorrow, do you expect to see herds of poodles roaming the plains?' What a sight that would be. As would massive packs of Shih Tzu sweeping across continents, chased by yapping masses of Scottish terriers.

In 50-100 years, most city streets would be overgrown, and man-made structures would soon degrade. After 200 years, most bridges would have collapsed, with those nice glass ones that have grown so ubiquitous being the first to go. Within 1,000 years most buildings would have collapsed. About 50 years after that, Michael McDowell's ego might finally have diminished to only trace levels.

In 500 to 1,000 years, most organic landfill waste will have decayed, the last stragglers presumably being half-finished Pot Noodles and the leftovers from a Chinese takeaway I had in 1993. Some plastics will stay on for many thousands of years after that, and glass will hang around for a while too. Some paper is also likely to survive long after the sophisticated technology has rusted away, so posing the horrendous possibility that while much of our modern wisdom will vanish, a future race will still be faced with having to read endless articles about Seoige and O'Shea.

It will take the carbon dioxide we've belched into the skies 1,000 years to return to pre-industrial levels, with the sea absorbing the rest over subsequent millennia. However, our radioactive waste will have the impertinence to hang around. Apparently, it may be two million years before some of that waste has returned to a safe level. It will be the fart that humanity leaves behind in the room.

So, that's it. A few bones and bits and pieces aside, we'll be noticed for having dirtied the place up a bit. If we are noticed at all. It's a wonder that the collective will of mankind doesn't take a slump at such a realisation. That mankind doesn't stay in bed all day, rising occasionally only to howl at the pointlessness of it all and to stick another Pot Noodle in the microwave.

It is bad enough to have your own deep well of existential angst of how even the act of passing on of your genetic material is only the addition of a grain of salt in the ocean of mankind. At least there was some comfort in looking around at the achievements of humanity: architecture, art, writing, some of the television that isn't Seoige and O'Shea and thinking, well, at least you were a part of that. And that would surely last. Only it turns out that we could build a tower block the size of Leitrim, and it could be gobbled up by Roscommon by the time the century was out.

And yet, it occurs to me that there is hope. The moon harbours evidence of our once having been there and it's not so easily covered over. NASA estimates that the astronauts' footprints could last a million years in the windless, dead landscape. The flags should last longer, as will all the other bits of spacecraft and a couple of golf balls that would pose interesting riddles for passing aliens.

And Sweden, rather bizarrely, announced this week that it plans to put a traditional red cottage on the Moon by 2011. So, it turns out that in millions of years' time, aliens may actually have some bed and board while they marvel at the achievements of a long extinct civilisation and figure out which way up the Ikea instructions should be held.

Loss of Four 'Wonderful Lads' Shocks Community

Alison Healy, in Threemilehouse

There was only one topic of conversation for people leaving morning Mass at St Mary's Church in the Monaghan village of Threemilehouse yesterday. They stood about in huddles talking about Saturday morning's crash that claimed the lives of four young men and left a fifth in a critical condition. Inside the church, parish priest Fr Joe McCluskey was contemplating the funeral

All that was left of the two Volkswagen Golf cars involved in a head-on crash near Threemilehouse in Co. Monaghan, early on Saturday, 21 October 2006. Four men aged between 19 and 21 were killed instantly in the crash; a fifth died later. Photograph: Tom Conachy.

arrangements for the men who lived within a mile and a half of each other.

The youngest of the four, Brian O'Neill (19), will be buried after funeral Mass at 11 a.m. in Threemilehouse today. First cousins Gary McCormick (20) and Ciarán Hagan (20) will be buried after 1 p.m. Mass today, while Dermot Thornton (21) will be buried tomorrow after 11 a.m. Mass.

Their friend John McQuillan (27) was still in a critical condition in Our Lady of Lourdes Hospital in Drogheda last night. He was a rear seat passenger in the car driven by Dermot Thornton that carried four men. Ciarán Hagan was travelling alone in the other car when the two Volkswagen Golfs crashed in a head-on collision, less than a mile outside Threemilehouse.

Inspector Pat McMorrrow attended the scene soon afterwards. 'I would say it was one of the most horrific accidents that Gardaí have had to investigate in recent times,' he said. 'Death was instant. They didn't have a chance at all.' He said there were very difficult scenes as families arrived and the news was broken to them. 'You can imagine the trauma at the scene,' he said. 'It was very bad.' Dermot Thornton's parents were on holiday in Lanzarote when they received the news while Ciarán Hagan's father was in France.

It was thought that the men had been socialising in the Threemile Inn in the village earlier that night, celebrating the next-day wedding of a friend. The wedding went ahead as planned in Northern Ireland on Saturday. At Mass yesterday,

Hundreds of mourners follow as the coffins of Ciarán Hagan (20) and Gary McCormick (20) are carried to St Mary's Church in the village of Threemilehouse, Co. Monaghan, yesterday. A third victim, Brian O'Neill (19), was buried earlier. Photograph: Niall Carson/Press Association.

Fr McCluskey prayed for the men, for the recovery of John McQuillan and for his mother Angela. This is not the first tragedy to hit the McQuillan family. John's father was killed in a construction accident a few years ago and his brother was involved in a motorbike crash.

Fr McCluskey said he didn't think the impact of the deaths had fully sunk in yet. 'They were all in their prime of youth and in their prime of health,' he said. 'It's not easy.' The deaths had numbed the local community, said Fianna Fáil councillor Benny Kiernan who is a former chairman of Seán McDermott's football club and knew all the men through his years of coaching.

'They were wonderful lads, lively lads, full of life,' he said. 'What I enjoyed about them was that, when I got onto the council, some people don't want to be seen talking to you, but them lads would always say "Hiya, Benny". It was a good sign about them. I would look upon that as being respectful.'

Dermot Thornton and Gary McCormick had both worked in Treanor Fireplaces while Ciarán Hagan had just returned from France where he was working for a local company. Brian O'Neill was attending Letterkenny Institute of Technology.

Danny Clerkin, chairman of Seán McDermott's football club, cut short his trip to Boston when he heard about the incident. He was at the Railway Cup final and said a moment's silence was held when the word came through. 'It struck home, the enormity of what had happened when it was mentioned so far away.' When he saw the men's friends at Mass yesterday, he half expected to see the four men with them. 'It must be hitting them terribly. They are only youngsters themselves.'

As neighbours queued to visit the families of the deceased yesterday, bouquets of flowers were piling up at the scene of the crash. 'I'm going to miss ya lads,' one card said. 'Can't describe the pain I'm feeling to have you taken away like this.'

MONDAY, 23 OCTOBER 2006

Political Will to Cut Death Toll Must Be Tightened

Paul Cullen

And so the appalling trail of death on our roads continues, followed, almost predictably by now, by copious hand-wringing and promises to improve safety standards. Government and the various safety bodies, seeing a glass half-full, tell us of measures introduced, checks carried out, arrests made and the latest improvement in the body count among a particular category of road-user.

The annual number of road deaths has dropped massively over the last 30 years. The figure was running at 600-plus in the late 1970s, and in only one year in the 1980s and 1990s did it fall below 400 – usually it was well above 400. It has been under 400 every year since 2002 and it should be again this year – the total to date is 303. Opposition politicians stress Ireland's inferior road safety record compared to other countries in western Europe.

The weekend's death toll has blown to pieces the Government's three-year road safety strategy, which aimed to bring the number of annual fatalities down to 300 by the end of this year.

The Road Safety Authority talks of having stopped the upward spiral but, in truth, this modest improvement has been achieved only by throwing considerable resources at the problem. In recent years, we've seen the introduction of penalty points and its extension, major public awareness campaigns including television advertising, the introduction of random breath-testing and the roll-out of a Garda traffic corps.

Each new measure has succeeded in driving down the number of fatalities. After random alcohol-testing was introduced, the number of people killed in September fell sharply, from 31 and 34 in the two preceding years to 19 this year.

However, these positive signs have proved temporary. The biggest drop was achieved when penalty points were introduced to much fanfare in November 2002, but the increased levels of driver caution lasted only six months. Over 250 people have lost their lives since then, because the improvements were so short-lived, according to one actuarial study.

Ireland recorded 9.3 road deaths per 100,000 population in 2004, well above the 5.6 recorded in the UK or 4.9 in The Netherlands. Our figures don't look so bad compared to overall EU averages, but only because so many countries in eastern and southern Europe have worse records.

The trend over time is also positive. Back in the 1970s, more than 700 people a year were dying on our roads. Between 1996 and 2005, the number of cars increased 41 per cent and the number of drivers 21 per cent, yet deaths fell 13 per cent. However, the same period saw big advances in car safety and growing affluence which allowed people to buy newer, safer vehicles.

According to the European Transport Safety Council (ETSC), political will is the missing ingredient in Ireland's woeful road safety performance. Ironically, the only time this will was provided – when the then minister for transport Séamus Brennan championed the penalty point scheme – a marked improvement in the figures was evident.

The problem is greater among certain categories of driver, and on certain types of road. A young male aged 17-24 is seven times more likely to be killed in a car crash than the general population. The poor state of rural roads is also a significant challenge, according to the ETSC, which has called for improvements to the road infrastructure. Ultimately, driver behaviour is the cause of most crashes and accounts for over three-quarters of road fatalities. Changing this, particularly among hot-headed young males, is proving as difficult a challenge as ever.

FRIDAY, 27 OCTOBER 2006

Pension Policies Require Radical Overhaul

Marc Coleman

It is the Godzilla of economic policy issues, looming so high above our heads we can't even see it: a faint stir of its future and significance was given in Germany last year when a political party – the Grey party, appropriately enough – was founded to represent pensioners.

The stability of the post Second World War era made traditional pension policies possible. An age expectancy hovering around the mid-70s was financially consistent with a retirement age of 65 and a defined benefit system. Families were strong and divorce less common, so that a good proportion of old people were cared for in the family, reducing the burden on the state of age-related health and care services.

A further factor in the good old days was that interest rates on fixed incomes – a mainstay for any defined benefit pensions regime – were attractively high. But as a recent conference in Dublin heard, pension policies need a radical rethink across Europe. Since the fateful year of 1925 – when the retirement age was set at 65 – the world of work has changed and changed utterly.

For a start, life expectancy is rising by one year a decade and, by 2025, the average worker will live 10 years longer than the average worker in 1925. Work today is far less manual than it was 80 years ago. And – hard though it sometimes is to believe – health provision is much better. Today's worker retires in far better shape and with far more years ahead of him or her than of old. But even more to the point is the fact that the age of lifelong employment is dead or dying. A pensions system institutionally designed around a job for life is one entirely irrelevant to the new economy we are entering.

Another issue facing pensions policy is international portability. Only about 2 per cent of the EU's population has worked in another EU country. With that proportion higher – and rising – among younger workers, governments must introduce pensions that are recognised between states.

For all of these reasons last week's conference on the future direction of pensions policy was a very timely one. It was unfortunately overshadowed by publication of the Department of Finance's pre-budget projections on the same day. That was a pity. The line up of speakers was extremely impressive, including Adair Turner (of the groundbreaking Turner report on UK pensions) and Karin Lissakers (chief adviser to George Soros on globalisation).

The quality of home-grown contributions was pretty good as well, even if a little less celebrated, and the speeches the conference produced were well worth a listen. Donal Casey of Irish Life made one of the most interesting, and perhaps controversial, observations: as well as being out of date for aforementioned reasons, the current preference for the defined benefit system only persists because those who benefit from the defined benefit system – older workers settled in stable employment – are better represented than those who don't in the corridors of power.

'The relative losers in the defined benefit model are people who move jobs regularly, who have more modest salary growth and who go part-time in their mid-careers,' Casey told his audience. With refreshing candour he admitted that the winners were people like him with more than 20 years employment in the one firm.

Hard-working 20 to 40-somethings – who may change jobs three times in their career – could lose up to half their pension benefits. This is because early transfer values – always the most valuable component of a pension package due to the time value of money – are sundered on changing jobs.

Underlying all aspects of the pensions problem is the fact that, while we have in this century achieved literacy in reading and writing, the number of people who are financially illiterate today is the same as in 1925. As Adair Turner pointed out, those people will find the rest of us increasingly unable to carry them on our shoulders: using estimates calculated in 2004, he showed that by the time today's 20-somethings hit 65 in about 40 years' time, they will expect to live another 23 years.

And for those relying on a tide of young immigrant workers to pay the pensions bill, he had further bad news: with globalisation come expectations for better living conditions and falling fertility rates. By 2020, fertility rates in Iran, Turkey and Brazil will fall below the critical level needed to keep dependency ratios stable. In most of Asia, this has already happened. In short, the pensions crisis is about to go global.

After putting the lid on the debate with the pronouncement: 'The future is defined contribution. There is simply no going back', Gerry Keenan of Irish Life Investment Managers started talking about the problems that this future poses – increasing lifespans and low contributions.

The fact is that there is only one solution to solving the pensions problem. A culture of personal responsibility coupled with strong tax incentives from the State. As Donal Casey said, we must get out of the mentality of giving up on our careers at 45. We must accept that work is not something to be endured, but rather an act of self-expression and self-validation in a world that needs our contribution.

Shifting to this culture will entail policy change in a whole range of areas. Corporate structures must flatten to give employees more ownership over their contribution. Life-long learning must be incentivised by the tax system and suppliers must ensure that the products they supply to mature students are well geared towards the kind of career development they need. No matter what the job, the work culture must be restructured so that the more one advances towards retirement, the less burdensome and more stimulating work becomes.

Such a shift will help a new generation of workers to accept the logic of defined contribution systems as well as the necessity to work a few years beyond the age of 65. Everyone deserves a comfortable and a generous retirement. But retirement is one thing. Prematurely copping out of life is another.

Keep On the Way We are Going and No Country Will Escape

Frank McDonald

There was a time, not too long ago, when only scientists and environmentalists were concerned about global warming. But with the publication in Britain yesterday of the Stern Review on the Economics of Climate Change, this concern has now crossed the professional species barrier.

No doubt sceptics will seize on the review as further evidence that economists are the purveyors of a 'dismal science'. But Sir Nicholas Stern is not someone who can so easily be dismissed; before becoming head of the British government's economic service, he was chief economist at the World Bank.

Also, the conclusion of his 580-page review is essentially optimistic. 'There is still time to avoid the worst impacts of climate change, if we act now and act internationally,' it says. However, if 'strong, deliberate policy choices' are delayed even by a decade, it would 'take us into dangerous territory'.

The Stern review is a clarion call for action, both nationally and internationally. At its core is an acceptance that, contrary to popular belief, the ecosphere that sustains life on earth is not merely a division of the economy. Quite the reverse, as the Scots would say – the economy is a division of the ecosphere.

As the review makes clear, unabated climate change risks raising average temperatures by more than five degrees Celsius from pre-industrial levels. 'This rise would be very dangerous indeed; it is equivalent to the change in average temperatures from the last Ice Age to today,' Sir Nicholas points out.

No country will escape. 'The most vulnerable – the poorest countries and populations – will suffer earliest and most, even though they have contributed least to the causes of climate change,' he says. Large coastal cities such as London, New York and Tokyo are under threat from rising sea levels.

'Climate change will affect the basic elements of life for people around the world – access to water, food production, health, and the environment. Hundreds of millions of people could suffer hunger, water shortages and coastal flooding as the world warms. So prompt and strong action is clearly warranted.

'Such changes would transform the physical geography of our planet, as well as the human geography – how and where we live our lives,' his review says. The scale of disruption 'would be similar to those associated with the great wars and the economic depression of the first half of the 20th century'.

That's why Sir Nicholas pleads that 'we must not let this window of opportunity close'. If we don't act, he warns, the overall costs and risks of climate change will be equivalent to losing at least 5 per cent and possibly as much as 20 per cent of global GDP each year, 'now and forever'.

By contrast, the cost of taking action to reduce greenhouse gas emissions to avoid the worst impacts of climate change can be limited to about 1 per cent of global annual GDP. 'People would pay a little more for carbon-intensive goods, but our economies could continue to grow strongly.' That seems to be a very small price to pay for saving the planet.

However, it will not be easy. What the review is mapping out, in effect, is quite a monumental

Wheelchair athlete Shaho Qadir pushes his chair over the finish line and walks across on his hands to finish in second place during the Adidas Dublin City Marathon on 30 October 2006. Photograph: Dara Mac Dónaill.

shift from an era of burning fossil fuels – as humanity has been doing for some 250 years – to a 'low-carbon economy', largely based on renewable energy. 'Ultimately, stabilisation [of greenhouse gases] requires that annual emissions be brought down to more than 80 per cent below current levels,' it says.

The magnitude of that task is daunting; it has been estimated that the Kyoto Protocol will only produce an overall reduction of less than 2 per cent. But Sir Nicholas maintains that cutting emissions 'will make us better off', as well as bringing huge business opportunities in developing new technology. 'According to one measure, the benefits over time of actions to shift the world on to a low-carbon path could be in the order of $2.5 trillion [€1.96 trillion] each year.'

The review proposes a three-point plan. The first – shirked by the Irish Government, at least in part – is 'carbon pricing through taxation, emissions trading or regulation, so that people are faced with the full social costs of their actions', with a common global carbon price across countries and sectors.

The second is technology policy, 'to drive the development and deployment at scale of a range of low-carbon and high-efficiency products'. The third is to remove barriers to energy efficiency and to inform, educate and persuade individuals about what they can do to respond to climate change.

The Stern review is being taken on board by the British government, with the likely introduction of a range of green taxes on aviation fuel and SUVs (sports utility vehicles) in a bid to change people's behaviour. But then, climate change has long been taken seriously by British Prime Minister Tony Blair. It also needs to be heeded in Ireland, not least by Taoiseach Bertie Ahern. For the past decade, his Government's attitude to climate change has been complacent, at best. Indeed, it has presided over the creation of unmitigated suburban sprawl which has only served to fuel our carbon dioxide emissions.

As Grian (Greenhouse Ireland Action Network) noted yesterday, the climate change-related measures announced in the last Budget – €20 million to purchase carbon credits abroad, €13 million for domestic renewable energy grants and €20 million for excise relief on bio-fuels – came to a derisory 0.04 per cent of our GDP in 2004.

That, and the Government's cowardly decision in 2003 to flunk the introduction of carbon taxes, is a real measure of how seriously the threat of global warming is taken here. It is long past time that the politicians, and all of the rest of us, woke up to the most overwhelming issue now facing humanity.

What's needed, according to Grian, is a substantive public process to tackle the problem of our emissions, including the establishment of a national commission on climate change – to bring an end to the 'inter-departmental feuding that has disabled effective national climate policy for the last five years'.

SATURDAY, II NOVEMBER 2006

Damning Verdict on Bush's Military Adventure in Iraq

Denis Staunton, in Washington

When it came, the storm that hit Congress was a category five hurricane that not only swept dozens of Republicans from office but wrecked the strategy that helped the party win elections since 1994. For President George Bush, it was, as he acknowledged last night, 'a thumping', but it was above all a clear and damning verdict on his military adventure in Iraq.

The president's first response to the Democratic victory was to announce the departure of Donald Rumsfeld as defence secretary, a move that will please critics in both parties and in the armed forces who blame Mr Rumsfeld's arrogance for much that has gone wrong in Iraq.

Less than a week ago, Mr Bush said that the defence secretary would remain in his job until 2009, but the president admitted yesterday that he was already considering a change at the Pentagon when he made that statement. In the final days of the campaign, numerous Republican candidates were calling for Mr Rumsfeld to go and senior military commanders had long ago lost confidence in their civilian leadership.

'He himself understands that Iraq isn't working well enough or fast enough,' the president said of Mr Rumsfeld yesterday. Mr Bush's choice as the new defence secretary, former CIA director Robert Gates, is a member of the Iraq Study Group, a bipartisan committee charged with coming up with a new US policy on Iraq. The committee, which is chaired by former secretary of state James Baker and former congressman Lee Hamilton, is considering ideas that have long been anathema to the administration, such as involving Syria and Iran in plans for Iraq's future.

Mr Bush promised yesterday to work with the Iraq Study Group and the new Democratic leadership in Congress to agree an approach to Iraq. He signalled that important changes were on the way at the Pentagon. 'There's certainly going to be new leadership. Bob Gates will bring a fresh perspective,' Mr Bush said.

For the Democrats, a change of policy in Iraq is essential if the party is to fulfil the mandate it received at the polls on Tuesday. Nancy Pelosi, who is set to become the first woman Speaker of the House of Representatives, said yesterday that

the election was a clear call for a new direction on Iraq. 'It's not about the Democrats in Congress forcing the president's hand. It's important for us to work in a bipartisan way with the president, again, to solve the problem, not to stay the course,' she said.

Despite the Democrats' comfortable margin of victory in the House, Ms Pelosi is likely to keep her promise to embrace bipartisanship, not least because it may be the best way to preserve a Democratic majority in 2008. Many of the new Democratic intake are moderates from districts long held by Republicans who will resist any attempt to push through radical measures that appeal to the left-wing, Democratic base.

The president has already suggested that he can work with Democrats on issues like education and increasing the minimum wage and a Democratic-run Congress could also work with Mr Bush to pass comprehensive immigration reform.

One of the most dramatic features of Tuesday's election was the collapse of Hispanic support for the Republican Party, which has been wooing that socially conservative community for more than a decade. Exit polls showed Hispanics favouring Democrats by 72 per cent to 27 per cent, almost

President George Bush walks away after announcing the resignation of Donald Rumsfeld at the White House on 8 November in the wake of poor election results in the mid-term Congressional elections for Mr Bush's Republican Party. Photograph: Win McNamee/Getty Images.

Spectators at a Halloween bonfire in Sallynoggin, Co. Dublin, on 31 October. Photograph: Eric Luke.

certainly on account of many Republican candidates' hardline stance on immigration.

If the new Democratic intake is more moderate, the remaining Republicans in Congress are more conservative than ever, with leading moderates such as senators Lincoln Chafee and Mike DeWine losing their seats. Moderate Republicans in the north east took the brunt of the Democratic onslaught, leaving the Republican Party more firmly anchored in the conservative south.

Republicans in the west paid a price for abandoning the political centre, with a prominent anti-immigration candidate, Randy Graff, losing to a pro-immigrant Democrat in Arizona – which also became the first state to reject a gay marriage ban.

Senator John McCain's presidential ambitions could benefit if Republicans conclude that they need a candidate who can reach beyond the party's base to independents and moderate Democrats. The shift of power this week that saw Democrats take a majority of state governorships could benefit the Democratic presidential candidate in 2008, bringing into play states that were until now strongly Republican.

Senator Hillary Clinton's sweeping victory in New York, which may also have helped Democrats to pick up congressional seats in the state, can only help her presidential ambitions if she chooses to run. Former president Bill Clinton's energetic fundraising and campaigning on behalf of Democratic candidates has helped to

Bridie Butterly, aged 80, from Skerries in Co. Dublin, who has been diagnosed with osteoporosis, working out with aerobic instructors from Contours Express in the Phoenix Park, Dublin. Photograph: Matt Kavanagh.

secure the loyalty of party officials throughout the country.

Many of the new Democratic congressmen and senators embrace an economic populism, with opposition to free trade and an emphasis on labour rights that is at odds with the Clintons' pro-business approach. Former vice-presidential candidate John Edwards could become the standard-bearer for the new Democratic populists in 2008, while Illinois senator Barack Obama's presidential appeal has grown during the recent campaign.

As Democrats prepare to move into their new leadership offices in January and Republicans are braced for a bitter round of infighting and recriminations, the US public will have little time to catch its breath before the campaigning starts again for the big prize in 2008.

FRIDAY, 10 NOVEMBER 2006

Measuring a Building by Lateral Thinking

WeatherEye: Brendan McWilliams

Mr Gradgrind, you may recall, was the gentleman in Dickens's *Hard Times* who had strong views on education: 'Now, what I want is facts,' he instructed. 'Teach these boys and girls nothing but facts. Facts alone are wanted in life. Plant nothing else, and root out everything else.' Gradgrindism of this kind tends to produce an intellectual approach to life which might be described as unadventurous; a more enlightened environment, on the other hand, results in a facility for lateral thinking.

Take, for example, the apocryphal student asked by his physics Prof during an interview how he might determine the height of a tall building using a barometer. Now the Prof clearly had in mind the phenomenon whereby atmospheric pressure decreases gradually with height above the ground. At or near ground level this rate of decrease is about one millibar, or hectopascal, for every 30 feet or thereabouts.

It follows, therefore, that if you have some means of measuring the difference in atmospheric pressure between two locations, you can estimate, with reasonable accuracy, their difference in altitude – in this case, a building's height. The response, however, was quite unexpected.

'I would take the barometer to the top of the building,' replied the student, 'attach a long rope to it, lower the barometer to the street and then bring it up – measuring the length of the rope. The length of the rope is the height of the building.' The nonplussed Prof suggested his student try again; this time the approach was mathematical.

'I could take the barometer to the top of the building, drop it from the roof, and time its fall with a stopwatch. Then using the formula $S = \frac{1}{2}$ at 2 (the distance fallen is equal to half the acceleration due to gravity multiplied by the square of the time elapsed) I could calculate the height of the building.'

Pressed for a less destructive methodology, the student's next suggestion involved the use of trigonometry: 'You could take the barometer out on a sunny day and measure the height of the barometer, the length of its shadow, and the length of the shadow of the building, and using proportions calculate the required height.' He then provided another method. 'Alternatively, you could take the barometer and walk up the stairs; as you climb the stairs you could mark off the lengths, and this will give you the height of the building in "barometer units".'

Perhaps his last suggestion was his most ingenious: 'I would take the barometer to the basement and knock upon the janitor's door. When the janitor answered, I would say: "Dear Mr Janitor, I have here a very fine barometer. If you will tell me just how high this building is, I will give you the barometer."'

TUESDAY, 14 NOVEMBER 2006

A Man Who Lives by his Words

Kieran Fagan

Words are like pebbles on the beach of history, shaped – sometimes misshaped – by thousands of years of wear and tear, use and abuse. Most of us just reach for words, using those that come to hand, not thinking how they came to be there, or what made them the way they are. Occasionally we, being Celts, take a word and send it spinning and bouncing across the waves of meaning. 'Come up Kinch, come up you fearful Jesuit!' Joyce did it all the time.

And on that beach, in weekly dialogue with *Irish Times* readers, colloguing sometimes – there's the odd flash of mischief – stands Diarmaid Ó Muirithe, lexicographer and etymologist. Those long grey words boil down to 'lover of language'. All his life he has listened to the way we speak. For the past 15 years he has engaged readers in a weekly column lifting those stones, identifying, opining, enlightening. The bazooka, that tubular anti-tank rocket, owes its name to a trombone-like instrument confected of two gas pipes played by a comedian-cum-musician in 1935, he tells us. 'The constant Gaelicisation of the good old English/Scottish word crack as craic sets my teeth on edge.' It harks back to a meaning it never had, boozing and high jinks, he insists.

There are exotic birds on this shore. Like blonde bombshell actress Joanna Lumley (my

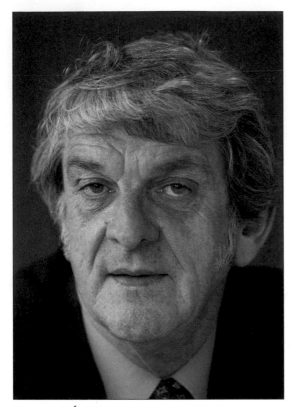

Diarmaid Ó Muirithe photographed by Matt Kavanagh.

description, not his). 'Isn't she just?' I try to ask. 'Yes, she's an egghead. We correspond about words.' He and Joanna took on the compilers of the Oxford English Dictionary about their description of the word 'fad' as being of unknown origin. Joanna maintained it came from the Malagasy language of Madagascar, which is based on the languages of the Malay Peninsula. He met Joanna Lumley through the British magazine *The Oldie*, edited by Richard Ingrams. There, too, he met the late Auberon Waugh, a 'nice, inoffensive, quiet man' whose rudeness in print was legendary.

Ó Muirithe is one of a precious circle of *Irish Times* contributors who speak directly to their readers – and their readers speak back. Others include Brendan McWilliams, Flann Ó Riain, Derek (Crosaire) Crozier, George Ryan and Michael Viney.

A trade unionist asks Ó Muirithe to explain how some workers get the sack, and others are fired. This goes back to medieval times, when a tradesman carried his tools around in a sack. At the end of the job he was handed his pay and his tools. If he misbehaved, he was given the sack. If he misbehaved badly he was dismissed and his tools burned. Hence fired.

When a player funks a tackle, why is a despairing voice from the terraces in Cork heard to cry despairingly: 'He have a touch of the higos', or 'he have the higo sh★★es'? Ó Muirithe finds the answer in a dictionary of Cork slang. The 'higos' refers to the Highland Light Infantry, 'a regiment despised by the Cork people and not known for their bravery'. An encounter with a travelling woman in Wexford yields another description for malfunctioning innards. 'The child has the tetters,' she explains, using an Old English word for ringworm.

There was not enough room to swing a cat. But the cat was not a furry creature hogging the fireplace. It was the cat o' nine tails used to whip miscreant seamen. Or was it? Did it refer to berthing small colliers, known as cats? The word cliché we owe to the French, and it was once a printer's tool, known in English as a stereotype, later being used to describe the hackneyed or stale. Now it has come full circle, as newspapers are full of clichés. The phrase 'stoney broke' we probably owe to an impoverished Irish adventurer, Andrew Robinson Stoney, who married an heiress for her money, but it was all in a trust fund, and he died as he lived, stoney broke. His tight-fisted wife, Countess Mary Eleanor Bowes, an ancestor of the late British Queen Mother, was 'partial to bouts of unbridled houghmagandie', which Ó Muirithe explains was poet Robbie Burns's phrase for 'how's your father?'.

Diarmaid Ó Muirithe is now 71. Though retired from his academic post teaching Irish in UCD, his mission never ends. It began in New Ross, Co. Wexford. He served 10 years as a primary teacher, then worked in RTÉ as a translator and bilingual journalist, read news on radio and TV for another 10, won the first Jacob's Award for a radio programme, *Idir Súgradh agus Dáiríre*, and his script helped RTÉ win the international Nordring Prize. He made 16 documentaries for TV, working often with producer Gerry Murray. He has had 12 radio plays broadcast. He is now a widower with five grown-up children and a scatter of grandchildren, and lives in Dungarvan, Co. Waterford. A retired horseman, he is still cross with the Oxford dictionary people about their derivation of 'Tally Ho' from an unattested French word. 'Clearly none of them ever attended a hunt, or they would know that in English dialect a tally is a fox's brush, or tail.'

Bite Without Spite

Kathy Sheridan

For his 13th and final book, Dr Ivor Kenny followed a friend's advice: first, no point-scoring and second, show sensitivity to people who might still be alive. That must have been a challenge for someone writing a business memoir in a tiny country? 'You just take out the un-nice things about them,' he says, dashing hopes of an elegant hatchet job on a blue chip name or three.

In a life devoted to clarifying the thinking and strategy of top-level managers, first as head of the Irish Management Institute, and later at UCD, he clearly became close to many of them. While he never got rich himself, he says – although 'rich' is relative, seated as we are in his privileged Dublin 4 enclave – 'the odd thing is that a lot of my good friends are people who are extremely rich and it doesn't in any way intrude into our friendship'.

There is point-scoring in the book, of course, though little of it is directed against his friends in business, except to chastise them for not making a decent case for themselves. Then again, he has never been shy about nailing his pro-business colours to the mast. Managers, he insists repeatedly, 'are the salt of the earth'.

Sitting opposite the genial 76-year-old in his bright, art-filled home, it is hard to believe that in the early 1980s, Ivor Kenny was dubbed 'the most dangerous man in Ireland' by Tomás Mac Giolla of the Workers' Party. No-one who lived through that era will forget the tenor of the times. The country, in Gay Byrne's immortal phrase, was banjaxed. The banks were hammering their customers with 20 per cent interest rates. Inflation was around 17 per cent. Up to 157,000 people were unemployed. PAYE workers – saddled with by far the greatest burden of taxation – were alive to the bitter reality of crippling tax rates minus the self-employeds' balm of self-assessment. Boats and planes out of Ireland were packed with angry, young emigrants leaving heart-broken families in their wake.

It was in this raw, stagnant atmosphere that Ivor Kenny became the angry, insistent voice of business. The Broadcasting Complaints Commission upheld a complaint about lack of balance on a *Late Late Show* entirely devoted to his book *Government and Enterprise in Ireland*. The BCC held that Gay Byrne 'clearly aligned himself with the views of three members of the panel – Ivor Kenny, Des Peelo and Tom Murphy'.

So Kenny had become a spokesman for – what? 'My enemies would say a spokesman for the new right, which is an organisation that doesn't exist. I've never found it. You'll find the old left because it's represented by the trade unions . . . they've retreated to the high ground of State monopolies.'

For added bite against the old enemy, he quotes John Monks, leader of the British Trade Union Congress: 'Trade unions are like gorillas in the forest suffering from a shrinking habitat.'

If business then was seen as an 'ogre', as he puts it, he returns the compliment to the trade unions. Asked to do a consultancy job on a 'very large Irish trade union' back then, he accepted, but never got to do it. 'That was because, for example, a trade union official in Galway had made off with large sums of money. In effect the trade union was run extremely inefficiently and very much on an old boys' basis. There were literally jobs for the boys in the trade unions . . .'

Six and a half pages in the book are devoted to the reproduction of a piece he wrote for the *Sunday Independent* in 1984, responding to a claim by the then taoiseach, Garret FitzGerald, that his government had turned the economy around. 'In that piece, I said, "You didn't turn the economy around; you reduced the increase in the loss."'

Fianna Fáil governments also come under the Kenny cosh. 'Charlie McCreevy said: "When I have money I spend it and, when I don't, I don't." This is such primitive economics. What you don't want from government is increasing the amount of money available for consumption. Back in the 1980s, I used to wake at 3 a.m. fuming about the incompetence of governments. We now have a different kind of incompetence, only masked by the torrents of money flowing into the Exchequer. There is no real accountability. Something like PPARS ends up on a Minister's desk, who effectively washes his hands of it and gets into a different department as quick as he can . . . Or there's denial, like the bloody voting machines. If that happened in business, there would be just awful consequences. Above all, the person responsible would get his ticket to leave.'

He takes well-aimed swipes at the Civil Service – 'a priesthood, dangerously remote from the affected publics'; at the Gardaí – 'a self-reinforcing priesthood'; at the institutional Church, for treating Eamon Casey with 'extreme cruelty'; at UCD for awarding honorary doctorates to six golfers, based on eulogies that were 'so thin'.

But knowing what we do now about corrupt politicians (bought by business, remember), wholesale tax evasion and banking scandals, surely business has a case to answer too, not only now but back in the 1970s and 1980s? The normally genial

Kenny bristles. 'During that time, I met very fine people like Ian Morrison of Bank of Ireland who had luminous integrity. There was not a breath of scandal around banking at that time, or Don Carroll and people like that.'

Did they shoulder a fair burden of taxation? 'With what?' he snorts. 'They were getting the pants taxed off them for goodness sake. The biggest single change in what we have now, the reason you, me, everybody has a lot more money now is because inward investment was attracted by the low tax rate and people have found out after long, painful learning that the less you tax people, the more income is generated.'

So business people were among the few trying to make an honest living? 'The business people – and believe it or not, the people at the top of corporations are people too, they laugh and cry and go to the toilet – they were suffering themselves from the heavy taxation. At that time there were a lot of disincentives to productivity and competition. There was still the weight of history of a Sinn Féin protectionist government.'

After some jousting, he finally concedes that business was 'pedestrian' then – 'we weren't really into exports' – then qualifies it by saying that 'business is a function of the society in which it works. It was a deadly society, hopeless, one that did not encourage enterprise or risk . . .' Moving swiftly on to the present day . . . He is as happy now as then, that Irish business – from which he excludes developers, 'for whom I have no particular respect' – is clean and caring, even if it has been bulldozed there by legislation.

'I know of no substantial business scandal in Ireland. We've had nothing like the business scandals of Enron – and you have to remember that everything like Enron calls forth a plethora of legislation . . . I think there is very little danger of people in business behaving obscenely badly.'

Could they treat their employees more fairly perhaps? Could Ryanair be regarded as a good employer for example?

Ivor Kenny in the garden of his home in Dublin. Photograph: Dara Mac Dónaill.

'First of all I think you're talking about a completely unique enterprise. And I don't know how it treats its workers except what I read in the paper. But the girls seem to stay with them. I've only flown Ryanair once and the hostess – now cabin crew – was as nice as you could meet anywhere else . . . I think to treat any human being in a beastly fashion is unforgivable. I've also said that the only way companies survive and grow is to build a real team and when that is not happening, what happens in business is that politics comes in and drives out substance. Once you get that, you're literally in an unmanageable situation because you don't know what people are thinking.'

A lengthy polemic towards the book's end calls capitalism's standard-bearers to arms, not to clean up their act but to learn to articulate their case from a moral basis.

'Rightists are neither angels nor devils. The right has its vice, and that vice is selfishness. New rightists mutter, "Let me rest; I lie in possession." State socialism has its vice, and that vice is envy. State socialists growl, as in Dr Faustus, "Why shouldst thou sit, and I stand?"' The deepest problem capitalism faces, he writes, 'is its estrangement from moral values. Wealth is created (or is not created) in accord with, and through, the expression of a particular set of values. The divorce of capitalism from the moral order results in the kind of demoralisation that faces businessmen today. The essence of the problem with Irish private enterprise is that it has no clear view of itself, no vision of the future, no articulated ideology. Faced with hostile ideologies (of which the archetype is State socialism), it has to fall back on a purely circumstantial defence.'

In other words, socialism, having cornered the market in priests, poets, philosophers and the odd

Golfer Pádraig Harrington with his wife Caroline after an honorary fellowship was conferred on him by Dublin Business School at a ceremony in the Royal Dublin Society on 21 November. Photograph: Eric Luke.

journalist, just happens to have more eloquent advocates. 'Businessmen, who could be the activists, the champions, of capitalism, fall back on "pragmatism", on "knowing how things work". Their pragmatism, divorced from any moral basis, fails to move hearts and minds other than their own.'

THURSDAY, 16 NOVEMBER 2007

A Landlord's Life

Apearl of wisdom about the stock market, attributed to Henry Ford, runs something like: 'When the shoeshine boy is telling me what stocks to buy, I know it's time to sell.' In the current sharp shock

to sales of second-hand properties, I suspect a similar sentiment among the people who really know property. But, come the moment when prices have dropped sufficiently, they will be buying and not selling.

By people who 'know' property I don't mean the standing army of fatigued economists from central casting, who pop up on TV coverage, with a soundbite about 'future trends'. Mostly under-employed by banks, but with inflated salaries to get media coverage for the bank's mortgage products, these gurus have little of value to impart to the people who know property.

The function of the bank pundit, God bless their floundering innocence about property, is – as mentioned – to get a brand mention for their employer in the fiercely competitive media war that has been waged for the past years of the boom. PR agencies are under hysterical pressure from their banking clients to get the guru onto the main TV news bulletins, where he/she will be captioned as being the chief or sub-chief economist of your promising bank.

Never mind that the latest 'survey' or 'new research' might not stand up to serious scrutiny. Property has been the new sex in news terms for a decade, which is a long time to keep it up but, hell, we're Irish and have a lot of catching up to do. So runs the thinking. It would be a poor news editor who did not assign a reporter, at the drop of yet another 'survey of property prices', to stick a mike in front of yet another prophet from your promising bank.

God help the unfortunate young PR trainee if the RTÉ news editor forgets to hold the caption on screen long enough to be recognised by those potential borrowers to whom the bank is pitching. I know whereof I speak, having been on the receiving end of said trainee's disconsolate wail, stopwatching her client on the main RTÉ bulletin and fearful of the reprimand from the banking client on the morrow.

It is to the national station's credit that it tries to vary the gurus and spread the exposure among the various lenders, who are vying to produce yet another newsworthy piece of (spurious) research which will get the required TV mention.

When I tell you there are literally billions of profits at stake here, you will understand the politics, and the spend on 'research' comes out of the marketing budget! The invitation to lunch is a standing one, as is the pressure on the hapless PR staffs to cajole, persuade and – yes, sometimes, to genuinely convince a busy TV news editor of the news worthiness of their client.

When I tell you that one mortgage of €200,000 will be likely worth €500,000 to the bank over its average lifetime, you will understand. Multiply by the million of borrowers over the next few years and you can see why the banks are so keen to have their 'economist' on air.

Crucially, these gurus are not directing their comments at the people who know property (PWKP). The PWKPs, I suspect, are sitting back and doing their sums, at the latest twist of the market. Yes, prices of second-hand properties have stalled – and will plummet. Yes, the agents' boards are up so long, the birds will nest in them come the spring.

Maybe they'll ask McDowell to take down a few 'For Sale' signs, given as he helped keep them up over winter and often finds himself up a ladder. Yes, the market is mesmerised by the great stamp duty debate. In spite of the best efforts of the industry, the buyers are holding off. And that, dear reader, is where the PWKPs come into their own. They do not need anyone to tell them when to

Jane Herlihy (3) from Glasnevin, Co. Dublin, arrives at the Mansion House on 2 November for the launch of the city's Christmas programme. Photograph: Brenda Fitzsimons.

move and buy at a discount. They will smell the moment as infallibly as the twitching nostrils of the ferret in the long grass. And the last to know about it will be your TV guru from your bank of promises.

SATURDAY, 18 NOVEMBER 2006

Keeping an Eye on the City

Frank McDonald

Timing is 'absolutely everything', as Maurice Craig discovered many years ago. When his marvellous book, *Dublin 1660–1860,* was first published in 1952, hardly anyone noticed. But by the time it was re-issued in 1969, there was a whole lot of new readers who were hooked on Georgian Dublin.

The battle for Hume Street was well under way, with eighteenth-century houses at the corner of St Stephen's Green occupied by a group led by Duncan Stewart and the late Deirdre Kelly. Even Charlie Haughey (then minister for finance) sent around a Christmas hamper, though he did nothing to save the houses.

Now aged 87, Dr Craig was delighted to see the tide turning. Though he never uses the term 'Georgian' because of its connotations of British rule, he had told the fascinating story of how Dublin was transformed into a grand neoclassical city, starting with the Duke of Ormonde's return in 1661.

It was, as Prof Mark Girouard notes in a foreword to the latest edition, 'a Dublin of warm hospitality and enjoyable rows, of bitter social and religious divides, of good parties, good stories and good funerals, of eccentrics and individualists, of bucks, bullies and rakes, of sudden wit and savage satire'.

Prof Girouard, an architectural historian like the self-trained Dr Craig, ranks *Dublin 1660–1860*

alongside Sir John Summerson's *Georgian London* (published seven years earlier, in 1945) as the firm foundations for 'a completely new way of writing about cities and the buildings in them'. What they had in common was a discipline based on meticulous examination of all sorts of sources such as building leases and regulations, analysis of building and town plans, and research into the lives of the landlords, politicians, clerics, merchants and 'people of fashion' who shaped the two cities.

Both books are enduring classics, Girouard writes, 'yet the different characters of their authors and of the cities about which they write lead to very different books: Summerson's shaped with restrained elegance and wit, Craig's a richer mixture of analysis rising to eloquence or dissolving into laughter.'

But Dr Craig says the first edition was 'far too early to attract the attention of anyone other than Elizabeth Bowen and a small number of people whose taste had been formed by Summerson's book, which had been out for a little while by then. We had the same publisher, Dennis Cohen, who was Jewish, of course.'

Cohen's literary adviser, John Hayward, had been at Magdalene College in Cambridge with young Craig. 'He had been exiled to Cambridge because he was an MS sufferer and lived in a chair. A great friend of T.S. Eliot, he went on to become a big name in the rare book world as well as working [with Cohen] at Cresset Press.

'Hayward said, "If you ever feel like writing a book, send it to us." I had collected a PhD for my work on [English poet Walter Savage] Landor, and learned from it how not to write a book. Because if you're trying to impress an examiner, you have to prove that you have not missed anything, and that's the perfect recipe for an unreadable book.

'It was after I came to Dublin to do the PhD at Trinity that I began to get seriously interested in architecture. I got hooked on the Casino [in Marino] and found that all the personal papers of

Maurice Craig with his cat at their home in Seapoint, Co. Dublin. Photograph: Brenda Fitzsimons.

Lord Charlemont were in the National Library. As a Protestant nationalist of the eighteenth century, he appealed to me, so I wrote a book about him – *The Volunteer Earl*.

'I sent it to Cresset Press, where Hayward read it and said they would publish it – provided that I wrote a book on Dublin. I had no thought of anything like that at the time. I think they expected a chatty book of literary gossip, politics and cultural history. What they didn't expect was that it would concentrate so much on architecture.'

While writing the book, Dr Craig learned to draw. 'Harold Leask [the State's first inspector of national monuments] taught me how to do perspective in 20 minutes – all you require then is exact observation and obedience.' Thus, he was able to draw all of the perspectives, elevations and plans in *Dublin 1660–1860*.

'It's not a book that I'm terribly fond of in some ways; I have written books that are much better. But I realise that the Dublin book has a special place. When I meet people, they say "Reading your book about Dublin changed my life," which is shorthand for changing the way they look at this. There was also a need for such a book on Dublin.

'Constantia Maxwell had done Dublin under the Georges, but it's quite clear that she never looked at buildings. But then, hardly anyone else did at the time, other than architects or engravers. The artist Flora Mitchell [whose *Vanishing Dublin* was published in 1966] couldn't draw. And if the artists couldn't draw, the laity were even less observant.'

Ironically, Mitchell's work and the 1969 edition of Dr Craig's book were both published by

Allen Figgis. His was one of a series of Irish reprints. 'All were flops except two, [Robert Lloyd] Praeger's *The Way That I Went* and my Dublin book. And I don't mind saying that had Figgis not reprinted the book, it would have been forgotten.'

He still detests the way it was produced. 'It was a horrible little book, which fell apart. But the 1980 edition is much better. Having used the paperback version of Peter Harbison's book *The Archaeology of Ireland*, I specified the material in the cover, which was a plasticised fabric that will stand up to an awful lot of punishment.'

He has high praise for Neville Figgis, however. After Dr Craig's wife, Agnes Bernelle, died in 1999, he decided to sell their Regency house in Strand Road. It was full of books, so he asked Figgis to help him get rid of a lot of them – including a very large Grierson Bible, printed in Dublin in 1715.

'He thought it was not a saleable item, and gave me £15 for it. Six months later, completely out of the blue, I received a letter from him saying it was a good deal more interesting than he had thought, and "enclosed please find a cheque for €1,000." Now who would do that, especially after a deal had been done? I think it's a beautiful story, and I tell it whenever I get the chance. An honest man is the noblest work of God, as the old saying goes.'

For the past six years he has been living in a small modern bungalow in the rear garden of Alma House in Monkstown, a nursing home opposite Seapoint Dart station. 'The entrance [to the station] is so secret that you wouldn't know it was there unless you tripped over it', he says, adding that his arthritis doesn't permit him to go out much.

Maurice Craig is a perfectionist. 'I would normally compose a sentence inside my head before putting anything on paper, and only occasionally produce a whole page in an afternoon. I never learned touch-typing, but I was able to rattle away on my old Royal portable for nearly 50 years.'

Although he now has an iMac, he finds the keyboard 'hyper-sensitive'.

He's also a stickler for detail, even of pronunciation. When I used the word 'research', pronouncing it as 'ree-search', he immediately corrected this 'Americanism'. He also corrected how I pronounced Belfast – which is, after all, where he was born – saying the accent should be on the second syllable, as in 'May the Lord in His mercy be kind to Bel-FAST.'

He maintains that anyone who lists Ireland's four provinces in alphabetical order is 'an ignorant fellow'. For him, it's simple: 'Ulster, Munster, Leinster and Connacht. North, south, east and west. Matthew, Mark, Luke and John. Or if you're blessing yourself – spectacles, testicles, watch and wallet!' (The watch, of course, being in your waistcoat pocket.)

As for Georgian Dublin, he thinks it has 'fared better than I feared. North Great George's Street has survived through individual effort and Mountjoy Square has been rebuilt in facsimile, although Henrietta Street is in a more parlous state. But I would be very worried about the Liffey quays' – the 'essential Dublin', according to the *Architectural Review*.

'I remember the brother of the French ambassador saying to me 60 years ago, "C'est un petit Paris." It was a huge compliment, as I understood immediately. So I think it's very important to keep the quayscape. In that context, Liberty Hall was a disaster, but I heard with delight that they're going to pull it down. It's not the right place for a high building.'

Dr Craig likens the vulgarity of much of what's been built during the 'Celtic Tiger' era to English Jacobean architecture, which he always regarded as 'hideous . . . simply because a lot of people who had very little architectural education became very rich very quickly with hideous results. It will correct itself in the end, although I won't live long enough to see it.'

Neither, I said, would I.

I'm a Bride, Get Me Hitched

TV review: Hilary Fannin

Not long ago, when our interest rates were lower, our bottoms were higher and some of the nation's well-manicured digits were tapping out the waiting time to their ripening SSIAs, a meso-morphic wedding planner in a silk shirt royally entertained us with an insider's look at big-cat Irish nuptials. Now he's back: *Brides of Franc*, a fly-on-the-newly-painted-wall series, follows Peter Kelly (aka Franc) as he executes espousals, ignites matrimonial matches and creates 'a fairytale' for those who are prepared to spend the GNP of a small republic on their 'big day'.

It's still highly entertaining to watch other people blow their budget on fripperies and to observe prospective brides and grooms invest great swathes of anxiety and emotion on napkin pleats, but somehow the programme seems a little darker and more sinister second time around.

Series two and Franc is looking alarmingly well-groomed, wearing a suit jacket decorated with designer graffiti and sporting an angular emerald on his pinkie. At one stage he stood in front of a mirror and casually flicked on his tie, revealing, on the carefully chosen accessory, a soft underbelly of pink silk lining. 'Franc loves his pink,' he murmured to his satisfied reflection.

Franc also loves his brides, and why wouldn't he? With the average (yep, average, according to Franc's team of planners) spend on a wedding being in the region of €30,000 – and often way, way in excess of that figure – the fantasies of young women, their dreams of a perfect day, their yearnings for a corner on the jigsaw of celebrity, are lucrative desires for a dream-maker.

Lorraine, this week's bride, admitted that after the difficult birth of her son (with fiancé Gerry), her cravings for perfection had intensified: she now wanted a Harry Potter-style wedding at Kinnitty Castle in Co. Offaly. To be precise, she wanted her guests to have a Hogwarts dining experience, presumably with sumptuous feasts magically appearing on golden platters, headless ghosts adorning the chandeliers and owls delivering the menus.

The infinitely more cautious Gerry, meanwhile, would have been satisfied with chicken or beef and a karaoke in the couple's local hotel in Navan. Thirty-five grand or so later, and having recovered from a nightmare in which Franc metamorphosed into a curmudgeonly Eddie Hobbs (separated at birth, those two), Lorraine was walking up an aisle decorated with flowering broomsticks, while back at Kinnitty Castle, an actor sat inside an empty picture frame waiting to direct 150 guests to the magically transformed 'great hall'.

Franc's creativity and professionalism are beyond doubt; a squat powerhouse of productivity, he is a master purveyor of bash and bling. He is, it would seem, as happy as a sand-boy with the current appetite for excess. But what I want to know is what happens Mr and Mrs Hitched when the candles are extinguished, the linens are tumbled into the industrial washers, the dress is encased in mothballs and the lilies that Franc scattered in the bridal bath are withered. What happens to Franc's brides when the clock strikes midnight, the credit-card company starts calling, the baby wakes up for his 4 a.m. feed and a flatulent Prince Charming can't find his glasses to nuke the bottle? Follow-up series, anybody?

'Three billion letters spell out the human code; we are looking for one letter.' As Detroit-based geneticists searched through the hieroglyphic structures of a single cell from a fertilised embryo, 10 times smaller than a pinhead, back in England Jill and Ian sat in their home surrounded by photographs of their beloved infant daughter, Ellie, who had died, aged just seven months, from the inherited disorder Gaucher disease.

Prof Robert Winston is back on our screens, this time with *A Child Against All Odds*, an exploration of the controversial subject of embryo selection, or 'designer babies' as the process is often emotively dubbed. Winston, who helped pioneer pre-implantation genetic diagnosis, a technique which allows fertilised embryos to be tested for genetic disorders, argued strongly and unequivocally for the process, one which offers couples such as Jill and Ian a chance to conceive a healthy baby. (Not shying away from the more controversial and ethically fraught aspects of the issue, Winston also followed Andrea and Glen, a wealthy Yorkshire couple who, having had four boys, wanted, as Andrea said, a girl to 'complete our little world'. The couple were accompanied on their trip to Cyprus for 'sex selection', a process which cost them £10,000 and which is not legal in the UK.)

What became searingly apparent from Winston's exploration was that, for the most part, this complex and nerve-wracking procedure is not a game played by whimsical couples looking to acquire pre-assembled blue-eyed, tap-dancing, blonde progeny. For many (including Andrea and Glen), the implantation process fails. But for Jill and Ian it worked, and Jill gave birth to a bloody, wrinkled, robust and healthy baby boy.

'Perfect? Designer?' asked Winston. 'He is only free from the plight of a specific disease; he now has the same chance in life as any other child.'

Speaking of celebrity and flatulent princes (were we?), David Gest snores in his hammock. This Gest is a CELEBRITY. We know this because he was once married to Liza-with-a-zee Minnelli and probably still is, theirs being a divorce case of epic proportions which will probably last longer than their marriage. Gest is also famous for his surgically enhanced eyebrows and a couple of scary peepers that have been somewhat over-emphasised by a gung-ho plastic surgeon. My personal infatuation is with his sparse but unrelentingly black hair that appears to be thatched on to his pate. Oh, and I almost forgot, he is also a record producer. But the main reason we know David Gest as a celebrity is because he is appearing nightly on our nervously dispositioned screens in the return of the return of the return of *I'm A Celebrity – Get Me Out of Here!*

Gest is a nightmare, with an idiosyncratic world-view that leads him to believe that some women (those who intimidate him or who remain unimpressed by tales of how he likes to play with Michael Jackson's snake) 'have their heads up their vaginas' or, perplexingly, 'vaginas where their heads should be'. This outburst of brutal physiognomic misogyny was apparently brought on by fellow jungle contestant and former newsreader Jan Leeming being, well, Jan Leeming (haughty, teary, pain-in-the-elegant-neck, high-maintenance, sixtysomething, with all her own wrinkles, who plans, somewhat unoriginally, to 'grow old disgracefully').

Young and lovely Myleene Klass, classical musician, former pop star and bikini-wearer, met with Gest's approval, however, while he seemed to view impressionist Faith Brown as an industrial-sized wet-nurse. There are 'pundits' out there who claim that this ant-eating, toad-licking, dunny-chucking nonsense is addictive viewing, and maybe they're right.

Morbid fascination will have many of us tune in from time to time, and I suspect that Tony Blair is getting nightly updates about his outspokenly critical sister-in-law, Lauren Booth, who has already told nine million viewers on the opening show that Blair is stepping down in January. Bush-tucker trial for you, young lady.

Abhorrent or addictive as you may find it, spare a thought for the unsuspecting Australian tarantulas that'll end up in some celebrity's sandwich. Outback arachnids must shudder with relief when these specimens of D-list celeb sapiens retreat to their urban webs and get on the phone to their petrified agents.

Wedding planner Franc, aka Peter Kelly, with some of his brides, who are prepared to spend an average of €35,000 on their wedding day. Photograph: RTÉ.

Some Men Just Want to Be Boys

Declan Kiberd

'In England', wrote the historian D.W. Brogan, 'being a schoolboy is an end to itself.' He was right. At the high tables of Cambridge University on every Sunday night, college fellows are offered a mouth-watering choice of desserts to close their meal, but almost all opt for rice pudding.

When once I summoned the courage (as I scoffed pavlova) to ask why, my dining partner smiled knowingly and said, 'It reminds us of matron and of school.'

Not that our country seems very different. In rural Ireland, until recently, you remained 'a boy' until you married, which could be late in life if you were waiting for parents to pass. A Dáil deputy for Louth back in the 1950s made an emotional plea for the rights of 'boys of 46 or 50 still waiting to inherit the land'.

The outbreak of laddishness in the culture of the 1990s breathed new life into the phenomenon. From Nick Hornby to Hector Ó hEochagáin, the

Donal Gallagher, brother of guitar legend Rory Gallagher, examines the Fender Stratocaster that Gallagher used onstage throughout his career, at the opening of Rockchic: The Life and Times of the Electric Guitar, at the National Museum in Collins Barracks, Dublin, on 23 November. Photograph: Frank Miller.

various types may be seen on TV. Even as child-hood seems to be rolled back and reduced, the idea of a boyhood lasting into late middle-age has taken further hold.

Some versions of the prototype are distinctly queasy: a current joke maintains that if Michael Jackson commits just one more infraction, the Pope will offer him a parish.

But most are viewed as examples of healthy high spirits – the sort of charming blokes who pro-pelled many a P.G. Wodehouse novel with their amusing attempts to avoid entrapment by a Gladys, who represented the awful prospect of 'settling down'. The image evoked by that phrase was of a corpse reclining into a coffin of complacency.

The cultural forces that have produced the 'new boy' are probably not all that different from those which generated Bertie Wooster or the Louth bachelor lads.

If you are chronically 'short of the readies' and cannot afford to pay the vast money now needed to secure a home of your own, the temptation is to go out and blow what money you have on cars, gadgets or gismos. Hence the strange, rather unnerv-ing, poster which this month advertised a display of such items in the RDS: 'Toys 4 Big Boys'.

Meanwhile, estate agents report that many of those taking out mortgages on first-time houses or apartments are single women in their 20s, who do not necessarily see such a move as coinciding with marriage or cohabitation. And some young men, less adept at planning or saving, are choosing to stay living in the homes of their parents.

The romantic poet Samuel Taylor Coleridge said that people should never put away childish things: the wisdom of life, he maintained, was to learn how 'to carry the feelings of childhood into the powers of manhood'. That was a plea for people not to lose their sense of wonder.

And it's true that many artists are great by virtue of maintaining contact with their inner child. 'A boy could have done that,' mocked a harsh critic of one of Picasso's early abstract paint-ings. 'Yes,' the artist chortled, 'but could a boy of 40 have done it?' I'm not sure that the 40-some-things who play Grand Theft Auto and read Superman comics are operating fully in the spirit of Coleridge and Picasso. But they are certainly haunted by the notion of a lost boyhood still to be recovered.

A similar explanation may lie behind the suc-cess this year of The Dangerous Book for Boys. This is a high-finish recreation for adult males by Conn and Hal Iggulden of the world of the old Victor and Wizard comics. It tells you how to make knots and treehouses or how to know the flags of all nations.

I happened to be clearing out the garage of my childhood home in the week that The Dangerous Book for Boys came my way. Every item I came upon – a blow football game, Subbuteo, a collection of Victorian pennies, a postage stamp album, a wooden drum – seemed to come out of the now-distant world reconfigured in the current bestseller.

It all bore in on me just how much the experience of boyhood has changed in the past 30 years. My father shared with me the pleasure of stringing a bow-and-arrow or of lacing a conker, as his father had done with him. But I don't under-stand most of my son's PlayStation games (even the Fifa soccer seems designed for someone with different wiring from my own).

Frustrated in the attempt to pass on the lore of old boyhood, many men in their late 40s and 50s are choosing to recreate it privately in their read-ing. Hence the demand for The Dangerous Book for Boys or for Ben Schott's miscellanies. Meanwhile, those 'big boys' still in their 30s commune with their lost (or never fully worked-through) youth in the hall of the RDS.

Perhaps the psychological truth behind much of this was captured in the Hugh Grant movie About a Boy. Like the central character in that film, all seem shadowed and haunted by the image of a boy, who is not only mysterious and persistent in himself, but who seems to call men away from childish play back into the real world of grown-ups.

Weasel Words

Kilian Doyle

Some weeks ago I promised the sensible people among you, the ones who've thumbed their noses at the Regplate Mafia and their newcarupmanshipping, that I'd broach the subject of purchasing a second-hand car. As you clever folk are doubtless aware, this can be a whole world of pain. The chances of a wide-eyed novice blowing their cash on a four-wheeled shed are more than slender. In fact, they are positively obese.

Sadly, space precludes me from explaining what to look out for when you actually go to see the car. In order to get to that stage, you have to first learn to decipher the hieroglyphics of classified ads. And here's where I come in. Be warned – not everyone is telling the truth. The gap between what sellers say and what sellers mean can be as wide as a bull elephant's backside.

A basic grasp of sellers' acronyms and euphemisms can help you avoid the heartbreak of stumbling upon what appears to be the deal of a lifetime and going, wads of cash in hand, to see what you think is your dream car, only to find out that it's a former dinghy that's been fitted with a lawnmower engine, pram wheels, a few garden chairs and seatbelts made of dessicated chow mein noodles.

Some lies are simply spotted. Immaculate Condition means the owner has just washed it. Showroom Condition means he waxed it too. 'Quick sale required' means the seller's neighbours have threatened to call the police unless his noisy death-trap of a rustbucket is moved from outside his house. Similarly, 'genuine reason for selling' translates as 'I've just come to my senses and realised this car is irredeemably rubbish.'

FSH is Fairly Shoddy Handling. A/C means the windows go up and down, or, in extreme cases, there is no windscreen at all. E/Seats is electric

seats. Not that they necessarily came out of the factory like that. It's just the oik who installed the glass-crackingly loud soundsystem, botched the wiring and every time you sit in the driver's seat, you get a strong enough electric shock to set your hair on fire.

One Lady Owner? This may well be true. But it neglects to mention the one lady owner has three teenage sons who've been using it to pull hand-brake turns on a local golf course. One old lady driver means the car will never have been higher than third gear and, consequently, the transmission will be knackered.

Needs minor overhaul? There is no clutch, gearbox or brakes. Needs major overhaul? There's no engine either. Or chassis. Poor condition? It's too bad to even bother trying to lie about. In fact, it is at the bottom of a lake.

Fuel efficient? It uses very little petrol. Only because it won't go more than a mile before breaking down. Quiet engine? It won't actually start. Runs smoothly? The handbrake is broken and it'll roll down any hill you leave it on.

Low mileage? It's either been clocked or was such a rubbish car from the beginning that the previous owner could neither afford to fix it when it broke down after three months nor find anyone stupid enough to buy it, opting to leave it to rot in a shed for the past decade instead.

Cars are usually only 'rare' because the particular model was so awful when it was new that nobody bought one. A restored car with no miles on the engine is one that wouldn't start again after it was stuck back together. A restored car with three miles on the clock is one that started, cut out just down the road and won't budge.

And then there's the real giveaway: Trades considered. This translates to – 'I am so desperate to get rid of this heap of junk that I'll swop it for anything that runs. And I mean anything.' Finally, remember this, the car buyer's Golden Rule – if, like anything in life, it seems too good to be true, it probably is.

Gabe Davies from Newcastle, England, surfing off the Donegal coast, near Bundoran, during the H30 Project on 16 November. The project brought together Irish and British surfers to ride the most dangerous waves off the coasts of Ireland and Britain. Photograph: Mickey Smith.

SATURDAY, 25 NOVEMBER 2006

Explosives, Gun, Knife and Abuse about a 'Sell-out'

Dan Keenan, at Stormont

It happened so suddenly. The figure of convicted loyalist killer Michael Stone was being bundled out through the revolving door of Stormont's Great Hall swearing at the civilian security staff who were surrounding him. They pinned him firmly to the ground, just in front of me. He bellowed 'No surrender' and what sounded like 'No sell-out Paisley' while cursing his captors, telling them to 'f*** off' and leave him alone.

Stopped in my stride by the melee, Stormont security staff approached, screaming 'get away, get away'. A few camera crews and photographers refused, staying to get the best shots.

Stone had tried to burst into Parliament Buildings carrying explosive devices, a gun and a knife. He had used a red spray can to scrawl some graffiti at the base of one of the stone pillars at the entrance. Within a short time, Stone was firmly restrained and on the flat of his back. A security officer held each of his limbs and a female officer appeared to be trying to talk to him.

Again the security officers shouted at me to clear the vicinity as others arrived on the scene. More security officers in civilian clothes insisted I move towards the side of Parliament Buildings, in the direction of the private entrance normally used by Assembly members. Already some of them and their officials were beginning to stream from the building out into the driving rain, ushered outside by insistent Assembly staff.

Confusion reigned, with those who had been following the goings-on in the chamber emerging clueless into the downpour. I could see Jeffrey Donaldson being placed in the back seat of what I took to be a civilian-style police car. It was then driven off hastily, its wheels spinning on the wet road. Seconds later I saw Peter Robinson in the rear of a similar car also being driven off at speed, lurching around the corners.

SATURDAY, 25 NOVEMBER 2006

Behind a Mother's Murder

Conor Lally

The cold winter breeze buffeted the young mothers pushing their wrapped-up toddlers in buggies. 'It is a shock, terrible,' said one eastern European twentysomething as she and her son looked on.

Security staff at Stormont's parliament buildings in Belfast restrain and disarm loyalist protester Michael Stone after he attempted to storm the entrance armed with a gun, knife and explosives. Stone later claimed that his aim was to murder Sinn Féin's Martin McGuinness and Gerry Adams. Photograph: Stephen Hird/Reuters.

Less than 12 hours earlier, a burst of gunfire had ended the life of Latvian mother-of-two Baiba Saulite (28) at her home in the Holywell estate, Swords, Co. Dublin.

As she lay dead in a pool of blood in the hallway of her rented house on Monday morning, members of the Garda Technical Bureau were dusting for fingerprints on vehicles outside the house. Other forensics experts, clad in white boiler suits, were taking measurements and photographing the scene. Any piece of evidence, no matter how small or seemingly innocuous, was recorded.

The State Pathologist, Prof Marie Cassidy, came and went. She carried out a preliminary examination before the dead woman's body was taken away, in a black body bag, for a full post-mortem.

As the week went on, the complex and sinister background to this case began to emerge. Baiba Saulite had come to Ireland searching for happiness and prosperity. She is leaving in a coffin. The path her life took in the six years between those two stages was a difficult one.

Friends this week described a warm and outgoing woman who was devoted to her two young sons. She worked part-time as a cleaner to supplement her social welfare. She prayed at the Lutheran church on Adelaide Road, Dublin 2.

From the city of Riga, she had travelled here with her Latvian boyfriend. Like most of the estimated 50,000 Latvians now in Ireland, they had no particular reason to leave their homeland other than to seek out new, greener pastures. Their relationship didn't survive the move and Baiba found herself single in Ireland.

She began dating a Lebanese immigrant, Hassan Hassan, who had moved to Ireland 20 years ago. They fell in love, married and had two children: Ali-Alexsandra, now aged five, and Mohamed Rami, aged three.

It was a difficult relationship founded on lies, according to Saulite's account. Hassan, now 38, told his then girlfriend he was Greek during the first two years of their relationship. She had expressed fears soon after meeting him that, as a Christian, she did not think marrying a Muslim was a wise decision. So he insisted he too was a Christian, of Greek origin. He neglected to mention he had once been married to an Irish woman.

At first they lived at Mount Andrew Rise in Lucan, Co. Dublin. Soon after the birth of their first child, Hassan admitted to his wife he was Muslim. Last year, after her children were held by their father during a custody battle, she went on RTÉ Radio 1 and explained how her husband's behaviour had changed after the birth of their first child.

'When the children were born he started acting in an Islamic way,' she said. 'He told us what we could eat, what we can't eat, what I have to wear, what I have to do. He wouldn't let me go out and see my friends, nothing.'

She said that Hassan insisted their children be raised in the Muslim tradition. The relationship disintegrated and the ensuing custody battle became extremely acrimonious.

In December 2004 Hassan was to have the boys for a three-day visit. But when the period ended he failed to bring them back to her, sending them overseas to Lebanon instead. She initiated legal proceedings against him to force her boys' return. But Hassan refused to comply with a Dublin District Court order to produce the boys. He was then imprisoned over the Christmas and New Year period.

When the first week in January 2005 came to a close, with no sign of her young boys, Baiba Saulite went on radio, thinking the children were still in Ireland, and appealed to the public to look out for them. The children were eventually returned to her. But personal problems and anxiety continued to afflict her until she finally suffered a nervous breakdown. Her relationship with Hassan became no more amicable. He made repeated threats against her and she feared for her safety.

Baiba Saulite in December 2004 with photographs of her two sons, Ali Alexsandra (left) and Mohamed Rami, after they were abducted by her estranged husband, Hassan Hassan. Photographs: Collins.

In February 2004, a large team of gardaí from Dublin's Blanchardstown and the National Bureau of Criminal Investigation swooped on a warehouse at Colbinstown near Kilcullen, Co. Kildare. They found about 20 top-of-the-range stolen vehicles, all of which were being stripped and prepared for export to eastern Europe.

Among the dismantled vehicles recovered were BMW, Mercedes and Fiat models as well as at least one Kawasaki motorcycle. The most expensive vehicle recovered was a €70,000 2004 BMW. The haul was valued at around €300,000. Many of the cars had already been completely dismantled and packed into a container ready for export through Dublin Port. Other vehicles had simply been cut in half for shipment. Gardaí believed those behind the racket were armed, but no guns were found.

Four men from Lebanon and Syria were arrested, charged and later convicted. One of them was Hassan Hassan. He is currently serving four years in Mountjoy for his role in the scam, which gardaí believe saw cars totalling up to €3 million in value stolen and exported before the ring was smashed.

With her husband behind bars, and the custody battle drawing to a close, Baiba probably believed her life and those of her children would improve. But in February a chain of events began that clearly showed she had reason to be fearful.

The Dublin Circuit Criminal court heard yesterday that a male solicitor, who represented Saulite in the custody case, had been receiving threats 'for quite some time' and was in 'honest fear for his life'. The solicitor's house was the subject of an arson attack last February, Sgt Liam Hughes told

Judge White during a bail application by Hassan to look after his two children in the wake of their mother's death.

Sgt Hughes also said that Saulite had contacted gardaí last Tuesday week and was in fear for the safety of her solicitor and for gardaí involved in the abduction case. Judge White refused the bail application. Gardaí say that because of Baiba's links to the solicitor she too was given security advice. However, they insist there was no direct threat against her life. Because of this, patrols were not stepped up around her.

When her car was petrol-bombed last month her landlord asked her to move out. She decided to take a two-bedroom townhouse in Holywell Square, Feltrim Road, Swords, Co. Dublin. Last Sunday night she stood in the hallway of that house with two friends, smoking a cigarette. A man walked up to the door just before 10 p.m. He produced a handgun and shot her twice at point-black range. She fell back into the hall and died as her sons slept upstairs.

The murderer fled in a black BMW driven by an accomplice. It was later found burned out in the nearby Birchdale estate. The identity of the person who pulled the trigger is unknown, but gardaí believe it could be a foreign national or a member of one of Limerick's crime gangs. Hassan has been interviewed by gardaí in prison to see if he knew of any person who would want to harm his estranged wife.

Gardaí say that since her killing they have learned Baiba had expressed concerns for her safety to friends and neighbours. An internal Garda inquiry is underway into the manner in which the threat to Saulite was treated in the months and weeks before her death. Gardaí insist they did not abandon her while offering protection to her Irish solicitor.

But two people who find themselves alone now are Baiba's sons. Rami and Ali are in the care of the State. Their father will stay in prison until 2009. Their loving mother is to be buried in Riga.

An immigrant's tale ended with bullets and a body bag.

MONDAY, 4 DECEMBER 2006

An Irishwoman's Diary

Deirdre McQuillan

'D, how wud u like 2 go 2 tuscany wit me 2 pick olives, end of oct 4 a week?' read the text received out of the blue in late September from my friend Prue Rudd in Offaly. It instantly brought to mind the dreamy, rolling hills of the Italian countryside far from the clamour of the city catwalks. 'Oh, yes,' I replied, 'I'm on the plane.' Three weeks later we were on the road to Arezzo from Rome for the beginning of the harvesting season.

Our destination was an organic farm in a panoramic-valley setting some 2,000 feet above sea level, four kilometres from the Renaissance hill town of Cortona. Prue had been twice before and loved it. The owners are two hard-working, idealistic Belgians, Luc Van Cauter, a former EU Commission parliamentary secretary and his wife, Brigitte Wyckhuyse.

After falling in love with the place in 1994, the pair decided to put down roots in Tuscany and restore the farm and its olive groves, an old plantation abandoned for 30 years. Their home is a converted watchtower, built in the thirteenth century and enlarged in the sixteenth century; their family comprises six donkeys and two dogs; their visitors are mostly Belgian professionals. They return to Brussels in December every year to sell their premier cru oil at private tastings.

Common methods of harvesting involve shaking the trees manually or mechanically or raking the fruit into nets. Their farm is one of the few in the area where olives are hand-picked in the traditional 'brucatura' way, the fruit never touching the ground. It is rigorous and labour intensive, but results in unbruised fruit and premium oil, necessarily expensive, with the highly prized low rate of acidity. In Ireland we never get such quality and freshness. For the newcomer, the taste and fragrance are a revelation.

Traditionally, harvesting in Italy begins on 1 November and finishes the week before Christmas when the pressing mills shut. Our team, including some Belgians, started in the olive groves each morning armed with little wicker panniers, or cistellas, around our waists and walking sticks for hooking down the branches. We worked from sunrise to sunset with a break for lunch at one o'clock. Systematically stripping each tree, we moved from the top terraces downwards, emptying the baskets into crates holding approximately 20 kilos, which yields up to three litres of oil. Ideally the fruit is pressed the same day. As we picked, Luc pruned.

Luc and Brigitte have about 800 trees, some laden with olives, others with sparse, recalcitrant fruit too high to trap. It became satisfying to find the plentiful ones and steadily denude them. 'Walk three times around each tree before you leave it,' commanded Brigitte, whose sharp eyes, I couldn't help thinking, looked just like small black olives. During the day we marvelled at the views, heard the distant cries of wild boar hunters deep in the forests and the peal of church bells echoing across the valley. Sunsets were breathtaking. It was immensely peaceful – 'time out of mind harvesting', as Patience Gray once described it. The road from the farm to Cortona is narrow and precipitous,

Flower buyer for Tesco Ireland Alison Kilpatrick inspecting the poinsettia crop at Uniplumo in Swords, Co. Dublin, with Elena Spencer (4) and Cormac Madigan (5). One in five Irish households will buy a poinsettia at Christmas. Photograph: Fennells.

better on foot than by car. On the way we looked forward to dinner served by our hosts, both accomplished and inventive cooks, who make use of wild and local seasonal ingredients. Memorable offerings included a carrot salad with garlic, lemon juice, oranges and olive oil; chestnuts baked in a bed of rock salt and a medlar tart. Parasol mushrooms were abundant, and fried with olive oil and butter were a meal in themselves. One evening we had small green fruits with fragrant and delicate flesh, a special gift from a neighbour; I later discovered they were pineapple guavas or feijojas.

There are many varieties of olives; the most popular in Tuscany have names like pendolino, leccino and frantoio. With an average life span of 500 years, their longevity is legendary; many trees can live up to 1,500 years. 'You plant for your grandchildren,' goes the saying. Homer called the harvest 'liquid gold', but the trickle from the first cold pressing is a vivid emerald green with an unmistakable aroma of grassy earth. Tuscan oil is peppery, spicy; oils from further south are sweeter, softer. The mills keep the pulp of the first pressing and press again, each pressing yielding oil of higher acidity and lesser quality, which is mostly what we get in Ireland. Unlike wine, oil does not improve with age and is at its peak in the first month after pressing, though it can keep for a year. Luc and Brigitte are understandably proud of their extra virgin oil which, at 0.1 per cent, has the lowest acidity in the whole region.

Italians place great value on the new season's harvest. On a trip to Cortona one evening we checked out a beautiful fabric shop (the area is as famous for textiles as for wine and oil). When the shopkeeper heard we were hand-picking olives, he was so impressed that he asked us to inform our hosts that he would swap some of his handmade fabrics for their handmade oils. A fair exchange, we thought, like our free board and lodging and a complementary litre to take home. As an earthy and satisfying way of experiencing Italy, who'd be a summer tourist after that?

The Gift of Giving

Irish Times Magazine: Róisín Ingle

It was lashing down as I walked down by Merrion Square, in Dublin. I was on my mobile phone, talking loudly about work, when a woman stopped me.

'You might be interested to know,' she said, as though what she had to say was more urgent than my conversation. This turned out to be correct, but I didn't know that at the time, and to be honest my first instinct was to ignore her. My second instinct was to listen, which turned out, as it sometimes does, to be the wiser one. 'You might like to know', she said, her tone not exactly friendly, 'that there's an old man down there who needs money. You might like to give him some.'

I asked the person at the other end of the line to hang on for a second and thanked the stranger on the street, mostly because I didn't know what else to say. Then I resumed my conversation, asking my colleague whether she had heard the woman. She had. And we laughed, because it was odd. Strange, you know, to be interrupted by a do-gooder on a mission when you are minding your own business, chatting on the phone.

I walked a bit farther, and, sure enough, an elderly, bearded man was sitting on the edge of the park railings. He had a hat in his hand, but he didn't look as though he was begging. He just looked defeated. The way people do when they are soaked and they've nowhere to go and their bones are aching and the wind goes right through them and it's no place for the old. My hand went into my pocket and my fingers found a forgotten fiver, and, because I'd been instructed to, I handed it to him. He took it, smiling and surprised, and secreted the note somewhere in the layers of clothes.

I did all this while I was still on the phone, walking at a pace so brisk it makes me ashamed now. It was too easy. I wasn't going to miss the

A man rinses soot from his face amid the debris of the fuel pipeline explosion near Nigeria's commercial capital Lagos on 26 December 2006. Photograph: Akintunde Akinleye/Reuters.

fiver, so the moment hadn't cost me a thing. I hadn't even wasted any of my precious time on the charitable transaction, multitasking as I was between appeasing my conscience ('You might be interested to know,' the woman had said, as though I was probably the type who wouldn't be interested in anybody except myself) and concluding my business on the phone.

Now, writing this, I want to know his name, his story, his situation. At the time, though, I just wanted to do what I was told, give him the money and dive back onto the cosy beanbag that is my life.

A girl called Sarah recently wrote to tell me of a similar experience she had on the quays in Dublin. She and her boyfriend have just moved from Galway to the capital. On their way to Soup Dragon, on Capel Street, they passed a man who was asking for money. 'I had my usual awkward moment,' wrote

Sarah, and her description of it will be recognised by anyone who has ever eyed a homeless person at a cash machine or outside a supermarket.

'Yes, I want to help, but what will he spend the money on, drink or drugs? And do I have any right to question what he spends the money on? Ideally, I would like to be able to give him food and shelter directly, without money changing hands. But if I went and bought him a sandwich, is he even hungry right now, and what fillings would he like in the sandwich? Surely someone has a right to decide what sandwich they get? But asking him is so patronising and awkward.' Her head spinning with questions, Sarah applied what she called 'the usual solution'. Avert eyes, keep head down, walk on. 'Which is no answer,' she wrote.

Sarah might just have found one, though. After eating at Soup Dragon she asked the lady

Farmer Fintan Nally transporting hay to feed his cattle during heavy flooding at Clonbonny in Athlone, Co. Westmeath, on 13 December 2006. Photograph: James Flynn/APX.

behind the counter for a €20 voucher. They don't normally do them, but she wrote one anyway, and, when passing by the man again, Sarah asked him if he would have any use for it. And he said he would.

None of us needs to be told that the best thing we can do for people who are out of home is to support charities such as Sophia Housing Association, Focus Ireland and the Society of St Vincent de Paul, organisations that are in a position to make a lasting difference to these lives.

But also, to make a temporary difference, couldn't Nude and O'Briens and the Bagel Factory and Starbucks and Café Bar Deli and all the other cafés around the country start making vouchers – call them Streetwise Vouchers – for us to keep a steady supply of in our pockets and our bags? A voucher that as well as providing the practical support of food or a hot drink might facilitate a conversation – a connection, even.

You'd have to consult the potential beneficiaries first, of course, but, as an idea, it strikes me as more considered and, therefore, more meaningful than, say, a €5 note thrust guiltily at an old man in the rain.

WEDNESDAY, 13 DECEMBER 2006

Gang Leader had Many Enemies

Conor Lally

On the morning of Friday, 6 September 1996, *The Irish Times* carried a graphic photograph on its front page. It was of Dublin man Michael Brady. He was pictured behind the wheel of his car outside his rented apartment in the Clifden Court complex on Dublin's Sarsfield

Quay. He had, as was clear from the photograph, been shot in the head.

Brady had raped and murdered his own wife, Julia, in their Clondalkin home in December 1985 after a day-long drinking binge. He had left her body in the living room of their house in Harelawn Park, Clondalkin, to be found by their young children.

He served almost 10 years in prison for the killing and had been released about 18 months before his death. Gardaí believed his killing was revenge for his wife's murder. They believe Brady was killed by Julia's brother, Martin 'Marlo' Hyland.

Brady's murder was Hyland's first serious calling card. In the decade between the Brady killing and Hyland's murder in Finglas yesterday, Hyland demonstrated a relentless appetite for serious criminality. He was known to every detective in the city, had an impressive property portfolio and was more involved in gun crime and top-end drug dealing than any other living criminal of his generation.

Hyland was originally from Cabra. He lived between his many houses in west Dublin, afraid that if he stayed in any one property for too long his many enemies would study his movements and target him. Hyland's big opportunity came with the shooting dead of drug dealer P.J. Judge outside the Royal Oak pub in Finglas. At the time, Hyland was working closely with Judge in running the latter's drugs empire in Finglas, Cabra and Ballymun. Following his boss's murder, Hyland took over the business.

In recent years he had become one of the biggest importers of heroin and cocaine into the Republic. He was also known to deal in firearms. He was involved in a major €2 million construction industry Revenue fraud which involved former members of the IRA.

When the Garda established Operation Anvil in 2005 to target organised crime gangs in Dublin, Hyland found himself at the top of the list of targets. But it wasn't until Anvil was up and running for a few months that gardaí understood the extent of Hyland's business.

He had become so big that a spin-off investigation, Operation Oak, was established. This involved members of the National Bureau of Criminal Investigation and the Organised Crime Unit. These were supported by the Garda National Drugs Unit, the Criminal Assets Bureau (Cab), the

Daryl Jacob and Duncliffe lead over the last flight before landing a novice hurdle at Ascot. Photograph: Julian Herbert/Getty Images.

Garda Bureau of Fraud Investigation and the National Surveillance Unit.

About 30 of Hyland's associates have been arrested under Operation Oak. More than €23 million worth of illicit drugs have been seized. In May his solicitor's offices were raided as well as a number of his houses. Financial documentation was taken for examination by Cab. In July firearms were seized in one of his Cabra houses.

In May, Operation Oak was intensified following the murder in Raheny, Dublin, of money launderer and drug dealer Patrick Harte (42), a Finglas native. Harte had flooded Finglas with

Young people signing a book of condolence for Anthony Campbell at St Michan's House in Greek Street, Dublin, on 17 December 2006. Gardaí say that Mr Campbell was murdered because he was in the wrong place at the wrong time. Photograph: Cyril Byrne.

drugs which had brought down street prices. Hyland was angry that his former friend was muscling in on his patch and he had Harte shot.

In August, when €400,000 worth of cocaine and nine firearms were seized near Athboy, Co. Meath, the drugs were traced to Hyland's gang. One of those arrested with the drugs was Drogheda man Paul Reay (26). Hyland feared Reay was about to turn Garda informer and ordered his killing. The father of three was shot dead three weeks ago. Such was his involvement in crime that Hyland, also a father of three, was suspected of playing a peripheral role in the shooting of Latvian woman Baiba Saulite in Swords last month. The killers may have received support from Hyland's gang, such as a stolen car or the weapon used.

Hyland had no major convictions. He had a lengthy list of motoring convictions. He once sued the *Sunday World* which described him as a major drug dealer. In 1999 he appealed the termination of his dole money when Cab began investigating him. He bought a winning Lotto ticket from a man known to him. He used the €250,000 winnings to explain his wealth.

MONDAY, 18 DECEMBER 2006

Widespread Public Sympathy for Gun Victim

Alison Healy

Hundreds of people have signed books of condolence in memory of apprentice plumber Anthony Campbell, who was shot dead on Tuesday as he worked in a house in Finglas, Dublin.

The target of the attack was drug dealer Martin 'Marlo' Hyland (39), who was shot dead at the same time. It is believed the young plumber was killed to ensure there would be no witnesses.

Mr Campbell's funeral arrangements were confirmed last night. His removal will be held at

John's Lane Church, Thomas Street, at 6 p.m. tomorrow with burial after 10 a.m. Mass on Wednesday.

The books of condolence were organised by Mandy Kavanagh, a neighbour of Mr Campbell (20) at St Michan's House flats complex, close to the Four Courts in Dublin's north inner city.

She said the residents had opened the books so that something good would come out of the death. 'We will give these to the Minister for Justice. He said on the *Late Late Show* that he can't tell the judges what to do, but isn't he the Minister?'

Ms Kavanagh said people wanted to see a change in the bail laws so that bail was not granted so freely. 'People are coming up with thousands of euros to get bail and we want to know where is all that money coming from? If people cannot prove where their money is coming from, they should be refused bail,' she said.

Ms Kavanagh and other neighbours will be standing outside the flats on Greek Street with a book of condolence again today and they expect to close the books tonight. Five books have already been filled.

'It's been great, it has. All sorts of people are stopping to sign the books. We've had doctors, tourists, foreign nationals. People are writing things like "We didn't know him but God bless him and he should never be forgotten."'

Ms Kavanagh said it was 'heartbreaking' to think of the effect of the killing on the young man's family. Mr Campbell was the oldest in a family of four children; the youngest is two years old. 'He was a lovely young fella, very quiet in himself but very obliging if you asked him to do anything,' she said.

Meanwhile, Fr Peter McVerry, director of the Welcome Home charity, has called for a more extensive witness protection programme to encourage the break-up of gangs. He said a properly resourced programme could cost €2 million per witness when Garda resources, relocation costs and living expenses are taken into account.

This would benefit gang members who wanted to get out of crime but feared the consequences. 'What holds gangs together is the cement of fear, so one way of dealing with gangs is to eliminate or reduce that fear,' Fr McVerry said.

SATURDAY, 16 DECEMBER 2006

What Chance has a Traveller Offender before an Irish Jury?

Kathy Sheridan

When the jury for the Pádraig Nally retrial was being empanelled in the Four Courts a couple of weeks ago, it was evident from the challenges to potential jurors that young women under 40 and young men dressed casually or in tracksuits were not in favour.

Each side may challenge up to seven potential jurors without having to show cause, armed only with details of occupation and what can be gauged from a person's appearance.

In this case the final selection of eight men and four women – including an engineer, an accountant and two electricians – had the look about them of mature home- and/or property-owners: pragmatic people, not the kind likely to be struggling with wet, liberal consciences. Does it matter? It could be argued that this was certainly a jury of Pádraig Nally's peers. But where did that leave the victim?

For any journalist (including this one) covering the first trial in Pádraig Nally's home county of Mayo, it was evident that sympathy for John Ward and his family was negligible. It was generally believed – with or without foundation – that no Mayo jury would send Pádraig Nally away if it could help it.

While the supporters of the 62-year-old farmer expected a very different reception in Dublin – 'no

Mayo farmer Pádraig Nally leaving the Four Courts in Dublin on 14 December 2006 after his acquittal at his retrial on charges of killing John Ward, a Traveller, who entered his farm and whom Mr Nally shot dead. Photograph: Cyril Byrne.

one understands rural Ireland,' said one – they were wrong. The atmosphere, even around the learned denizens of the Four Courts, was no different.

Few defendants on a manslaughter charge can have received such a congenial welcome around the courts as Pádraig Nally; handshakes in the yard from court employees and visitors, hooting car horns from drivers on the city quays, phone cameras whipped out in the nearby pub for pictures with the Mayo man, dinner bills picked up by total strangers.

On this evidence alone, no Irish jury could be considered truly representative if several members at least did not set out with a bias against Travellers. In a speech last week the Minister for Health, Mary Harney, noted – presumably with facts to hand – that Travellers 'still confront enormous discrimination' at many levels of Irish society. What chance, then, has an offender from the Traveller community against juries made up of settled, relatively prosperous people?

After the verdict the confused response of one woman probably encapsulated the mood of much of the nation: 'Nally shouldn't have got off – but I'm glad he did.' She said for all 'the politically-correct craw-thumping there is an air of quiet satisfaction' about the outcome. 'Poor, defenceless old people in the countryside are being terrorised – which is nearly the worst thing you can do – and there's no doubt that Travellers are often, if not almost always, involved.'

She is 'fed up' of Traveller representatives 'saying that it's only a small number who are involved in criminality'.

'Their numbers in prison are disproportionate; their response will be that it's because they're disproportionately under suspicion – but I think people really are pretty tired of all that.'

Again and again the charge is made that Travellers know all about their rights but what about their responsibilities and obligations?

With each new Traveller incident, such as the despoliation of an amenity area like the Dodder, or tonnes of waste left behind on a public sports ground, or small towns being forced to shut down at the eruption of murderous feuds involving slash hooks, pickaxes and shotguns, public attitudes harden. Publicans tell stories of vast, intimidating Traveller groups taking over a premises.

Traveller women themselves talk quietly – never openly – about extreme violence within their community. Some of the most violent crimes

in Co. Mayo in the past decade have been attributed to Travellers, although they have not been proven to be responsible. During the trial in Castlebar last year a priest became visibly upset while telling this writer that elderly people living alone in the area 'have no lives . . . because they live in daily terror'.

The High Level Officials Group, set up to replace the Traveller Monitoring Committee, has also expressed concern at 'reports of violence, intimidation, and organised crime [such as drug dealing and smuggling] involving members of the Traveller community', and even the emergence of 'no-go areas' as a result of intimidation of State officials.

Writing here last week, Felim O'Rourke of Sligo Institute of Technology pointed to the fact that the promotion of the 'Traveller Economy', part of official policy for many years, 'ignores the

The sisters of murder victim Siobhán Kearney (from left), Anne Marie, Aishling, Caroline and Brighid, hold a vigil outside her home at Goatstown in Co. Dublin on 10 December 2006. In June 2007, a man was charged with the killing. Photograph: Bryan O'Brien.

fact that the so-called Traveller economy is part of the black economy and may even in some cases involve illegal activities'. Meanwhile, PAYE workers, forced to work harder for every cent, find each one rigorously scrutinised by Revenue. Thus, to the dismay of decent Travellers and their supporters, public attitudes to their community in general have moved inexorably and dangerously from quiet prejudice to barely-concealed venom.

It was in this atmosphere of real, anecdotal and/or unproven wrongs that the case against Pádraig Nally for the homicide of a Traveller came before two Irish juries. The question posed this week was whether a body of 12 Irish men and women existed that was capable of withstanding such prejudice within themselves or from external pressures.

Yet the fact is that the jury – expected to fold within a few hours in the face of stern direction from the judge and Nally's previous conviction – ploughed on for nearly 16 hours over three days.

Just a couple of hours before the verdict they came back looking pale and weary to ask a particular question which suggested that some at least were still battling to objectively weigh the true extent of Pádraig Nally's mortal fear, as he pumped the second and fatal shot into John Ward's back from only four or five yards away, a man who was already limping from the first shot to the buttock, badly beaten and fleeing for his life down the road.

After the verdict, Paddy Rock, a loyal Nally supporter, dismissed the suggestion that this was ever a Traveller issue. 'This is an issue where an intruder came into a man's home . . . where somebody crossed over a boundary to try and do what they did on Pádraig.' The fundamental question is whether any Irish jury, in a grossly anti-Traveller climate, could assess such a case in that way?

Despite the prosecution's contention that Pádraig Nally was 'seeking to put Mr Ward out of circulation and to ensure that he would not again plague Mr Nally', the farmer's consistent plea was self-defence: that Ward's four or five known visits to the area had made him agitated and fearful, and that when he finally came upon Ward in his yard and shot him, Nally felt he was then fighting for his life.

A man with John Ward's deeply disturbed psychiatric history, his known propensity for violence, his approximately 80 previous convictions for offences including burglary, trespass and assaulting gardaí, the fact that on the day of his death his body contained a cocktail of drugs – some prescribed, some not – suggest that Pádraig Nally may well have had reason to fear for his life, whether or not Ward was a Traveller, and particularly if he truly believed that 'reinforcements' for Ward were imminent.

But would Pádraig Nally, living a fairly solitary life in an isolated area, have been quite so fearful to begin with; would he have fired that first shot if Ward had not been a Traveller and therefore identified with the heinous deeds of others in his community?

That isolation and sense of helplessness were no doubt hugely exacerbated by the fact that when Pádraig Nally sought help – twice – from his nearest Garda station, no one was on duty to hear his worries and offer reassurance.

And if outstanding warrants against John Ward for serious offences had been promptly executed, would the man still be alive today?

SATURDAY, 16 DECEMBER 2006

'Welcome to Shannon. All Weapons Must Remain on Board the Aircraft'

Tom Clonan

As Atlantic storm-force winds and rain whip across Shannon Airport's runways and terminal buildings, Christmas trees and ribbons of festive lights sway crazily in the maelstrom. Despite the atrocious December weather, all of the American military flights due at Shannon are on schedule for today.

Since March 2003 – and the invasion of Iraq by US and British forces – approximately half a million US soldiers have travelled through Shannon airport.

'An average of 3,000 US personnel pass through here on a weekly basis. At busy times, like Christmas, that average goes up to 5,000 soldiers per week,' says US army Maj Chris Sabatini, who is based full-time at Shannon airport. He is the liaison officer between the US military's European Command (EUCOM) based in Stuttgart, Germany and the Shannon Airport authorities.

Most of the soldiers are bound for service in Iraq and Afghanistan. An occasional aircraft brings US troops to Germany and elsewhere in Europe.

In the duty-free area today, approximately 200 troops, in distinctive, well-worn desert fatigues, are browsing the many souvenir stands and perfume counters in the main foyer. These soldiers are mostly from the US 82nd Airborne Division, returning home after a tour of duty in Iraq. They arrived on an ATA flight from Kuwait City this morning and are due to fly to McGuire Air Force Base, New Jersey.

The returning soldiers are visibly relaxed, with a large number queuing for drinks at the Sheridan Bar in the open plan duty-free area. The first soldier I approach – at random – is Staff Sgt Debbie Ochsner (40) who has been serving with the 82nd Airborne Division in Baghdad. Deployed to Iraq in April of this year, Ochsner says she is returning to her home town Fayetteville, North Carolina, to be with her two sons, aged eight and 14.

She has bought Irish souvenir T-shirts for the boys and she has also bought a 'worry stone' in the duty-free area. 'I'm carrying the worry stone as a reminder of my husband, Robert. He's still in Iraq, serving with the 82nd Airborne,' she says. She is being sent home early to the US on compassionate grounds following the death of her husband's younger brother, James, aged 36, who was recently killed in action in Afghanistan.

Ochsner then shows me a silver bracelet she is wearing with her brother-in-law's name engraved on it, along with the date, time and location of his death. 'We've all got them,' she says, 'to commemorate family members we've lost in the war.' She adds that she was unable to see her husband during her tour of duty in Iraq, even though they were both serving 'in-country' at the same time.

'It's part of the sacrifice military families have to make,' she says. She plans to spend Christmas with her mother, who has been minding their two sons since she was sent to Baghdad eight months ago.

The next soldier I meet in the Sheridan Bar is Staff Sgt Fran Smith (44), who was serving in Baghdad with the 263rd Air Missile Defence Unit. She says she has been in Iraq since October 2005. Her daughter, Vicky (24), has just given birth to a baby girl. Arriving in Shannon is 'surreal', says Smith. 'After all that time in the heat and dust of Baghdad, to see the green, green grass of Ireland is so strange to me. It's also strange to go home as a grandmother,' she adds with a laugh, 'and not to have to carry a weapon – for now.'

Also in the Sheridan Bar are Sgt Maj James McDowell (45) and Sgt First Class Steven Edmondson (34) from Brooklyn, New York. They both claim Irish ancestry. Both are finishing a one-year tour of duty in Iraq with the newly configured Joint Improvised Explosive Device Defeat Organisation (JIEDDO) based in Baghdad.

'So many of our guys and gals are getting taken out with IEDs [improvised explosive devices] in Iraq that we've started a whole programme to wise them up to the threat,' says McDowell. 'We start stateside by briefing them in our training centres in Louisiana and California about the IED threat. Then we tell 'em again in Kuwait just before they deploy to Iraq, but they don't really pay attention until they're in-country in Iraq.

'Then they see IEDs rolled up in foam rubber and dipped in cement to make the bombs look like rocks – then they pay attention real fast, because it's

Sheep have the road almost to themselves in the Sally Gap area of Wicklow on 15 December 2006 when motorists heeded AA warnings to avoid the area due to snowy conditions. Photograph: Frank Miller.

life or death. We've also come across hollowed-out kerbstones or dead dogs and cats stuffed with high explosives and detonated by remote control when our troops come by.'

All of the troops agree that the ubiquitous Humvee – the standard US military transport vehicle in Iraq – is especially vulnerable to IEDs. One soldier refers to them candidly as 'death traps'. Before he heads for the departure gate, McDowell points out that new medical advances being developed in the field in Iraq, such as powerful powdered coagulants designed to stem arterial bleeding, are saving lives among US troops badly injured by IEDs.

An ATA announcement calls the US troops to board their return flight to New Jersey. Within minutes, the duty-free area empties of US troops. They file silently towards their departure gate,

many carrying hastily wrapped gifts, soft toys, dolls and teddy bears for children they have not seen for more than a year.

The photographer and I follow them to the departure gate. However, *The Irish Times* is not allowed to go on board the ATA flight. We are informed apologetically by an ATA employee that 'there are weapons and dogs on the flight and it isn't very photogenic'. When I inquire about the 'weapons' and 'dogs', I am informed that the troops sometimes carry their personal weapons, 'minus the ammunition', on board for ease of transport back to their home installations.

As for the dogs, a departing US soldier explains: 'We regularly get army dogs on the flights. Most of them are trained to sniff out bombs or drugs. They're not allowed off at Shannon to get air or exercise because of Irish Department of

Siki and Winnie, from the Children of Soweto drama group, pin red ribbons on one another at the unveiling by President McAleese of the Rose Project sculpture in St Stephen's Green, Dublin, to mark World Aids Day on 1 December 2006. Photograph: Alan Betson.

Agriculture rules about dogs. Which is a pity, because they get real excited in there when they smell the fresh Irish air and sometimes they pee on the carpet.'

As he disappears into the air-bridge he quips, 'Hey, make sure you tell your readers that it isn't just the troops that are enthusiastic about the Shannon stopover.'

Within 45 minutes of the departure of the ATA flight to New Jersey, another ATA flight from the US Marine Corp's Camp Lejeune in North Carolina lands at Shannon. On board are members of the US Marine Corps Regimental Combat Team 2, 2nd Marine Regiment, bound for deployment to Al Anbar Province, Iraq.

As the ATA Boeing 757 aircraft taxies to the arrival gate, *The Irish Times* is given permission to board the aircraft. With the aircraft door just opened, the sight inside the aircraft is a little unusual. There are no passengers crowding the aisles, reaching for hand-luggage in the overhead cabins, as is the norm among civilians prior to disembarking an aircraft.

Instead, stretching right back to the rear of the aircraft, there is row upon row of crew-cut marines in identical combat fatigues sitting in total silence. The ATA announcer on board the aircraft states, 'Folks, good morning, welcome to Shannon. You're going to be on the ground here for 45 minutes. The bar and the duty-free are available and there is a smoking section just straight across from the bar. All weapons must remain on board the aircraft, and that includes gun holsters. Thank you.'

The marines leave the aircraft in near silence and head straight for the duty-free area – and the

Sheridan Bar. Their commanding officer, Lieut Col Andrew Smith (41), says the marines are on their way to Al Anbar province for a year-long deployment. Lieut Col Smith, whose family is Irish-American, explains that he brought his family to Ireland to stay in Adare Manor this summer, 'as a last family vacation prior to my deployment to Iraq'.

With a daughter named Shannon, Lieut Col Smith smiles as he describes the significance of the Shannon stopover to the US Marine Corps: 'Shannon, for every US marine, is the highlight of any transit to Iraq. The people of Ireland are genuine and warm and it's always nice to land here. Plus, you get the benefit of a pint of Guinness,' he says. 'It's always special to touch down here as you go in harm's way. For marines in transit, if they

know they're landing in Shannon, it's a very big deal for them.'

These sentiments are echoed by Capt Conlon Carabine (34) of the 2nd Marine Regiment. 'If you were to poll the US Marine Corps, 99 per cent of them would say that Shannon is the stopover of choice when passing to or from Iraq or Afghanistan.' Capt Carabine describes how Shannon has entered the informal culture and vernacular of the US Marine Corps, with the airport becoming synonymous with service in Iraq for most US soldiers.

'I'll tell you this, leaving Kuwait, leaving Iraq to come back to the United States and you'll land in one of two places, either Hahn in Germany or Shannon in Ireland. Everybody, without exception, wants to land in Shannon and celebrate with

Sick Tinker Child, *an oil painting by Dublin artist Louis le Brocquy, was sold for €820,000 at the Adam's Irish art auction on St Stephen's Green in Dublin on 5 December 2006. Photograph: Matt Kavanagh.*

a Guinness. It's not just the Guinness though. The Irish and the American populations are tied together at the hip. We're inextricably linked since the Famine, I guess. More than any other European country, especially since the 1840s.'

The mood among the marines departing for Iraq is noticeably far more sombre than that of those returning to the US. When asked about leaving his young family of four children at Christmas, Lieut Col Smith is philosophical about the sacrifice his family has had to make for military service.

'Of the last four Christmases, I've spent one at home. I spent last Christmas in Al Anbar Province, Iraq. Sure, my kids are curious as to why their Dad leaves around the Christmas timeframe, but that's just how the cards play out. They're old enough to know the risk, and they do ask about Iraq and what's going on there.'

Capt Carabine describes the ferocity of combat experienced by the 2nd Marine Regiment in Al Anbar province in their previous deployment, during which they sustained many losses in battles with insurgents in the city of Khaim, close to the border with Syria. 'These guys don't just stand and fight, some of them are prepared to stand and die in battle.'

Capt Carabine, who was married in August, describes to *The Irish Times* the difficulty of leaving family behind in the US, especially at Christmas. 'I'll tell you, I've been shot at multiple times and it takes more courage to say goodbye to loved ones going to a combat zone, going away to war.'

Capt Carabine, who spent his summer holidays as a child with cousins in Foxford, Co. Mayo, is philosophical about the risks in Iraq. 'Fear isn't an issue for me. I would say there is some anxiety with losing some of the troops under one's command. As far as myself is concerned, dying or getting hurt, I'm not afraid. To be honest, I do not fear death or getting hurt. There's anxiety, but not fear.'

Capt Carabine and Lieut Col Smith barely have time to finish a pint of Guinness before they are called to departure Gate One and their departure to Kuwait City and Iraq. As a steady stream of young marines boards the Boeing for Iraq, their dun desert combats seem poignantly out of kilter with the howling wind, driving rain and green, green grass of Shannon.

SATURDAY, 16 DECEMBER 2006

A Fairytale Steeped in Truth

Joe Cleary

> *It was Christmas Eve babe*
> *In the drunk tank*
> *An old man said to me, 'won't see another*
> *One'*
> *And then he sang a song*
> *'The Rare Old Mountain Dew'*
> *I turned my face away*
> *And dreamed about you*

The single of 'Fairytale of New York' was first released in December 1987, reaching number one in the Irish and number two in the British charts that year. Now, nearly 20 years later, Shane MacGowan's and Jem Finer's masterpiece has established itself as the soundtrack to Christmas for a whole generation, and as one of the great secular carols of our times. With the exception of Joyce's 'The Dead' or Patrick Kavanagh's 'Advent', no work of the twentieth-century Irish imagination has managed to illuminate a particular sense of Christmas so well, as that song has done.

> *Got on a lucky one*
> *Came in 18 to one*
> *I've got a feeling*
> *This year's for me and you*
> *So happy Christmas*
> *I love you baby*
> *I can see a better time*
> *When all our dreams come true*

The excitement in the crowd during the Durkan New Handicap Hurdle at Leopardstown Race Course on St Stephen's Day 2006. Photograph: Alan Betson.

Fairytale's success – artistic and commercial – owes much to its combining of several genres. It is at once a twisted love song, an emigrant ballad and an anthem to the capital city of the twentieth century. And it is perhaps for that reason that it is the only 'Christmas classic' that one can hear without wincing in July.

Maybe 'Fairytale' is also the best-known Pogues song because it sounds more like a mainstream pop song than most of their works do. Its lush melodies clearly make concessions to the schmaltziness of the Christmas-song genre, and the lyrics trade on the combined appeal of romantic love, New York and the American Dream to create a winning formula. It lacks the punk aggressiveness of some of their more rambunctious classics – 'The Sickbed of Cúchulainn', 'Sally MacLennane' and 'If I Should Fall From Grace with God' – and the republican politics and the macabre delirium tremens of many of their standards.

But even if it sounds 'soft', 'Fairytale' is still a complex emotional package. The wonderfully slow, low-key piano lead-in is followed by the sudden surge of raw energy when the whole band comes in and the tempo speeds up and Kirsty MacColl's high-pitched voice edges aside Shane MacGowan's more wistful tones. Then the two leads spar magnificently, trading foul-mouthed insult ('You scumbag/ You maggot/ You cheap lousy faggot') for abusive put-down ('I could have been someone/ Well so could anyone').

The song manages a deft tightrope-walk between starry-eyed hope and world-weary disenchantment. The city evoked in 'Fairytale' is neither a dazzling urban wonderland nor a spiritless wasteland. Instead, the song juggles both the utopian and the dystopian sides of the modern metropolis, weaving sinuously between a youthful sense of big-city excitement and promise ('You were handsome/

You were pretty/ Queen of New York city') and a jaded atmosphere of burnt-out wretchedness ('You're a bum/ You're a punk/ You're an old slut on junk/ Lying there almost dead on a drip in that bed'). Very few pop songs, let alone Christmas songs, have nearly this edge or range.

Like many of the best Pogues songs, 'Fairytale' draws on an Irish tradition of the carnivalesque-violent knockabout or donnybrook – jousts of verbal wit, boasting, insult and repartee, and an outsized or grotesque indulgence of carnal appetite, whether for food, drink or sex. The tradition is of great antiquity, but in its modern form it has survived chiefly as a ballad tradition that records a peasant or plebeian sense of anarchy and excess that must be understood as a comic-serious riposte to the brutalities of colonial poverty and scarcity, or to the travails of migrant communities swept by domestic economic underdevelopment into the great industrial maws of England, Scotland and the United States.

In this tradition may be numbered masterpieces as various as *Fled Bricend, Cúirt an Mhean Oíhe, Ulysses, Finnegans Wake, King Goshawk* and *At Swim-Two-Birds.* The comic street songs that it inspired continued to be performed into recent times by the likes of the Dubliners or the late Frank Harte.

This tradition's spirit of gargantuan festive exaggeration features, in its most basic physical forms, in several Pogues favourites, such as 'The Irish Rover' or 'Fiesta'. In somewhat more politicised versions, such as 'Galway Races', the same sense of bibulous bonhomie is married to a demotic republicanism that celebrates the mingling of 'the Catholic, the Protestant, the Jew, the Presbyterian' in the festive, non-working license of the race-meet.

> They've got cars big as bars
> They've got rivers of gold
> But the wind goes right through you
> It's no place for the old

> When you first took my hand
> On a cold Christmas Eve
> You promised me
> Broadway was waiting for me

The music of the Pogues was always connected to ideas of carnival and excess, and it is appropriate then that their single greatest hit should be a song about New York, the capital of capitals, on Christmas Eve, that late-twentieth century carnival of carnivals that has become a byword for demented 24-hour shop-till-you-drop extravaganzas of mass consumption.

'Fairytale of New York' is a tribute to 'the American Dream' that New York incarnates. The city's allure depends on the idea that the United States offers the abundance beyond appetite that was always central to carnival's appeal. Yet, though its affection for the US's most swinging city is sincere enough, 'Fairytale' also shows the Pogues at their slyly subversive best, and the song's tribute to Christmas, New York, and the American Dream are all double-edged.

'Fairytale' is, after all, a Christmas song that simultaneously manages to be an exceptionally foul-mouthed anti-Christmas song. It is a tender love song that is also a biting duet of mutually reciprocated disappointment. And it is an aria that invokes the city it hymns not as a place where emigrant dreams come true, but as a dream-busted landscape of the down-and-out – the lonely, the drug-addicted, the drunken, the homeless, the old, the incarcerated.

The wonder of New York is that it offers all of the extravagantly exaggerated carnal promise of the old mythical lands of Cockaigne. Yet, while acknowledging this, 'Fairytale' is never so mesmerised as to forget the alienation behind all the hype. In sum, what we get is not a Sinatra-type eulogy to Manhattan's capacity to take one from 'vagabond shoes' to being 'king of the hill/ top of the heap', but rather a remarkable duet between an English socialist and an Irish republican hymning

Sound of the season — bell ringers of St Fin Barre's Cathedral in Cork rehearsing for New Year's Eve 2006.
Photograph: Daragh Mac Sweeney/Provision.

not so much the US itself as the dreams of abundance that emigrants have always attached to the country – dreams that the Empire State has always successfully exploited, and only rarely redeemed.

> *You were handsome*
> *You were pretty*
> *Queen of New York City*
> *When the band finished playing*
> *They howled out for more*
> *Sinatra was swinging*
> *All the drunks they were singing*
> *We kissed on a corner*
> *Then danced through the night*
> *The boys of the NYPD choir*
> *Were singing 'Galway Bay'*
> *And the bells were ringing out*
> *For Christmas day*

Songs take their meaning, however, not just from their own words or music, but also from cultural contexts. When 'Fairytale' was released in 1987, the Irish economy was in the doldrums and Northern Ireland was an unacknowledged warzone. Ireland, North and South, was a production line for the low-skilled, turning out labourers and childminders, barmen and waitresses, hotel-workers and janitors for London, New York, and Boston.

Back then, whole sections of New York's north Bronx were populated by recently arrived 'New Irish', living, often acrimoniously, between older, more assimilated Irish-American and Italian-American communities and African-Americans and other poor migrant peoples – Dominicans, Mexicans, Jamaicans and Puerto Ricans.

In the one-roomed Irish bars that studded the streets snaking from Bedford Park and Webster

Avenue across Mosholu Parkway to Bainbridge Avenue, Gun Hill Road and northwards up to the more gentrified and 'whiter' districts of Woodlawn and McLean Avenue, the Pogues were rarely off the jukeboxes. In the run-up to December 25th, the few with Green Cards (and savings) returned home for Christmas, while those without Green Cards or savings or yen for home hunkered down for another makeshift festive debauch in Gotham.

The 'Fairytale' combination of jaunty excitement, nostalgia, acrimony and washed-out despair is of that time and place. The young Irish who congregated over Christmas week in the Roaring Twenties, the Phoenix, the Black Thorn, the Village, Ireland's Thirty Two, Fiona's, Fibber Magees or Rumours, knew the economic and the emotional condition that the Pogues had captured.

> You're a bum
> You're a punk
> You're an old slut on junk
> Lying there almost dead on a drip in that bed
> You scumbag, you maggot
> You cheap lousy faggot
> Happy Christmas your arse
> I pray God it's our last

Today, the 'New Irish' are home. Ironically, many of them now employ people who are themselves labelled the New Irish and when Irish people travel to New York these days it is often on those demented overseas shopping extravaganzas that mark the time of the Tiger. And if Ireland has changed, so has New York. The al-Qaeda bombers of September 11th punctured as great a hole in the American Dream as they did in downtown Manhattan. New York may have been the capital of the twentieth century, but it is unlikely to be the capital of the twenty-first.

But back in the 1980s, when the Irish were still a dirty job people, the celebration of lumpen excess that was the trademark of so many of the Pogues songs had a radical edge. They sang of the unrepentantly shiftless world of the 'undeserving poor' – ne'er-do-well navvies, brawling republicans and free-spending rakes. To many here it all smacked of a wretchedly stereotyped Ireland of Victorian caricature, but the songs played back then to Irish communities from Queens to Cricklewood that had some idea of what it was like to be one of the hod-carrier peoples of the world and, as such, to be associated with lawlessness, fecklessness, squalor, spongerism, the wrong side of emigration law, and terrorism.

This Christmas, most Irish-born people over 40 will have either experienced emigration themselves or had family members who went away; few under 30 know anything of it. To them, the notion of the Irish as migrant menials, spongers or terrorists seems distinctly 'foreign'. And so, when 'Fairytale' plays in the shops of Temple Bar, Tullamore or Templemore, it may well be the 'New Irish' who now most viscerally appreciate its curious mix of expectancy and despondency.

> I could have been someone
> Well so could anyone
> You took my dreams from me
> When I first found you
> I kept them with me babe
> I put them with my own
> Can't make it all alone
> I've built my dreams around you

When the bubble bursts here, will the cycle of emigration begin again? One hopes not; it would be a remarkable achievement if that cycle of human export could be relegated to folk-memory and folk-song. But for now at least, 'Fairytale' can be a reminder to the rest of us that capitalism – in New York, here, wherever – divides its spoils no less unevenly today than two decades ago. And when our home-grown neoliberals summon up the sorry ghost of the 1980s to remind us we have never had it so good, MacColl's and MacGowan's duet can be a reminder that not all back then was misery and despair; there was also resilience and resistance.

WEDNESDAY, 20 DECEMBER 2006

Judge Casts a Cold Eye on Haughey's Life

Miriam Lord

In life, he bade farewell to a turbulent political career and settled into comfortable retirement. He held open days for charities at his lovely home. The dark memories faded. There was talk of the presidency. The future looked good for the former taoiseach. Then the past came calling and ripped gilded posterity from his grasp. The nation reassessed. Second time around, judgment was less kind.

In death, the pattern is repeated. Twice this year, the career of Charles Haughey has been assessed, with very different outcomes.

The first assessment was delivered on a Friday in June, from the side of a hill in a chilly north Dublin graveyard. The second was distributed on a Tuesday in December, from a suite of cosy offices in Dublin Castle. (Yesterday, to be precise.) The first, spoken by Taoiseach Bertie Ahern at Charlie's graveside, was heavy with admiration and emotion. There was a note of defiance in his voice as he recalled with pride, and a catch in his throat, the man he called 'Boss'.

Nobody expected Bertie's words at the funeral of his old friend and mentor to be anything other than generous and kind. But the manner of his eulogy, conveyed in a pitch verging on the aggressive, raised eyebrows. The only thing the Taoiseach didn't do was organise a national

Charles Haughey's legacy — printer Leonard Swords delivering copies of the Moriarty Tribunal report at Dublin Castle on 19 December 2006. Photograph: Matt Kavanagh.

whip-round to get a statue of Charlie erected in the GPO next to the dying Cúchulain.

The second, written by Mr Justice Michael Moriarty, is not constrained by the bonds of lifelong friendship or political loyalty. While Bertie Ahern drew on a Fianna Fáil lifetime to compile his report, Mr Justice Moriarty had a mere nine years in a tribunal chamber to concentrate on his. He has looked at the 'Haughey Years' – times when Bertie was busy forging his career and picking up tips from a populist master – with a dispassionate eye. When not examined through the green-tinged lens of the Soldiers of Destiny, the Charles Haughey that

Taoiseach Bertie Ahern as seen by caricaturist Peter Hanan at the end of 2006.

Michael Moriarty sees is far less heroic than the figure Bertie Ahern wants us to remember.

That is not to say these two very powerful men – Taoiseach and High Court judge – disagree on everything. They don't. They are in hearty agreement on one point: Charles J was a very hard and diligent worker. (It's when it comes to the nature of some of that work, and the beneficiaries, that these distinguished gentlemen part company.) Of the two assessments, the report Michael Moriarty produced after nine years is a more unforgiving exploration of 'The Squire's' interesting life, or 'extraordinary journey', as the awestruck Bertie put it last June. In mitigation, the Taoiseach only had 15 minutes to deliver his conclusions on CJ. The judge had the luxury of 700 pages.

'He was a legend, and a man.' – Ahern.

'Devalued the quality of a modern democracy.' – Moriarty.

It's very difficult to reconcile the two Charlies.

There's Bertie's 'Boss' – the hero. 'Charlie had a steadfast love for this country,' trembled the Taoiseach at the graveside. 'This love was a central element of his political life. He was patriotic to the core. He had a great respect for every aspect of the life of this country – our noble heritage, our rich culture, our ancient tongue – and a special interest in historical and literary matters.' (Bertie forgot to mention how CJH also had a great devotion to amassing large amounts of money, spending it lavishly, then forgetting he ever got it.)

There's Michael's witness – the liar. The judge doesn't feel any need to wax lyrical about him. Just straight facts will do. He categorises Haughey's reign as 'a dismal period in the interface between politics and business in recent history'. The facts back him up. In his report, Mr Justice Moriarty charts the years of 'clandestine donations'. He reckons, conservatively, that Haughey amassed over £9 million above his normal entitlements between 1979 and 1996.

And how much would that be worth in today's money, judge? Again, no hyperbole or tales of old Ireland from Michael. That, he concludes, would be in the region of €45 million. The money was sloshing into the taoiseach's coffers as fast as he could spend it. Sadly, as the report notes, Charles Haughey wasn't fussy about where that money came from.

'If the definition of a patriot is someone who devotes all their energy to the betterment of their countrymen, Charles Haughey was a patriot to his fingertips.' – Bertie.

'Unbelievable – Bizarre – Unprecedented.' – Mr Justice Moriarty. (He nearly got the full house in the course of his report, but he just couldn't manage to slip a 'grotesque' in there too.)

June, 2006, and it's Bertie again. 'Today, I recall his singular combination of love for great literature and great politics.' Yesterday, Michael recalled his singular pursuit of cash, his improper interference with the Revenue service at a time when the country was on its uppers and his regrettable attempts to 'saddle others' with responsibility for some of his financial affairs.

'Have no doubt that the ultimate judgment of history will be positive. He was one of the most consequential of Irishmen. And when the shadows have faded, the light of his achievements will remain.' That's Bertie, ever the optimist.

And the achievements will, deservedly, remain. But after the Moriarty report, the shadows are there forever too. They include the 'elements of fear and domination engendered by him in individuals in both the public and private sector'. And the tribunal's finding that he failed to co-operate at all stages.

Still. We're all human. The Taoiseach could have been talking about any man, not just Charlie, when noting, 'He could err, but he was always valiant.' CJ's errors are well documented, but where is the valour in pocketing substantial subscriptions

Nadine Crotty, a first-time homebuyer, watching finance minister Brian Cowen on TV in Buswells Hotel, Dublin, delivering his Budget across the road in Dáil Éireann on 6 December 2006. Photograph: Dara Mac Dónaill.

left over from a fund to pay for a best friend's liver transplant? Michael Moriarty can't find it.

In fairness, sentiment and loyalty allow Bertie to say what he likes at his friend's graveside. But, after the publication of yesterday's report, one suspects not many will agree with the Taoiseach's assertion that 'he was one of us'. Raking in 171-times his actual wages? Bullying a major bank? Telling the little people to tighten their belts? Brazenly denying the obvious in a witness box? Profiting from a friend's misfortune? One of us? Back to Michael, before the apologists start. 'It would be quite unwarranted to conclude that "everyone was at it".' Unless, perhaps, you were connected enough to be 'one of us'.

THURSDAY, 21 DECEMBER 2006

Haughey Memorial Card sent to Thousands of Sympathisers

Stephen Collins

The memorial card for Charles Haughey has been sent out to friends and sympathisers in the same week as the publication of the Moriarty tribunal report into the financial affairs of the former taoiseach. The card quotes the Thomas Davis poem 'My Grave'.

Thousands of the memorial cards were sent earlier this week to those who had sympathised with the Haughey family after the death of the former taoiseach last June.

The card includes a photograph of a smiling Mr Haughey under the heading: 'In Loving Memory of Charles J Haughey, Abbeville, Kinsaley, Co. Dublin.'

Under the photograph is a quote from the Psalms:

*Happy the man who delights in the law of the Lord
And meditates on His law day and night.*

*He is like a tree planted near running water
That yields its fruit in due season, and whose leaves
shall never fade.*

One side of the card quotes the Thomas Davis poem 'My Grave' in full. It reads:

*Shall they bury me in the deep
Where wind-forgetting waters sleep?
Shall they dig a grave for me
Under the greenwood tree?
Or on the wild heath,
Where the wilder breath
Of storm doth blow?
Oh, no! oh no!
No! on an Irish hillside
or an opening lawn, but not too wide;
For I love the drip of the wetted trees –
I love not the gales, but a gentle breeze,
To freshen the turf; put no tombstone there,
but green sods, decked with daisies fair;
nor sods too deep, but so that the dew,
The matted grass roots may trickle through.
Be my epitaph writ on my country's mind;
HE SERVED HIS COUNTRY, AND LOVED
HIS KIND
Oh! 'twere merry unto the grave to go,
if one were sure to be buried so.*

FRIDAY, 22 DECEMBER 2006

Winter Begins Slow Farewell After Long Night Closes

Eileen Battersby

Long before daybreak, the signs were good. The heavens were casting off the Dickensian fog that had shrouded the Boyne Valley, and many other areas, during a 48-hour spell of damp, murky weather that

A stream of golden sunlight passes through the window box and along the passageway leading into the burial chamber of Newgrange on 21 December 2006 during the winter Solstice on the shortest day of the year. Photograph: Alan Betson.

made one suspect that time might be better spent re-reading *Bleak House* than waiting for the sun.

As the Newgrange watchers and Save Tara protesters gathered at the Stone Age monument, one of the finest passage tombs in Western Europe, knowing smiles set the tone. After two dull mornings in which the Boyne itself had been invisible, the optimists had been rewarded.

A formidable trio consisting of nature, the ancients and global warming had decided on an impressive Christmas present – a golden sunrise. Night suddenly became day and the monument and its resident battalion of sentry-like standing stones emerged from the purple darkness.

The air was cold but dry, perfect. Early arrivals noted the appearance of a handsome black Labrador. Too busy to notice the lone rabbit that froze statue-like before darting into a nearby hedge, Nick seemed businesslike, deliberate, impressively self-possessed. Two years of age, he is

an experienced sniffer dog – his brief to check out the monument. Down the passageway he went, indifferent to the archaeology but intent on his task.

On leaving the monument, he walked down the hill, his Garda handler at his side, and settled down with a sigh. Sharing the back of the van was his good-looking sidekick, Hesky, a German Shepherd, eager if far less a specialist. 'He does patrol work,' said his handler. Nick sighed again. Trained by the British Metropolitan police, he is an ambitious character who needs a challenge.

The chosen few, those who had won Solstice tickets as well as the usual Government Ministers, filed by on their way into the mound. The rest of us waited, aware the show had already begun. Beneath a brightening sky, the warm pink turned to yellow as a blister of orange on the horizon began to take shape. The tree-lined ridge across the valley seemed to shimmer. By 8.45 a.m., the sun

Electrical contractor John Bonfield changes a Christmas light bulb over Silver Street, Nenagh, on 9 December 2006, after storms destroyed a large number of the town's seasonal decoration bulbs. Photograph: Fergal Shanahan.

was poised to break free. No light ever seems as bright or as sudden as that on a Solstice morning. This is the sun that rises after the longest night.

A woman wearing a pair of balloons began to sway and wave her arms at the sun. 'Is she trying to levitate?' asked an onlooker. 'I hope not,' answered his companion, 'but that one over there might set herself alight.' Oblivious to those of us watching the sun, stood a forlorn acrobat with a hoola hoop. A number of cups attached to it were blazing.

Meanwhile by 8.51 a.m., on cue, the sun was displaying an emphatic sense of purpose, and had broken free of the horizon. Within five minutes, it was well clear of the ridge and was casting a bright light over the valley. The river, which had been a swollen torrent, for day had become a silver ribbon.

Faces turned away from the sky to the quartz-faced monument. A great beam of yellow was pouring through the roof box. Cameras were held aloft as were mobile phones – all recording the moment. The light began to withdraw, its mission completed. Suddenly the party that had been inside the chamber made its way out. As the first figures descended the steps, the sun moved behind the clouds. Nature and ancient man had said enough, winter had symbolically begun its slow farewell.

SATURDAY, 6 JANUARY 2007

Ancient Beijing Being Lost in Welter of Rebuilding

Clifford Coonan, in Beijing

A bitterly cold wind is gusting down this ancient Beijing laneway, but the two old friends don't care as they happily set out a couple of stools and a trestle table to enjoy a steaming plate of jiaozi meat dumplings.

The sun is shining, and the wind makes the air fresh – it's good for your health, they say.

Despite the diners' upbeat tone, these are troubled times for Beijing's hutong laneways, which once fanned out around the city to form a graceful network of passageways lined with traditional courtyard houses, grey Ming dynasty environs filled with atmosphere.

Only one-third of Beijing's hutongs still exist – most have been demolished or partially destroyed, according to a recently released survey. The devastation of ancient areas such as Qianmen, which used to house some of Beijing's oldest traditional courtyards and alleyways, bears out the report's findings. Qianmen has lost many laneways, some of them dating back to the thirteenth century, to make way for new developments.

As well as being the main form of urban construction in the 'northern capital' of Beijing, the hutongs have for centuries provided a framework for vibrant local communities, as knife-sharpeners, coal merchants and fruit-sellers moved up and down their precincts plying their wares.

Down one winding laneway filled with wafting scents of Mongolian-style pork being barbecued on skewers, Wang Jian, a 70-year-old retired carpenter, is chatting with his neighbours. Wang says his house is a bit draughty at this time of year, but he'd never dream of leaving the hutongs. He never married and has no children, so his neighbours are like family to him, particularly as he gets older.

'I love my neighbours and friends. There's a great feeling of community here in the lanes. My brother is disabled and in a wheelchair and he's had a lot of help from the neighbours,' he says.

The word hutong itself is originally a Mongolian expression meaning 'well': in early Beijing, communities grew up in the streets leading to the wells. During the early Ming dynasty (1368–1644), there were 458 hutongs in Beijing; the figure rose to 978 during the Qing dynasty (1644–1911).

The latticework of streets housed the eunuchs of the imperial household, the markets for coal, jewellery or goats, historical columns dedicated to the unicorn or the courtyards of the Wendefang, or Literature and Morality district.

By the 1980s, when China began its opening-up process, there were 3,679 alleys in Beijing, but since then rampant development has destroyed many of them – the number of hutongs has fallen by 40 per cent since then as town planners clear the precincts to make way for roads and gleaming office blocks.

Some courtyard houses on the laneways have been cleared and set aside for purchase by rich Chinese, and foreigners keen to have that authentic Beijing experience. However, a recent auction of courtyard houses was a failure, because of a lack of clarity over who owns the houses – title can be controversial in many cases.

But still the destruction continues. The areas due to be demolished are marked with the character chai, which means demolish. The pace of destruction was expected to slow as 2008 neared, but new chai signs are still going up.

While some of the development is linked to projects for the 2008 summer Olympics, which are being held in the capital, much of the old city has been knocked down as part of the broader redevelopment plans to make Beijing into a world-class city.

Chairman Mao Zedong started the process in the 1950s, when he moved many factories into the city. But the Great Helmsman's impact on the hutongs has been dwarfed by efforts to redevelop the capital as a world city, complete with world-scale office buildings in the Central Business District in the heart of the city and the new signature

Beijing's hutongs under a recent fall of snow. Many hutongs or alleyways are being torn down in an effort to modernise Beijing ahead of the 2008 summer Olympics. Photo: Guang Niu/Getty Images.

Olympic buildings springing up on the sites of ancient communities.

A survey by the Beijing Institute of Civil Engineering and Architecture examined about 1,320 traditional streets and lanes and found that 15 per cent had been destroyed to make way for new buildings. Another 52 per cent have managed to retain something of their original condition but have suffered serious damage. For example, many have had the traditional courtyard houses destroyed, while only one-third of the hutongs have retained their original character.

Sun Xiulan (30) has only recently moved to a house in a laneway near the Bell Tower, in the increasingly trendy district of Houhai. 'I moved here a year ago and I really like it. It's very convenient and it's cheap to live here too. My child's school is near here. The neighbours are very friendly, though I'm always out and about,' she says. 'I don't like tall buildings, and if they build skyscrapers, I'll never manage the rent.'

Locals worry that Beijing has lost something of its essence as an old capital city, even though many of the resettled residents are quite happy about being moved from cramped courtyard houses, often with multiple families in a building, to modern apartments with great facilities. But they do complain that the community spirit is gone. There are also cases of corrupt developers pocketing their compensation money, and armed thugs have been involved in illegally moving out some of the more stubborn residents.

Alarmed that there may be nothing of Old Beijing for the visitors to see during the Olympic Games, the government has introduced restoration guidelines for the hutongs, requiring that they be rebuilt with original materials and retain their original grey colour. Many courtyard houses are being rebuilt with interior toilets, and communal toilets along the laneways have been dramatically upgraded.

'I hope they rebuild these old hutongs and the courtyard houses. They'll be a lot nicer to live in than they are at the moment. Although I am a bit worried if they rebuild the houses, I won't be able to afford to buy a new one,' says one elderly woman.

FRIDAY, 12 JANUARY 2007

Sad Irony of Ervine's Passing

Fionnuala O'Connor

The sudden death of David Ervine this week – far too early for a still youthful, vivid personality, but well after his star had dimmed – removes another of the players who helped blaze the path for the Belfast Agreement and what followed. There is a sad appropriateness about the final departure of the last prominent 'loyalist fringe' figure.

David Ervine was a great man for the wonky rhetoric. He hated the suggestion that loyalist paramilitaries might have had their moment in politics, but he would have admitted that the timing of his last exit could be called the opposite of glad confident morning.

It has been a trek. There is a litany of names once central, now long gone from the Northern stage. Several have died: Tony Blair's first secretary of state, Mo Mowlam; IRA veteran Joe Cahill; now Mr Ervine. The late Mary Holland, almost as much player as commentator, wrote (in this space) with grace, insight and authority derived in part from matchless knowledge of the principal figures, but in the main from a yearning to see an end to violence and a lessening of bitterness.

Others have been shuffled off by the remorseless rhythms of political life. The Women's Coalition had a brief hour of prominence, like the loyalist fringe contributing more to the Good Friday negotiations than their size warranted.

These are the last few months at the centre of events for Mr Blair, who bounced into the North

The coffin bearing the remains of Progressive Unionist Party leader David Ervine stops at his office on the Newtownards Road in east Belfast after his funeral service in the East Belfast Mission on 12 January 2007. The funeral was attended by, among others, Sinn Féin president Gerry Adams and foreign minister Dermot Ahern. Photograph: David Sleator.

all of 10 years ago to seize hold of events handled so tentatively by John Major, his predecessor as prime minister.

It is almost as difficult to predict the shape of things to come post-Blair, in terms of British government involvement, as the shape of the DUP post-Paisley. But there will be no replicating the intensity of the Blair involvement, the commitment of a new prime minister with a majority far in excess of anything his successors are likely to win.

The youthful Mr Blair embarked on a shiny new project full of danger. The shine disappeared long ago. The danger, depending on your point of view, is now damage woven deep into the fabric of the state, or is all but dissipated.

Mr Major had none of Mr Blair's advantages. Forced to evaluate the potential of a peace settlement while IRA violence continued, himself the target of a mortar attack on Downing Street which missed him by yards and with a dwindling majority and fractured party, he nonetheless made some determined moves. It also emerged that while he and his Northern secretary, Sir Patrick Mayhew, were rubbishing the very idea of contact with republicans, government representatives had been secretly meeting Martin McGuinness and others.

Sir Patrick usually seemed made for his moment on stage, but the senior lawyer's assurance and command of language dissolved in the face of exposure. When it came out that 'no contact' meant repeated contact, a press conference in Stormont Castle witnessed a man in shock, pale and stumbling, unable to face down the journalist who broke the story, Eamonn Mallie. The unhappy performance ended abruptly, his forgotten spectacles glinting on a table as the Northern secretary rushed off.

When Mr Blair goes, the only remaining main players from the original cast will be the Sinn Féin leaders. Unless we count Ian Paisley. After the first careless rapture of denunciation, the DUP leader cut an isolated and increasingly discontented figure, as deniable back-channels became ceremonious and prolonged negotiations reported by the world's press. The man at the centre of events, David Trimble, more often looked stressed than jubilant, but he clearly relished the deference he was accorded as head of the largest unionist party, by the prime minister and successive taoisigh though not, of course, by some of his own colleagues.

The man whose efforts had urged Irish, British and American governments to see the potential for a settlement and who helped Gerry Adams across the barrier of distrust and distaste, John Hume, went into negotiations exhausted. He emerged spent, his dominance of nationalism eroded. SDLP deputy leader Séamus Mallon carried much of the burden.

Mr Trimble, Mr Hume and Mr Mallon look on now from the sidelines. There was a scene at night outside Stormont as the Belfast Agreement was being finalised when it appeared that the sideline was the final Paisley destination.

He arrived to shout about treachery in the darkness as Mr Trimble prepared to sign up, and was heckled by loyalist paramilitaries turned enthusiasts for talks. 'Dinosaur', they shouted. David Ervine came out to quieten his own followers and ask them to allow an old man to speak.

The peace process has many ironies, few greater than that Ian Paisley is more vocal and more powerful than ever while, to the regret of many, the voice of David Ervine has been stilled.

Towards a Leaner Future

Jane Powers

In times of crisis I attempt to comfort myself that my worries are written so minuscule on the face of the earth that they are meaningless. I'm just like a tiny ant in a field, making no difference at all to the big scheme of things. This insignificant-ant-person idea is certainly a consolation, and is a fine device for getting past life's sticky patches, but it doesn't take into account our capabilities as human beings.

As humans we have built civilisations beyond the wildest insect dreams, by harnessing the earth's resources to the twin engines of science and technology. For the past century those engines have been driven mainly by fossil fuels, and for the past 50 years almost exclusively by oil. Our hydrocarbon-powered journey has raised us higher than we would ever have expected. The introduction to the 1969 Whole Earth Catalog – an educational and inspirational guide for environmentalists, hippies and proponents of sustainability – noted: 'We are as gods and might as well get good at it.'

Thirty-eight years after those words were written, it is a moot point as to whether we ever got good at it. Oil's near-magical energy has allowed us to produce more food than we ever would have thought possible, and (in the time since the publication of that issue of the Whole Earth Catalog) to almost double the population of the world. It has given us mobility: 95 per cent of transport is powered by oil, propelling us to the farthest corners of the earth – and to the supermarket that is just a little too distant to be reached on foot. It brought us the products on that supermarket's shelves, from hundreds or thousands of miles away. It fuels industry, and runs and heats (or cools) our homes, our hospitals, our schools, our places of work. Oil – so cheap, so convenient, so powerful – has driven our lives for the past few decades. From one point of view we are indeed as gods, living in a golden era.

All eras have to come to an end, and our age of oil is no exception. We may be in our glory days now, but peak oil – the point at which we have less oil left in the ground than the amount that we have already taken out – is either here already or will be upon us within the next couple of years. (The experts, who include erstwhile oil executives among their numbers, give different predictions, but all are near enough to put a stop to our gallop pretty soon – or at least to have some of us thinking about reining in.)

Peak oil doesn't mean that the stuff will run out in the near future, but, because we've already consumed all the easy-to-get-at stocks, it means that the second half of this resource will be harder and harder to extract and thus more and more expensive. At a certain point it's better, both environmentally and economically, to just leave it in the ground.

That's the oil situation, and it will take all our wit, inventiveness and intelligence to ensure that our descent down the far side of the peak is a smooth one rather than a painful crash.

We have another urgent motive to stop squandering oil: climate change. We all now know that greenhouse gases, including carbon dioxide, are emitted when we burn fossil fuels, causing the average global temperature to rise: we've seen an increase of 0.6 degrees in the past century. And while we in the comparatively chilly north of the planet may welcome the idea of growing grapes and figs outside, the effects in the south are already calamitous. Floods, erosion, desertification and crop failure threaten the existence of our fellow human beings.

The poorer nations in Africa and Asia are now bearing the brunt of our love affair with oil combustion. And it's only a matter of time before the adverse effects here will be apparent to even the thickest of sceptics. It's no coincidence that our summers are drier, that our winters are wetter and that floods are more common. Just imagine this:

add another degree or two to our newly balmy temperatures and rain forests will die, sea levels will rise disastrously (thanks to melting polar caps and glaciers) and millions of people will be displaced all over the world. Surely that is enough to drown out the denials?

Or maybe it's not. Climate change and peak oil may be rumbling relentlessly towards us like a pair of runaway buses, but we can't actually see them, so it's easy to pretend that they're not there. We have to make a leap of faith. As George Monbiot compellingly writes on climate change, we have to realise that all the figures and graphs and projections that are generated by scientists actually pertain to our ecosystem. The ecosystem: that's planet earth, the place we live, my home and yours, and of all our children. If an out-of-control bus were crashing through our walls we'd grab our kids and run like hell – or, if it were too late for that, stand in front of the bus ourselves, to protect the next generation. But there is no bus; it's just a metaphor for a catastrophe waiting to happen. So instead we strap the children into the car and drive them the kilometre to school.

No one wants to change, and, even more so, no one wants to change first. We all know the argument: 'Why should I stop driving the kids to school – or stop taking weekends in Paris or Prague, or start turning down the thermostat – when your man across the road drives a four-litre Range Rover and flies to Dubai or Cape Town or New York at the drop of a hat?'

Here's one answer: because those climate-change and peak-oil graphs give us undeniable evidence that we have to. And here's another: because it's less painful and less stressful to make changes voluntarily now rather than desperately and resentfully later. And here's a third: because it's better to do it while we still have some relatively cheap and accessible oil.

With this oil we can fabricate the framework for a leaner future. In the coming era we will have to lead our lives in a more efficient and sustainable

A sunny and mild Sandymount Strand in Dublin on Christmas Day 2006. The draft United Nations climate report said the Gulf Stream, which brings warm waters to the north Atlantic and keeps Ireland temperate, was likely to slow but not enough to offset an overall warming. Photograph: Bryan O'Brien.

way. We will need to make modifications to our transport networks, to our houses and buildings, to our electricity generating systems, to our industries, to almost every imaginable sector. We need to spend the oil of today wisely, in order to secure our tomorrows.

Different voices say that we must cut our carbon-dioxide emissions by varying amounts in order to avoid a calamity. The Stern Review on the Economics of Climate Change suggests a 25 per cent cut by 2050, with an ultimate figure of about 80 per cent, while Monbiot, in his book *Heat: How to Stop the Planet Burning*, suggests a 90 per cent cut by 2030.

The figures are academic to a lay person, but they indicate the same thing: it is time to power down. Some of our needs are already being met by renewable energies, such as solar, wind and water power, and by geothermal pumps, which tap into the relatively steady temperature just under the earth's crust – providing heating in winter and cooling in summer. Yet none of these have the potency of oil.

Biofuels – either in the form of biomass (solids such as woodchip and miscanthus) or as liquid ethanol or biodiesel – will, in the future, power more of our transport, heating and electricity generators. But such crops need fuel for processing, and, more importantly, their cultivation could occupy valuable space required for growing food. Nuclear power is sometimes suggested as a solution to our coming energy deficit, but I'm not alone in never wanting to see a nuclear power station in Ireland, for many, many reasons.

Which brings us again to the inescapable conclusion that we have to cut our energy use dramatically. We already know the obvious: turn off the lights; turn down the heating; insulate our houses; walk, cycle or take public transport instead of driving; fly less; recycle and reuse; compost our waste. These are no-brainers, and many of us have already incorporated them into our lives. Yet these energy-conservation measures will not, on their own, ensure a bearable and sustainable future. Depending on how we react now, we are on the brink of either a disaster or an adventure. We can choose to go over the edge screaming and clinging to every single comfort and meaningless luxury we've grown used to in the past couple of decades or we can gird our loins, make plans, get educated, get prepared and do this thing together.

I know, I'm a little embarrassed by the rallying cry too, but having a common purpose makes this project 100 times easier – or, if everybody felt the same on this island, about six million times easier.

The internet is available now in almost every house, and contains a lifesaving treasury of information on how we might move into a slimmer and more oil-free future. The Post Carbon Institute (www.postcarbon.org), the Community Solution (www.communitysolution.org) and the Foundation for the Economics of Sustainability (www.feasta.org) are just three starting points.

Our lives and the lives of future generations depend on our learning about climate change and peak oil now, on our taking action now, on our lobbying our politicians now. Our future depends on our becoming more self-sufficient and learning to grow our food and repair our belongings. It depends on our valuing the possessions we have and not hankering after every little thing that we haven't. It depends on changing our mindset from a selfish one to one where we work together to save this planet and its resources – Mother Earth, who gives us everything we have.

The way to achieve much of this is right in front of our noses – and outside our doors. The more we can meet our needs within the immediate vicinity, the less resources we use, and the less waste and emissions we create. Buy local products, eat local food, do local things: that is, build a community.

We are facing the most serious crisis in our lives: one where we can, to go back to the beginning of this article, in fact, learn from the ants. One ant on its own is of little consequence and has little future. But when that ant joins with thousands and millions of others it helps to build interlinked, harmonious and long-lasting colonies.

This is a slightly edited version of Jane Powers' introductory article to the Irish Times Magazine *edition of 13 January, which she edited, and which was devoted to environmental issues.*

TUESDAY, 16 JANUARY 2007

'Waiting is the Hardest Thing for Families'

Michael Parsons, at Hook Head, Co. Wexford

The seaside village of Duncannon was deserted yesterday as grey choppy seas pounded the beach. In the harbour, fisherman Alan Foley (20), dressed in yellow oilskins, sat mending his nets beside the *Alma-May* trawler, which was tied up in port like most of the local boats. He said the weather was 'too bad to go out today. There's no let-up.'

Last Thursday he and two friends took part in a search of shoreline around the Hook and Baginbun in the hope of finding survivors. Mr Foley, from the nearby village of Ramsgrange, began working as a fisherman at the age of 16, like his 'father, uncles and grandfather'. He described the last week's events as 'an awful tragedy', but added: 'you have to keep on fishing.' He described the sinking of the *Père Charles* as 'a freak accident'.

Overlooking the harbour, at the Star of the Sea church, Fr John Nolan, parish priest of Duncannon, said 'people are frustrated that weather conditions are hampering the search'. He added that 'recovering the bodies would bring closure'.

Throughout the day, the weather changed from squally showers to clear patches, but visibility was reasonably good for the search of the shoreline. At Kilmore Quay, in a glass-fronted office facing the Saltee Islands, harbour master Capt Phil Murphy said patrol units from the Coast Guard were out walking 'from Carnsore Point right down to Dunmore – a huge area to search'. He said they faced some difficulties when walking on cliff tops because of the strong winds and also that some of the rocky outcrops of the shoreline were very slippery. Most of the local fishing fleet was tied up in harbour because of the weather.

'In the fishing industry, people know tragedies like this will happen at sea, but that doesn't lessen the effect of it. The waiting is the hardest thing for families,' Capt Murphy said.

The narrow road out to Hook Head was sprayed with foam from huge waves crashing on to the rocks beneath the lighthouse.

Builder Stephen O'Leary (44) from Bannow was on his lunch break and looking out to sea where two trawlers appeared to be fishing in rough seas. He had taken part in a search of the shoreline last Sunday. 'There are a lot of people out walking the shore – there's a lot of coastline to cover.' He said he hoped the bodies would be found soon as 'there would be some consolation for the families'.

In the small fishing village of Slade, an experienced fisherman who did not want to be named expressed pessimism that divers will be able to enter the *Père Charles* today. He believes that 'the divers won't be able to go into the boat because underwater visibility won't be good enough after all the gales' and 'a few days fine weather would be needed' first.

He said he had lost his friend, who was skipper of *The Rising Sun*, a trawler that sank in an earlier tragedy. 'You wonder in the fishing game will you ever go back, but eventually you have to get on with life and keep going.'

Martin Corbett and Ross Lewis of Chapter One in Parnell Square, Dublin, celebrating on 25 January 2007 following the awarding of a Michelin star to the restaurant. Photograph: Alan Betson.

SATURDAY, 20 JANUARY 2007

C'mere With My Phone

Róisín Ingle

Just to recap some of the ways I have parted company with mobile phones over the years. There was the time I left one down the back of a cinema seat during a woeful Uma Thurman movie that wasn't worth the price of the ticket. It was then stolen by a fellow cinema-goer, obviously hoping to recoup something from a lost afternoon. There was also the moment when, smothered with a cold, I dropped one into a hot whiskey by my bed. Hot whiskeys are not medicinal for mobiles, it turns out. Then there was the day I dropped one down the toilet. Thankfully, the phone didn't disappear around the U-bend, but when it floated back to the surface it was dead. To conclude this litany of loss and destruction I'll just say there was a period when I would dig around in my bag for the phone and be more surprised to find it than not.

The other day it was gone again. I've got into the habit lately of checking behind me when I leave a place. In this way I've started to minimise the snail trail of life debris I seem to spew. I especially check the taxis I am vacating because that's the number one place I've left my phone in the past. This check-before-you-go tactic has meant I've mislaid fewer items recently. Foolishly, I really thought I'd left those lost days behind me.

I know I checked that taxi last week. Gave the back seat the once over. When I got home, though, the phone wasn't there. The first step in the drill, as any serial mobile-phone loser will know, is to phone the phone. It rang, which is always a hopeful sign. A young man answered. 'Who's this?' he asked. 'My name is Róisín. I think you have my phone.' 'Ah, yeah, I do,' said the gentleman, who sounded uncannily like Rats from Paths to Freedom, which made me warm to him immediately.

'My name is Alan. Found it down the back of a taxi, so I did.' 'Oh, great,' said I. 'Just let me know where you are and I will come to pick it up.' 'Ah, no,' said he. 'You see, I'm on a train, going down the country, and I won't be back until tomorrow. I can meet you tomorrow if you like.' 'Fine,' said I, wondering why Alan didn't just give the phone to the taxi driver but not saying that, in case I antagonised him and he decided to throw the phone out of the train window.

'C'mere to me,' said Alan. 'How come you have Louis Walsh's number on your phone? I think I will give him a ring for the laugh.' 'Ho, ho, ho,' said I, panicking slightly now, which gave rise to

this unseasonal Santa Claus impression. 'Please don't do that, Alan. But thanks for minding my phone. I'll call you tomorrow.'

Alan seemed like a nice fellow. A bit of a joker, sure, but at least my phone was safe. An hour later I got a call from my sister-in-law. She had texted me to say she couldn't make a meeting we'd planned, and the reply went something like: 'That's it, you wagon. We are finished.' Alan was clearly having lots of fun with my phone.

The next day, as arranged, I rang Alan. He was in Portarlington, in Co. Laois, visiting his family. 'The thing is, Róisín,' he said, 'I don't honestly know if I'll be back in Dublin today. I've had a few drinks, if you know what I mean.' I did. It was 3 p.m. I began to want my phone more earnestly. 'Alan, will you be back in Dublin tomorrow?' said I, keeping my voice even. 'C'mere to me; I'm not very reliable, really, Róisín.' At least he was honest.

Drastic measures were called for. I found a taxi company in Portarlington (thank you, J&S Cabs) that had someone going up to Dublin later that day. For a fee they would pick the phone up from Alan and drop it to me in the city centre later that evening. I rang Alan to tell him. 'Nice one,' he said. 'By the way, I keep trying, but I can't get that Louis Walsh on the phone. He must be very busy.' 'Ho,' said I, 'ho.'

I was with my mother during these exchanges, all of which had taken place on her mobile. She was worn out by the Alan phone saga and wanted to go home. Unfortunately, we were sidelined by some soup-testers on Grafton Street, who persuaded us to taste some instant soups and say whether we liked, moderately liked or didn't like them. When we eventually reached her apartment I discovered I'd left her mobile phone in the soup-tasting place. Her response is unprintable.

We managed to recover her phone, and later that night a white stretch limo pulled up outside the Central Bank of Ireland. The driver handed me my mobile. I immediately scanned the recently dialled numbers. Alan had tried to get in touch with Maeve Higgins from *Naked Camera*, RTÉ's Katriona McFadden and, several times, Louis Walsh. I may finally be cured of my acute mobile–phone-loss syndrome. So c'mere to me; thanks, Alan.

SATURDAY, 20 JANUARY 2007

The Age of Gogan

Tony Clayton-Lea

He says he always wanted to be a DJ, from the very first time he started listening to Radio Luxembourg in the early 1960s, when he would listen to the likes of Alan Freeman, the pop picker's pop picker. The family owned a newsagent shop in Fairview, and he would be helping out. A woman called Maura Fox, who worked in advertising, would buy a newspaper every day, and when he discovered that she had something to do with producing sponsored radio programmes on RTÉ, he plucked up the courage and asked for an audition.

The family thought he was mad. The brothers were off being accountants and priests and marketing executives and here was yer man, the boyo, wanting to go into the entertainment industry. Heads were shaken and sighs were heard.

His mother was heard to ask, 'Will you not get a proper job?' The entertainment industry? Wasn't that somewhere in New York or London? He passed the audition. There were lots of sponsored radio programmes back then, and he was given a

Larry Gogan. Photograph: Matt Kavanagh.

part in a soap called *The District Nurse* – he played a young lover, or something like that. But he didn't want to be an actor, he really wanted to be a DJ, and so eventually he went to see RTÉ radio producer Bill O'Donovan, who was the one who sent him off to get a tape recorder – which he bought on hire purchase – to practise and practise over and over again.

'The first thing I did was a commercial, on a Craven A programme – imagine they had cigarette companies sponsoring programmes! And then in RTÉ the spot advertising thing was starting to happen, and they put me up for a programme called *Morning Melody*. I auditioned and got it. They phoned to tell me, but I thought it was some of my pals setting me up. That was the first live music programme I ever did. God, even the commercials were live.'

'Does it seem a long time ago? It does all right. In another way, though, it just flashes past.'

Larry Gogan sits back in one of the high chairs in the RTÉ Radio Centre staff canteen, sipping from his cardboard mug of Starbucks. Colleagues come over and congratulate him on his birthday (it isn't – it's a running joke that never fails to elicit a few head turns), but most of the time the most popular and longest-standing pop music DJ in Ireland, possibly in Europe, takes it all in with the kind of serene calm that we have come to expect from him.

He looks well for a man in his late 60s (or is it early 70s? No one knows for sure – Larry fudges the age issue with a smile and a shrug), still hale and hearty. He will be on the receiving end of a Meteor Award in less than two weeks' time, and then from March his 2FM show will be shifting from weekdays to the weekend. The Meteor Industry Award is for his significant contribution to Irish music and also for his unwavering support to up-and-coming acts. It is, he says, 'lovely to get it'. He received an Irma award in 2005 (again for his contribution to Irish music) and thought that would be the end of the gongs. But no, he smiles, when he heard that another one was in the offing, he 'was amazed and delighted'.

If the reasons behind his move from weekdays to weekends seem obvious, Gogan neither confirms nor denies the whispers on the industry grapevine: that 2FM is once again tardily playing catch-up with other stations, that marketing strategists and statisticians are now taking control over the type of music 2FM will deliver across the airwaves, that the target market of 15- to 34-year-olds don't want to hear someone of Gogan's vintage, standing and professionalism.

'A good song is a good song,' he says about the tyranny of the play-list. And, you might add, a good DJ is a good DJ, so what's the problem? He's saying nothing on the topic, and is neither bullish nor contrite about what may or may not be the logic behind the shift.

Physically, he says, daily shows 'weren't getting to be too much at all, not at all. Not in the least'. He fumbles for words, allowing a situation whereby anyone can read between the lines if they so want. 'It doesn't take a feather out of me, whatever I do,' he says. 'I'm looking forward to the weekend shows – they're two three-hour shows, long shows, and they'll still have Just A Minute, the Golden Hour, and all that kind of stuff.'

And yet it does seem that 2FM have finally signed off on the end of an era. Gogan's comment on this is so non-committal it's hardly worth mentioning, but it highlights a facet of his personality that has endeared him to many generations of radio listeners – the man is wholly affable, non-confrontational.

'I've had a very happy life,' he says. 'I had a happy childhood, a very happy marriage for 39 years, and am having a happy time on the radio, so I can't complain.' Does it upset some people that he is clearly not dysfunctional? 'It does, I think.' A chuckle. 'But I never had anything like that in my life. People say to me that I must have had terrible rows in RTÉ, but I never had any rows at all. I never fight with people at all. Couldn't be bothered.'

He also couldn't be bothered with leading a high-profile life. Living in the same house in

Templeogue, Dublin, for the past 40-odd years, Gogan is an extremely modest and down-to-earth figure in an industry renowned for its high quotient of ego and bullshit. Whatever showbiz pals or stories he has he keeps to himself. It was different in the 1960s, he says, when his star status meant that he was besieged by fans wherever he went.

'It was incredible – you couldn't go anywhere. Television was new – Ireland was effectively one-channel land then – and the places would always be packed. We really would be the stars. Outside Dublin in particular was amazing. You'd go down the country to open a supermarket and there'd be hundreds of people pulling out of you. It was a novelty, and something completely new to me. That kind of attention is not to be taken seriously, though. I was never driven by ego – I just thought it was great crack.'

He was, he implies, never one of those people who'd be clubbing it around town, aching to get their face and name into the gossip columns. 'Ah, no, you wouldn't be reading about me having been in Lillie's or Renards,' he says. 'I was never really into them, to be honest. Myself and Florrie [his wife, who died several years ago] just liked to spend time with the family and maybe going out for a meal or on holidays. We had five kids, remember, and that grounds you.'

Apart from music, he has no other passions. He says he never had any other hobbies, was never into sport, and hates gardening. 'It really is music,' he says. 'I mean, there's the family as well, I'm very much a family man, but mostly it's music and being a DJ.'

TUESDAY, JANUARY 23 2007

An Irishman's Diary

Frank McNally

The image of actress Drew Barrymore romping naked through a cornfield is of course every Irish tillage farmer's nightmare. As if crows, mildew, and the effects of heavy rain are not enough of a threat, they must now also worry about Hollywood bad girls trampling their crops. That is one result of Ms Barrymore's admission to a US magazine that, on her frequent trips to Ireland, she likes to 'rip all [her] clothes off and just run in the wheat fields'.

Then there's the issue of trespass. The actress claimed the nude romps allowed her to feel 'at one with nature'. Unfortunately, her attitude is likely to place her at two with the Irish Farmers' Association, which has long campaigned against incursions on private land, even by fully-clothed walkers.

The Barrymore case breaks new ground, legally and every other way. But the insurance aspect must be considered. Running naked through a cornfield, romantic as it sounds, can be a fraught activity, carrying the risk of everything from a sprained ankle to severe chaffing. I speak from personal experience here.

Ms Barrymore would hardly sue for compensation. And if she did, it would be difficult to prove that the owner's duty of care extended to foreseeing the possibility of a Hollywood starlet running buck-naked through his fields. Even so, I think it's fair to say that just thinking about this prospect will now keep some farmers awake at night.

But however hard it is, we must always try to look on the bright side, which is surprisingly easy in this case. Because worrying as it may be to farmers, the actress's admission – which has been widely reported in the US media – is potentially the most exciting development for Irish tourism since Riverdance. The two are not unconnected, I suspect. It was Riverdance that finally made Ireland 'sexy'; now, anything goes. At the very least, Ms Barrymore may have identified a new 'niche' tourist experience that we can market alongside fishing and golf.

Another potentially positive side effect of her interview may be a renewed interest in small-scale tillage farming. When I was a child, wheat and barley fields were still common in the northern half of the country, and a beautiful sight in July and

Model Baiba Neilande displays Irish jewellery at the Showcase Ireland press launch in the Morgan Hotel, Dublin, on 5 January 2007. Photograph: David Sleator.

August. With the trend towards specialisation, however, the crops are now concentrated in the south.

While ranchers there will undoubtedly react to the latest development by erecting fences, I suspect it may encourage smallholders elsewhere to grow an acre or two of wheat, on the off chance that Drew Barrymore might be passing sometime and fancy a run. (Incidentally, I presume that when she said 'wheat', she was using the term generically. Thanks to its distinctive 'whiskers', barley would be even more stimulating than wheat for a nude runner. Or so I'm told.) A third indirect benefit might be increased international interest in this newspaper's former sister publication, *The Irish Field*. I'm not trying to teach the new owners to suck eggs. But perhaps now would be a good time to launch a special naturist supplement.

More generally, it is gratifying to think that Ireland's cornfields are a safety valve in Ms Barrymore's continuing attempt to deal with the pressures of fame. She told the same magazine that her Irish adventures would surprise people because 'I'm so responsible now'. But as she approaches her 32nd birthday, responsibility is a recent acquaintance. Born into an acting dynasty, she was destined for childhood stardom and achieved it in ET. Barely had ET phoned home, however, than her descent into addiction began. She tried alcohol at nine, marijuana at 10, and cocaine at 12. She was in rehab by the age of 13, and temporarily exchanged the Hollywood lifestyle for work in a coffee shop before making a comeback.

For a time during the 1990s, the actress was famous – as now – for taking her clothes off. She posed nude for *Playboy,* and 'flashed' David Letterman on air. At the height of this exposure, Stephen Spielberg sent her a quilt as a birthday present with the message, 'Cover yourself up' – advice she seems to have taken by remaining clothed for longer periods since.

A Costello on her grandmother's side, Barrymore has strong Irish roots and her love of wheat may date from the August 2001 honeymoon

in which she toured Galway, Limerick, Tipperary and Kerry. Sadly the marriage lasted only a little longer than the harvest. Barely had the winter wheat been sown when her husband filed for divorce.

Commercial tillage farmers apart, most people will welcome her new maturity, for which – even at a time of rising wheat prices – minor crop damage seems a price worth paying. Of course in future, she and any other nubile Hollywood starlets planning this sort of thing should first alert the landowner (and the nearest newspaper photographer), so that proper arrangements can be made.

They should also be mindful of frightening wildlife. The corncrake prefers wetlands, thank God. But as any birdwatcher knows, Irish wheat fields can be home to the meadow pipit, the corn bunting, and a wide variety of tits (behave yourself, reader). Once these considerations are met, a certain amount of naked romping could be a healthy thing.

If nothing else, Ms Barrymore has given us the most plausible explanation yet for the mysterious 'crop circles' discovered from time to time in Ireland and Britain, and sometimes attributed to aliens. I'm not saying she caused them all herself. But is it possible that ET was running after her?

WEDNESDAY, 24 JANUARY 2007

Funeral of Dink Brings Thousands on Streets

Nicholas Birch, in Istanbul

Up to 50,000 mourners gathered in front of the office of Dink's newspaper, *Agos*, where he was shot dead last Friday by a 17-year-old high-school dropout. 'You have left your loved ones, your children and your grandchildren, but you did not leave your country,' Dink's wife, Rakel, said as she stood by her husband's coffin before the cortege set out on the five-mile walk to Meryem Ana church on the other side of the old city.

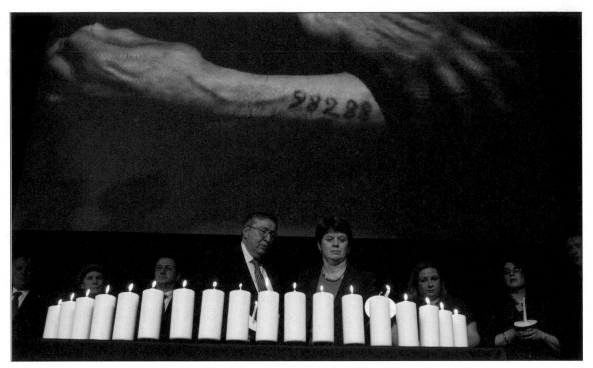

Joe Katz and the wife of the Israeli ambassador, Rita Evrony, both children of survivors of the Holocaust, lighting candles during the Holocaust Memorial Day ceremony at the Mansion House in Dublin on 28 January 2007. Photograph: Cyril Byrne.

'Whoever the killer was, I know he was once a baby,' she added, her voice breaking. 'Unless we can question how this baby grew into a murderer, we cannot achieve anything.'

At the time of his death, Dink was being prosecuted for openly criticising the Turkish state's refusal to discuss what happened to at least 600,000 Ottoman Armenians killed in 1915. Suspected gunman Ogun Samast, who was arrested on Saturday, reportedly told interrogators that Dink's writings provoked him to commit murder.

Though Dink made no secret of the fact that he considered the events of 1915 genocide, he always described his main aim as helping to bring about reconciliation between Armenians and Turks. To an extent he achieved that in his death. Despite having no diplomatic ties with neighbouring Armenia, Armenian officials were invited to join their Turkish counterparts for the funeral.

Turkey's government has also signalled its willingness to change an article of its criminal code that makes 'insulting Turkishness' a crime, something it had refused to do before despite heavy pressure from Brussels.

Among the marchers, though, the mood was more sombre. 'If we can at least get the government to get rid of this law, that will be a start,' said Oktay Durukan. 'And I'd like to think the BBC was right this morning when it said Turkey was mourning Hrant Dink, but I'm not sure it's true.'

Waiting for Dink's body to be transferred from the church to the shared Greek and Armenian graveyard at Balikli, on the Marmara sea, one woman said that only outside pressure would keep the momentum going. 'We've been calling for change in this country for decades, and almost nothing has happened,' she said, declining to give her name.

The Right Reverend Alan Harper, Church of Ireland Bishop of Connor, is embraced in St Patrick's Cathedral in Dublin by his wife Helen at the announcement on 10 January 2007 of his election as Archbishop of Armagh and Primate of All Ireland. Photograph: Brenda Fitzsimons.

'I don't know,' countered Ege Edemer, a 29-year-old translator. 'Can you remember the last time so many people gathered in support of freedom of expression?'

SATURDAY, 27 JANUARY 2007

Strong Leadership Needed on Thorny Issue of Immigration

Breda O'Brien

They carry out operations on our hearts. They serve our food. They clean our schools. They build our houses. They design our software. All around us, immigration is changing the face of Ireland.

Enda Kenny was charged with using the 'race card' as an election ploy, and even worse, having the temerity to use the adjectives 'Celtic' and 'Christian' to describe our heritage. Apparently, 'Celtic' and 'Tiger' are fine, but 'Celtic' and 'Christian' are evidence of being hopelessly out of touch, even if you are suggesting that our Christian heritage should help us understand and empathise with the challenges of immigrants.

Elements of the media seized with glee on his comments about crime and road safety, as if that was all he said about immigration. He also said that you would have to have a small mind, a very short memory and a very hard heart not to welcome the strangers trying to make better lives for themselves.

Strangely, it didn't generate the same headlines. A debate about immigration is long overdue. Immigration is a reality for a decade now, and for the foreseeable future. Yet any debate will have to begin with looking at our own sometimes flawed perceptions.

Take the oft-quoted statistic that 10 per cent of the population is now foreign-born. The 2002 census estimated that 10.4 per cent of the population were foreign-born, but this included significant numbers of people born abroad to Irish parents, or born in Northern Ireland, and a huge number born in Britain.

Tentative estimates suggest that about 9.4 per cent of the population in 2006 were non-Irish nationals. We do have a very large influx from new member states of the EU, but there are still large numbers of British citizens and those from longer-standing EU members. The perception that there is a massive influx of other races is not accurate.

A debate about immigration will be painful, because it will raise many questions about our own identity. We used to have a firm fix on our own identity, even if elements of it were a curious mixture of victimisation and triumphalism. Our identity has become much more slippery in recent years.

Archbishop Dr Seán Brady, according to a poll in the *Sunday Tribune*, struck a chord with his statement that Irish culture had become much more crass and aggressive. Are we going to blame newcomers for that? Or is that the kind of culture we want them to adopt? Most people, including most immigrants, would agree on the need for a shared culture and shared values in order to prevent anarchy. But what exactly are our values?

Successful integration will be dependent on a lot of practical things. At the moment, we still have a model of immigrants as temporary workers.

A new system of permits was announced this week and Minister for Employment Micheál Martin announced that high-skilled 'green card' workers would generally be eligible for permanent residency after two years.

However, as far as I am aware, there are only two routes to legitimate long-term residency in Ireland. One is by naturalisation after a period of five years' residence, and is completely at the discretion of the Minister for Justice. The second is permanent residency for EU nationals and also involves five years' residence. Becoming an Irish citizen may result in the loss of legal ties to their country of origin, a route that most people would not wish to embark on.

Do we need a permanent residency channel that could be awarded to certain categories of immigrants straight away? If we view all our immigrants as being a temporary little arrangement why should they invest energy into integrating? We have a serious lack of joined up thinking on immigration. Fine Gael has proposed a minister of state attached to the Taoiseach's department with responsibility for co-ordinating state services involved in immigration.

As a proposal, it has some merit, and there are valuable precedents such as the Office for Children. However, it would probably be an impossible task for a junior minister. We should start with a centralised office for collection of data. We have a crazy situation in this country where we do not really know what we are dealing with. Take, for example, the situation regarding newcomer children. Under the National Development plan, 550 new language support teachers will be appointed. However, we have no accurate data on the number of children who will require language support. Currently, one teacher is appointed in a school for 14 newcomer children, two for 28, and in highly exceptional circumstances, one other such teacher and no more may be appointed – even if you have a further 150 children who need such help. Support for a child is also only available for two years, which is fine if you are a child in junior infants. If you come at age 11, it only scratches the surface.

The Department of Education recently revamped its definition of disadvantaged schools. However, the number of children without English as a first language was not one of the new criteria for assessing the level of disadvantage. Frankly, this is also mad, because lack of English poses such extraordinary challenges for students and schools. The Irish Primary Principals' Association says that one in five schools is catering for up to 10 nationalities. They estimate that in some urban areas, up to 60 per cent of the pupils are from non-English speaking backgrounds.

Moreover, what was wrong with the Fine Gael leader's suggestion that our Christian heritage should help us to understand the plight of immigrants? Welcoming the stranger is a key part of Judaeo-Christian teachings. How are we supposed to welcome other cultures if we are in firm denial of our own cultural roots?

Mind you, Fine Gael would have had more credibility if they had a fully worked out policy on immigration, including how much money they are willing to invest in integration. The party's riposte to that criticism is that they wanted to start a debate.

However, given that this issue needs real leadership, a fully articulated policy that focused less on potential crime and more on potential benefits, would have been a fine place from which to start.

SATURDAY, 3 FEBRUARY 2007

Latest Assessment Injects More Certainty into the Debate

Frank McDonald, in Paris

So now we know. The warming of the world's climate system is 'unequivocal', and that's not what scientists are saying. It has also been accepted as a fact in Paris this week by the representatives of more than 100 countries on the UN's Intergovernmental Panel on Climate Change (IPCC).

'Unequivocal' is the most powerful word in its latest assessment of global warming, based on hard evidence of increases in air and ocean tempera-tures, widespread melting of snow and ice, and rising sea levels. And this trend is set to continue, even if we manage to cut greenhouse gas emissions.

IPCC scientists are now 90 per cent certain that these emissions — mainly carbon dioxide (CO_2) — are to blame for causing climate change. Using different scenarios, they project that global average surface temperatures will rise by 3° within a century, changing the world we live in. 3° doesn't seem like much, but it equates to the difference between our era and the last Ice Age.

As Dr Kevin Trenberth, head of climate analysis at the US Centre For Atmospheric Research, said: 'If you came back in 100 years, it would be like Startrek — you would be on a different planet.'

A New Zealander, he was one of the 600 scientists who drafted the IPCC's report on the physical science basis for climate change. A veteran of the IPCC process since its First Assessment was produced in 1990, he agreed that what has really changed since then is the level of public — and media — interest in the issue.

Dr Trenberth, who is based in Colorado, will be in Washington DC next week to give evidence on global warning to committees of the US Senate and House of Representatives. 'We have to recognise that it's happening. All scientists can do is to try to present information. It's up to politicians to decide what to do.'

It is remarkable that the Fourth Assessment's 'mid-range projection' of a 3° increase in temperature by 2100 is exactly the same as the forecast made by the First Assessment 17 years ago. This time, however, it is supported by much more sophisticated computer models, as well as what's been happening since 1990.

Eleven of the last 12 years rank among the dozen warmest years on record since instrumental measurements began in 1850. According to Dr Susan Solomon, co-chair of the IPCC working group that produced yesterday's report, the world will warm up by 0.2° per decade with the rise in greenhouse gas emissions.

The projected increase of three degrees by 2010 is based on a doubling of CO_2 concentrations. But even if emissions were reduced to 1990 levels, the rate of warming would still be 0.1° per decade, because of the time-lag in adjusting the climate system. A warmer world is therefore inevitable, whatever happens. 'Warming would continue for centuries due to the timescales associated with the climate system, even if greenhouse gases were stabilised,' Dr Solomon said.

And if the average global surface temperature climbed higher, and this continued for a thousand years, the Greenland ice-sheet would disappear altogether, she warned. Like all IPCC scientists, she is scrupulous about sticking to the science and declined to be drawn on what should be done to combat global warming, either in the context of the Kyoto Protocol or the wider UN Convention on Climate Change.

But what to do is the obvious, and increasingly urgent, issue. If we go on the way we're going, the changes will be even more disastrous than they might be otherwise. What the IPCC has done is to inject more certainty into the debate; no longer is it credible to challenge the fundamental fact that climate change is already upon us.

There will always be sceptics, paid or unpaid. The American Enterprise Institute – a neo-conservative think-tank based in Washington, which has received funding from Exxon-Mobil – was report-

Some of the 254 gardaí who graduated on 2 February 2007 on parade at the Garda College in Templemore, Co. Tipperary. It was the largest group to graduate at the same time. Photograph: David Sleator.

ed yesterday to have sent letters to scientists and economists, offering them $10,000, plus expenses, if they were prepared to write articles debunking the IPCC's latest findings.

But the working group's report went through a rigorous process. Not only were there 600 authors from 40 countries involved, but it was also 'peer-reviewed' by a further 600 scientists and then the 21-page summary for policymakers was gone through over the past week in Paris by representatives of 113 countries.

Peter Stott, of Britain's Met Office, who is a member of the IPCC working group, said the world now had 'an opportunity to prevent many of the climate changes this report discusses and avert a

lot of their more serious impacts. We can even bring the temperature back down by pulling CO_2 out of the atmosphere,' he said.

And even though the scientists couldn't be 100 per cent certain that human activity is to blame for global warming, Achim Steiner, executive director of the UN Environment Programme, said there was every reason to act on it. 'Every individual can go out the front door and cut emissions without reducing their quality of life.'

The drip-feed release of the IPCC's Fourth Assessment of climate change will also keep the issue high on the international agenda this year. Reports from other working groups on the impacts of global warming and what measures might be

Joe Stuart (left), Arts Council press officer, and Helena Gorey, curator, examine fixings behind John Gerrard's portrait, Mary, *a 3-D rotating piece on display at the Arts Council offices in Dublin on 1 February 2007. Photograph: Alan Betson.*

taken to deal with them are to be published in Brussels next month and in Bangkok in May.

MONDAY, 5 FEBRUARY 2007

Organic Shrine to the Loaves and Fishes

Aidan Dunne

It's a bitterly cold day in Palma de Majorca and the artist Miquel Barceló, wrapped in a dark woollen coat and a white scarf, is hunched against the chill winter air. Hunched as well, perhaps, against the questions of dozens of journalists, all of them assembled for a preview of his epic ceramic installation in a chapel of the city's fine cathedral – officially inaugurated by King Juan Carlos on 2 February. A formidable building in warm yellow stone, still incorporating its fourteenth-century Gothic origins, and replete with rows of flying buttresses, the cathedral is proudly situated over the harbour, looking out on the Bay of Palma.

Thirty years or so ago, Mallorca's then most famous resident artist, Joan Miró, proposed designs for a set of stained-glass windows. Somewhere along the line there was a failure of nerve and the scheme was never pursued, which makes it one of the great missed opportunities of public art patronage: Miró and stained glass being a marriage made in heaven.

As though making up for this lapse, at the end of 2001 Barceló was enlisted to make an altarpiece. It was a brave initiative on the part of Bishop Teodor Úbeda (who sadly died before the altarpiece was installed), but it didn't come out of the blue.

The process had begun when Barceló, probably Spain's most celebrated living artist and a Majorcan, was approached about accepting an honorary degree from the University of the Balearics – it was duly awarded last Thursday. But

what he would really like, he said, rather than just accepting a degree, was to do something in Majorca. One possibility was a retrospective exhibition in the cathedral.

And, it was suggested, Barceló might like to design some gargoyles – that assignment is still outstanding, but the artist doesn't think it will ever happen now. Perhaps it's become a bit superfluous. In the meantime, he realised the cathedral didn't make an appropriate venue for an exhibition. The bishop offered him the Chapel of the Holy Sacrament, a substantial chapel to the right of the high altar, as the possible sight for an artistic 'intervention'. Barceló proposed making an ambitious altarpiece, and his proposal was accepted.

There remained the problem of funding. In the end, a foundation was established, comprising representatives of a veritable array of civil and cultural bodies. The theme, the miracle of the loaves and fishes, was suggested by the bishop and Canon Pere Llabrés, and enthusiastically embraced by the artist. It fitted him like a glove, he said. The finished work is an organic whole but falls into a triptych arrangement: on the left the sea, on the right the land, in the centre an evocation of 'frontal humanity' with emblems of mortality and a spectral figure of the wounded Christ. The walls are alive with teeming shoals of fish, with a profusion of crusty loaves and ripe fruit.

Barceló, who was born in 1957, is an engaging character, omnivorously interested in things, and forthright in his speech. Physically he is compact and contained, with a wide face and bright, lively eyes. He came to prominence at a relatively early age as a bold textural painter. He was, he has said in the past, part of a post-Franco generation that yielded relatively few artists but was central in the process of opening Spain up to the outside cultural world. His own initial popularity coincided with the international success of Neo-Expressionist paintings across Europe.

Barceló's achievement was to look both outward and in, forward and back. His hugely

Altarpiece by Miquel Barceló in the cathedral of Palma de Majorca. Photograph: Agusti Torres.

energetic style of painting, combining geometrical underpinning with thick, amorphous swathes of meaty pigment, often on ambitiously large scales, looked equally related to Anselm Kiefer's portentous historical statements and Antonio Tapies' grittily textured compositions, redolent of the worn façades of the buildings in Barcelona's Gothic Quarter. From there, one could trace a lineage back to the sombre strain at the heart of classical Spanish painting.

As with many artists who rose to international prominence in the midst of the 1980s revival of painting, Barceló has utilised the momentum gained to propel his career since, even though the fashion-conscious gaze of the art world has to a large extent shifted elsewhere. To his great credit, Barceló has continued to engage in increasingly ambitious projects on a wide variety of fronts, and his gutsy approach to the Palma Chapel was reputedly instrumental in winning him what may well be – though it is as yet unconfirmed – his next large international commission, for the UN in Geneva.

He spends much of his time living in Mali – work made there will feature in a show at Imma next year. His chapel in Palma drew attention from the press, and from television and radio networks, in Spain, Germany, Italy, the US, and indeed Ireland, partly because of his international profile, and partly because a church commission on such a scale, and of such aesthetic ambition, is these days extremely rare. Hughie O'Donoghue's Passion cycle, for example, had a secular patron.

At first hand, the enormity of what Barceló took on in the Chapel of the Sacred Heart is breathtaking. Early on, when a friend asked him how he was planning to do it, he replied simply: 'By doing it.'

Inevitably, comparisons with Michelangelo and the Sistine Chapel come to mind. Barceló's chapel is not on that scale, or in that league, it has to be said, but it's audacious and impressive.

It's also, strikingly, as a documentary on the project makes clear, a solo effort. That is, inevitably

he worked with ceramics experts, led by Vincenzo Santoriell in Italy, and the five stained-glass windows were made in the studio of Dominique Fleury in France. But he didn't just devise a scheme, make a maquette and hand it over to the technicians. Far from it. It's fair to say that everything about the work was shaped by his vision of both the process and the desired result.

To a remarkable degree, what we see in the chapel – some 300 square metres of ceramic sculptural façade – is the product of his dogged, day-in, day-out, hands-on effort. He says he regarded the clay as analogous to paint, and in practice he treats the whole piece as a painting, albeit one of daunting magnitude.

Established in a huge studio space in a village close to Naples, he worked long days for four months continuously during the spring and summer of 2003. A cold spring gave way to a sweltering summer – so hot that he had to work by night rather than during daylight hours. Footage of him negotiating elaborate scaffolding and grappling with clay, clad in a sleeveless vest and dripping with sweat, recalls Bruce Willis's character in *Die Hard*.

Early on he decided, with a stroke of genius, that he would not structure his ceramic in conventional, regular panels of clay. Instead, he wanted it to form a continuous skin cladding the interior of the chapel. Hence the enormous, sloped scaffolding seen in the documentary, clad with a clay membrane. A gamble was involved here.

Barceló watched anxiously as the clay dried and cracks and fissures opened up across its surface. Isn't art all about observing nature, he observed wryly. In effect, the clay was dividing itself into irregular panels, bounded by lines and spaces that form part of the finished work. Paradoxically, they pull the whole thing together, as well as providing an intimation of time and mortality.

The process of creating his imagery was exceptionally physical and demanding. He improvised a whole battery of tools and effects, using his bare hands, kitchen implements, air compressors, even boxing gloves, the latter employed to punch rotund mounds into the surface from behind – for he worked the clay from both front and back, as he explained in gleefully ribald terms. He even threw lumps of clay at the surface. Ultimately, he is a spontaneous artist, which meant he was under huge pressure, working with clay that dried out with every passing minute.

As you encounter the installation, at eye level, you are treated to a lavish feast of three-dimensional imagery: packed masses of myriad fish species and crustaceans, jumbles of clay amphora, heaps of loaves and fruit. Barceló clearly fell in love with one particular device, that is: poking through a bulge in the clay, by which means he evokes, variously, the gaping eyes and mouths of fishes, the incisions etched into the tops of baked bread, and the splitting of overripe fruit. He does all this with a conjuror's flourish that is hardly surprising when you remember that he has been consistently interested in, and excited by, the transformation of materials entailed in the artistic process.

There are resonances of Spanish Romanesque art, and of Roman murals, for that matter, and much more besides, in what he has made. In terms of religious iconography, the installation might be viewed as an iconoclastic departure from convention, but it relates strongly to the Spanish tradition of vast sculptural altarpieces or *retablos*. As John Moffitt notes in his history of the arts in Spain, these monumental architectural schemes of densely packed, painted sculptural reliefs derived their names from the Latin *retro tabulus* (behind the altar table).

They date from the Middle Ages and the Renaissance, and were 'for a long time the main theatre for collective Spanish artistic endeavour'. They were not peculiar to Spain, but the Spanish made them their own or, if you prefer, went to town on them. Some things have changed. The medieval *retablos* embodied a fierce level of religious commitment.

Barceló is considerably less committed when it comes to describing the religious status of his own

retablo. 'It is not a religious work of art,' he says flatly. 'It's a work of art located in a cathedral.'

THURSDAY, 8 FEBRUARY 2007

Tabloids Let the Cat Out of the Bag on Bertie

Dáil Sketch, by Miriam Lord

Another morning in Drumcondra, and Bertie's fork is poised above the modest kipper on his breakfast plate. He's always been partial to a bit of red herring.

A flunkey nervously approaches. 'Time to take your tabloids, Taoiseach,' he announces with a weak smile, placing the newspapers behind the teapot with a trembling hand. He quickly withdraws, and scuttles in under the stairs behind a large framed portrait of Charles J Haughey. He waits.

It doesn't take long. 'Ah, for jaaay-sus sake!' Bertie's seen the paper. What fresh health hell is this? It's a photo of Louth hospital's €2 million CAT scan machine, the one which, back in the heady days of the 2002 election campaign, Bertie promised to deliver in jig time to the voters of Dundalk.

There it is, five years later, still in cardboard boxes and unceremoniously parked in the sterile and controlled environment of the hospital laundry room. Finally arrived in November. The picture – it spoke volumes – put Bertie right off his kipper, and he looked in a right bad humour by the time he arrived in the Dáil chamber.

While his Ministers joked with each other, a thin-lipped Taoiseach appeared lost in his own thoughts, keeping to himself and examining his fingernails. When Enda Kenny rose, he has the offending newspaper article in his hand.

Bertie heaved a heavy sigh and started chewing a knuckle. Enda outlined the embarrassing details of how a precious CAT scan machine in a laundry room has joined the Government's expanding pile of dirty linen.

The Duke of York, Prince Andrew, with the Taoiseach, Bertie Ahern, under a portrait of Éamon de Valera, in the Taoiseach's office at Government Buildings on 5 February 2007. Photograph: Eric Luke.

Minister for Foreign Affairs Dermot Ahern, whose constituency base is in Dundalk, spoke urgently into Bertie's ear. In between explaining the situation to his boss, Dermot roared at the Opposition. 'You don't know because you're ill-informed. You're ill-informed.'

'How. Is it really a washing machine?' scoffed Fine Gael health spokesman Liam Twomey. Dermot was disgusted. 'It's a good story, and you're trying to ruin it.' The Opposition couldn't get over the craziness of the situation. 'What the hell is going on?' boomed Enda.

The Minister for Sport decided to wade in and impose some authority. 'You're a tabloid party

with a tabloid leader,' yelped John O'Donoghue. 'A tabloid party.'

That's all Bertie needed. He began chewing the knuckles on his other hand, glowering up from under his eyebrows. Slowly, he got to his feet.

Millions spent on the ailing masses of Dundalk. Much done. The CAT scan machine only arrived in November, and the place needs an electrical upgrade before it can be commissioned. You can't just plug it in.

He never explained why this preparatory work wasn't done earlier, given that the equipment was promised since 2002 and the public spent two years fundraising for the machine before the HSE stepped in and picked up the tab.

Still, it's almost ready to go now. After further questioning from Enda Kenny, Bertie said he was sure all the staff required to operate it would be made available.

'Before the election,' predicted the Opposition.

Bertie talked up the qualities of this 'highly-sophisticated machine'.

'In a laundry room,' came the reply.

'If yis are interested in just playing tabloid headlines, well that's alright, there's no point in me answering,' whined miffed Bertie.

No wonder he was in bad humour. Nothing he said yesterday could erase the image of the CAT scan machine in the cardboard boxes in the hospital laundry.

It's an image voters will remember when statistics fade. Word of advice to the Drumcondra flunkey: stay under the stairs.

SATURDAY, 10 FEBRUARY 2007

Queen of the Green

Orna Mulcahy

Getting a sneak preview of the new Shelbourne Hotel, on St Stephen's Green in Dublin, wasn't easy. There were phone calls to the Marriott people who will run it, phone calls to the developer who built it, phone calls to the PR firm that will promote it and phone calls to the hotel's historian, who has been monitoring the changes to the grand old lady of the green.

Hang on a minute. The hotel's historian? Is that a full-time job? Yes, it is, but then this is the most extravagant refurbishment in town. There has been nothing like it since Charlie Haughey renovated Government Buildings, in 1991. It has taken two years and a reported €83 million, and it's still not quite ready.

The Shelbourne was meant to open in time for the Ryder Cup, last September, then it was to open for Christmas and now the opening has been put off until 'later this month', missing today's rugby international and St Valentine's Day, a lucrative night for restaurants.

Inside, armies are at work. The restaurant is not quite finished, light fittings need replacing, hundreds of paintings and prints are stacked in hallways and teams of people are polishing the mahogany doors, laying carpets and testing the technology in the white-and-gold ballroom, which can accommodate 350 people. There will be a few all-nighters before the white blinds are raised and the doors are swept open by young men in grey livery and traditional pillbox hats.

The question is will people like it? After all, it's our hotel. When it was sold first to a bank and then to a consortium of property developers and hoteliers a few years ago, many of us felt just like the author Terence de Vere White, who wrote: 'I would be very angry if anyone laid hands on the Shelbourne Hotel. It was and will always remain the archetypal hotel, built at a time when people understood the souls of hotels and theatres and public houses.'

Quite right. For more than 175 years it had hosted Dublin's high and low society, any celebrity who came to town and all the hangers-on you might chance to meet in a long night at the Horseshoe Bar, where, as one Dublin wit put it, 'women with a past met men with no future'.

In 1922 the hotel provided the setting for one of the defining episodes in Irish history: the drafting of the Constitution under the chairmanship of Michael Collins. When the social season mattered, the big events happened at the Shelbourne: riotous hunt balls, for example, and, on one occasion, a party hosted by the owners, the Jury family, for 200 of their closest friends – in the kitchen.

A favourite haunt of Princess Grace of Monaco, it heaved with actors and writers in the 1950s. Later on it became the favourite meeting place for spin doctors and PR handlers, the corners of the Lord Mayor's Lounge bristling with worthies being interviewed by journalists. Retiring captains of industry were given their golden hand-shakes in the Constitution Room, on the days when it wasn't being used for government press conferences and legal dinners. The mezzanine floor, behind the lift, was the legendary setting for hole-in-the-corner business deals and illicit gropings.

Even so, it was all a bit tired and in need of an overhaul, much as it had been in Thackeray's day, when the author noticed that the window of his room was propped open by a sweeping brush. That was in 1842. By 2004 the corridors were so uneven that the room-service trolleys had developed minds of their own.

Few people except elderly solicitors taking their families out for lunch at Christmas ventured

The Shelbourne's Horseshoe Bar. Photograph: Bryan O'Brien.

into the fusty dining-room, and you had to wait a lifetime for stewed coffee and a sandwich in the Lord Mayor's Lounge. And although a hard core of legal and political types were fiercely loyal to the Horseshoe Bar, Dublin's new millionaires had drifted off to the Ice Bar at the Four Seasons, in Ballsbridge, to swill champagne and smoke Cohibas. Sure, it was alien and out of town, but the bar was fun and the service impeccable.

They'll all come back to the new Shelbourne. It's spectacular. 'Budget? Everyone keeps talking about the budget. There was no budget,' says historian Michael O'Sullivan, the hotel's historian, who is guiding us through the hotel with Liam Doyle, the Kildare man who returned from the US 18 months ago to manage the hotel.

'This is all bespoke,' says O'Sullivan, waving a hand towards gilded plasterwork, intricate radiator covers and glistening chandeliers. 'When you are restoring an old girl and giving her a new wardrobe there can be no budget.' The dapper O'Sullivan, who has written a book on the hotel, as well as biographies of Mary Robinson and Seán Lemass, was given a blank cheque to buy art and artefacts for the hotel. He's very keen on the grand-old-lady-of-the-green concept. 'Not just new clothes,' he says, 'but a new steel corset, too.' The hotel has been rebuilt from the inside out, so that the corridors no longer creak. It's good for the next 200 years.

There are some major changes. First of all, take a look up the staircase. You can see all the way up to the sixth floor, a view that was intended by the Victorian architect John McCurdy, who was responsible for the last Shelbourne revamp, in the 1860s. It's a stunning sight that was blocked in 1906, when the hotel's famously temperamental hydraulic lift was installed. The lift is gone and the view is dazzling, past each landing decorated in ice-cream colours.

The Horseshoe Bar has been faithfully restored to Sam Stephenson's 1957 design, and it's sad he's not around to see it. It's all reassuringly familiar, but will it ever be the same again?

The fact is, there is a brand-new bar, and it is going to be packed from day one. Called Number 27, it's a vast L-shaped room with views onto the street, gorgeously ornate plasterwork, blazing chandeliers and a long bar where you can order more than 100 wines by the glass and nibble, if you will, on lobster lollipops.

It's aimed at winning back drinkers from the Ice Bar, the Merrion's Cellar Bar and the new and trendy Dylan, in Ballsbridge, and you'd want to book a table right now: that one over in the corner with the view of the green, or the sofa just inside the door in front of the open fireplace – no puttering gas flames but real logs, one of three open fires that will warm the ground floor. Smokers will have a rooftop terrace that is still under construction on the mezzanine level.

Beside the lobby, the Lord Mayor's Lounge is all set to offer the 'hushed, intimate luxury of deep cushioned lounges, low tables and discreet attentive service'. In reality it's a disappointment, with dreary burgundy and green armchairs and suburban table lamps providing an inappropriate setting for abstract paintings by Barrie Cooke, Breon O'Casey and Hughie O'Donoghue. On the plus side, the coffee will be Illy, not the stewed brew of old served in pots that would burn the hand off you. Tea, in hand-sewn silk bags, will be flown in from San Francisco.

The tour continues through to the restaurant, which is now behind where the lift used to be. Called the Saddle Room, for old times' sake, and as a homage to the racing fraternity that has always gathered here (at one time the hotel porters were notorious tipsters), it will be a steak-and-seafood place where you can have, say, a dozen oysters at the marble-topped bar along with the house cocktail – a strawberry-and-rhubarb-flavoured-vodka concoction – before heading to the restaurant, an intriguing layout with numerous corners and cul-de-sacs with tables for two, four and six. It's all very tasteful until you get to two booths lined with studded gold leather, which look like the inside of a designer handbag.

The reception is at the back of the ground floor; here the marbled space is dominated by two brilliant life-size diptychs by Cian McLouglin of characters from Samuel Beckett's *Waiting for Godot*. These more than make up for the 'hotel art' that dominates the bedroom corridors. We're also glad to report that political cartoons by Martyn Turner of *The Irish Times* will reappear in one of the private dining-rooms.

The ballroom and its adjoining reception rooms, which are now accessible from inside the hotel, have been exquisitely decorated by Christina Fallah, a London-based designer. These salons and private dining-rooms have to be the most beautiful the hotel has ever seen, with their elegant arrangements of Georgian Irish furniture, gilt-framed

Staircase of the refurbished Shelbourne Hotel in Dublin, which reopened in February. Photograph: Bryan O'Brien.

portraits and fabulously restrained white-on-white paint schemes and light fittings. And to think that one of them once housed the hotel gym.

On to the bedrooms, designed by Frank Nicholson, a veteran of the Ritz-Carlton division of Marriott International. The rooms so far completed are predictably luxurious, if a tad on the small side, and executives will be able to plug in any number of gizmos. Beds are high and piled with pillows. The feel is traditional, and those lucky enough to stay at the front of the hotel, in the 'heritage rooms', will have marvellous views over St Stephen's Green. Room rates will start at €320, with 'heritage' rates starting at about €410. Room only.

Finally, to the Constitution Room, with its deep-green silk-damask walls, billowing gold curtains and austere furnishings, including the table and chairs used for the drafting of Bunreacht na hÉireann, which O'Sullivan unearthed in a warehouse in England where many of the Shelbourne's furnishings had been stored after the hotel was sold to its current owners by Royal Bank of Scotland, in January 2005. It's a perfect room, full of gravitas.

The neighbouring meeting-rooms have been converted into Georgian-style sitting-rooms that one wants to move into immediately. A shame to think that they are going to be used for PowerPoint presentations and drug-company beanos, but then, after all, the Shelbourne is not just a glorious bit of social history; it's also a five-star hotel.

MONDAY, 12 FEBRUARY 2007

Grand Hopes Slammed

Gerry Thornley, at Croke Park

Ireland 17 – France 20

Wonderful, unforgettable occasion. Lousy finish. A great day except for the last two minutes, as Paul O'Connell succinctly put it. That is life, and that is assuredly sport, but after Croke Park had fairly crackled and throbbed for 80 increasingly dramatic minutes yesterday, somehow *c'est la vie* couldn't possibly encapsulate the crushing emotions at Ireland's sporting citadel. The majority of a raucous 81,500-plus crowd were simply numbed.

The bounce of a ball was a popular refrain afterwards, not least by the Ireland coach, Eddie O'Sullivan, and as Croke Park witnessed yesterday, the bounce of a rugby ball can be particularly capricious and cruel.

An Irish team that had dug deep to extract a big second-half performance from a slow, sluggish, nervous start, had seemed to have done enough when Ronan O'Gara, scorer of all their points, edged them 17-13 in front entering the penultimate minute of the match.

That would have been dandy. Bring on England in a fortnight's time for a Six Nations summit meeting. Bring back Brian O'Driscoll and Peter Stringer too. The Grand Slam was, fleetingly, very much on.

But France, as they did for much of the first half and again in what was for Ireland a harrowing, truly nightmarish endgame, still had to trust their 21-year-old outhalf Lionel Beauxis to leave his hanging restart just beyond the 10-metre line. They still had to compete for the ball to force the ricochet infield. Yannick Jauzion and his alert backs still had to claim that dastardly bouncing ball, and when stopped in the right corner, they still had to puncture a heavily populated green wall.

In their desperation to drift across and not be outflanked, John Hayes, Neil Best and company were checked a little flatfooted, but Vincent Clerc still had to take on the responsibility, and possess the ability, to cut through and score. They made full use of that one bounce.

France's captain, Raphael Ibanez, scorer of their first try, had revealed that they'd had a team meeting to explain and discuss the historical importance of Croke Park to Ireland. 'We know that the Irish will be very disappointed because it is part of

Vincent Clerc leaves a trail of Irish jerseys in his wake, as he skips through the Ireland defence to score the late and decisive try that dashed Irish Grand Slam hopes and spoiled for the home fans what was otherwise a wonderful and historic day in Croke Park on Sunday, 11 February 2007. Photograph: Ray McManus/Sportsfile.

their history, but sometimes you meet the French,' he reasoned, with a beaming Gallic shrug.

The reality is that Ireland did not play especially well from the start. They will assuredly lament not having a real go and perhaps making even more daring use of their backs and, at the end, they know better than anyone that they had the winning of the game, had they secured the restart or kept Clerc and co. out.

That will only add to the pain.

A first Six Nations title in 22 years is still feasible if Ireland win their remaining games, and having England play at Jones's Road next Saturday week under the evening lights is still going to make the hairs stand on the back of the neck. Eddie O'Sullivan reminded us as much afterwards.

Maintaining that 'the boys had played their guts out and it was a cruel way to lose a game of rugby', he added: 'We've got 13 days for our next game here at Croke Park against England, and we can't just roll over and die now because we lost a game like that.' Yet it was hard to warm to that particular theme there and then, even, no doubt, for the coach himself.

For the French it was a joyous win and showed the motivation hosting the World Cup is already providing them. That is their holy grail. Afterwards, their head coach, Bernard Laporte, admitted: 'Our primary goal was to ensure that Ireland will not be coming to the World Cup as the champions of Europe.'

O'Sullivan said he would welcome the meeting in the pool stages of the World Cup, but at the Stade de France the majority of the 80,000 crowd will be singing Allez les Bleus, not The Fields of Athenry.

Though it seemed merely a minor detail here, this was undoubtedly a significant psychological blow for the French with the Coupe du Monde in mind.

For much of the first half it was the French who rose to the occasion, found their free-flowing, touchline-to-touchline rhythm, controlling the ball much better and taking the game to Ireland.

Grateful to be only 13-11 in arrears at the interval after a superbly worked try – O'Gara looping around Ireland's outstanding player on the day, David Wallace – Ireland played with much more aggression and intensity in the second half, crashing into the French in contact or at ruck time.

There still could have been more precision in the handling and the linking though, had the finest player of this or perhaps any Irish generation not

Ireland's Donncha O'Callaghan (left) and Isaac Boss (centre) after the final whistle sealed a 20-17 victory for France in the first rugby international to be played at Croke Park, on 11 February 2007. Photograph: Alan Betson.

been obliged to rest a hamstring in the stands, they might well have found a way through for the decisive try. Instead, they were left open to a last-ditch mugging, and they were cruelly mugged.

Ireland might have had a penalty (with referee Steve Walsh, already playing advantage) when Marcus Horan supported Hickie's snipe close-in and was tugged by Imanol Harinordoquy and slightly blocked by Clement Poitrenaud when failing to gather his own chip-ahead. But the advantage had been played and Ireland might also reflect that they could have deliberately knocked on, à la George Gregan, and taken the first three points on offer.

It's a moot issue, as is Walsh's decision to haul back Gordan Murphy when making off for an 80-metre intercept try.

To his credit, O'Sullivan refused to find grounds for debate in the performance of the Kiwi official. Mr Walsh does not look as if he suffers a crisis of confidence when he gazes in the mirror, but O'Sullivan is right: Walsh is a good referee.

Alas, chances like this and days like this don't come along often. It just underlines how difficult Grand Slams are to come by.

TUESDAY, 13 FEBRUARY 2007

Minister on a Mission: A Week in Zambia with Mary Hanafin

Seán Flynn, in Lusaka

Tuesday, 6 February – Lusaka

It has only nudged past 6 a.m., but even at this early hour the Zambian education minister is on the tarmac at Lusaka airport awaiting the arrival of Mary Hanafin and her entourage from Ireland. Dressed in a vivid green suit with an orange tie, the minister, Prof. Geoffrey Lungwangwa, is a big, physically imposing man. Until September last, he was a vice chancellor of the University of Lusaka but after the November election he was appointed minister.

Zambia is a democratic state and one that has not been afflicted by the kind of tribal conflict that has scarred much of Africa. The visit of the Irish education minister is big news in Zambia; half a dozen reporters and a camera crew from state television are on hand to record the moment. In a bleak VIP area, the Zambian minister talks of Ireland's rich contribution to his country – the work of missionary priests and nuns for more than half a century, the commitment of Irish aid workers and, not least, the development aid flowing from the Irish Government.

Ireland is giving €22 million this year. Some €8 million is targeted towards education where Ireland, along with Holland and Norway, is among the key donor countries. Zambia is 10 times the size of Ireland with more than double the population. But government spending on education is minuscule. Zambia is spending about €200 million per year; Ireland invests €8 billion.

En route to the Irish Embassy we drive down Los Angeles Boulevard, formerly Saddam Hussein Boulevard. The change symbolises Zambia's drift towards the American way, but a billboard along the route points to an old failing. 'Succeed the right way – not the corrupt way', reads the slogan set against a picture of a wealthy businessman in his Mercedes.

At the Irish embassy an official explains how Zambia continues to languish in poverty despite its bountiful supply of copper and its rich arable land. Zambia is ranked 165th among 177 states in the UN quality of life index; Ireland is fourth.

Despite the 10-hour flight from London, Mary Hanafin has no respite before a full day of engagements. It is the first hint of what will become a feature of the week – Hanafin's perpetual motion.

At the office of the Zambian ministry of education, there are more hints of the challenge facing the state. There are old Olympia typewriters and those clunky 1970s-style filing cabinets. You wonder what conditions are like out in the schools when the ministry muddles through with this level of equipment.

Wednesday, 7 February – The Copperbelt
A 6 a.m. start means we reach Ndola in the Copperbelt by 8 a.m. The Irish team is anxious to press ahead with meetings but everything must wait – President Levy Mwanawasa is on the tarmac. He is returning to Lusaka after a visit to the region.

It is a bizarre scene. Over 200 people are on hand to mark his departure with traditional music and dance. The roads all around have been closed for two hours and no one leaves the tarmac until the great man is safely airborne. Mwanawasa is only

Education minister Mary Hanafin meets pupils at Mama Monty Basic School in Kitwe, northern Zambia. Photograph: Gareth Bentley.

the third president since Zambia gained independence from Britain in 1964. Kenneth Kaunda, the father of the nation, dominated Zambian politics until Frederick Chiluba, the leader of the workers' union defeated him in the midst of an economic crisis in 1991. Chiluba is currently facing corruption charges.

After the long wait we arrive at the Copperbelt secondary teachers' training college and hear of the challenges facing teacher education in Zambia. They are formidable; the entry requirement for teachers is just five O levels, the broad equivalent of a good Junior Cert result. The colleges of education, such as this one, often face the burden of training teachers in subjects they have not studied in school – such as the sciences. Failure rates of up to 40 per cent of all final years have been recorded.

The college for 200 students is dilapidated and sparsely furnished. Morale is not helped by the bleak prospects facing the class of 2007. Teachers are poorly paid (about €90 a month) and full-time employment is scarce. Most of all, the teaching profession is struggling to cope with the devastating impact of Zambia's HIV/Aids pandemic. One-in-five teachers was said to be HIV positive in one survey. The Zambian teachers' union says an average of 1,000 teachers have succumbed in each of the past two years. Appropriately, there is an HIV/Aids resource room in the college, but the young social worker who runs it seems downbeat about the future.

We travel onward to the Mama Monty School in Kitwe. It has over 2,000 pupils. Upwards of 60 pupils are squeezed, three to a desk, in one class. Despite the bleak economic backdrop, the pupils seem remarkably ambitious, telling Mary Hanafin how they long to be engineers, accountants and psychologists. No one has the faintest notion where Ireland is so the Minister helpfully rolls out a map and locates our small island.

Hanafin is in her element in this classroom setting. She has visited over 400 schools in the past two years and she has an instinctive feel for saying and doing the right thing and pressing all the right buttons.

Three hours later, we have reached Ndola, where the Catholic diocese runs an integrated Aids programme supported by Irish Aid. A homecare programme provides practical assistance to those whose families have been ravaged. Volunteers work alongside the bereaved, allowing them to work in the markets or to continue in school if they are orphaned.

The field visit to homes is a harrowing experience. A 16-year-old boy, Benjamin, tells us how he is rearing his two siblings alone after the death of both parents. Hanafin is upset and shaken as a volunteer explains how HIV/Aids has become a weapon against education. Now, the challenge is to turn things round – to use education as a weapon against the disease.

Thursday, 8 February

A flight on a six-seater Cesna brings us across southern Zambia to Livingstone, the home of the Victoria Falls. A provincial minister, Joseph Mulyalta, is on hand and a royal welcome is rolled out.

Mulyalta was educated by Irish priests and worked for a time with an Irish businessman. With his easy charm and his ready one-liners he is more like an aspiring US senator than a provincial minister in one of the world's poorest countries.

But his mood darkens when half an hour later, a student at the local teacher-training college has the temerity to raise the bleak job prospects for graduates during an open forum. Mulyalta calls it an internal matter and continues with what sounds like a 10-minute party political broadcast.

The mood among staff and students at the

Louis le Brocquy (right) viewing his exhibition, Early Heroes Later Homage, *at the Hugh Lane Gallery in Dublin, with his son Pierre, who curated it. The retrospective is in honour of the painter's 90th birthday and focuses on his early and later works. Here, they are looking at* Girl in Grey, *an oil on canvas from 1939. The display runs until 30 March. Photograph: Eamonn Farrell/Photocall Ireland.*

David Livingstone College is surprisingly upbeat. We meet two students from Stranmillis teacher-training college in Northern Ireland. They tell of the desperately poor literacy standards out in the schools and the huge hunger for learning among the children and their parents.

One of the lecturers, Benson Mangu, completed a Master's in educational leadership and administration in UCD last year under an Irish Aid fellowship scheme. He explains the desperate lack of computer equipment and appeals for second-hand computers from the Irish teacher-training colleges. 'We have two hands rushing for each mouse,' he says.

His contribution – with its passion and commitment – is typical of what flows from every member of staff. It is a glimpse of sunlight after the rain.

That hunger and passion for education resurfaces at the Mapenzi Community School. Here, many of the pupils walk four miles or more to attend lessons. The principal, Emmanuel Mainza, and his staff work on a voluntary basis in the school, supported by the Franciscan Missionary Sisters. One 82-year-old sister explains how she has spent all of her life in the missions – in Ethiopia, Uganda and here in Zambia. For these nuns, the Hanafin visit represents a kind of affirmation – a signal from the people of Ireland that the work of 141 missionaries in Zambia is valued back home.

In the searing heat the Minister joins the kids in a traditional African dance. Despite the poverty and the shadow of HIV/Aids, there is an infectious joy in this place way out in the bush. The school takes its name from its village, Mapenzi, meaning suffering. The new name of the school will be Chileleko – meaning blessing.

Friday, 9 February
Fr Michael Kelly is a slight, softly-spoken Jesuit from Tullamore, Co. Offaly. He is also one of the most remarkable people that one could wish to meet. His story is one of a lifetime dedicated to the poor since moving to Zambia in 1955. He is a Zambian citizen.

Today, he is being honoured by a new initiative in his name. The Father Michael Kelly Bursary, sponsored by the Irish Government, will allow Zambian students to undertake postgraduate study in Aids/HIV.

Fr Kelly's research work has largely focused on how education can be used as a shield against the disease. His central message is how HIV/Aids is less prevalent where education is available. He has also challenged the orthodox view of the Catholic Church on the use of condoms.

His acceptance speech is delivered with a great humility but it is also very powerful. He talks despairingly of how those of us in the West have become tired of the Aids battle and moved on. Here in Zambia, the pandemic is having an impact on every aspect of society; teachers are dying, students are dying. He recalls the final words of one mother to her eight-year-old son before she fell to the disease recently. Make sure you always stay in school, she told him.

The launch of the bursary in mid-morning marks the final official event of the Hanafin mission. Already this morning she has paid a private visit to a local community school where orphans of those afflicted by HIV/Aids are educated by the Presentation Sisters.

This afternoon, the Minister spends over two hours mingling with about 200 members of the Irish community. She works one end of the room, takes lunch and then meets anyone who might have missed out on a chat or a photo – or both.

The Michael Kelly Bursary is the only new tangible element to emerge from the visit. But it seems clear that the Irish commitment to Zambia can only deepen. In a joint statement, both the Minister and her Zambian counterpart commit to enhanced co-operation in the key area of teacher education. There will be more money and more support, but the scale of the challenge in education and much else is formidable.

Reflecting on the visit, Mary Hanafin points to the huge potential of this place, once one of the richest states in southern Africa. 'What will stay with me,' she said, 'is how this country is struggling to meet that potential when it comes to education and overall governance.'

McSalad? We don't Give a Toss

Present Tense: Shane Hegarty

In 1999, a bright spark in McDonald's product development division had a fine idea. It would sell salad in a container that would fit just perfectly into a car's cupholder. The Salad McShaker would be healthy eating on the go. But customers soon noticed one minor, yet vital, flaw. Despite millions of years of evolution, humans had utterly failed to develop the ability to drive a car and eat a salad at the same time.

In 2006, McDonald's introduced another new item on its American menus. The Snack Wrap was tested and re-tested until what emerged was a tortilla that is the perfect width to eat single-handedly while driving. And the consistency of the sauce is perfectly calibrated so that it won't drip on your pants while you do this. Given several aeons, nature itself couldn't have designed a better Snack Wrap.

The success of this non-drip, non-crash hunk of grease and calories is among the reasons McDonald's global sales are at a 30-year high –

Writer Cecelia Ahern and broadcaster Ryan Tubridy wrestle over a copy of her latest book at the shortlist announcement for the Irish Book Awards 2007 in Dublin on 31 January 2007. Photograph: Eric Luke.

only a short time after many wondered if the golden arches were on the verge of collapse.

In 2002, the company suffered its first quarterly loss in its history and its stock dropped 56 per cent in just 10 months. It was the time of Fast Food Nation and the McLibel trial, and a growing perception of McDonald's as the epitome of all that is bad about modern food and food production; of a vile culture of consumption and disposability; an obesity epidemic; and of unthinking corporations targeting our children.

McDonald's had hamburgled our culture and the alarm had finally gone off. And yet, from that low point it went on a roll. Sales are up in the US, Asia and, gradually, in Europe. And the major part of its resurgence has not been the salads, or little bags of fruit, or because the McCafé on Grafton Street acts as a walnut-panelled fig leaf for the greasy-fingered reality of the restaurant behind it. It's bouncing back because people still love burgers.

There are accompanying factors. It has arrested its virus-like growth around the world. (Although it will still open a store somewhere in the world every day of this year.) In the US it's adding customers through opening 40 per cent of its stores 24 hours a day. It sells a quarter of all that country's fast-food breakfasts, making the Egg McMuffin – with its egg that looks like it's been laid by a squashed chicken – an unerringly integral part of the American morning diet.

It has benefited from a resurgent US economy, because more people at work means less people eating at home. And it has also pushed what we know as the Eurosaver menu, and which is called the Dollar menu in the US. It might not always be good food, but it's at better prices.

You'll need the extra change for the snack dispenser in the cardiac ward.

But mostly, it has realised that man cannot live on salad alone. In fact, salad sales have dropped over the last two years and in the UK the company's attempt to re-market itself as health-conscious has been blamed for its inconsistent performance there.

'I think we had allowed a belief to grow that we were going to morph our way into a health food shop,' said its UK chief executive. 'That was never going to happen. We are proud of core McDonald's. The burger business is at our heart.'

The salads have served a purpose, though. They 'cast a favourable glow over our brand and the rest of our menu', explained McDonald's chief financial officer back in 2004. In other words, throwing a bit of greenery about the place made it look like much less of a junk-yard.

Burger King – which has avoided much of the flak fired at its great rival – is also having a pretty good time. As with McDonald's, its profits have jumped in Ireland. And with that has come cockiness. It has proclaimed that 'there is life in the burger', and announced internal research which, it claims, says that people are fed up with being told what to eat and where to eat it.

It should hope so, because Britain is introducing a ban on the advertising of junk food to children and Burger King, which previously spent about £3 million (€4.5 million) a year trying to entice British kids, will no longer be allowed tell anyone under 16 what to eat and where to eat it.

But those who still find their way into the restaurant will have the option of the recently-added Double Whopper meal which, at an average 1,500 calories, isn't far short of the daily recommended intake, but which has all the salt needed and several grams of trans fats (the cigarette tar of fast food). The introduction of this followed McDonald's super-sized World Cup burger, which weighed in at 40 per cent larger than the Big Mac.

Both burgers illustrate a new defiance among the chains, mirroring a US trend towards fatter, more filling burgers to cater for a hungrier, fatter population. Evolution may not have given us the ability to simultaneously eat lettuce and drive a car, but it has given us a deep craving for fat that has not yet been satiated.

Karen Fitzpatrick wearing a dress by Untold, House of Fraser's new own-brand range, which was unveiled at the House of Fraser spring/summer collection fashion show at the Dylan Hotel in Dublin on 20 February 2007. Photograph: David Sleator.

MONDAY, 26 FEBRUARY 2007

Everyone Wins on Perfect Day

Gerry Thornley, at Croke Park

Ireland 43 – England 13

A certain brew don't do rugby matches, but if they did . . . . From the tingling anticipation of Ireland's delayed entrance, the respect afforded 'God Save the Queen', the lusty support of the crowd throughout and an utterly masterful dissection of the auld enemy from one to XV in every sector of the game, you couldn't have dreamt it better. Everyone bar England was a winner: the country,

sport, rugby, the GAA and Croke Park, and most thrillingly of all, of course, this exceptional Irish rugby team. As the song says, just a perfect day.

First and foremost, Ireland's best display in the RBS Six Nations in aeons was founded in the disappointment of the defeat to France, and most especially in the fear that they might leave Croke Park with two defeats from two. Eight hundred years of pain, 80 minutes of pleasure, as one wag put it, but this actually had little or nothing to do with history or anthems.

For sure, nothing concentrates Irish minds or teams quite like the sight of all-white opponents, but this was all about doing Irish justice to this venue – which can rarely have seemed more wondrous than on this day. The force with Ireland on Saturday was almost mystical.

Paul O'Connell dominates another line-out early in the second half of Ireland's record 43-13 victory over England in their Six Nations Championship match at Croke Park on 24 February 2007. Photograph: Cyril Byrne.

'As Brian alluded to yesterday, we owed everybody a victory. We owed ourselves, we owed the Irish rugby public and we owed the GAA, who opened the doors to Croke Park,' said Eddie O'Sullivan yesterday. 'That brings pressure, and I'm very happy that the team did deliver a performance under pressure that was even better than we expected.'

As one banner put it, 'Even God won't save you today,' and as one suspected, as even Brian Ashton had feared, England paid for that French defeat. Ireland might not have brought such physical aggression and held such unrelenting focus for 80 minutes on Saturday had they come off with a win over France – though, then again, they performed mightily under a different pressure on Saturday – but they still would have put this vastly inferior, relatively poorly-prepared English side to the sword.

Hence, the nagging suspicion lingered that as

much as any year in Ireland's rugby history, this should have been another defining step toward a Grand Slam. A third Triple Crown in four years is in the offing come Murrayfield in a fortnight, which is no mean achievement, but it might seem slightly hollow, simply because, as with the autumn, this performance reminded us that this Irish team can aim higher than that.

'Of course you look back now and say "what if?" But you can't dwell on it,' said O'Sullivan.

'You can't unring a bell. As my mother used to say, Lord have mercy on her, there's no point in crying over spilt milk, and that's what the French game is now.

'We can still win four out of five, and England will have France in Twickenham, and that could open the championship up again. If you go on and win the next two matches it will always be in the back of your mind, but right now I'll take that and win the next two matches.'

It's France's title to lose now, but nonetheless the England captain, Phil Vickery, told O'Sullivan on Saturday night Ireland can go to the World Cup as real contenders after their first 40-pointer against England, and a four-from-four haul since England themselves became world champions. The reward for the Irish players was a frozen dip in the Forty Foot in Dún Laoghaire yesterday.

The crowd were almost as good as the team, and were a barometer of the performance.

Ireland's delayed entrance might have seemed a tad discourteous but was mild payback for Martin Johnson's stand-off in Lansdowne Road four years ago. The determination to afford England's anthem respect was as much a statement by a country as it was by an Irish sporting audience, as were the lusty renditions of Ireland's anthems and, at times of clear supremacy, 'The Fields'.

'We were aware that when the anthems finished we needed to win a game here. Everything else was right about the day,' said O'Sullivan, who expressed his regret at not being able to shake Martin Corry's hand.

'When God Save the Queen finished, Corry applauded the Irish crowd. I thought that was a fantastic gesture on his part. I've huge regard for Martin, and I have even more now.

'Despite people expressing opinions contrary to what happened yesterday, everybody did the right thing. It was a great sports occasion and I'm absolutely delighted that rugby was the occasion, and we're really chuffed with ourselves to have been involved in it.'

Fears there would be a mass invasion by English chariots proved unfounded. It seems Irish fans weren't inclined to make a financial killing, preferring instead to witness a sporting one, though, talking to Irish supporters, it's clear the English fans' recent crash course in Anglo-Irish history may have prompted them to down colours. In the hospitality afforded our English friends, there were shades of 1973 all over again, even

down to England's performance echoing John Pullin's memorably self-deprecating remark about not being good but at least turning up.

Even Jonny Wilkinson was made to look ordinary, which was hardly surprising with so little quality ball and such a plodding midfield. The expensive gamble by the RFU and Brian Ashton in fast-tracking Andy Farrell with such indecent haste looks profligate in the extreme.

Not only in midfield, but pretty much everywhere – bar Harry Ellis at scrumhalf and David Strettle on the wing – England were ponderous and pedantic, at times even pitiful.

About the only irritants were the Mexican waves as O'Sullivan broke with practice and emptied the bench; the edge briefly ebbed from the endgame until Isaac Boss's late, late try.

Having presided over Ireland's record defeat to England a decade ago, so Brian Ashton presided over Ireland's record win over England on Saturday; indeed the heaviest defeat and highest score conceded in England's championship history, eclipsing the 37-12 loss to France in 1972 and 33-6 defeat to Scotland in 1986.

Thinking back to recent tonkings, Ireland owed England one. How times change. Thinking back to 10 years ago, not only did Ashton pick a bad time to be Ireland coach, he possibly picked a worse one to be England coach.

Not so Fast Eddie. Whatever about Ashton's game plan, O'Sullivan's worked a treat here.

FRIDAY, 2 MARCH 2007

Mr Ed

The Ticket: Donald Clarke

Nothing more forcefully dispels the myth that the US is a classless country than a meeting with a Yale man. George W Bush, William F Buckley and Tom Wolfe all attended the prestigious

Connecticut university. Fictional Yalies include Niles Crane, brother of the more famous Frasier, and Mr Burns from *The Simpsons*. The combined alumni of Oxford and Cambridge look like a gang of street sweepers by comparison.

'I grew up going to public school in the suburbs,' Edward Norton says. 'It wasn't a rich cultural life. I did have a bohemian family. But the world around me wasn't rich in culture. When you go to Yale from that environment you suddenly encounter a richness. Suddenly there is the spectrum of opportunities.'

Ed Norton is a versatile actor, to be sure. His breakout performance as a devious psychopath in 1996's otherwise unimpressive *Primal Fear* showcased an uncanny ability to swing from sweetness to ferocity. He executed a similar form of psychological alchemy in *Fight Club*. He travelled in the opposite direction – from racist skinhead to caring brother – in *American History X*. But despite all this mayhem, Norton has never quite lost the straight-backed self-confidence of a man who has schooled well.

Sitting upright on a sensible chair in the Dorchester Hotel, Norton speaks in the slightly pinched voice that Yalies undoubtedly use when upbraiding Harvard grads for wearing white after Labour Day. His job today is to promote two fine new films. In *The Painted Veil*, an adaptation of a W Somerset Maugham novel, he stars as a repressed English doctor sweating his way through 1920s China. *The Illusionist,* slighter, but more entertaining, casts the actor as a magician at odds with powerful forces in the Austro-Hungarian Empire.

Norton, a true professional, is impressively articulate and open to jokes, but gives the impression that he is – to journalists at least – reluctant to reveal too much of the inner Ed.

'Well, you know this is a necessary evil,' he says, gesturing towards my notebook. 'How I feel about this side of the business depends on how I feel about the film. If I feel that the film provokes interesting discussions, then that's not so bad. That seems to be the case here.'

Edward Harrison Norton was raised in middle-class Maryland by a father who was a prominent lawyer, and his late mother, an English teacher. The piece of familial trivia quoted most often in profiles of Norton tells us that his grandfather, James Rouse, developed America's first shopping mall. Edward studied history at university, but, as the years progressed, found himself drawn to the arts.

'I was not the sort of guy who would have known instinctively what he wanted to do at 21 or 22,' he says. 'It was all very compelling at that age: travelling, learning languages. And I never had that sort of tunnel vision where I saw only one way forward. But eventually you find yourself turning down one option in life so that you can pursue another – acting in my case – and then you realise maybe that is what you should do.'

Instilled with an interest in classical theatre after catching a performance of Ian McKellen's one-man show on Shakespeare, Norton made his way to New York to dream of Coriolanus while ushering and waiting tables. Two breaks – one modest, the other huge – eventually propelled him into the top rank of actors. Firstly, Edward Albee, one of America's most revered playwrights, caught a glimpse of Ed and cast him in a production of his play *Fragments*.

Then, in 1996, Norton delivered a near-legendary audition to secure the role of a disturbed altar boy accused of murder in *Primal Fear*. Stuttering and twitching, his tone veered dramatically from pacific to ostentatiously demented. He reputedly scared the casting director half to death. Norton's performance in the humdrum thriller secured him his first Oscar nomination. Rapidly hailed as one of the great actors of his generation, Edward went on to date a dazzling array of famous women. Courtney Love, Salma Hayek and Drew Barrymore have all accompanied him up red carpets at one time or another. Yet, like many performers of his generation, he claims to hate all the celebrity palaver. (He never answers questions

Jane Gilheaney (centre) watchers her sister Martha (left) and Dolores Reilly go through their steps on Sliabh an Iarainn overlooking Ballinamore, Co. Leitrim. Photograph: Brian Farrell.

about his love life, so look away now if you're seeking the skinny on life with Courtney.)

'I don't think I am unique in being that way about fame,' he says. 'It is a generational thing. My peers from the New York school of actors – Phil Hoffman, Sam Rockwell, Adrien Brody – have always had a more ambivalent attitude to fame. We have a more cautious relationship with "All That". But, you know, I think that world is changing a little. Some of the shine seems to have gone off it. Just look at the Oscars this year. It is beginning to look overcooked and vulgar.'

Be careful you don't bite the hand, Ed.

'That sounds contemptuous, I know. I am not contemptuous of an industry celebrating itself. But once a year is enough. We seem to do it 18 times a year. Also, I hate to say it but the taste being reflected doesn't reflect my own generation's taste in film. Sometimes a great film like *Capote* will end up in there. But we seem to be looking at a baby boomer's take on things that has nothing to do with our own.'

I'm tempted to point out that *The Painted Veil*, which Norton produced with his co-star, Naomi Watts, looks like the sort of film a baby boomer's parent might have made, but I refrain. It's a decent piece of work, and I have read that Norton can turn flinty when professionally challenged. Nobody has quite suggested that he has Sean Penn Disease or Russell Crowe Condition, but reports from the set of his films do tend to use words such as 'uncompromising'. So, does he regard himself as difficult to work with?

'No, I don't think so. Difficult is a strange word. If you mean difficult in terms of objecting to the size of your trailer or how cold the M&Ms are, then you are talking about something that deflects energy from the work. But, to me, challenging the assumptions that may be in the work is putting energy into the project. A good actor has to do that, and a good director knows the difference between those two definitions of difficult. I would say this: the films people respond to most are those where I have had a good relationship with the director.'

Really? The dispute between Norton and Tony Kaye, the director of *American History X*, has formed the basis of a minor Hollywood legend. Kaye has suggested that, after the studio objected to the director's cut, Norton took it upon himself to re-edit the film to his own tastes.

'He's an east coast privileged young man whose grandfather invented the ice-cream cone, or whatever,' Kaye, a famously immodest English commercials director, said of Norton a few years later. 'Which is why he's on the cover of *Vanity Fair,* or Vanity "Unfair", a little quicker than me. I was going to take Hollywood by storm, and I would have, but for that buffoon.'

Norton smiles wryly when reminded of the dispute. 'I think what was going on there was to do with Tony projecting what was going on inside himself onto other people. The process of that film was great. Then he got into this dispute with the studio and lumped me into it all. He did an interview recently and somebody suggested he thought that *American History X* was shit. He said, "Oh no, I think it's great."'

Maybe so, but Kaye still called Ed a buffoon. That's not nice. 'Oh, I think it is a performance piece for Tony. Actually, I think his whole life is a performance piece.'

Edward Norton is now successful enough not to have to worry about what Tony Kaye thinks. Currently living in New York, where, in between environmental work, he is writing a film adaptation of Jonathan Lethem's novel *Motherless Brooklyn,* Norton can rest easy in the knowledge that his name appears towards the top of every casting director's wish list. Yet he insists on seeking out less mainstream projects. In 2005 he produced and starred in *Down in the Valley,* an eccentric amalgam of urban satire and existential western. Now we

have *The Illusionist* and *The Painted Veil*. What drove him towards these two projects?

'Well, I think that the interesting thing about these two characters for an actor is that the way they are, at the beginning, is very different to how they are at the end. They change, but not in big dramatic moments. The changes happen in very fine shavings. That is very challenging. The work I did here with Naomi Watts is more intimate than the work I have done with any other actor.'

The key to Norton's success is, perhaps, his stated determination to turn every part into a character role. Though he takes the lead in both films, there is a notable lack of showiness to the performances. From time to time he allows himself to sink into the background.

'The generation of actors that included Dustin Hoffman, Morgan Freeman, Robert De Niro and Gene Hackman all inverted the paradigm that a leading man had to look like Tab Hunter,' he says. 'My friends in the business, people like Liev Schreiber, take the same attitude. We think of ourselves as character actors.'

Thank you, Dustin and Gene. Perhaps the baby boomers weren't such a bad influence after all.

SATURDAY, 3 MARCH 2007

Keane Aptitude should not Surprise Us

Sideline Cut: Keith Duggan

There may well be a little bunker in Roy Keane's garage reserved as a burial ground for the various trophies and baubles he has picked up over his football career. It is amusing to think of the Corkman striding briskly into the family storeroom — an ordered place, one imagines, with the lawnmower spit-polished and the wax jackets and galoshes used for Trigger's walks arranged just so — and tossing his

Manager of the Month award into a cubby-hole glittering with old FA Cup medals, innumerable Premiership trinkets, Player of the Year trophies and a couple of old United shirts.

There will be plenty of years to mount them on green baize, but for now he has other fish to fry. Keane's poorly concealed impatience at being singled out as Championship manager for February was predictable. It is a bit like being announced over the PA as man of the match with a half-hour left to play. Anything can happen.

All old sportsmen have a touch of the superstitious. The last thing he wants is to jinx a good run for Sunderland with a token award that is basically a sponsorship wheeze and, as he says, ultimately means nothing.

Not for the first time, the bread-and-butter Championship league has become infinitely more fascinating than the more glamorous Premiership as the race for promotion heats up. A league table featuring eight teams within five points of each other going down the stretch of 10 remaining games: that scenario promises the kind of pyrotechnics and human drama the Premiership – for all its hype – simply cannot deliver.

In the Premiership, the vast majority of clubs are guided by the chief principle of simply staying up. In the Championship, teams are more gung-ho, driven by the ambition of getting into the big league. And look at the clubs chasing down promotion: Preston; Mick McCarthy's Wolverhampton; Stoke City; Cardiff; West Bromwich Albion.

These are all old-stock football towns, redolent of bygone eras when wealth and talent were more evenly distributed, and after years and even decades of languishing in the doldrums, they are within shouting distance of the big time once more.

Into the mix come Roy Keane and Sunderland. It is no real surprise that Keane has taken to management so smoothly and impressively. The lazy stereotyping of Keane during the more turbulent on-field and off-field episodes of his playing career always overlooked the fact he studied and learned from everything that happened to him.

As John Giles pointed out on the radio a few nights ago, the English press, in particular the tabloids, never tried or particularly wanted to understand the passions of the Manchester United man beyond the easy caricature of The Wild Irishman. The boozy nights of Keane's youth, the colourful, uncompromising turn of phrase and the menacing on-field persona gave them plenty of fuel, and even when he turned zealous in his approach to the game, he was often regarded as some kind of oddball.

As Keane himself noted in the aftermath of the mid-summer World Cup madness of five (!) years ago, 'I have this image – the robot, the machine, the winner.' During the hysterical debates that gripped this country during the fallout from that 2002 World Cup, there were spurious attempts to portray Keane as the embodiment of the new, affluent Ireland, where winning and getting ahead was the only thing. This always seemed wrong to me on two counts.

To begin with, Keane was reared in the old school of English football culture. Signed from Cobh to the unique and strange environment of Brian Clough's Nottingham Forest dressing-room, Keane thrived under the direction of the egocentric genius then in the twilight of his career. 'When I go,' Clough once quipped, 'God is going to have to give up his chair.' Who knew if he was joking?

Keane was ebullient on the pitch and off it and, as he admitted in his biography, was delighted to discover a flourishing drinking subculture when he signed for Manchester United in 1993. Ferguson's team were top dogs then, playing and partying hard. Reminiscing about those traditional days in a long *Observer* interview in 2002, Keane said, 'When we went out for a so-called meal, you wouldn't even see a sandwich.'

He also agreed that maybe the boozing was something of a crutch to help him overcome an essential shyness, an aid used by those other Irish folk heroes George Best and Paul McGrath with far more ruinous consequences. Keane decided drinking and football could no longer mix, and he became painstaking and rigorous and unforgiving in his preparation for games. Those two worlds collided explosively in Saipan.

But in Clough and Ferguson, Keane was blessed to be mentored by towering figures on the English football landscape, both of whom remained steadfast products of their own environment while imposing their personalities on their clubs.

Keane is like that in the sense Cork has never left him and never will leave him. In his Nottingham days, he would race for an evening flight so he could drink late with his childhood pals from Mayfield. He watches Cork play Gaelic games and gave a long talk to the hurlers during last summer's championship. It has been said that in the old days he used to listen to Irish ballads before matches: rebel songs and the like.

Who knows whether that is true? But it seems clear the further in life Keane has travelled, the more important his home has become to him. And although he has always been ambitious, his aspirations were always predicated on what was best for club and country. Glory came his way but he never explicitly sought it out and hardly craves it now. Those early rejection letters wised him up to the fact he was never going to catch the eye as an individualist, and so he set about becoming the most competitive, the smartest and the hungriest player on any field. He bossed and inspired more technically-gifted colleagues to greater heights. Countless players have testified that Roy Keane made them better.

And though he must have enjoyed the sportsman's pride in victory, it was always about the team, which was why he could continue to play his heart out for United in the Champions League semi-final of 1999 in the full knowledge the second booking he picked up against Juventus (after stretching to retrieve a wayward pass from a team-mate) would rule him out for the final.

And so – after reuniting with Niall Quinn and taking over a Sunderland team that had a zero-for-five record in league and cup upon his arrival – the beginning of Keane's managerial life would undoubtedly merit bon mots from old Big 'Ead. Ferguson must secretly be revelling in the prospect of managing against his old protégé.

When Keane was originally spoken of as a manager, the common reaction was that he would simply blow his fuse when things went wrong or at the shortcomings of lesser players. But Keane's tirades were always triggered by what he saw as ineptitude or unfairness. Now that he is in control, such problems won't arise. As for the players, what young professional worth his salt would not want to play under someone of Keane's stature? Another big test lies ahead against West Brom today, and Sunderland could yet fall short.

But the marvel is not where Keane the manager might stand at five o'clock today but where he may be in five years' time.

FRIDAY, 9 MARCH 2007

Telling Lies about Japan's Ugly Past

David McNeill, in Tokyo

Once a week, anger and the call of the past drag Gil Won-ok from her bed in a suburb of Seoul, South Korea to the Japanese embassy in the city. The frail 78-year-old is haunted by memories of what happened to her as a teenage girl when she was raped daily by dozens of Japanese soldiers in a Second World War 'comfort station', a chilling military euphemism for a rape factory. 'I was in so much pain. Sometimes I didn't know if I was going to live or die.'

Her fellow Korean survivor, Lee Ki-sun, was snatched by troops while on an errand for her father and raped daily for seven years, leaving her unable to have children. She was tied with a rope to three other women, forcing them to wash, sleep and go to the toilet together. 'At night all four of us were raped. Five men a night raped me. The soldiers alternated, so there were different men each night.'

Week after week for 15 years, the Korean 'comfort women' have stood with protesters outside this embassy to demand recognition from the Japanese government. Now, instead of an apology, they have received another official denial. Japanese prime minister Shinzo Abe says there is 'no evidence' to prove that the women were coerced. The denial — reversing the Japanese government's long-term official position — has enraged the women. 'The Japanese government is lying,' said Gil Won-ok yesterday. 'They can't make this go away by lying about it.'

Elderly women all across Asia tell similar stories. In the Chinese province of Shanxi, Guo Xi-cui was just 15 when she was taken from her village and held in a 'comfort station' for 40 days. She said Japanese soldiers stood watching as 'two or three men' held her legs. 'They spread them until I was injured and then they raped me. When they sent me home I was not able to sit properly.' Her screaming nightmares regularly woke her family for years afterward.

Adelaide grandmother Jan Ruff-O'Herne and her friends were rounded up 'like cattle' from a Japanese concentration camp in Java and taken to a comfort station. 'We were given flower names and they were pinned to our doors,' she told Australian TV recently.

According to Amnesty International, thousands of women from China, Taiwan, Korea and

Former South Korean comfort women, who were forced to become sex slaves by Japanese soldiers during the second World War, chant anti-Japanese slogans at a protest in front of the Japanese embassy in Seoul, 7 March 2007. Photograph: You Sung-Ho/Reuters.

THE IRISH TIMES BOOK OF THE YEAR

other parts of Asia – most under 20 and some as young as 12 – were 'enslaved against their will and repeatedly raped, tortured and brutalised for months and years' by the Japanese wartime military.

Thousands died in painful, unrecorded silence after a lifetime of torment until a small group of Korean victims began to speak out in the early 1990s, starting a tide of testimonies. Ms O'Herne remembers watching the women on TV. 'I thought, now is my time to speak out.'

The issue of 'comfort women', however, has galvanised the Japanese right, which denies government involvement in the women's enslavement. 'The women were legal prostitutes in brothels who were earning money for their families,' says revisionist academic Nobukatsu Fujioka.

Prof Fujioka is one of the leading figures in a burgeoning Japanese revisionist movement that embraces academia, popular culture and much of the ruling Liberal Democratic Party (LDP). The project that unites them is, in effect, a conservative revolution: an attempt to overturn much of the accepted wisdom about what took place during Japan's rampage across Asia in the 1930s and 40s.

Twelve out of 18 members of Japan's current cabinet belong to a political forum that wants to 'rethink' Japan's history education and backs many of Prof Fujioka's views.

About 120 law-makers want Japan's official position on the 'comfort women' issue reversed. The Society for History Textbook Reform, an organisation Prof Fujioka helped set up in 1997, has sold 800,000 copies of a revisionist high school history book that denies well-documented war crimes like the enslavement of the 'comfort women' and the rape of Nanjing. Before coming to power, current prime minister Shinzo Abe was one of the society's better known supporters.

The revisionist denials are flatly rejected by many Japanese historians, who insist the military command organised Asia's network of comfort stations. 'The military decided when, where, and how "comfort stations" were to be established,'

says Yoshiaki Yoshimi, a professor of history at Tokyo's Chuo University. '[They] implemented these decisions, providing buildings, setting regulations and fees, and controlling the management of the stations.'

Former Japanese soldiers have also testified to their involvement in mass wartime rape of Asian women. Hajime Kondo, who was stationed in China from 1940-1944, recalls kidnapping a woman in Shanxi Province and taking turns with his colleagues in raping her. 'They raped her in the order of length of service, so my commander said: "It's your turn next." So I did it. The woman's clothes were ripped off and her eyes were just staring. They were blank.' He says the thought that gang rape was wrong 'never occurred' to him until he had his own family. 'I wondered then how I could have done such a thing 40 years ago.'

The deniers, however, have grown in strength since a landmark 1993 statement by then chief cabinet secretary Yohei Kono, during a period of relative weakness for the LDP, that the military was directly involved in setting up the stations and enslaving women. That statement has never been accepted by the right, which has campaigned relentlessly to have it reversed.

Now, with the prospect of a US congressional resolution calling on Tokyo to 'formally acknowledge, apologise and accept historical responsibility' for the comfort women, they have sprung into action again. A delegation of LDP politicians is due to travel to the US to seek to have the resolution quashed.

Mr Abe's blunt denial has surprised and embarrassed some of Japan's powerful US friends: John Negroponte, US deputy secretary of state, did little to hide his unhappiness in a trip to Tokyo last week, calling the treatment of the sex slaves 'most deplorable'. But the prime minister's supporters in Japan, who have been waiting since his election last year for him to fly the nationalist flag, are heartened.

Some say his plummeting approval ratings at home following a series of political blunders have convinced him to go for broke, with key elections looming next month. 'If he is true to his beliefs and says what he feels his popularity will rise,' says Mr Fujioka. 'He should show which side he is on.'

MONDAY, 12 MARCH 2007

Decline of Wales into Pits a Lesson for All

LockerRoom: Tom Humphries

Caught the end of the Ireland v Scotland game on Saturday and there was Denis Hickie celebrating the Triple Crown. I drove through the local estate later that evening and there were kids out playing on the green in St Vincent's jerseys and tracksuits. They were playing rugby. It's not a long-term problem for the GAA. I ran the kids over, but the sight of them still haunts me.

First, back to Denis Hickie. Later we'll tie in the kids. Et voila, we'll have made a point.

This column hardly needs to trumpet its inadequacies, prejudices and failings when it comes to rugby, but we kind of like Denis. Once, at Dublin airport, he came up to me and inquired politely as to why I didn't like rugby. He had the modesty to state who he was and what he worked at, a precaution which might have saved us both some embarrassment.

I defended myself, not too convincingly perhaps, by saying I had nothing against the game itself and could, if pressed, bear to sit still for 80 minutes of rugby on the television. It was just the entire premise of the Irish game and its habit of feeding itself on class structure which I had grown to hate. (Usual note: Yes, it's changing. Yes, Munster are great.)

Denis seemed a little baffled, but he said generously that he knew what I meant about some of the 'bullshit' and we shook hands and have never seen each other again. He seemed like a

decent fella though, and one of my little perversions ever since is to keep an eye on what he is doing while completely ignoring everything else going down in the world of Irish egg-chasing.

I wished afterwards that I could have explained to him in more detail the depth of the disaffection some of us feel towards Irish rugby. I don't know any other sport on the Irish landscape which divides people so greatly. Rather than rugby being the heartbeat of the nation – or whatever twaddle was being trotted out about it after the England game – I know that a large number of people whom I like and respect actually take a pleasure in seeing the Irish rugby team being beaten.

It's not a pleasure that would stand up to meeting those guys as individuals, and it is a prejudice which is constantly challenged by the Irish team's generally open policy with the media, wherein even those of us who are unstirred by it all have learned to identify more with the individuals who play the game then we have the surly cabal which seems to form the heart of the Irish soccer team.

And none of us felt any different after the *God Save the Queen* thingamajigger in Croker. Just amused at the presumption of the rugby world that because the occasion was special unto them it was special unto the nation. All that is by the by anyway, because the weekend's rugby reminded me in an odd way of a time long ago before I became devout in my antipathy towards rugby's failings. After Denis Hickie won the Triple Crown I broke the habit of a lifetime and stayed sitting in my chair and just watched the telly.

Wales were playing Italy and it was a calamity. I'm fascinated by what Italy brings to the fusty home countries set-up, but I have a lingering childhood affection for Welsh rugby. Back when I was a kid and there were only three TV channels, you were limited in the range of sporting icons you could take an interest in. Ali. Best. Leeds United, etc.

And Welsh rugby seemed special. Genuinely the heartbeat of a nation. I liked Ireland when

Tony Ward was playing. I didn't like England because I was a knee-jerk red-blood patriot from the time I could run. I hated Scotland mainly because I don't really give a damn what a Scotsman wears under his kilt and because the Scottish rugby world seemed even more twee than our own. And the French with Rives, Skrela and that little madman Jacques Fouroux? Okay, not bad.

But I liked Wales. *Bread of Heaven* in Arms Park? Whoa! I'd even marvel at Max Boyce and his big leek. I liked the accents and the JPR sideburns and the sense of adventure. I even liked *Rugby Special* on winter Sundays when it came from some muddy field in Neath or Pontypridd and great heaving scrums of men who I imagined to be straight up out of the nearest mineshaft did battle in front of packed houses.

I've never quite managed to rid myself of that soft spot for the romance of Welsh rugby and am always surprised by the little spark of interest that the sight of that vivid red jersey sparks in me. Watching them on Saturday was a sad business. It's true they were the victims of some odd refereeing, but who is to say their incompetence wouldn't have secured the defeat anyway.

It seems almost inconceivable that the team which won the Grand Slam just two years ago has fallen apart so quickly and irrevocably. Back then, although Wales seemed a little lightweight, they had adventure and abandon, they'd restructured the debt most of which hung over them because the Millennium stadium was built, and their drastically pared down club system seemed not such a bad thing after all.

The Welsh, though, even in the old days of the three Grand Slams in the 1970s, always seemed to be better losers then they were winners. Winning just re-affirmed their view of themselves as a chosen people. They could be a little unbearable about it. Losing, even on Saturday, brought out the gracious side of their nature.

Since the Grand Slam it's been nothing but misery. Gareth Jenkins seems as overwhelmed by

his job as Steve Staunton does by his. Jenkins has delivered a win over Canada and a win over the Pacific Islands as the only successes of his first 10 games.

And that seductive team of 2005? Gavin Henson is gone it seems, mistrusted or injured most of the time. Rugby needed the boost that a good-looking guy who admits to shaving his legs could have given it. Gareth Thomas got chucked out of the captaincy in the wake of that whole Mike Ruddock thing.

And so after a season when there has been more poppycock, nonsense and high falutin' bullshit spoken about rugby and its place in our world, perhaps the real story is that of Wales, the one country among the home nations who derived a genuine sense of wellbeing from success at the sport, the one country who could claim to have built a culture around the sport is in crisis.

The national team and its muddled affairs are just the tip of the iceberg. Professionalism and the mismanagement of the Welsh RFU have hit the game hard. You dip in out of interest to the post-nuclear world of Welsh rugby and it is a vastly changed landscape from that which we watched on those *Rugby Special* afternoons with Nigel Starmer-Smith and Bill McClaren. The game no longer feeds a people's identity and self-image, it's not woven into the community.

The big lesson for the GAA this spring is not from Croke Park and the anthems, nor does it lie in the mealy-mouthed lack of reciprocation on other issues on which the GAA might have expected some generosity. No, the lesson is in the valleys and in how easily a game which took its place for granted can be banished from the heart in the space of a generation.

The threat is never really from other sports. The pitfalls are as banal as money and mismanagement and not giving kids something to fill their imaginations with.

And those blazers who I might have rolled my eyes at when talking briefly to Denis Hickie a few years ago are damn good at avoiding those pitfalls. We would all watch and learn a thing or two.

Bray Puts Ireland on World Map

Richard Gillis, in Kingston

They said Ireland had nothing to contribute to this World Cup. They're not saying that any more. Certainly not the world's media, who were clamouring for the attention of Ireland's leading players after the drama of their match against Zimbabwe on Thursday. It is fair to say that they're not going to win the tournament, but they are winning friends.

Straight after the game on Thursday, captain Trent Johnston, coach Adrian Birrell and man-of-the-match Jeremy Bray sat before a mass of microphones, fielding questions in the sweaty confines of the post-match press conference centre behind the Sabina Park's enormous North Stand.

The lady from *Sports Illustrated* wanted some face time for a feature on cricket in Ireland. Fox, Sky and the BBC competed with ESPN and Indian

Ireland's Dave Langford-Smith celebrates World Cup cricket victory over Pakistan on St Patrick's Day, 17 March 2007 at Sabina Park in Kingston, Jamaica. Photograph: Pat Murphy/ Sportsfile.

journalists from Zee TV all looking for quotes. The front page of the *Gleaner,* the Jamaican national paper, led with Ireland's exploits. Andrew White's final over is on YouTube.

The relationship between sporting celebrity and the press is defined by tedious power games and mistrust on both sides. Set against this backdrop, Ireland's cricketers come across very well indeed. It is no small compliment to say they talk like real people. They smile and are open and thoughtful; a breath of fresh air.

Unsurprisingly, it was Bray who received the most attention. His extraordinary century rescued an Ireland innings that after a terrible first hour was in danger of capitulating, taking any hope of further progress in the tournament with it. 'You looked like Matthew Hayden out there,' said the guy from the *Hindustan Times,* comparing Bray to Australia's record-breaking opening batsman of the past decade. 'Who are you? Where have you been?'

It was a good question. But not one the club cricketers around Dublin need answering. He spent the nine years flaying them to all corners of Leinster before spending last season playing for the Eglinton club in the northwest. But the Hayden comparison is intriguing. How is it that someone who can play an innings like that, under such pressure, on the biggest stage in the world game, did not make it in the pro ranks?

Sitting in the more relaxed environment around the Ireland team's hotel the next morning, the 33-year-old Bray talks of his days in the brutal playground that is Australian state cricket. It's a familiar tale of early promise going unfulfilled, or unfairly ignored, of missed opportunities that caused him to fall out of love with the game in his mid-20s.

At 19, Bray was considered one of the brightest prospects in New South Wales, a cricketing stronghold based on the highly competitive Sydney club circuit. He scored heavily in an Australian under-19 team that contained future Test players

Brad Hogg, Jimmy Maher and Shane Lee, brother of Brett. Ricky Ponting was selected for the team but not released by Tasmania, his state team. Above him in the pecking order for the New South Wales team were the Australian Test openers Mark Taylor and Michael Slater.

'I was dejected because I wasn't selected for games when I thought I should have been. I thought they stuck with their golden boys over me at a time when I was scoring more runs,' he says, before balancing it with some self-analysis. 'I probably enjoyed the party lifestyle too much,' he says, laughing.

He came to Ireland in 1998 with his Irish wife, settling in Kilkenny. 'I wasn't really going to play cricket when I came to Ireland,' he says. 'I'd lost enthusiasm for the game. A mate persuaded me to go along to the Phoenix club in Dublin. I went, enjoyed the guys' company and it went from there.'

He has spent the subsequent years plundering runs, first for Phoenix, then the Clontarf club. Last summer he played for Eglinton in the northwest, which demanded a four-and-a-half-hour commute. The rationale behind the move was financial.

Bray says there is a market for talent in club cricket, and balances work as a fitness instructor with his cricket commitments. He says the premium offered in the northwest outstrips what he could make in Leinster.

'The standard is not as high, but it is hard and aggressive cricket. I enjoyed my time up there, but it is a long way to travel. A lot of the clubs in Dublin can't afford to pay anymore. They were funded by wealthy businessmen, but they're finding they're not getting a return for the outlay.'

He says he's undecided about where he will be playing this season. 'It all depends on a few things,' he says laughing, rubbing his fingers in the universal gesture for money. After his performance this week, he won't be left in the shop window for long.

Ireland's Andrew White, who bowled the winning ball, celebrates beating Zimbabwe at the cricket World Cup played at Sabina Park in Kingston, Jamaica, on 15 March 2007. Photograph: Morgan Tracy/Inpho.

MONDAY, 19 MARCH 2007

Band of Brothers Stumps the World

Johnny Watterson, in Kingston

When Ireland captain Trent Johnston lofted the winning six into the bleachers, the entire team bolted from under the new stand at Sabina Park.

It was the end of not one match but two that had whittled down to fraught endings of who blinks first, a couple of wickets, a handful of runs. The first was Zimbabwe. This time, though, it was Pakistan. Ireland had felled one of the sport's Redwoods in arguably the biggest upset the cricket World Cup has seen.

No longer the gutsy, glorious losers, Ireland took a step up and into history. They had made the ascent of their Everest more manageable by bowling out the opposition for 132 runs on Saturday, and then proceeded to scale it as the cricket world watched on in disbelief.

The week had not been all unrestrained celebration, and there was a moment early in the match against Zimbabwe when a vulture glided down from the Blue Mountains overlooking Kingston and soared over the ground. In Irish minds then, fears were there were going to be some bones to pick over. Ireland were 89 for five against the group's other 'weak' team.

That downbeat ending wasn't the journey this

team had sought. It didn't represent the hopes of the hard core of fans who travelled each match day in convoys of buses and cabs into the rundown side of town.

Beginning in morning darkness from their base on the Montego Bay side of the island, the ritual has been to snake over the hills in the centre of the island, cut through the rain forest, bisect the slums of Spanish Town and drive to the suburbs of Kingston, a city the locals affectionately call Baghdad.

But the Irish team dared to dream and the supporters bought into some great, unthinkable thoughts that a side of World Cup debutants could sup soup with cricket royalty and wrangle their way into the second phase of this competition.

After next Friday's final pool match against the West Indies, Ireland will probably meet England in Guyana in the first match of the Super Eights phase. Not a soul saw this coming.

At the forefront, Railway Union's Niall and Kevin O'Brien reluctantly accepted the heaped praise. The brothers, part of a clutch of five O'Briens who were all nurtured in the Sandymount ground alongside their international hockey-playing sister, Ciara, held Ireland's middle order together in the midst of the Pakistani bowlers' assault, Niall earning man of the match for his courageous 72 runs.

For times during the bombardment the two met in the middle of the wicket, their only place of relative tranquillity as an increasingly anxious Mohammad Sami made it his business to run up the wicket after a delivery to deliver a few choice words in open demonstrations of hostility.

'It was just a matter of cricket for me,' said Niall. 'Verbals? There were no verbals. I'm a very quiet individual,' he added, tongue firmly in cheek. 'Conditions suited the bowlers and we had to dig deep. Beating Pakistan in the World Cup is brilliant, but when you are out there it's just bat and ball.'

It was hoped that Ireland would at least ask a few questions of Pakistan. Instead, they set the

former world champions a stiff examination and ultimately brought this competition to life. Scotland and Bermuda had been humiliated in their opening games, which again threw the spotlight on the perceived uselessness of the minnows. But on the lush Kingston wicket, Ireland picked two Pakistani scalps for 15 runs, then five for 58. It continued. Six for 72. Seven for 103 to increasingly frequent versions of *Ireland's Call, The Field's of Athenry* and *England, Are You Watching?*

At that point Pakistan were certainly more spliff than biff, and when lower order batsman Rao Iftilkhar made the lonely walk from the locker room to the crease to try to repair some of the damage his more illustrious front-end hitters had left him with, he had the look of a child called to the front of the class for a public scolding. All out, and the brothers, watched by their former international father, Brendan, then stepped up.

'It can't get better than this,' said Kevin. 'I did the easy job. Niall did the hard work. It's the best I've ever seen him bat. The whole world was watching. I'm only a nipper in the game. I've only 10 caps and I'll listen to anything anyone has to say. But today was incredible and we deserved it.'

TUESDAY, 20 MARCH 2007

Turning Green Overnight

Heartbeat: Maurice Neligan

I am not about to head for the hills just yet. In fact, I don't think I'll be leaving my carbon footprint on that trail any time soon. Was there not a prophesy that at the end of the world, Ireland would sink beneath the waves and everywhere else would be consumed by fire? I think that was promised by St Patrick. It's not much of a choice really – roasting or drowning.

However, the story would fit with the more apocalyptic versions of the ultimate outcome of global warming. They are scary. Even our prescient ruling elves are among those committed to reducing greenhouse gases. So much so that they are jetting all over the world on the feast day of the aforementioned Saint to spread the word. The carbon footprint consequence of this diaspora is, of course, not mentioned. That is for the little folk.

Can you imagine it? Close your eyes and visualise our latter day missionaries, spreading their wings around the world, converting unbelievers to the cause. Saints and the occasional scholar, coming from the land that abolished the plastic bag and the smoke-filled pub; aren't their green credentials impeccable?

In earnest of their intentions they are about to forswear the Government jet and replace it with a hot air balloon. There'll be no shortage of fuel for that. Indeed they'll be using the same fuel for ministerial cars and still have enough left to light the country. We won't need low energy light bulbs at all.

It may occur to some cynical folk that this is a pretty seismic conversion on the part of a Government previously not noted for its interest in conservation or alternative energy. Indeed, had the same incentives been available for the supply and development of such sources, as are available to horse breeders and property developers, we might truly be among world leaders in this field.

We have a White Paper on the subject, not before its time I might add. It is long on aspiration and pious hope but offers little in the way of practical attainable outcomes. I fear that like many such papers and expensively commissioned reports it will prove to be just another white elephant.

Last week I wrote that consensus does not equate with certainty. It is true also of this problem. There are many eminent scientists who do not accept the conclusions being drawn from the undoubted global warming, and plausibly argue that the world has been here before.

Anybody lucky enough to have seen Channel Four's recent deeply-researched documentary, *The Great Global Warming Swindle,* will have been left with food for thought. I'll stay in the foothills for a while yet. Maybe when the Maldives disappear, it will be time to take a hike!

All of the above, of course, has nothing to do with the impending election and the possibility that the Government might need Green support in its aftermath. They're terrible foolish folk these Greens and, like the rest of us, are reputed to have come down in the last shower.

I read today that the Progressive Democrats have launched a poster campaign claiming major improvements in the health service. As the youngest authority would put it, 'Yeah, right.' The Tánaiste says, 'Evidence of major improvements in health is mounting up every day. The huge energy that Mary Harney has put into this job is paying increasing dividends.'

The Minister for Trolleys is sorting out the nurses, the consultants, the NCHDs, the GPs, the paramedics, even the bugs (MRSA). Isn't she wonderful? I am reminded of George Eliot's hen which 'may all the while be sitting on one addled egg; and when it takes to cackling will have nothing to announce but that addled delusion'.

I know of no medical or nursing folk who share that delusion. The same newspaper also carried a description of the current situation in Our Lady of Lourdes Hospital in Drogheda where conditions and staffing levels across a wide range of disciplines are described as dangerous and unacceptable.

Remember folks that this is where Dr Neary worked. Recommendations by Judge Harding Clark in the aftermath of that debacle have not yet been implemented, yet the Minister for Trolleys has seized on that one case to bring in a Medical Practitioners Bill, designed to establish ministerial control over this ancient and honourable profession.

This is a situation that appertains nowhere else in the world. If passed, it seeks to gag the profession from speaking out about system failures and would allow dictates from the Minister on purely ethical matters – such could come from a deeply conservative or a freely liberal Minister; I need hardly outline some of the permutations possible. Meanwhile, back in Drogheda the discerned defects remain unheeded.

Stories like these from hospitals around the country give the lie to the ministerial boast of improvement. George Bernard Shaw wrote that 'Optimistic lies have such immense therapeutic value that a doctor, who cannot tell them convincingly, has mistaken his profession.'

This does not apply to politicians. Nonetheless, to claim 'improvements' when the dogs in the street know the converse to be true reflects little credit and much insensitivity on the part of the person making them.

But things are good for you, Tánaiste? The gardaí are in their box, crime is eliminated, and Thornton Hall was good value. You're the man!

THURSDAY, 22 MARCH 2007

Teenage Lives out of Control in Sea of Drugs and Violence

Kathy Sheridan

There were no gasps of outrage or disbelief when the jury delivered a verdict of manslaughter against 21-year-old Kelly Noble in the Central Criminal Court yesterday. Before lunch, the seven men and five women had found Noble guilty of unlawfully producing a knife in the course of a dispute or fight in a manner likely to intimidate or inflict serious injury.

Shortly after lunch, just 14 minutes after Judge Barry White had told the jury that he would accept a majority verdict, they were back.

At mid-morning, the father, siblings and friends – about 10 in all – of the 19-year-old victim, Emma McLoughlin, had filed in. Noble, by contrast, was noticeably alone for most of the trial,

Kelly Noble. Photograph: Garrett White/Collins Court Pictures.

looking tired and older than her years with a broad swathe of blonde through her dark hair, occupying herself by making notes in a spiral pad and chewing sweets. The reaction to the verdict showed that there were no winners in the court.

Evidence in the trial, including children's testimonies via videolink, painted a picture of teenage lives out of control in a sea of drink, drugs and violence, of a world where binge drinking in a field seemed the pleasant option on a sunny summer's afternoon, and of a child predestined to self-destruct where early intervention might have saved her.

The McLoughlin family made it quietly known in recent days that they were unhappy at the portrayal of Emma during the trial as a violent, volatile young woman. But a former school principal in Laytown, Maurice Daly, described how he had given a written warning to the board of management in 1998, that pupils and staff were not safe when Emma was around. He was also anxious to point out that although the school had requested an assessment of Emma in 1996 when she was 10, it was not until three years later that she was diagnosed with Attention Deficit Hyperactivity Disorder.

Her sister, Shona, told gardaí how her sister had kicked her unconscious and broken her jaw in a fight over a mobile phone. The court also heard of numerous dealings with the gardaí over the years, as well as allegations of an assault on a 12-year-old neighbour and seven-year-old child.

Outstanding charges against Emma were due to be heard the month after her death. There were suggestions in court that she also bore the scars of violence on her own body. At just 19, she was already the mother of two children, both in care.

Sitting in the dock was her eventual killer, Kelly Noble, at 21 also the mother of two children, the older of whom was raised in the family home while Kelly's mother, Jacqui, was under investigation (with an accomplice) for the murder of Kelly's father, Derek Benson, in 2000.

When Jacqui Noble was jailed for life in February 2004, Kelly was just 18. Now both Jacqui and Kelly Noble are in prison and carry the label of killers.

As Kelly was being taken back to prison yesterday afternoon, pending sentencing on 14th May, the McLoughlin family and friends stood in the Round Hall, courteous but saying little. Asked during the trial was she remorseful, Kelly Noble said: 'I have more than remorse. If I could turn back the clock, I wouldn't have gone to the shop.'

As always, when a tragedy unfolds before the courts, the old questions present themselves. Who facilitates the supply of alcohol and drugs talked about by children in this trial? And what is the true level of violence behind closed doors in Irish families?

[On 24 May, Kelly was sentenced to 10 years imprisonment for manslaughter, with two years suspended.]

Gaelic Gourmet

Lara Marlowe, in Paris

In a country that regards cuisine as an art form on a level with music or literature, it seems astonishing that a farmer's daughter from Co. Antrim, a mother of four with no formal training, should become 'the queen of culinary publishing', as *l'Express* magazine calls Trish Deseine.

The rave reviews don't end. 'She has reconciled women with cooking, relieved the guilt of chocolate addicts, shaken the publishing world,' says *Elle* magazine. 'Through love, this blonde Irish tornado plunged into French cuisine.' Deseine's *Je Veux du Chocolat! (I Want Chocolate!)*, published in 2002, is the most successful of her nine books, selling 300,000 copies. It is written with humour — one chapter is entitled 'Chocolathérapie' and is sprinkled with Anglicisms.

In her restaurant reviews for *Le Fooding* website and *Le Régal* food magazine, Deseine delights in creating hybrid words such as 'les gastro-pubs' and 'polentarisé'. She dislikes the French term *cuisine ménagère* because the word for housewife is so dreary. So whenever possible, she substitutes 'le home cooking'.

For her last book, *Ma Petite Robe Noire (My Little Black Dress* — about food, despite the title), Madame Figaro praised Deseine's 'very feminine and very sensual' approach to cooking. There is a certain coquettishness in the anecdotes Deseine slips into her cookbooks. The cover photograph shows her shoulder-length blond hair, warm smile and *décolleté* to advantage, and Marie-Pierre Morel's photographs of Deseine's dishes make food look, well, sexy.

At the end of the month Deseine will travel to Beijing to collect the World Gourmand award for Best French Cookbook for *Ma Petite Robe Noire*. Last November the same book won France's most prestigious cookbook award, the Lamazille, named after a famous French woman chef from Périgord.

In the midst of a messy divorce, the recognition meant a lot to Deseine. 'It was as if they'd said, "You are one of us,"' she says. 'I was being rejected from one family and brought into another, which is even more macho and patriarchal [than her husband's French family].' Deseine's informality, the way she can joke about dropping a steak on the floor and then washing it under the tap, is a key to her success in France. She refuses to revere 'the different age' of French chefs, of Bocuse, Robuchon, Escoffier. The complexity and formality of their cuisine alienates too many people, she says.

'French restaurants are not fashionable any more in London,' Deseine continues. 'People think the best cooking now comes from Spain and London; it's not true. Go to little French towns and look through the windows, then go to Kirkcaldy or Coleraine; there's no comparison in the quality, variety and amount of love and care that goes into it.'

Deseine learned cooking by watching her former mother-in-law and her ex-husband's French aunts. 'It was a great way of getting to know people, like talking about the weather back home,' she explains. The title of the first book she's written in English, *Nobody Does It Better,* to be published by Kyle Cathie in London in May, is testimony to her belief in the excellence of French cooking.

When Deseine set out to write *Ma Petite Robe Noire* four years ago, she 'was looking for a useful, kitchen-bible sort of thing. I love articles in women's magazines that say, "Your ideal wardrobe is this. All you need is a navy blazer and you're set; if you have this, you're equipped."' Though the concept was abstract for a cookbook, her French publisher, Marabout, bought it.

The book's 160 recipes are organised like a fashion treatise: the basics (from roast chicken to crispy beef salad); accessories, including various sauces and side dishes; 'la petite robe noire' – the dish that's sure to dazzle, whether it's brioche with caviar and crème fraîche or chocolate cake. The chapter on *tenue de soirée* (evening dress) contains cocktail recipes.

A childhood French teacher seems to linger in the background of every Frenchified foreigner. Deseine's was called Mr Snowball, and she was 12 years old and named Patricia Stevens when she developed a schoolgirl crush on him at Belfast Royal Academy. Thanks to Mr Snowball, 'writing in French and getting it right is still my biggest motivation and pleasure,' she says.

When she was growing up in Northern Ireland, 'our parents instilled in us the idea that we were charmed and lucky to be living in the country,' Deseine recalls. 'The countryside was beautiful. If it hadn't been for the Troubles it could have been good.' In the event, her childhood was unhappy; it was always understood that she and her two brothers would settle abroad.

Deseine's father was very involved in the farmers' union. Her mother was an activist in a unionist party. 'It was stalwart, Protestant Co. Antrim. Social life revolved around the party, the bridge club and the church.' The Stevens children were bused to school in Belfast. 'We had to be escorted to the bus stop. There were stones and bottles thrown at us,' she says. 'It was extremely violent. My father owned land over Cave Hill in Belfast, where bodies were dumped. Some of his employees were taken to jail. When you're a child and people tell you it's a normal place, you know it's not.'

By comparison, France seemed 'hugely exotic and romantic', she says. Deseine was smitten with Paris on a school trip at the age of 14. She studied French literature at Edinburgh, where she met a young man doing a year's voluntary service promoting French food and wine in Scotland. She loved him because he was French, she says; he loved her because she was not.

When they were newlyweds in Paris, Deseine worked for the Northern Ireland tourism office. 'We had difficulty identifying what our product

Trish Deseine, one of France's most popular food writers. Photograph: Deirdre Rooney.

was,' she says. 'Our strategy was: Are you going to the South? Would you not like to pop up?'

Though she has spent half of her 42 years in France, Deseine doesn't feel French. 'I have a British passport,' she says. 'When I was brought up, it was drummed into me I was British. I don't feel any nationality . . . I'm not French, and I don't feel Northern Irish. My agent [Ivan Mulcahy] is Irish.

My best friend [Greg Delaney] is Irish. I'm always joking that I want the Irish to tell me I'm Irish.' Growing up, the South always seemed freer, easier, more romantic. The southern Irish people I met seemed so laid back.'

Though she has no desire to return to Northern Ireland, Deseine is relieved that the Troubles are over. 'I love the fact that the goalposts have moved, that the rest of the world has caught up with them and that Northern Ireland's little problems don't matter any more, that the harsh realities of the world has Northern Irish people saying maybe we shouldn't be involved in this kind of thing.'

In 15 years of marriage, Deseine had four children: Corentin, Timothée, Tanguy and Victoire. She and her ex-husband have been awarded custody on alternate weeks, an increasingly common practice in France. 'My life is completely schizophrenic,' she says. One week she is shopping, cooking and taking the children to school from the former family home in the affluent Paris suburb of St-Germain-en-Laye. The next week she is a single career woman living in the apartment she bought in Paris's 20th arrondissement, a sixth-floor walk-up with a view over the rooftops.

Many of Deseine's friends are activists in 'le Fooding', which she describes as 'a gastro-intellectual movement started seven years ago by two young food critics who decided to upset the apple cart, to showcase new French talent'. Followers of 'le Fooding' see food as 'a style choice', she says. 'They set up events, picnics and parties. Before Christmas they hold la Semaine du Fooding, with *bars clandestins* and *tables d'hôte* in designers' kitchens. It has a huge following.'

Personal experience has turned Deseine into a feminist, because of the double standards applied to men and women, she says. Her ex-husband's family are in the food industry, and she began writing recipes to promote their products. She was pregnant with Victoire when Marabout, a division of France's largest publishing house, Hachette, 'discovered' her at a food fair in 2000. Her first book, *Petits Plats Entre Amis (Small Dishes Among Friends)* sold 150,000 copies.

'As soon as a woman starts overshadowing the man, the whole balance shifts, especially when a woman leaves a man,' Deseine says. 'You feel the weight of French society against you.

Accommodations can be made in a couple, but the family has to be sustained. Most of the sacrifices are expected from the woman.'

Reading Deseine's books and restaurant reviews makes even the unsophisticated palate water. She has come a long way from the farm in Co. Antrim, but her favourite meal remains 'my mother's roast chicken, stuffed with bread, parsley and onion.' For dessert, she likes the French cake called opera – 'layers of coffee-soaked sponge and chocolate butter cream, topped with chocolate glaze'. She'd savour the meal with a bottle of Condrieu, a white burgundy. 'With a slight taste of resin, it goes down very well with foie gras,' Deseine says. 'It has been described as the sexiest wine in the world.'

Mouldes Mariniere for four ...

'This is a very communal dish. There is a camaraderie attached to eating *moules frites*, mussels steamed in wine and herbs and served with chips. At the Braderie de Lille, a huge seven-day autumn flea market that invades the entire city and is France's largest public gathering, over 500 tonnes of mussels are consumed. Their empty shells are piled up on the pavement in front of each restaurant, in a competition to find out which place was most popular with hungry visitors.

'At home, mussels are often pre-announced to guests as the raison d'être of the evening. "Come tonight, I'm cooking *moules frites*," your host will say. And, just as with *raclette* or *crêpes* or a leg of wild boar, or *pot au feu*, the gathering is defined and justified by the food being served. Rejoicing in and sharing it is the only goal.

'My children love mussels. It's an attraction-repulsion thing, something I have exploited over and over to get them to try things: it starts as a 'bet you won't eat that' challenge and then, miraculously, they discover they love the taste. They also love the way you can use one empty-hinged shell to pinch out the next mussel, the fact that there are often little hitch-hiker crabs hiding inside and the way each empty shell can be neatly slotted into the next one, bending a shiny, black purple garland around their plates.'

2kg mussels (avoid the pre-cleaned and pre-packed variety, and buy them as fresh as you can. In France, choose 'bouchot', the best, grown on wooden posts)
50g butter
2 tbsp sunflower oil
1 garlic clove, finely chopped
2-3 shallots, finely chopped
Good handful curly parsley, finely chopped
2-3 glasses dry white wine
Freshly ground black pepper

Clean the mussels: under cold running water, scrub them and pull off the gritty beard. Discard any that are open and do not close as you press on them.

In a very large, deep saucepan, heat the butter with the oil and gently sweat the garlic and shallots. Add the parsley, white wine and some pepper and bring to the boil.

Throw in the mussels, put the lid on and cook for two to three minutes. Give the pan a shake or dig down to the bottom once or twice with a ladle to make sure they cook evenly. The mussels are cooked when the shells are open and the flesh is tender.

Discard any mussels that have remained closed, then with a large slotted spoon transfer the mussels to deep plates. Ladle the glorious cooking liquid over them and serve.

Other tasty possibilities are cooking the mussels in pastis instead of wine, or, for *moules à la crème*, adding a few tablespoons of crème fraîche to the cooking liquid after the mussels are cooked.

Recipe taken from *Nobody Does It Better: Why French Home Cooking Is Still the Best in the World*, by Trish Deseine, which will be published in May by Kyle Cathie, €36.50.

TUESDAY, 27 MARCH 2007

New Partners Survive a Nervous First Date

Deaglán de Bréadún, at Stormont

You had to pinch yourself to make sure it was real. Was this happening or had someone put LSD in the coffee?

Were we seeing things or was Ian Paisley really sitting alongside the former adversary, Gerry Adams? Were we hearing things or was the Big Man really making all those conciliatory statements?

The leader of the Democratic Unionist Party has a booming voice but yesterday it was the content of his remarks that made an impact. It was like the tolling of Big Ben, only much more portentous. Bong! A date for the resumption of Stormont had been agreed with Sinn Féin. Bong! The DUP wanted the best future for 'all' the people of Northern Ireland – which has to include nationalists. Bong! The meeting with the former acolytes of Satan in Sinn Féin had been, wondrous to relate, 'a constructive engagement'. Bong! There would be 'regular meetings' between the DUP leader and Martin McGuinness to prepare for their jobs as first and deputy first minister.

The DUP leader has a penchant for quoting the Good Book but his pronouncements yesterday might yet earn 'Big Ben' Paisley the status of a political prophet. Who would have predicted this final twist in the career of Ulster's number one fire-and-brimstone preacher, 'Doctor No' himself, the man whose middle name was 'Never'?

Paisley was a hard act to follow yesterday but the Sinn Féin leader did his best. The Adams speech had been discreetly circulated to reporters beforehand so there were no surprises. There was the usual sprinkling of quotes in Irish but for the

Ian Paisley (left) and Gerry Adams sit at the same table in Stormont, Belfast, on 26 March 2007. Photograph: Paul Faith/Press Association.

benefit of his new partners, Gerry helpfully translated 'Tús maith leath na hoibre' into 'A good start is half the work'.

The two men were sitting close together and, at the end, Adams looked expectantly at Paisley, like an eager but nervous suitor on a first date, clearly hoping for some physical contact to round off their brief but heady encounter – but the handshake was not forthcoming. Maybe some other time. Even hard-boiled journalists who had seen many false dawns were impressed. Spines that had been crooked over typewriters and laptops for years, cranking out bad-news stories about the Troubles, felt a little tingling of excitement and anticipation. For once the remark about 'History in the making' had real substance.

At a press conference later, Peter Hain looked like a man who had won the political equivalent of the Lotto. Reporters taunted him about his threat of 'devolution or dissolution' by 26 March. Hain didn't care and replied, in effect: Deadline, schmedline, I've got the ancient enemies talking and soon they'll be moving in together, thank you very much.

On a day that two estranged communities finally sealed a peace deal, it seemed somehow appropriate that the politician overseeing the process at local level was South African and had come into politics as a campaigner against apartheid. The Northern Secretary doesn't do emotion in public but he came close to it yesterday. 'Those pictures of Ian Paisley and Gerry Adams will resonate around the world,' he said. 'We saw something today that people never, ever thought would happen.'

Now there's even talk of 'Paisley: The Movie', with reports that Hollywood is getting in on the act and looking at fellow Ballymena man Liam Neeson for the title role. But it's not time to wrap up the script just yet. Hard talking will take place between now and the new devolution deadline of 8 May. Remember, Northern Ireland has a history of taking two steps forward, one step back. But whatever happens, nobody who was there on the day will quickly forget 26 March.

Keeping the Faith in New Orleans

John Moran, in New Orleans

In a famous old hotel at the Royal Street entrance to the French Quarter, the little black waitress approaches my table. She has a warm smile and an unexpected greeting. 'Top of the morning,' she says, mysteriously. Whatever gave the game away? I wondered. Was it the curly hair? The rosy cheeks? Not a bit of it. Lucille had been oblivious to all clues of Irishness. 'If a guest looks friendly,' she explains, 'I always say that.' So just a coincidental bit of the old Blarney, but nice.

Over a strong coffee in that literary landmark Hotel Monteleone, I wondered though, if Lucille's felicitation might be some kind of a survival from a time the Irish and African-Americans were the largest minority groups in the city, often sharing the same districts where both practised voodoo, worked the riverboats, and miscegenation was not necessarily the crime it was elsewhere.

When heartbroken Irish writer Lafcadio Hearn fled here in 1877, he was running from a storm that had overwhelmed him in Cincinnati, Ohio. Hearn had been sacked by his newspaper, fiercely criticised and ostracised as a moral delinquent. His crime was to 'live openly' with a former slave, Alethea 'Mattie' Foley, whom he had married at a time when to do so was illegal in Ohio.

In New Orleans, Hearn immersed himself in the mysterious world of local culture and his reports were widely read throughout the US. His prodigious output of translations, literary journalism and colour sketches recorded black music and culture, and captured forever the Creole and Cajun traditions that fascinated readers. He was rumoured to have had an affair with voodoo queen Marie Laveau, and he first introduced – among significant others – the word 'zombie' to the English language.

Hearn's funky New Orleans literary oeuvre helped create a secret garden of romance which was tended over time by others, until its exotic flowering into the collective imagination where it settled and bloomed as a fabulously wild orchid that the world took to its heart.

Into this steamy ambience down the decades were drawn writers, painters, poets, musicians, as well as free spirits, innumerable eccentrics, sundry street characters and legions of lost souls. Under a hypnotic spell of moonlight and magnolia, hot cuisine and voodoo queens, it became the Big Easy, a shady haunt where the Bible Belt unbuckles, a Caribbean carnival washed up on the American shore.

Hearn had a tough time at first in New Orleans, and although broke, suffering from dengue fever and missing Mattie, he wrote in a letter to a friend: 'But it's better to live here in sackcloth and ashes than to own the whole state of Ohio.'

As a fan of Lafcadio and a lover of New Orleans, I was happy to return as one of a small Irish press pack invited for a research visit to meet the tourism people of the New Orleans Metropolitan Convention and Visitors Bureau (gulp) for the launch of its worldwide campaign to re-focus attention on all the good stuff the place has to offer.

Our two-day tour took us to the heart of southern sensibility, the Ogden Museum of Southern Art. Its wonderful collection brings vividly to life all the contrasting colours, textures and shapes of the old and new South. For me, the strongest feelings were not evoked by a painting, but a window. I noticed it looked out onto the interstate highway where, days after Katrina broke the levees in August 2005, bedraggled refugees huddled and baked on a flyover in a heat-haze, becoming universal emblems of abandonment and despair, and sounding the alarm bells at the shocking frailty of civil society in vulnerable cities.

Ogden director Dr Richard Gruber and chief curator Dr David Houston told us that in the

Joan Blake from Dalkey, Co. Dublin, with her new all-island free travel pass which was launched for older people, North and South, on 2 April 2007. Photograph: Cyril Byrne.

darkest days and months after the deluge, a time when people had few places to gather, the Ogden became a communal meeting point. On a street where parking tickets are issued by the coastguard, Katrina survivors did well to discover as fine a refuge as this. If art is sometimes an act of survival, in the Ogden it's also an act of hospitality.

For the consolations of cuisine, the Irish press pack dined in the divine trinity of legendary French Quarter restaurants: Brennan's for breakfast, the Court of Two Sisters for its jazz brunch, and dinner at Arnaud's, which is as well known a line here as breakfast at Tiffany's (the film was based on a novella by local writer Truman Capote).

The big push for new and lost tourism is a vital one for the city. Tourism is the lifeblood of the New Orleans economy, with many tens of thou-

sands of jobs depending on it directly or indirectly. It is of particular importance to the 200,000 evacuees, roughly half the pre-Katrina population, who have yet to return.

While the attractions of the Warehouse District, the French Quarter and the Garden District are intact – indeed in some cases enhanced – there's still a painful legacy from hurricanes Katrina and Rita, and a mountain of work still waiting to be done in the Lower Ninth Ward, Gentilly and Lakeview.

One of our hosts from the Visitors Bureau is Christine DeCuir, who had to abandon her home when the waters rose in the Lower Ninth Ward. She went to live with relations in her hometown of Opelousas, Louisiana, three hours' drive from New Orleans. An African-American, DeCuir and

Aoibheann Crawley, aged 6, a pupil of Scoil Naoimh Éanna, Carrickmacross, Co. Monaghan, who won third prize in the 'six years and under' category with her painting The Pig Race *in the 2007 Texaco Children's Art Competition, the results of which were announced at the Hugh Lane gallery in Dublin on 3 April 2007. Photograph: Bryan O'Brien.*

her youngest daughter Ashlie had just moved home the night we spoke in Arnaud's.

'I'm so happy to be back in my house,' she says, 'even though it's not completely finished. I'm just thankful to God for keeping my family safe and sound until we can reunite again. I was delighted to return to work, as I'm the only one who can put my house back together while my family is still displaced.'

DeCuir is critical of some of the media for negativity, and for not giving the full picture of people in places such as the Lower Ninth Ward. 'The best thing was the way people got together as

a community and helped each other out,' she says. With other New Orleanians you can sometimes sense a malaise, a heavy weariness with the slow pace of reconstruction, and on occasion you sense pangs of frustration and anguish. But, like Christine DeCuir and little Lucille, they're a hardy lot in this troubled old town.

Another such person, who has been working throughout in New Orleans Parish and the Lower Ninth Ward, is Fr Joe Campion, an Irish-American Jesuit priest. Fr Campion is with the Josephite Order, which serves the African-American community in the US. His people come from Co. Kilkenny.

'Fr Joe', as he's affectionately known, is a cool cat who likes a laugh, but there's a simmering anger when talk turns to the unconscionable delay in rehousing families. 'The people of this area understand the vast devastation wrought by hurricanes Katrina and Rita. But they also feel the blow of Hurricane Politics. Inefficiency, incompetence and enduring corruption have dramatically hampered progress.'

Fr Campion believes the ethnic make-up of New Orleans will change dramatically. 'African-Americans will probably still constitute a majority, but that number will be far less than it was pre-Katrina (70 per cent).' He says more and more Hispanics will work on the reconstruction and then decide to stay.

Our driver, former Times-Picayune reporter Jeff Richard from Baton Rouge, says before Katrina, Mexican immigrants mostly didn't cross the Sabine River, which forms much of the boundary between Texas and Louisiana and was once part of the national border between Mexico and the US. Back then it was Americans crossing the river, and in the other direction. The tide turns.

Fr Joe Campion says that despite the slow pace of recovery beyond the tourist vista, there have been some notable improvements since Katrina. 'Slowly, the infrastructure is changing for the better . . . but people need grants, not loans. I see a strong resolve in so many to get their lives and homes back in order. They press on each day, and get a little bit more [work] accomplished.'

But there are other problems, such as serious concerns about crime; complaints of a lack of federal engagement, particularly in terms of releasing funds for rebuilding homes; stories of failures of civil and judicial administration; and a tradition of political 'malfeasance'. With regard to the latter, while being escorted around Arnaud's museum, our host points to a picture on the wall: 'That's our former governor,' she says drily, with a resigned drawl. 'He's in jail.'

While for New Orleanians, storms on the horizon are nothing new, this year's hurricane season brings more than the usual insecurity. Last year the Gulf of Mexico area was protected by the El Niño effect, which blew storms back into the Atlantic. But meteorological experts say El Niño has now completed its cycle, and with the hurricane season starting in May a number of powerful elements are now combining to make New Orleans more vulnerable than ever to hurricanes.

For one, the protection formerly provided by Louisiana's vast southern wetlands is vanishing, having been turned into a vast honeycomb of canals and pipelines to serve offshore oil wells. Prior to Katrina, *National Geographic* magazine reported that the State of Louisiana loses 25 square miles every year – 33 football pitches every day – to coastal erosion.

However, most scientists say the greatest threats are not hurricanes or coastal erosion, but rising sea levels caused by global warming. Most of New Orleans is below sea level, and some scientists warn that unless global warming is reversed, by the end of the century the city will be bypassed by the gulf coastline.

Global warming is also heating up the waters of the gulf, scientists say, which has increasingly boosted the strength and frequency of hurricanes – as always the most pressing and immediate concern. If there's a 'Big One' this year, some fear the levees Katrina's tidal surges didn't break might now be breached. Also, Katrina was barely a category three hurricane when it landed, and its malevolent eye actually missed New Orleans. So what if the next one is a direct hit, and a category four or even a five?

Maybe in some smokeless room in Washington DC all these factors have already been mulled over. Maybe if there's a Big One this year and the city is flooded again, low-lying areas – mostly inhabited by African-Americans – will officially be abandoned. Maybe that's why funding for rebuilding is so slow in arriving.

The tourist areas are as safe and beguiling as ever. However, unless industrial impact on coastal erosion is challenged, and unless we all tackle Al Gore's 'inconvenient truth' on global warming, we will witness the beginning of the end of New Orleans as we know it. If, that is, the claims of scientists are correct.

It is sad to think that in any malign scenario the community that will lose out is that which has for generations provided the joys and con-solations of the best of jazz and blues, from Mahalia Jackson to Louis Armstrong, from Fats Domino to Wynton Marsalis, and others such as Muddy Waters, who migrated north from the Mississippi Delta but looked back south in so many songs for thoughts of home to lift the blues of exile.

In today's more benign reality, visitors are flocking back to the city. The weekend saw the 21st Tennessee Williams Literary Festival, and again it was a sell-out. Next up is the New Orleans Jazz and Heritage Festival (Jazz Fest) at the end of the month, featuring Van Morrison, Allen Toussaint, Norah Jones, Dr John and Jerry Lee Lewis, to mention just a few.

Meanwhile, back in Le Cafe in the Hotel Monteleone, Lucille Williams works away, still waiting for her home to be rebuilt in the Ninth Ward, while she lives in a trailer. Her two adult daughters are in Houston, Texas, still waiting to return.

Lucille looks into her crystal ball for answers to the Irish guest's queries about hurricanes, coastal erosion and global warming. 'You know, honey,' she declares, 'the Lord gives us more than enough to worry about each day without upsetting our-selves with all that stuff.'

'And He always provides . . . well, almost always,' she concedes with a giggle – looking scarcely half her 56 years. In the home of jazz, it looks like they always find a way to beat the blues.

You keep the faith now, Lucille.

Ahern and Paisley's Handshake Melts Away Decades of Suspicion

Miriam Lord, at Farmleigh

They said it could never be done. After decades of bigotry and hatred and sus-picion, the shattered lives, the heart-break and the hurt; the fear, the cyni-cism, the false dawns; the oceans of empty talk and the acres of newsprint, the god-awful spirit-sapping sameness of it all. Was this it? Could this really be it? Yes. Pinch yourself. Remember the date: Easter Week, 4th April, 2007. A momentous day in Irish history and joy it was to be there.

It took an epic journey to prove it, but politics truly is the art of the possible. For years, as the tor-tured progress of the Northern Ireland peace process stuttered along, politicians and pundits talked of choreography. Positive developments seemed less important than the race to spot which party put a foot wrong.

There was no such talk at Farmleigh House yesterday, where the choreography was purely celestial. The grounds, bathed in glorious spring sunshine, carpets of daffodils and blue wood anemones provided a fitting backdrop for the extraordinary events to come. Three minutes to 11 and word came through: 'They're at the gate.' Two cars rolled up the gravelled driveway. Taoiseach Bertie Ahern emerged from the old mansion, patting down his jacket as he waited to welcome his guest.

No big ceremony was laid on for Ian Paisley. His presence supplied the fanfare. Bertie bustled over, a wide smile on his face. Dr Paisley, the old warhorse, sprang from the car and met him halfway. 'Good morning!' boomed the leader of the Democratic Unionist Party. 'I have to shake this man's hand! Give him a grip!'

With arm outstretched, he made an enthusiastic lunge for the Taoiseach. They shook hands. Bertie grasped the top of Big Ian's arm. Big Ian gave Bertie a manly wallop on the shoulder. They were like two auld farmers at a mart, striking a deal over a bullock. The media looked on, dumbstruck. Ian Paisley of the Free Presbyterian Church, the Dr No of hardline Northern unionism, in Dublin and doing business with the leader of the Irish Republic in a building built on the proceeds of beer.

And that was it, the moment in Ireland's history we thought we would never see. Seismic, earth-shattering and over in a minute – but the symbolic importance of that handshake cannot be underestimated. Countless lives and lifetimes to get to here. But at last, when Bertie met Ian, courage and hope finally got the chance to shine.

The meeting took place in the Library room. They sat opposite each other at a small square table. They ate egg and cress sandwiches and drank pots of tea. The mood was friendly and very relaxed, like they had been having these little tête-a-têtes for years. The two men discussed practical issues, such as investment projects and tourism initiatives. Dr Paisley, who had previously only visited the

Northern Ireland First Minister designate the Rev Ian Paisley with Taoiseach Bertie Ahern at their meeting at Farmleigh House in Dublin's Phoenix Park on 4 April 2007. 'Good morning!' he boomed striding towards Mr Ahern. 'I have to shake this man's hand! Give him a grip!' In a remarkably warm and inclusive speech, Dr Paisley declared that there should be no hedges between our two countries. Photograph: Dara Mac Dónaill.

Pope's heathen South to protest, marvelled at the growth of Dublin. The atmosphere was friendly. There were no awkward moments.

Next month, Ian Paisley takes office as Northern Ireland's first minister, sharing power with Sinn Féin. The soon-to-be legislator and his vastly experienced Dublin counterpart swapped ideas. They talked about the Battle of the Boyne site in Co. Louth. Bertie invited Ian to visit it with him. Ian accepted and said he might even drop in for a preliminary look on his way home.

Their meeting went on longer than intended. Afterwards, they walked together into the sunlight. The media scrutinised their body language. It was good. Taoiseach Ahern was beaming. Dr Paisley looked very relaxed. Bertie spoke first.

'At this important time in our history, we must do our best to put behind us the terrible wounds of our past and work together to build a new relationship between our two traditions.' Big Ian nodded in agreement. 'The future for this island has never been brighter. I believe that this is a future of peace, reconciliation and rising prosperity for all.'

Then it was the Doc's turn. We remembered the man who spat fire and venom at politicians from the South. We remembered the man who marched to Carson's statue and swore 'No Surrender!' We remembered the man who was jostled and jeered when the Belfast Agreement was endorsed by the people of the North and we remembered the survivor who used that unswerving opposition to revive his political fortunes.

The voice is not as strong as it once was, but the preacher can still impart a message. 'Some say hedges make the best neighbours, but that is not the case. I don't believe we should plant a hedge between our two countries,' he began. Journalists who have been writing about Ian Paisley for 30 years looked on in wonder. Was this really happening? As he spoke of being a proud Ulster man, it was hard not to feel moved. Spellbound, we waited for the 'but' to arrive. It didn't.

'We both look forward to visiting the battle site at the Boyne, but not to refight it,' said Dr Paisley with a chuckle. This was incredible stuff. 'I look forward to future meetings and trust that old suspicions and discords can be buried forever under the prospect of mutual and respectful co-operation.' Truly incredible. When he finished, there was silence. The journalists looked at each other in disbelief. Nobody even attempted to ask a question.

What they really wanted to do was applaud. Afterwards, old hands wandered about, shaking their heads. 'Is this a dream? Am I dreaming?' asked UTV's Ken Reid. We weren't dreaming. Bertie gave Ian a book about Farmleigh. Ian gave Bertie a book written by his wife Eileen called *Take a Break*. Four hours later, the Government published its report on the Dublin/Monaghan bombings that killed 33 people in 1974.

Ian Paisley's meeting with Bertie Ahern will forever stand as a magnificent milestone in this island's troubled history. It was a privilege to be there.

FRIDAY, 6 APRIL 2007

The Art of Good Friday

Eileen Battersby

Emaciated and stained with his blood and sweat, a man hangs from a wooden cross. Nails have been driven through his hands. A crown of thorns has been forced onto his head. His flesh is livid. He is dying, or perhaps he is already dead. At his feet, a weeping woman laments. It is his mother. Their agony is one of the most dramatic episodes in human history; it is, according to Christian ritual, atonement for the sins of mankind.

The image of Christ's brutal death has inspired artists throughout the centuries and the crucifixion is central to all Christian art. Even should the sun shine on this most solemn of days, Good Friday creates its own muted tone and many composers have captured the appalling beauty of a mother's sorrow. Somehow the sky will seem to darken, and many people will pause and consider, whether with certainty or doubt, and they may experience the communal guilt of a debt unpaid.

About 1512, the great German Renaissance artist, Mathis Grünewald (circa 1465-1528) completed the central panel of the *Isenheim Altarpiece* for what was a leprosy hospital, and the disease is reflected in the colouring of Christ's skin. The Europe of Grünewald's life was frequently swept by outbreaks of the Black Death; plague was a fact of daily life and he would die of it in Halle, soon after fleeing Frankfurt.

His altarpiece has been acclaimed as the final masterpiece of the Middle Ages and Grünewald's merciless depiction of Christ's physical suffering, from his torn head, parched lips and oozing side, to his twisted broken feet, represents the first attempt to convey the reality of his dying. Prior to this, beauty invariably countered realism. An earlier artist, Italian Andrea Mantegna (circa 1431-1506) allowed the formal compositional grace of his version of the Crucifixion to overshadow the horror.

But Grünewald, who after centuries of neglect would influence many twentieth-century German expressionists, including Otto Dix, preferred realism. In his final representation of the Crucifixion, completed about 1525, the tormented Christ is huge. Grünewald was a religious man, who only painted sacred subjects and left no known pupils or followers. God, not man, preoccupied him.

Whereas Albrecht Dürer, with whom he was friendly, looked to the wider world of the Renaissance, Grünewald, who was also a gifted hydraulic engineer, remained concerned with his spiritual life. Both men died in the same year, 1528.

The *Isenheim Altarpiece* has an elaborately complex design, incorporating statues of saints as well as panels, including a double set of folding wings which open and close, revealing and concealing, according to the church year, various episodes of Christ's life. Most of the other panels, such as the Annunciation and the Resurrection, testify to his expressive, vibrant use of colour. But his Crucifixion is dark and eerie, the background is empty. It is as if the world has closed down.

Within a few years of Grünewald's death, a child was born in Crete in 1541 and grew to show artistic promise. By the 1570s, having studied in Venice and Rome, El Greco had settled in Toledo and he became synonymous with religious art, although he also painted portraits.

The painters of Europe have left a rich social history, a visual narrative; the earthy power of kings and merchants is well represented, alongside religious themes. The passage of the Crucifixion story in Irish art has been a long and constant one. 'The Crucifixion, being a central theme of Christian thought', writes archaeologist and art historian Peter Harbison in the introduction to *The Crucifixion in Irish Art*, 'is the only religious event or scene that has been represented in Irish art in virtually every century from the year 800 down to the present day.'

He has assembled a thoughtful selection of 50 contrasting examples, ranging from tomb panels and figures carved on a high cross, to the twentieth-century stained-glass windows of Harry Clarke and Evie Hone, and argues that prior to the ninth century, the Irish artist had been drawn to the abstract and the stylised. The earliest representation of the human figure in a natural form can be seen on the surviving high crosses. The crucified Christ appears on the west face of *Muiredach's Cross* at Monasterboice, Co. Louth.

It is interesting to contrast the approach adopted by the craftsmen who carved the high crosses with the more fantastical style perfected by the monks in their richly decorated illuminated manuscripts. But then, the illustrations served as decoration, not narrative. Harbison notes 'the Celtic love of stylisation and geometrical decoration'. But the emergence of the craftsmen who made the high crosses represents not only the beginning of an Irish sculptural tradition, itself important in the context of European

The High Cross and round tower at Monasterboice cemetery. Photograph: Matt Kavanagh.

art, but it is also evidence of changing artistic attitudes towards depicting the human form.

Among the examples selected by Harbison is the cross at Dysert O'Dea in Co. Clare. Dating from the twelfth century, the Christ figure, although depicted with arms outstretched and clad in a long robe, appears more triumphant than defeated. In the south transept of St Mary's Protestant Cathedral in Tuam, Co. Galway, now stands the *Market Cross,* which until 1992 occupied the centre of the town. This cross is composed of two segments. The head, dating from the 1150s, depicts a crucified Christ, but one wearing a king's crown instead of a ring of thorns.

Above the doorway of the late twelfth century round tower at Donaghmore, Co. Meath, a simple crucifixion figure has been carved. On one flat stone the upper body has been depicted, while the legs, on the keystone of the arch of the window, are narrow and twisted. A far more sophisticated rendition is to be found on a Gothic tombstone standing in St Columba's Church of Ireland, in Kells, which notes a change in the iconography.

'Instead of Christ's two feet being side by side and nailed separately to the cross,' notes Harbison, 'they are placed one above the other and pierced with a single nail.' The figures on the tombstone suggest it is of Norman origin and it is believed to be one of the earliest identifiable representations of the Crucifixion on an Irish tombstone.

Metal workers also depicted the Crucifixion on shrines and bronze plaques. The *Leabhar Breac,* or *Speckled Book*, now housed in the Royal Irish Academy but written in Co. Galway between 1408 and 1411, chronicles the birth, life, passion and resurrection of Christ. According to Harbison, this great manuscript contains the only representation of the crucified Christ to be found in the later medieval texts. At the side of the Dublin-Navan road stands a wayside cross dating from the later fifteenth century. On it, the crucified Christ appears more peaceful than tormented.

A far more primitive wayside crucifixion cross carved in granite is *St Valery's Cross* at Fassaroe, Co. Wicklow. Dating from the mid-seventeenth century is the *White Cross* at Athcarne, Co. Meath, an example of sculpture rather than stone carving. It is an unusual work. The short crossbar of the cross creates the impression that Christ's arms reach skywards, above his head, while the depiction of the feet, shown side by side, rather than one on top of the other – indicating the use of one nail – returns to the pre-Gothic style.

There is a particularly gruesome late-sixteenth century stone crucifix built into the north wall of the Catholic church in Johnstown, Co. Kilkenny. A bizarre sense of movement is conveyed, suggesting

real torment. Surreal peace and destiny fulfilled is the mood of Mainie Jellett's *The Ninth Hour* (1941), a wartime oil executed on a panel, housed in the Hugh Lane Municipal Gallery of Modern Art in Dublin.

Harry Clarke's famous *The Crucifixion and the Adoration of the Cross*, dating from 1920, is a formal and elegant narrative in rich purples, blues and reds spanning three vertical lights. Visual artists across the centuries have considered the story of one man's death on a wooden cross and have made images that stay in the mind.

For all the power of the visual image, the life blood of Passion Week is the music of Bach. His Passions – reserving his celebratory *Oster Oratorium* for Easter Sunday – add to the legacy established by earlier masters, such as Palestrina, Lassus, Victoria, Monteverdi and Scarlatti, who were inspired in turn by the Passion Week, its traditions and rituals.

A century before the birth of Johann Sebastian Bach, the Spanish composer Tomás Luis de

A typical summer's day in Sandycove, Co. Dublin . . . 5 April 2007. Photograph: Cyril Byrne.

Victoria (1548-1611) published *Officium*, his music for Holy Week. This is a Renaissance sound and it is one of the most complete cycles of music for Holy Week by a single composer and it is probably the most cohesive work of Renaissance polyphony. Victoria's subtle, melancholic and elegant contribution surpasses even that of his great peers, Lassus and Palestrina.

His set of 18 *Responsories for Tenebrae* are particularly appropriate for today and tomorrow, Holy Saturday. Victoria was a quiet man. Having excelled as a chorister, he was patronised by Philip II, and sent to Rome. He knew Palestrina. For all his success in Rome, Victoria yearned to return to Spain and did.

Dietrich Buxtehude (1637-1707), master organist and composer, so inspired an admirer, one JS Bach, that he famously once walked 200 miles to Lübeck to visit him. Buxtehude's *Memra Jesu nostri patientis sanctissima (Most Holy Members of the Body of our Suffering Jesus)* is a cycle of seven cantatas, each addressed to a different part of the crucified Christ's body. The listener will be struck by the long instrumental passages.

There is also, of course, the lingering influence of the early German master Heinrich Schütz, born exactly a century before Bach. All roads led to Bach and it is his Passions, that of *St John* (1724) and the majestic *St Matthew Passion* (1727), with its glorious arias, which have come to dominate Passion music. Yet, it is interesting to also recall Scarlatti's graceful treatment of *St John Passion*, which is more in the tradition of Monteverdi's operas than of Bach's masterworks.

A man fulfils his destiny and obeys his father. The death is brutal but inspiring. Christian man continues to contemplate the privilege and the debt and the mystery. Is it wonderful or shocking, or probably both? Western artists have created a glorious legacy by drawing on this drama. A mother weeps for her son. A young Italian composer, Giovanni Pergolesi, was drawn to the mother's suffering.

His response, *Stabat Mater,* arranged in 12 sections, was his final work completed in 1736, the year of his death, aged 26. It has remained the definitive *Stabat Mater* and caused Rossini to initially refuse a commission in 1831, simply because he felt Pergolesi's version could not be bettered. For all the rich flourish of his subsequent treatment, Rossini was right.

From the Golden Age of early English music, as pioneered by John Taverner, Christopher Tye and Thomas Tallis, to the European Renaissance and the early Italian Baroque composers, who played a part in shaping God's musician, JS Bach, and on to Mozart's *Requiem* and Haydn's *Die Sieben Letzten Worte unseres Erlösers am Kreuze,* there are musical riches to suit the mood of this symbolic day, a good day to die on, a fine day to be born on, as Beckett liked to remark.

Pergolesi's eloquent *Stabat Mater,* one of the most influential works in musical history, articulates a mother's grief and could open a door for many engaged in a vigil of faith.

The Crucifixion in Irish Art, by Peter Harbison, is published by Columba Press, €18.99. Among the best recordings of Pergolesi's Stabat Mater is the Academy of Ancient Music's version, conducted by Christopher Hogwood, and featuring soprano Emma Kirkby and counter-tenor James Bowman on Decca (1989).

TUESDAY, 17 APRIL 2007

'He Chained up some of the Doors . . . and Started Shooting'

Denis Staunton, Washington Correspondent

Engineering student Josh Wargo was sitting in a second-floor classroom at the Norris Hall building of Virginia Tech's sprawling campus at about 9.30 yesterday morning when he heard a series of loud bangs followed by screams. 'We heard almost 40 or 50 shots. They were going on from the time we heard them and jumped out the window until almost two minutes later. When I landed, I was in a daze, standing outside of the building. Then I heard shots going through glass – that's when it hit me that I had to get out of there,' he said.

While Wargo and his classmates fled, the horror continued inside as a gunman described by witnesses as a young man of Asian appearance wearing a maroon cap and a black leather jacket shot more than 50 people, killing at least 33.

Gene Cole, who has worked in Virginia Tech's housekeeping services for more than two decades, was on the second floor of Norris Hall when he saw a person lying on a hallway floor. As Cole approached, a man wearing a cap and holding a black gun stepped into the hallway. 'Someone stepped out of a classroom and started shooting at me,' Cole said. He fled down the corridor, then down a flight of steps to safety. 'All I saw was blood in the hallways,' Cole said.

Earlier yesterday, shortly after 7 a.m., a gunman believed to be the same young man entered West Ambler Johnston, a co-ed dormitory on the other side of Virginia Tech's campus. Some witnesses said he was looking for his girlfriend and when he failed to find her he shot one person dead.

Aimee Kanode, who lives in a room one floor below where the first shooting happened, said that at about 8 a.m., someone knocked on her door and told her to stay inside. 'They had us under lockdown. They temporarily lifted the lockdown. The gunman shot again,' she said.

While police and emergency services focused on the dormitory building, the gunman made his

A student cries during a convocation a day after the killings at Virginia Tech in Blacksburg, Virginia. Photograph: Kevin Lamarque/Reuters.

way across campus to Norris Hall, walked into a classroom, and started shooting. Hector Takahashi was in class in a nearby building, talking with other students about the incident at the dormitory. 'Then all of a sudden, we were like, "Whoa – were those shots?"' he said.

Details of what happened inside Norris Hall remained unclear last night and authorities would not confirm reports that the gunman lined up his victims against a wall before shooting them.

Student David Jenkins suggested the killings had been more random. 'From what I heard, he chained up some of the doors so people couldn't get in and he basically was just going to every classroom trying to get in, and just started shooting inside classrooms,' he said.

Jenkins, who heard the earlier shots at the dormitory, said that one of his friends was in one of the classrooms targeted by the gunman. 'He was very fortunate. He said every single person in the room was shot, killed and was on the ground. He laid on the ground with everyone . . . he played dead and he was okay,' he said.

Police and Swat teams converged on Norris Hall, ordering everyone to remain inside and locking down the campus for three hours after the shooting ended. Authorities confirmed that the gunman then shot himself dead. The dead and wounded were rushed to nearby Roanoke, where hospitals struggled to cope with the sudden rush of trauma wounds, while the medical examiner's office waited for reinforcements before carrying out autopsies.

With more than 25,000 full-time students, Virginia Tech is Virginia's largest university, with more than 100 buildings over 2,600 acres. Last August the opening day of classes was cancelled and the campus closed when an escaped jail inmate allegedly killed a hospital guard off campus and fled to the area near Virginia Tech.

Last week the university received two bomb threats and when they heard the first reports of yesterday's shootings, some students were sceptical.

'At first I thought it was something like a joke because going through something like this twice in one year didn't seem possible,' said 18-year-old Dennis Hollich.

WEDNESDAY, 18 APRIL 2007

Piper's Lament: Emigrant's Final Wishes Realised at Graveside in Spiddal

Denise McNamara, in Galway

The final request of a woman whose unclaimed body lay in a London morgue since her death on Christmas Day, was realised yesterday in the Connemara village of Spiddal.

In her will, Irish-born Marian Marriot asked to be buried in the west of Ireland in an area untouched by industrial development, beside a stream and a meadow. She also wanted the lament of a piper to ring out as they laid her in the ground. She died aged 70, penniless, in London on Christmas Day, from peritonitis and emphysema and was without friends or family.

When the social services in the UK found among her items an old membership card from the Irish Club in London, they rang the club in February. Owen Murphy, vice-chairman of the club, knew Ms Marriot as she was honorary secretary for a time. He believes she had relatives in southwest Ireland and her maiden name was Butler. Her parents were said to have a coffee plantation in east Africa.

She was a marvellous debater, recalls Mr Murphy, and the pair won a debating competition in the 1970s. Then they lost touch. He believes she had lived in a bedsit off Fleet Street, where she said she worked as a freelance journalist.

Máirtín Ó Fatharta plays a lament at the graveside before the burial of Marian Marriot at Tulach Bhuí cemetery. Photograph: Joe O'Shaughnessy.

The Irish Club decided to donate £1,000 to carry out her last wishes. They appealed to the London Irish community to help defray the costs involved in burying her in Ireland. Tulach Bhuí Cemetery in Coilleach, Spiddal, overlooking the sea was chosen as the burial ground.

Parish priest of Spiddal, Msgr Brendan Kelly, told the congregation who gathered in St Enda's Church yesterday there were two striking elements about the case of Ms Marriot. 'There's the lamentable loneliness of a life, which we can all understand and identify with, and then there's the goodness that will overcome everything.'

A small plaque will mark the spot where Ms Marriot was laid to rest.

THURSDAY, 19 APRIL 2007

And Here is your Host . . . The Religious Rite-Wing Radio

Newton's Optic: Newton Emerson

That was The Monkees with 'I'm a Believer' and you're listening to Jeremy Sweater on Host FM, Ireland's first openly Christian radio station. Later we'll be asking if the Central Bank is a money changer in Temple Bar, then studio guest Michael McDowell will read from his favourite Biblical passage, Ephesians 3:7, Whereof I was made a

Ann Ryder, a patient at Roscommon County Hospital, standing in support of the striking nurses on 13 April 2007.
Photograph: Frank Miller.

minister, according to the gift of the grace of God. We'll also have a specially commissioned hymn for listeners in Galway, 'Water friend we have in Jesus', all coming up after the *Good News and Weather*.

But first a quick look at the international headlines. By the rivers of Babylon, a bridge fell down, yea George Bush wept, when he remembered Zionism. In Britain, defence secretary Des Browne has been summoned before God for inscribing the Ten Commandos. Finally, chess grandmaster Garry Kasparov has been arrested by Russian authorities. Well, Garry, that's what you get for sacrificing a bishop.

Just time now for a quick reminder that Host FM is funded partly by donations, so be sure to cast your bread upon the airwaves. We also want your texts and emails on the latest Bertie Ahern scandal. Is it easier for a rich man to pass through

Manchester Airport than to be needled by the *Sunday Independent*? While you're mulling that over, feel free to enter today's text competition. Was it Jesus of (a) Nazareth (b) Nasa or (c) Naas? Entries charged at €5. If you're under 18, don't forget to ask for forgiveness.

On the line now we have Father John Curie from the Congress of Righteous Indignation, who will recite the parable of the wealthy merchants who squandered their gold on a foolish venture instead of giving alms to the poor . . . oh, we seem to have lost Father Curie there. Moving on to today's meditation and our topic is the nursing strike. Jesus said: 'Take up thy bed and walk.' Or was it the Virgin Mary Harney? Either way, the Lord's purpose is clear. This item was brought to you by Very High Insurance Ltd, your escalating stairway to heaven.

On the subject of miracles we'd also like to share this scriptural reflection from Isaiah on the Rev Ian Paisley's recent conversion: And the government shall be upon his shoulder, and his name shall be called Wonderful Counsellor, the Mighty God, the Everlasting Father, the Prince of Peace. I think that sums up everyone's feelings really, don't you?

Time now briefly for some traffic and travel. Drivers on the M50 are warned that the Red Cow off-ramp has been paved with good intentions; Iarnród Éireann advises Arklow commuters that a bus substitution service will be coming to carry them home and passengers on the stranded Holyhead ferry have rowed the boat ashore, hallelujah. In a moment we'll be joining our faith broadcasting partners at 1453 Muslim Wave for the *Equality Authority Hour*, brought to you by a Broadcasting Commission licensing requirement. But not before we've played a special request for all the boys and girls at St Priscilla's Teacher Training College who'd like to hear 'Body and Blood', the latest single from slightly edgy yet still clearly harmless Christian rock group, Testify.

So turn down those hearing aids, oldsters, and get ready for some happening praise in the house! First though, the 'Angelus'.

WEDNESDAY, 25 APRIL 2007

'Whatever it was, they must have Felt Very Alone'

Carl O'Brien, in New Ross

Dressed in black and numbed with shock, Mary Dunne is sitting in front of a small coal fire and struggling to comprehend how she lost four family members over the weekend. 'I'm devastated, completely heartbroken. I'm trying to put a brave face on it for the rest of the family,' she says, as she grips her daughter's hand.

'It was bad enough to lose my son James last month, but now I've lost my son, my daughter-in-law and my two lovely grandchildren. They say you shouldn't have to bury your children – well, you certainly shouldn't have to bury your grandchildren.'

Crowded into the sitting-room of the small family home near New Ross, Co. Wexford, other family members and friends are still coming to terms with the deaths of Adrian and Ciara Dunne and their daughters Shania (3) and Leanne (5).

Their grief is also tinged with anger over what they see as the failure of State authorities to contact them when concerns were first raised on Friday evening. Adrian's sister Bridget says it was an opportunity lost for the family to intervene and potentially avoid the tragedy. 'If they had told us, we'd have gone down to the house and we wouldn't have left for the whole weekend. There's no way we'd have allowed that to happen.'

Mary remembers hearing about how social services weren't available to help Sharon Grace and her two daughters before they died two years ago. Now, she says, her family has been failed by the same system. 'I thought that case was terrible. I couldn't understand why they didn't do something about it. I never for a moment thought we'd be affected by something like that. Nothing seems to have changed.' The Dunne family says there wasn't even the faintest warning in previous weeks as the tragedy unfolded on Monday morning.

Adrian had been his normal self, they say, talking about sports and how the Wexford hurlers would do this year. Ciara was the same vivacious person who would light up a room when she walked into it with her pulsating personality.

Among the last to speak to Adrian was his brother Sebastian (18) last Saturday evening. 'He was slagging me about girlfriends, because I never seem to hold on to one for that long, and we were talking about the result of the matches,' he recalls. 'He also told me about a job going as a caretaker. The last thing I said was that I'd talk to him later.'

Sebastian recalls discussing suicide with Adrian, at the funeral of their brother James (30), just under a month ago, but it was only to firmly rule it out as an option. 'He told me that he'd never do anything like that. He said he'd never be able to do it and, anyway, he wouldn't cause even more grief for Mammy.'

Some relatives have discussed the possibility of a suicide pact between Adrian and Ciara. As difficult as it is to contemplate, Bridget thinks it is a serious possibility. 'I don't think Adrian would have done that on his own. It may have been a joint decision between the two. There's no way he'd have done it on his own. They were extremely close.'

His brother says only something like the fear of being separated from their children or having them taken into care could have prompted their actions, but there is no evidence this was considered by social services.

Adrian and Ciara's marriage appeared to be a perfectly normal, loving relationship. They met in their early 20s while taking college courses in Stillorgan in Dublin about seven years ago. Ciara was doing a childcare course, Adrian was finishing a communications and journalism course.

Adrian was visually impaired, suffering from a hereditary eye condition, but it had never prevented him fully enjoying and participating in life. The Dunnes had been taught by their mother to look beyond their disabilities and live the same lives as others.

'We've always been an open family here, we talk about everything,' says Mary, 'but whatever it

John Burke, a technician with Bedrock Theatre, in Meeting House Square in Dublin's Temple Bar, with props from their production of Samuel Beckett's Breath *about to be shipped to Paris for their performance in the Irish Cultural Centre in Paris in May. Photograph: Brenda Fitzsimons.*

was, they must have felt very alone. I do feel more could have been done. There are still so many unanswered questions.'

Shocking Reminder of the Fragility and Complexity of Human Behaviour

Tony Bates

In the past week I have been asked twice by the media to try and shed some light on human tragedies of staggering proportions. First there was the massacre in Virginia, and now the death of an entire family in Monageer. Both of these events involved violence in the context of some form of mental health crisis. It seems reasonable therefore to ask so-called 'mental health experts' to make sense of what happened or at least to offer some insights that may ensure these tragedies might never happen in the future.

But let me declare from the outset, particularly in relation to the Dunne family, I am as shocked as any of you and I don't know why this happened. I believe this story will unfold in the coming weeks and months and that we may gradually achieve some understanding of what occurred and put in place protections within our communities to reduce the likelihood of it happening again.

But there are no simplistic explanations for the above tragedies and there are no guarantees that we can rid our world of irrational, unpredictable, heart-stopping shocks. The best we can hope for is that these traumas reveal to us more clearly how complex and fragile we are as a species and how we need to respond more effectively as a community to those in extreme distress, before their desperation carries them beyond our reach.

The community in Monageer will never be the same again. A sudden trauma like the death of the Dunne family is an overwhelming experience that breaks all the rules and generates intense anxiety.

In addition to their experience of loss for each person who died, and died needlessly, they will experience a loss of trust and safety in the world. How can they, or any of us, be sure that this won't happen in our own family? The world they wake up to every day, with its normal ups and downs, has become dangerously unpredictable. The absence of some easy explanation that would help to make this tragedy bearable adds enormously to their sense of loss of control.

People need enormous care in the aftermath of trauma. For most of us, in the days following a crisis, our greatest need is for comfort. Analysis can come later.

What we need at this time are opportunities for connecting with one another and extending emotional and practical support wherever we can. The more that a community can share their experience of shock and loss with one another, the greater their chance of working through the shock and not allow it to tear them apart.

In time, there will be questions to ask and reflect upon. What really happened within this family to bring about such horror? Were there early warning signs that could have been picked up on and responded to more constructively?

We can ask these questions with the goal in mind of finding someone to blame, or we can ask them in order to discover ways of improving our systems of care within each community. It is tempting to find a scapegoat and lay the responsibility for all that happened at some individual's or agency's door. I sense we do this more to avoid facing the truth that human beings are far more prone to irrational behaviour than any of us would care to acknowledge; that life is full of shocks and that there is no guaranteed way for any of us to stop the pain. What we can do is to acknowledge this truth and provide supports for people to engage with and work through tough times.

The southeast has had more than its share of tragedies, notably deaths by suicide. As a consequence it has established a wealth of services and counselling facilities each committed to suicide prevention in their own particular way.

The Dunne family was visited by a number of individuals and agencies in the days before the tragedy. Concern was raised by the priests in particular and communicated to others. But perhaps in this situation, these caring initiatives needed back-up support from specialist services which might have brought relevant expertise to complement their efforts.

What we may learn from this tragic incident is that there is a role for flexible, outreach teams in our services that can be mobilised to support community workers and families where there is a mental health crisis. When people feel at their lowest, it is often the time they are least able to leave their home and seek help from statutory agencies.

Outreach or homecare teams are a standard feature of mental health services in many countries. They are described and recommended in our mental health policy 'A Vision for Change'. Undoubtedly, we will be grappling with the questions raised by this crisis for some time. Individuals, communities, and services will be asking hard questions and generating ideas for building more caring communities.

Hopefully this will lead to a deeper appreciation that everyone has something to give, and that working together in an integrated way enhances our capacity to bring care and support to those who need it the most.

SATURDAY, 28 APRIL 2007

A Terrible Beauty

Editorial

W@ would da gr8 poet William Butler Y8s have made of da news dat txt spk is chngin da way da yung ppl rite? Easter, 1916 mite

2day read like dis: He, 2, has bin chngd in his turn, Trans4med utterly, A trrble buty is born.

Da st8 chief examiner sez dat da standard of English is droppin cos 'text messaging, with its use of phonetic spelling and little or no punctuation, seems to pose a threat to traditional conventions in writing'. He sez dat xam answers r 2 short cos 'candidates seemed unduly reliant on short sentences, simple tenses and a limited vocabulary'.

N response, da Assoc of Secondary Teachers in Irel& sez der is no need to panic, dat 'rigidity or conformity with received standards is not the first port of call in judging a piece of writing or, indeed, speaking' & dat 'language changes as the world changes: it cannot be set in aspic'.

It is tru dat der is a chng in da way we commnc8. Da Irish sent 4.4bn txts last yr, or 1,053 txt 4 evry 1 in the St8. We own approx 4.5m mob phones, & cos 96% of 11-12 yr olds hav a phone, in little tym Irish teens have lrnd to adapt 2 abbrev8d lingo. Dey find it ez 2 switch between txt spk & traditional langwge.

It is a fascin8n trend, a gr8 shift in da way ppl rite & 1 dat has bin driven by nu tech. B4, tho, txt spk woz ltd 2 txt msgs & Bebo sites. Now it is affecting both Jr Cert and Levn Cert xams. Dis mns it is bginnin to dsplace Stablished use of English, ncludn da logicl & conceptual found8ions of da langwge.

Da rulz of English grammr r bein ignored & may b 4gotten. Dis cant b good 4 educ8nal standrdz, or 4 how yung ppl undrst& da language dey spk & rite evry day. Txtin is best regRded as a parllel funcshnl langwge with its oan rules & wit, rather dan 1 dat by in10tion or de4llt dsplces convenshnl English.

& in da long term, it cud affect da lingo of biz and even cultr. Will ppl pay 2 c an actor deliva da gr8 line: '2b or not 2b, dat d Q.'

1 day, mayB, all of Da Irish Times will b rtn lyk dis. But not on Mdm's woch! 4 now, txting is still just as hard to rite as it is 2 read. Which is da rison y dis editorial is on da shrt side.

A bust of the late Dick Walsh, former political correspondent of The Irish Times, *which was unveiled in the new Irish Times Building on 18 April 2007 by the Editor, Geraldine Kennedy (left), with Deaglán de Bréadún, Father of the Irish Times National Union of Journalists Chapel (branch), Ruth Kelly, Mr Walsh's widow, and Emmet Malone, chairman of the newspaper's Editorial Committee, which was founded by Walsh. Photograph: Dara Mac Dónaill.*

MONDAY, 30 APRIL 2007

Fianna Fáil's Early Start gives Impression they're on the Run

Miriam Lord

It just looked wrong. No matter what way they spin it in the coming days, yesterday morning was a disaster for Fianna Fáil. As far as the start of the election campaign is concerned, the party took its advantage to the Phoenix Park and promptly handed it to the opposition on a plate.

They planned this short course race down to the very last detail, hoping to gain valuable early ground by bursting from the blocks and leaving the rest of the field standing. Surprise is a wonderful weapon. But strangely, in the course of a bizarre few hours, it seemed as if Fianna Fáil had turned it on themselves.

This long-awaited day was one of unexpected contrast. It began with Taoiseach Bertie Ahern scuttling to Áras an Uachtaráin as the Sunday city still slept. His mission was to ask President McAleese to dissolve the 29th Dáil, and he carried it out in a manner that verged on the furtive. Dawn calls to a very small number of media personnel heralded what should have been a momentous event. Instead, it was almost as if Bertie was embarrassed to be seen out so early.

THE IRISH TIMES BOOK OF THE YEAR

Still, at least he did Mrs McAleese the courtesy of allowing her to do her Constitutional duty before she departed for America.

Around the city, and around the country, activists from all parties roused themselves and attacked the lampposts. Meanwhile, Enda Kenny was on his way to Knock airport, preparing to board a flight to Dublin. It was midnight in Mayo when he got the first call saying it was very likely the Taoiseach was about to name the date.

Labour, the Greens and Sinn Féin turned on the power in their offices at first light. Election machines were oiled and ready to go. They got to work as soon as the news was official. The PDs were first out of the traps at 11 with their manifesto. Tánaiste McDowell, his usual ebullient self, declared that he hadn't been surprised by the Taoiseach's daybreak flit to the Áras. He was fighting fit and ready to go.

Before the launch, he posed for photographs on the Liffey boardwalk with deputies Liz O'Donnell and Fiona O'Malley. As Minister for Justice, he could be confident he wouldn't be troubled by the drug addicts who like to loiter around the riverside walk.

Once the all-important images were recorded, Michael made his way across to the Morrison Hotel and joined the throng of candidates, handlers and shiny young PDs. He presented his party's pledges to the nation. Seven in all, and introduced by Michael in the proud tones of a man about to unveil seven new wonders of the world. 'Don't Throw it all Away' was the slogan on the backdrop. The manifesto, said the Tánaiste modestly, is called 'From Good to Great'. A little slide-show accompanied the exposition.

So what fresh goodies were on offer from the junior government partner of ten years' standing? Lower taxes, fairer stamp duty, better healthcare, protection of the environment, a tough approach to crime and a promise to 'reward pensioners'. After a spirited contribution on the health system by Mary Harney, it seemed churlish to ask whether the pensioners' reward would be for staying alive, or staying on trollies.

The slides were all nice images of children and families. There was one of the Tánaiste with two Garda reserves. All three were laughing with their arms out in front of them at mid-chest height, like they were doing the hokey-pokey. The PDs are giving everyone in the country a free manifesto magazine.

Minister McDowell experienced some media leakage as journalists rushed off to make Enda Kenny's gig across the city. It was held outdoors, on the steps of their election headquarters.

Despite his sleepless night and early flight, deputy Kenny was full of beans, leaping out of his car and punching the air. His hair, some of the ladies present observed, seems to have found its level and is settling down. In brilliant sunshine, IndaKinny indulged in fightin' talk. 'Your time is up!' he told the Government. He offered 'fourteen fundamentals' to trump the seven pledges.

There was much talk of destiny, before he went off to present the government with their P45, officially bagging first silly photo opportunity of the election for Fine Gael. Enda Kenny's performance may be the key to the campaign. He appeared relaxed yesterday and up for the fray. Time will tell.

Labour were supposed to start with a silly photo opportunity of their own at the Molly Malone statue. Leader Pat Rabbitte arrived at the bottom of Grafton Street in his battle bus. Then he formed a line with deputies McManus, Burton, Costello and Shortall and they walked up the street.

Like a big human sweeping brush, they moved quickly along. As a walkabout it was pointless; they talked to no one. But there were photographs taken at the flower stalls and Pat accused Bertie of 'chickening out' of calling an election for 17 May and wondered why he 'slunk out to the Park in the early hours of the morning'.

Back in headquarters – it's sure to be a hit with the media, as it's next to Doheny and Nesbitt's pub

Bertie Ahern leaving the stage after launching Fianna Fáil's election campaign at the party's headquarters in Dublin. Photograph: Bryan O'Brien.

and above Burger King – he bagged the first silly prop of the campaign. He turned on a 'digital clock' for a 'Countdown to Change'. Labour is 'brimful of ideas designed to create a new society in Ireland,' said Pat. People want change. 'It's very evident from the doorsteps and the supermarkets.'

There is a large white message board just inside the door. A 'Message of the Day' was scrawled in red marker: 'It's the future, stupid. P.S. Don't forget health.' All very upbeat, confident and enthusiastic. It was the same story at the Greens and the Sinn Féin press conference, which took place about the same time.

And so, to Fianna Fáil in their impressive headquarters in the Treasury Building near the Grand Canal Dock. The atmosphere there could best be described as subdued. There was tension in the air.

Even the irrepressible PJ Mara seemed a little reserved. This was nothing like the launch five years ago, when everyone was buzzing and Mara kicked things off with a mischievous 'It's show-time, folks!' What followed was quite strange. Following a low-key introduction by press director Mandy Johnston, the Taoiseach walked from behind the backdrop onto the small platform in the conference room.

He seemed a little out of sorts. He read from a script without passion or animation. He highlighted his Government's achievements, then ran though a mini-manifesto of promises. It wasn't a long speech, and for the day that was in it, it was decidedly dull. When he finished, he didn't wait for questions, but shot back through the opening in the backdrop, leaving an audience of bemused journalists staring into the silence.

Bertie came into the refreshment room for a little while, shaking hands and making small talk with the media. He was pleasant and said he hoped to see everyone on the campaign trail. But there was awkwardness there. Everyone knew it was because of the Mahon Tribunal. He didn't stay long. No questions answered, but lots more lingered.

Events in Dublin Castle today will determine how the campaign pans out for Bertie. For Fianna Fáil, the battle is on hold.

The best laid plans of mice and men . . .

FRIDAY, 4 MAY 2007

Parlon Gives All the Right Answers Down Home on the Range

Kathy Sheridan

Hi there folks. Welcome to Parlon Country. Rolling hills, lush parkland, galloping great Georgian houses, ancient castles, horses, artists' studios, birdsong, the usual quota of yelping sheepdogs, whole packs of yapping designer dogs and a swathe of unfeasibly prosperous, grinning voters, ripe for a chat on a gleaming doorstep, SUV, tractor or trailer.

Most are already home or nearly there in the sun-dappled, late afternoon. M50 madness? N4 neurosis? Nah. Not in Parlon Country, cowboy. Makes ya jess wanna lean against a big oak tree, tip back the ole sombrero and light up a Marlboro.

On days like this, you think sleepily, the Parlon department of decentralisation and dissent could do worse than run bus tours of south Offaly for Dublin-centric civil servants . . . So when someone turns ugly (and we don't mean Charlie Flanagan, running an annoyingly blistering campaign, according to Parlon's posse), it just seems durned well inappropriate.

Like the woman who conducts a vocal stand-off from an upstairs window and lets fly about her recent hospital incarceration. Good thing the hospital was neither Tullamore nor Portlaoise. Disaster averted. Sort of. It did mean having to defend Mary Harney, and not for the first time . . . 'She's only been in power two and a half years and reform takes a while.'

Hours later though, it was the Biffo who accused him of trying to shut down rural Ireland that he was smarting about: 'Blueshirt, I'd say. Bit of a chip on his shoulder . . .'

He was straight with the elderly PD voter who raised Bertiegate. After the pleasantries (he's a natural, leaping out of cars, racing up driveways, jumping walls, then looking like someone with all the time in the world), she brooded: 'You'd wonder Bertie won't come out with an answer . . . something?' 'Maybe he hasn't one,' said Mr Parlon.

Afterwards, he swears that the PDs have not been briefed about it and that he isn't familiar with the detail, but concedes that 'it all sounds a bit strange . . .' Certainly now, it's a very uncomfortable position for him and the party. 'On the other hand, I've met a thousand people in the past four days and a few have made a bit of a crack, but not one has said: "I won't vote for you if you're associated with that man".'

But isn't he the president of the watchdog party? 'I've never said that. I don't regard myself as a watchdog. Last time round, the Taoiseach briefed Michael McDowell, who bought the story and didn't upset the applecart. Now though, it does sound bad.'

Moving swiftly on, more gates, more gravel, more running and jumping, before being totally laidback on the doorstep. 'I love this, love it. If only there wasn't so much at stake.'

We light on a real-life hombre sitting in his back garden doing something with a horse collar. 'I'm not much bothered with voting,' he says in a rural English accent. Despite a palpable apathy, Mr Parlon persists. 'You mightn't be bothered, but I am. You can register 15 days before polling day.'

Suddenly, the target straightens up: 'Do you support foxhunting?' Pause.

Mr Parlon decides: 'I do.'

'You sure?' asks the hombre. Parlon eyes him squarely. 'I let them cross my land. I've no problem with it at all.' Bingo! Our man is a huntsman, made redundant after the English foxhunting ban, now employed by a nearby hunt. 'It was Ireland or America,' says his wife. Job's oxo.

Suddenly, there's a rush to the office in Birr for a mystery meeting. A quick visual confirms that it's Des Kavanagh, chief executive of the Psychiatric Nurses' Association (PNA) and the PNA's local chairman, Seán Melia. It lasts under 30 minutes.

Possibly inspired by the PNA men, he bets on a horse in Ballinrobe (it lost, but then a black cat runs in front of the car). Later, in Birr, a man in a fine, new house asks about decentralisation progress ('beyond the point of no return') and about the paucity of gardaí in the town ('there's so many guards passing out' nowadays, he says, that Mr McDowell reports that he hasn't time to acknowledge each one individually 'and it's almost "give me a five" as they pass').

A friendly woman agitates about her three grown children in Dublin and Galway who can't get home on a Thursday to vote (no fret; there will be Parlon buses if you know the password). Another sympathises on the death of his mother after a lengthy illness a couple of weeks ago. It may be one reason why he seems edgier, a little more

Taoiseach Bertie Ahern with his first grandchildren, five-week-old Rocco (left) and Jay and their parents, Georgina Ahern and Nicky Byrne, at the Grand Hotel in Malahide, Co. Dublin, where the new arrivals were shown publicly for the first time. Photograph: Matt Kavanagh.

nervous than expected, despite his 16-strong polling crew out this evening.

A recent Red C poll tips him for the fourth seat with Charlie Flanagan getting the fifth and Seán Fleming to lose his seat. He's taking nothing for granted: 'At 53 it would be a big kick in the arse to lose my job.'

Time for a quick chat with Tony McLoughlin, the fiercely independent county and town councillor who wants to know if Fine Gael and Labour were drunk when they promised to provide 2,500 new hospital beds – 'equivalent to nine Tullamore hospitals' – before adjourning to Kennedy's pub.

It's after 11pm when the team scatters. Then it's home, home on the range . . .

FRIDAY, 4 MAY 2007

Showtime Is More Like a Showdown As Bertie Is Browned Off

Miriam Lord

Standing amidst the wreckage of a disastrous first week, Bertie Ahern prepared to face the most difficult challenge of his leadership career. Shell-shocked troops to the left of him. A hostile media to the right. His once-strutting officers arrayed on either side – like they were about to be shot at dawn.

Fifth-year students from The Teresian School in Donnybrook, Dublin, including twin sisters Abigail and Joanna Cornwell and Aoife Quinn, have some unseasonal fun in the snow courtesy of a snow machine installed at the RDS in Dublin for the launch of the programme for this year's BT Young Scientist & Technology Exhibition 2008. Photograph: Matt Kavanagh.

The mood in the Mansion House was as upbeat as a dentist's waiting room. Party advisers, battalions of them, tip-toeing around the margins. The room was dark – it suited the tense, subdued atmosphere. Security men patrolled the aisles.

Happy days? Emphatically not. When Fianna Fáil launched its manifesto in 2002, the happy spirit was summed up in one word by PJ Mara: 'Showtime!' Yesterday felt more like a showdown. As Bertie read his script, Cabinet colleagues looked glum. Nobody noticed when he came to the end.

'I'll now take questions, ladies and gentlemen,' said the Taoiseach. It was only then that the huge number of supporters in the Round Room realised he had finished, and clapped. In the meantime, PJ Mara had shimmered from the shadows and materialised before a microphone at the edge of the stage.

From the off, this was not an easy experience for Bertie. Questions over the party's U-turn on the stamp duty issue were raised. Recent comments by a party backbencher that Fianna Fáil was getting 'hammered on the doorsteps' were brought up. The Taoiseach handled them well. The supporters, outnumbering journalists at what was supposed to be a press launch, perked up.

It didn't last. A reporter questioned his credibility before the electorate in the light of the un-answered questions about his personal finances. Ministers sank down further in their seats, while the supporters, seated in the main down one half of the room, glared over, shaking their heads at the impertinence. Clearly uncomfortable, in apologetic tones, the Taoiseach admitted that in Fianna Fáil, 'in the past, there were individuals' who might not have operated to the highest ethical standards. The shade of Charles Haughey loomed large, while his former adviser PJ Mara stood by.

In this highly charged atmosphere, Bertie battled on. 'I don't think there's any problems hanging over my head,' he declared. 'I have to deal with these issues as we go forward, and I will.' Another question on stamp duty. It wasn't just his personal finances that were under attack. Minister for Finance Brian Cowen, who had categorically stated there would be no big announcements from Fianna Fáil, remained expressionless as the Taoiseach tried to extricate his party from this policy promise.

'Can the minister tell us what it tastes like to eat his own words?' asked RTÉ's Bryan Dobson. He got no answer.

This was damaging for Fianna Fáil. In normal circumstances, the stamp duty U-turn would be hugely embarrassing, but this wasn't normal circumstances. On the scale of calamities, it wasn't the worst.

It was a case of: ask all you want about stamp duty, just don't ask about the 'stamp duty issue' that Bertie claimed swallowed up some of the £30,000stg in cash he got in relation to a rented house.

But the money quickly resurfaced. Why should voters wait until after an election to hear an explanation about his personal finances? Had any of his ministers asked him to clarify the situation? Said ministers were looking like stunned mullets. Even Dick Roche's smirk vanished.

Then Vincent Browne got the microphone. What followed was an absolutely astonishing exchange between the journalist and the Taoiseach. It lasted 12 riveting minutes, punctuated by heckles and applause from the Fianna Fáil claque and a few ineffective bleats from PJ Mara as Browne got stuck in.

Why didn't he tell Bryan Dobson in that clear-the-air interview last year that Michael Wall called to his office in 1994 and gave him a briefcase containing £30,000stg in cash, three days before he expected to become Taoiseach? At the time, Mr Wall was renting a house to Bertie Ahern and his then partner, Celia Larkin.

'That money was not money for me. It was money for his affairs, in his house. I hope that answers the questions.' A party officer went to take the microphone, but Vincent had no intention of relinquishing it.

Megaphone in hand, South Kerry Independent TD Jackie Healy-Rae heads through fields outside Kilcummin, Killarney, as he begins his quest for re-election. Photograph: Don MacMonagle.

'No, it doesn't,' replied Vincent. And he took it from there. Bertie repeated that this was Mr Wall's money. 'It isn't credible,' asserted Vincent, explaining why. 'It was Mr Wall's money administered by Celia Larkin,' insisted the Taoiseach. Nothing at all to do with him.

Or as Bill Clinton might have put it: 'I did not have financial relations with that woman.' Bertie stood his ground. He thrust an arm out to silence the supporters when they started to heckle. Vincent went from the suitcase of cash to the Taoiseach's own money – that £50,000 he managed to save in a 12-month period when he says he was so strapped he had to rely on handouts from friends.

Last November, with stated reluctance, he tearfully said he had to think of his children's education. Why had he put a portion of that figure into a house he didn't even own, that was only a few years old? 'It ain't credible,' repeated Browne.

But the Taoiseach stuck to his story. His fighting spirit went down well with the supporters. Brian Cowen shushed them. That money was his own money, bristled Bertie. He was entitled to spend it any way he liked. When PJ tried to intervene, he was reminded how Charles Haughey had sought to silence the media when his finances were under question.

Finally, as journalists heaved their jaws off the floor, the duel ended. A measure of the disaster that was this manifesto launch was the look of relief on Fianna Fáil faces when talk turned to the nurses' strike.

Whatever the outcome of this election, this public interrogation of a taoiseach over his financial affairs at his own party's manifesto launch will be seen as one of the defining moments of Irish politics. Amazing stuff.

Bertie hits the country today to repair the damage. He has enough time to do it, if the country is of a mind to listen.

Sarkozy Victory 'Extraordinaire' Like a Screenplay

Lara Marlowe, in Paris

'C'est extraordinaire!' is Nicolas Sarkozy's favourite expression. He uses it most often to describe real or imagined criticism of himself, as in: 'When I talk about the nation, I'm accused of being a nationalist. When I talk about immigration, I'm accused of being a racist. When I talk about patriotism, I'm accused of being a fascist. C'est quand-même extraordinaire!'

Whatever one thinks of Sarkozy, you've got to hand it to him: his victory in the French presidential election last night may not have been a surprise, but it was nothing short of extraordinaire; the real-life culmination of a Hollywood screenplay entitled 'The Fabulous Destiny of Nicolas Sarkozy'.

Roll the clocks back a few years. Bernadette Chirac, the outgoing first lady who was allegedly gifted with infallible political judgment, told her entourage that Sarkozy would never become president of France. He was too short, too foreign-looking and had no provincial roots, hitherto a requirement for every French leader.

Nothing predisposed Sarkozy to becoming the sixth president of the Fifth Republic. As the extreme right-wing leader Jean-Marie Le Pen ungraciously reminded France during the campaign, three out of four of Sarkozy's grandparents were foreign.

On his father's side, he is descended from minor Hungarian aristocracy; his father, Pal Nagy Bosca y Sarkozy, used to tell him: 'With a name like yours, you'll never get anywhere in France.' His maternal grandfather, who raised him, was Benedict Mallah, a wealthy Jew from Salonica.

Sarkozy failed the entrance exam to 'Sciences Po' because his English wasn't up to scratch. Unlike the failed socialist candidate Ségolène Royal – and most of the country's political elite – he did not attend the École Nationale d'Administration (ENA). That was probably a blessing.

Taunting the socialist benches of the National Assembly, Sarkozy once said: 'You don't talk like the people do; that is why you lost them.' Sarkozy's directness may be his greatest advantage. Time and again, voters have told me they liked him 'because they understand what he says.'

The French are also fascinated by Sarkozy's thirst for power; if he wants it so badly, he must deserve it. There's a good dose of revenge in Sarkozy's ambition. 'Je vais les niquer tous,' (I'm going to screw them all) a fellow journalist once heard Sarkozy mutter repeatedly during a helicopter journey.

Despite Sarkozy's outsider status, there now seems to have been a certain inevitability to his rise. Within months of joining the Raffarin government as interior minister in 2002, he became the most popular member of the cabinet.

Action – or at least the media semblance thereof – was the secret to his success. Tony Blair's government was furious with France for allowing thousands of Kurds and Afghans to pour across the English Channel? Sarkozy closed the camp at Sangatte. French lorry drivers threatened an umpteenth strike? Sarkozy broke the strike in one day, by threatening to confiscate their licences.

When the former prime minister Alain Juppé founded the Union for a Popular Movement (UMP) in November 2002, Sarkozy insisted that Juppé be given a two rather than three-year mandate as leader. Was he already plotting his own take-over of the party?

He and his wife Cecilia refused the seats reserved for them in the second row at the launch, ostentatiously placing themselves front and centre. A year later, Sarkozy announced he intended to succeed president Jacques Chirac.

There followed a battle of Shakespearean – or Oedipal? – proportions, with Sarkozy constantly vaunting his superiority to Mr Chirac. The president's rule was 'a house of cards' on the verge of collapse, Sarkozy told the 237 right-wing deputies he invited to dinner shortly before Bastille Day, 2004.

Chirac made a last attempt to call the unwanted upstart heir to order. 'I take decisions; he executes them,' Chirac told the nation in his annual televised interview.

Having provoked Chirac, Sarkozy then adopted the same strategy he would use during the campaign against Royal; he played the poised statesman who refuses to respond to aggression.

Against the better judgment of his closest advisors, including his wife, Sarkozy resigned from his post as finance minister to stand for president of the UMP.

Commentators widely compared his November 28th, 2004 'coronation' as head of the party to Napoleon Bonaparte's lavish consecration almost exactly 200 years earlier.

Napoleon-like, Mr Sarkozy spoke of his 'grand design'. Unlike Royal, who asked voters what they wanted, Sarkozy told them what they needed. The losing socialist candidate accused Sarkozy of 'brutalising' France. She failed to understand that the country may be at a stage where it wants to be 'brutalised'.

Sarkozy promises to share his energy, determination and confidence with the country, as if by blood transfusion.

The outline of Sarkozy's presidential programme was already present in his November 2004 acceptance speech: the rehabilitation of work, revision of the 35-hour week and the welfare system, the abolition of death duties so the French can pass on 'an inheritance built by the sweat of the brow.'

When Sarkozy finds himself out of sync with the French mood, he never publicly changes policy. He opposed the law banning the wearing of Islamic headscarves in French schools, but shut up when he saw how popular it was. He proposed US-style affirmative action to integrate French minorities, but stopped talking about it when it raised hackles. His condemnation of French 'arrogance' in opposing the invasion of Iraq went down badly, so during the campaign he repeated that the US had made a grave error.

France's new president is a man of paradoxes. The son and grandson of immigrants, he takes pride in having expelled record numbers of would-be immigrants from France. He is a tough crimebuster who yearns to be loved; a short man who once scratched out his height on his driver's license, and mysteriously appeared the same height as George W Bush (who is some 15cm taller) on the re-touched photograph of their meeting. The self-styled 'spokesman of the people' is fascinated by pop stars, celebrities and millionaires.

The reactions of two acquaintances this weekend seemed to summarise national schizophrenia about Sarkozy. An elderly woman who holds dual French and Irish nationality told me: 'I can't help liking that young fellow – he's so un-French!' She even romanticised the 'look of sadness' she always detects in his eyes.

A neighbour in central Paris, a businessman whose company trades in Asia, told me he'd go early to the polls, then leave the country until the celebrations blow over. 'I can't stand the thought of France being in Sarkozy's hands for the next five years,' he said. 'He and his gang are mafiosi. I don't want to hear and see the sarkozystes gloating.'

The country that Nicolas Sarkozy is about to take over is a land of hope and fear. Will he teach the French the merits of hard work, usher in prosperity and full employment by the end of his five-year term, as promised? Or will he cow the press – a process that has already started – inflame race relations, pit rich against poor and preside over war on the immigrant banlieues? These possible outcomes, positive and negative, are part of the Sarkozy paradox.

And they are not mutually exclusive.

Day of 'History Without Drama' Goes As Planned

Gerry Moriarty, in Stormont

'The Troubles,' said Tony Blair. 'Not so much a dispute as a way of life.' Which was a good description of what Northern Ireland, these islands indeed, had endured through 40 years of awful conflict, much of it bloody.

Even after yesterday the legacy of bitterness and sectarianism and criminality will remain with us – but to ever diminishing degrees, is the general hope. Regardless, yesterday marked the symbolic ending of that dispute.

It was unquestionably a huge moment in British-Irish history, in the history of unionism and nationalism, in the relationship between the North and South, a fitting climax to the long, gruelling, often heartbreaking years of negotiations to get to this point.

So why was there an underlying sense of anti-climax about the occasion? At least that was the feeling some of us had. The principals – Ian Paisley, Martin McGuinness, Bertie Ahern, Blair – acted properly, they spoke well, they provided positive images, there were apposite quotes. Yet, somehow, the day didn't quite match the occasion.

Perhaps that's as it should be. All the hard work was done beforehand. There was no suspense about the day, as there was on so many other days when hopes were shattered or results fell depressingly far short of expectations. 'It was history without drama,' to quote one commentator.

Northern Ireland's new start had to work from the outset, which is why Paisley and Peter Robinson on one side, and Gerry Adams and

Northern Ireland's First Minister Ian Paisley (left) and Deputy First Minister Martin McGuinness after being sworn in at Stormont. Photograph: Paul Faith/PA.

McGuinness on the other, and all their most senior strategists, through the benefit of bitter experience, nailed down the script in advance. There would be no deviation from each side's carefully rehearsed roles. No surprises. We've had enough surprises.

Will it work? There is no reason why it shouldn't. The omens are good. David Trimble was always in thrall to his own Ulster Unionist dissidents, many of them now in the DUP, and, of course, to Paisley himself. But Paisley is in thrall to no one except his God and, perhaps, his wife, Eileen. Who can challenge Sinn Féin? Not republican dissidents, not the SDLP who, in any case, want this project to succeed.

This Executive has the imprimatur and goodwill of the main parties at Stormont, of the British and Irish governments, of George Bush and the White House, and even of the IRA leadership. It was significant that sitting in the VIP gallery just seven seats from Tony Blair and Bertie Ahern were the most senior of republicans, Brian Keenan, Brian Gillen and Bobby Storey.

There was no handshake between Ian Paisley and Martin McGuinness yesterday but we knew that would be the case. It was what Paisley and McGuinness said and did that was important, signalling an ability to work together in a business-like manner. Pushing for more would have been counter-productive. Easy on the hype, heavy on the pragmatism, was the sensible approach.

In the Assembly chamber yesterday morning, Paisley and McGuinness and their Ministers made solemn commitments. They affirmed pledges of office to promote the interests of the entire community; to participate fully in the Executive, and in the North-South Ministerial Council and the British-Irish Council; to observe the 'joint nature' of the Office of First Minister and Deputy First Minister; and to uphold the rule of law and support the police and courts.

If they meet these challenges, as they pledged to do, then Northern Ireland should have a stable future. When Blair, Ahern and Northern Secretary

Peter Hain squeezed into the couch in Paisley's office after the Assembly proceedings, flanked by the now properly installed First Minister and Deputy First Minister in their comfortable armchairs, the mood was unforced, genial and relaxed.

Others, though, asked the question: What was it all about? Did the powersharing Sunningdale agreement of 1973, wrecked by the likes of Paisley and the IRA, not offer as much as was achieved yesterday? Could the intervening loss of life not have been avoided? Over recent weeks the First Minister and Deputy First Minister have addressed that question without providing a coherent explanation as to what it was all about. More than 3,700 people died in the Troubles and many, many thousands more were physically or emotionally damaged by that violence. That suffering would 'not be erased from our memories', Paisley promised. They would 'look to the future to find the means to help [the victims] heal', said the Deputy First Minister.

Northern Ireland has travelled a long, tortuous, terrible journey over almost 40 years to arrive at yesterday's powersharing agreement between the most trenchant of political rivals. It was indeed a big day, but in deference to the dead and scarred and in anticipation of the hard work ahead, it was an understated occasion that indicated a real possibility, as the Taoiseach said, of a 'new era of mutual respect and peace'.

WEDNESDAY, 16 MAY 2007

Party Leaders' TV Debate Could Prove Decisive

Noel Whelan

Exhaustion is setting in, as the politicians, party apparatchiks and political media have been keeping campaign hours since Easter. After the disorientating early Sunday morning start to the election proper, many

were hoping that the May bank holiday weekend would bring an opportunity for respite.

The Progressive Democrats put paid to that, however. Last Sunday, for the second weekend in a row, journalists were roused early. This time it was to a city centre hotel where, to the surprise of many, the Tánaiste announced that he and his party were not after all pulling out of Government. Instead, McDowell demanded public answers from the Taoiseach about his personal finances.

The Progressive Democrats tried to explain away the uncertainty about whether they would pull out of Government by blaming it on a frenzy of media speculation. The media, on the other hand, pointed to divisions within the Progressive Democrats and/or a change of mind on McDowell's own part as the more accurate expla-nation for the weekend's confusion.

The Progressive Democrats and their leaders were either typically indecisive or reckless in their media management. It was naïve of them to think that, at the height of an election campaign, they could ignore a gathering media storm and retire to a house down the country to calmly deliberate over their options. It's hard to come to any con-clusion other than that last weekend's events have further damaged the Progressive Democrats' already difficult election prospects.

Martyn Turner's election.

The upshot of last weekend's happenings was the promise from the Taoiseach that he would make a full statement about the purchase of his home during the campaign. There are indications that the commitment to make the statement was extracted as much at the insistence of some of his own Ministers as at that of the Progressive Democrats.

A Fianna Fáil press conference had been scheduled for noon last Sunday but was postponed to 3pm – a crucial three hours that not only allowed time to absorb what McDowell had said, but also to allow senior Fianna Fáil Ministers, including deputy leader Brian Cowen, to meet Ahern. It was from that meeting that the strategy of promising a full statement evolved.

Taoiseach Bertie Ahern addressing the two houses of the British parliament, the House of Commons and the House of Lords, in the Palace of Westminster. Photograph: Eric Luke.

As a result, the payments controversy was parked for the rest of this week and it will probably stay parked for at least some of next week. It allowed the Taoiseach the space to focus on his attendance at Tuesday's historic event in Stormont, on paying tributes to his friend Tony Blair, who announced his retirement on Thursday, and then on meeting with Ian Paisley at the site of the Battle of the Boyne yesterday.

For five full days now the campaign has refocused on the issues. As a result, the campaign has been more worthy but less interesting. Much of the morning press conferences has been given over to reheating previously announced policies and revisiting marginal differences between the parties. There are very few real differences between the parties – even Sinn Féin has now signed up to the low-tax consensus.

The distinctions, such as they are, between the parties and their promises to the electorate have been well rehearsed for several months, and most of them had their first outings at the series of party conferences this spring.

Of course, the payment controversy will resurface, at least temporarily, whenever the Taoiseach publishes his statement. Some doubt whether a statement can be produced that is consistent with what he has already said on the complex sequence of payments, whether publicly in the Dáil and to Bryan Dobson last autumn, privately to the Tánaiste, or to the tribunal in a supposedly private session four weeks ago.

Those close to Ahern, however, are confident that such a comprehensive statement can be produced. No precise time has been given for its release, although it will probably have to come before the head-to-head television debate now scheduled for next Thursday.

Much of what Fianna Fáil has had to say about the media pursuit of this story has, frankly, been over the top. However, just because they are paranoid does not mean that some in the media aren't out to get them. For some journalists, this is personal – they are biased against the Government parties or against Ahern specifically. The attention given to this story is out of proportion to the public's interest in it, but there are a number of reasons for this.

Although complicated, it is a potentially dramatic story. There is a sense that some in the media enjoy exercising the modern power of the fourth estate – seeing it as appropriate that they, rather than the electorate, should decide whether Ahern will be Taoiseach again. However, most are pursuing this story out of grander journalistic motives. Their worry is that if Ahern is re-elected Taoiseach and shortly thereafter the tribunal reveals information that, if the voters had known it in advance, would have changed the election result, then the Irish media would have failed to do its job and would look foolish.

Having been submerged in the payments controversy for its first phase, subdued by a low-key policy debate in the second phase, the campaign is now entering its final crucial stage in which the question of leadership will be front and centre. There will be more exchanges on policy every day next week and more polls next weekend, as well as next Thursday's televised debate between Ahern and Enda Kenny.

In 2002, the leaders' debate was held just three days before polling. This time around there will still be a full week between the broadcast of the debate and the opening of polls, including the crucial last weekend of the campaign.

On this occasion, the debate is a match between two contenders who, yesterday's TNS/mrbi poll confirmed, stand evenly matched in their prospects for the top job. In a campaign where leadership is now the key issue, the televised battle of the leaders could be decisive.

WEDNESDAY, 16 MAY 2007

Thanks, Bertie, You Did Us Proud

Miriam Lord, in Westminster

Yes, Bertie Ahern from Drumcondra. That was you. Guest of honour in the Palace of Westminster, like statesmen Yeltsin and Mitterrand and Clinton before you, fêted by the Commons and the Lords and thoroughly deserving of your place in history, writes Miriam Lord, at Westminster.

No one man or woman brought about this wonderful new era for the Republic of Ireland, Britain and Northern Ireland. But you've more than done your bit. This day, Bertie, was for you.

There was something about him yesterday, sitting pensively in the gilded surrounds of the Royal Gallery as the illustrious assembly stood and applauded him. Him, Bertie, the boy from the northside.

He had just notched up another historic milestone as the first Taoiseach to address the joint houses of parliament. Tony Blair, not half an hour earlier, had paid him the most glowing, heartfelt of tributes. His words went far beyond the normal call of commendation.

The guest list was an impressive roll call of British and Irish politicians past and present. The warmth of their welcome for Bertie was generous and genuine. Yet, for a few moments, it was as if the man they had come to honour was a bit taken aback by it all. He remained in his chair, as the speaker of the House of Commons, applauding, moved in from one side and Tony Blair, leading the ovation, moved in from the other.

Both men appeared to be signalling the same thing: 'Get up!' Eventually, almost reluctantly, Bertie Ahern got to his feet. No big smiles, although he must have been delighted. He must have been the proudest man in the room.

Yesterday evening, he was back in his Dublin North Central constituency, knocking on doors, looking after business. People on the Navan Road, who had been watching the Taoiseach on the six o'clock news in the houses of parliament, opened their doors to find Bertie on the step.

People who claim to know him would say that cementing his place among his own has always been what drives him. Even now, as one of the biggest vote getters in the country, he obsessively pounds the pavements on his own patch. Even now, when the mother of parliaments has gone out of its way to recognise him as a political great, he still worries.

While Mr Blair spoke of his 'formidable' role in the Northern peace process and the development of his country's economy, the Taoiseach's fingertips fidgeted.

What was he thinking? Not far away, sitting in the front row to his left, was Fine Gael leader Enda Kenny. He looked good. Afterwards, when the two prime ministers left, deputy Kenny was surrounded by well wishers. Former Conservative prime minister John Major shook his hand. 'Go for it, man! Go for it!' said John.

What was Enda thinking? They know how to lay on a good ceremony in Westminster. Staff looking like they've stepped off the set of a BBC costume drama, resplendent in black tails and white tie. Bertie arrived with Tony at the Sovereign's Entrance, just like the Queen does at the opening of parliament. A fab'lus hall – as Albert Reynolds might have put it – providing a magnificent setting.

It was clear that Tony, who has run his race and will step down next month, wanted to do well by his 'personal friend', who is still very much in the political running and in the thick of a tough general election battle. 'There is no side to Bertie,' he said, recalling negotiations on the North. 'He would absorb the harsh, occasionally insulting words.' At this point, the Taoiseach looked up with a rueful smile. One suspected his mind was more on current travails.

'I often say to people I have met many big political leaders over my 10 years in office but I have never met a bigger one than Bertie Ahern.' Tony and Bertie. A great double act. Tony, bowing out, doing his best for his old pal.

The Taoiseach spoke of a shared history and a new partnership between the two nations. It was a wonderfully well-crafted speech and he delivered it well.

There was a sense of two men rounding off a decade of fine achievement, recognising that their unique political relationship is coming to an end. 'Tony Blair has been a true friend to me, and a true friend to Ireland.' You could feel the emotion in Bertie's tone. As he concluded, he quoted John F. Kennedy when he addressed the Dáil. Ireland, he said then, 'is an isle of destiny. . . when our hour has come we will have something to give to the world.' There was a quiver, a slight catch in his voice as he invoked the iconic spirit of JFK.

'Ireland's hour has come,' said the Taoiseach. 'A time of peace, of prosperity, of old values and new beginnings. This is the great lesson and the great gift of Irish history. This is what Ireland can give to the world.' The crowd rose to him – northern secretaries, past and present. Gordon Brown – PM in waiting. John Hume, Peter Sutherland, John Major, Neil Kinnock, Ken Clark. Lords and ladies, honourable members, ambassadors.

Writer Edna O'Brien, motor racing mogul Eddie Jordan, rugby great Keith Wood, fashion designer Paul Costelloe, actor Fiona Shaw. Bertie's friend Des Richardson was there with his wife Fran, along with property developer Seán Dunne and his wife Gayle.

This was a great occasion. Bertie's occasion.

And yet . . . other matters rumble on at home. Enda Kenny gave an interview on the lawn outside. 'I wanted to be here, as an Irishman and the leader of my party,' he said. 'It was a fine speech, well delivered.' The Taoiseach, his rival, was entitled 'to real public credit, and it's richly due.' Deputy Kenny was speaking 'as one who looks to be taoiseach'. Here, perhaps, was one reason for why Bertie looked so pensive. With one part of the double act going, and Bertie having achieved the pinnacle of political achievement, there was a sense yesterday of things coming to a natural conclusion.

He will not want that view to go abroad. But maybe, that air of modesty about the Taoiseach had more to do with the man who is still not quite sure of his place. History is sorted, without a doubt, but is Bertie? Hence yet another Dublin Central canvas last night, crazy as that might seem.

Let's be parochial for a moment. From this particular Northsider: Thanks, Bertie, you did us proud.

MONDAY, 21 MAY 2007

Harrington Ends the Drought

Philip Reid, at Adare Manor

Finally, belatedly, the demons of a quarter of a century of golfing frustration have been banished. But, in typical Pádraig Harrington fashion, he did it the hard way.

There wasn't a still heart in the vast expanse of Adare Manor yesterday as the Dubliner eventually captured the Irish Open title in a play-off, outlasting a stubborn Bradley Dredge – cast in the role of spoilsport – at the first extra hole.

On a day that somehow managed to share heavy, wintry rain with glorious sunshine, Harrington fulfilled another part of his golfing destiny. It was, though, a roller-coaster ride of the white-knuckle variety, with the victory secured only in sudden-death when Dredge discovered that the river Maigue, which fronts the 18th green, is not as angelic as its picture postcard appearance. It was an expensive discovery for the Welshman.

So Harrington, the poster boy of Irish golf, delivered. And, in claiming the top prize of €416,660, he ended the 25-year drought since John O'Leary's win. But it was tough, and not always pretty. Still, it was one to savour, another to add to the list of achievements that include Ryder Cups, World Cups and the European Tour order of merit title.

Where does, or can, it rank? 'I'd put this as an equal to what I've achieved. The World Cup, unbelievable. The Ryder Cup, unbelievable. This is at the top of the pile, no question about it . . . but I wouldn't set it apart. It's there, or thereabouts,' said Harrington.

Coming here as the highest-ranked player in the world in the field, and with the weight of a nation's expectations to contend with, Harrington shot a final round 71 to Dredge's 68, the pair finishing tied on 283, five-under, and he saw off his chief rival with a par five on the 18th, the first play-off hole. Dredge, who had played superbly, took a seven, and his battle was finally over.

All day, those spectators – the crowd was officially recorded at 23,150 – who had followed Harrington's fortunes barely had time to draw breath before one twist was followed by another in the unfolding drama.

At one stage, England's Simon Wakefield threatened to infringe on the duel between Harrington and Dredge, only to falter with three bogeys coming in to finish alone in third place, four strokes adrift. Otherwise, it was one man against the other, just as it had been when the pair went head-to-head in last year's Dunhill Links when Harrington won.

After a nervy start from both players in the final grouping, when the crowd's enthusiasm and expectations couldn't but be felt by the pair, it seemed Harrington had struck the vital series of

Crowds watch as Pádraig Harrington plays his second shot to 15th hole during the final round of the Irish Open at the Adare Manor Hotel and Golf Resort in Co. Limerick. Photograph: Andrew Redington/Getty Images.

blows with some stellar, world-class shots from the seventh to the ninth. In that run of holes, Harrington went birdie-birdie-eagle to Dredge's birdie-birdie-birdie.

Harrington's play over that stretch was sublime: on the seventh, he hit an approach with his hybrid club to 25 feet, and only barely missed the eagle putt; on the eighth, he hit a sandwedge approach – after Dredge had put his to four feet – to two feet; and, on the ninth, the Irishman, with 245 yards to the flag, hit a five-wood approach to 12 feet and sank the eagle putt. It put him four shots clear, but instead of seeing off Dredge, it only signalled the start of the really hard work.

While Harrington failed to record another birdie and dropped a shot at the 11th and 17th, Dredge, with four birdies and two bogeys in that stretch, grabbed the momentum. Dredge chipped in for birdie on the 14th and sank a long putt on

the 15th to go one behind. But his charge, it seemed, had come to an end when he bogeyed the 16th.

Dredge's response, though, was to hit an approach from thick rough on the 17th to two feet. It forced Harrington, in the middle of the fairway and with a wedge in his hands from 129 yards, to be aggressive. He overshot the green, finished in heavy rough and failed to get up and down. Dredge rolled in his birdie putt and, suddenly, the pair were level. And when the 18th was shared in par, there was nothing for it but to extend the fight.

Throughout the tournament, Harrington had used five-wood off the tee. But the game plan hadn't yielded birdies and, so, in the play-off he switched to driver. The result was a pushed shot into rough, just a matter of yards from where Dredge had also put his tee-shot. It was what followed next that decided the outcome: Dredge's recovery ran over the hazard line and, although still dry, left him with an awkward stance and a tough shot over the river.

Harrington, meanwhile, saw his second shot come up short of the river in the rough. Dredge's third shot failed to clear the bank on the far side, but was visible – and just about playable – on the riverbed.

With Harrington on the fringe of the green in three, Dredge had no option other than to attempt a miracle recovery shot. It just about found the grassy slope above the bank. His fifth shot finished just off the green and, finally, the golfing gods were imparting their blessings on Harrington.

Dredge failed with his chip-in and eventually recorded a double-bogey seven to Harrington's five. 'It was just so frustrating to give it to him the way I did in the end,' lamented Dredge, whose late birdies – three in the last five holes of regular play – had been met with polite applause from galleries very much in support of Harrington.

In the end, though, Harrington got what he wanted. 'This is the tournament I wanted to win more than any other, bar a major. So, it is majors next, no question about it . . . and hopefully my game is capable of going on to win not just one, but more.'

More immediately, Harrington's win means he heads to the BMW PGA Championship at Wentworth this week with the tantalising prospect of chasing a €1 million bonus should he add that title to the Irish Open. 'I'm the only one with a chance of winning a million euro, but I wish it was being played somewhere else,' quipped Harrington.

In truth, for Harrington, the money is secondary. Really. It is winning titles that matter most. And, in that greater scheme of things, getting his hands on the Irish Open title and adding his name to those of Fred Daly, Harry Bradshaw, Christy O'Connor Snr and O'Leary, who preceded him, provides him with a place in history.

Bertie Will Win as We Dislike Risk

John Waters

The Irish race has many unique qualities but two in particular will become important in these four days: our dislike of taking risks and, in times of misfortune, our love of blaming someone other than ourselves. Faced with a choice between taking responsibility or not, we will always choose the latter.

We are poised at a moment of uncertainty when, following 10 years of prosperity, we are unsure if it is going to continue. If we change the government now and things subsequently begin to go badly, we will have nobody to blame but ourselves. Our sense of having made a mistake will haunt us forever. There may or may not be a connection, but we will never know for sure. If we don't change the government and things subsequently go wrong, we can blame the government. This suits us better. Not only is not changing the government less risky; it is also the option which allows us to pass the buck.

The consequences of these tendencies will become partially visible in the opinion polls up to Thursday, and overwhelmingly on Friday as the votes are counted. It reminds me of the 1992 general election in the UK when, for much of the campaign, Labour under Neil Kinnock seemed set to sweep Margaret Thatcher from office. So certain was Kinnock that he began to celebrate before the campaign was over.

But the British people, though embarrassed to admit it, were still under Nanny's spell and, while telling the pollsters one thing, snuck into the polling booths to say something else. Through the long summer night of the count, certainty turned to disbelief, and then to wonder, as Thatcher swept back to power.

Duncannon beach in Co. Wexford during the 'Light in the Windows of Time' ceremony by Buí Bolg, as part of the Bealtaine Festival 2007. Photograph: Dylan Vaughan.

Bertie is no Thatcher, but in many respects the connection he has made renders him better adapted to harvesting the invisible, ineffable sentiment of the voter's private heart. Most of us, certainly most over about 35, regard the prosperity of the past decade as an accident. We don't know where it came from and certainly don't feel we deserve it. We have a strong suspicion that governments of the day, regardless of hue, had little to do with it. But we can't be certain.

Bertie, therefore, is the right man in the right place. He's one of us: he doesn't know what happened either, but has come to personify our sense of simultaneous bemusement and hope. Although he makes speeches from time to time implying that he knows what's going on, we see this as no more nor less than one would expect from a politician.

Other politicians declare themselves certain they know what they are doing, and this scares us. What if one of them pulls the wrong lever or throws the wrong switch? Bertie knows not to make sudden moves or take too seriously the idea of being in control. Bertie is Bertie, and even though this condition baffles every attempt at description, we have come to anticipate precisely its effects.

Thus, the significance as a force in this election of last week's intervention by Tony Blair is incalculable in terms of the affirmation it provides of a view of Bertie which most us have come to gradually, but still have difficulty in admitting, even to ourselves. Blair is in awe of Bertie, precisely because the greatness of Bertie's political talent is equalled only by its invisibility.

Bertie converts ordinariness into political capital and skill. Blair appreciates this because his own talent is close to the opposite: he sparkles and vibrates in ways that make him a focus for intense admiration or dislike. In contrast to Bertie, he draws attention to himself as an essential element of his appeal. Blair stands out, Bertie blends in. Blair stopped being 'Tony' a long time ago. Bertie will always be 'Bertie'.

The media misunderstand Bertie, but nevertheless the allegations about his private finances emerged from an intuitive desire to strike at the understated connection he has forged with the Irish people. The purpose was not merely to insinuate something dodgy, but to undermine the whole edifice of Bertie's exaggerated ordinariness. But the media-supervised discussion in the public square operates to rules that have only a small space in the hearts or hearths where political sentiment is forged, so the intrusion of crude allegations born of Watergate Syndrome has had a range of effects which may, in the end, cancel one another out.

Some people may respond to the mess of Bertie's personal finances in the black-and-white manner of a *Liveline* discussion, but most of us, secretly, see a reflection of our own lives, of the miracle of monthly financial survival that somehow we manage to pull off. And this also, interestingly, resonates with our sense of the public finances, with the miracle of the Celtic Tiger.

Once again it helps us to understand and, perhaps perversely, trust Bertie without necessarily being able to say why. This goes some way towards explaining why we will renew our embrace of him on Thursday.

He still has life in our affections and nobody has come along to take his place.

TUESDAY, 22 MAY 2007

My Life is in Politicians' Hands

Orla Tinsley

I watched the Ahern v Kenny TV debate unfold. I was particularly interested because I am still unsure as to where my vote will go. Being a teenager in the throes of exams I am bombarded with calls to 'rock the vote'. It is easy to spurn such rocking, particularly when voting is on a Thursday, in the middle of university exams.

However, I have a very personal interest in this election, a selfish one at that. It concerns my life and the lives of many of my peers, so I've taken time away from study to write this.

I needed treatment in hospital last April for my cystic fibrosis. I have had this illness since I was three days old. Ireland has the highest incidence of CF in the world and yet we have the poorest facilities. In their debate, Bertie Ahern made light of the fact when Enda Kenny said that a 30-year-old machine was in use in a brand new hospital. The Taoiseach quipped under his breath that it was impossible as it was a new hospital.

But he doesn't understand. Machines are exchanged, underfunded and overused. Just like the nurses, doctors and patients who are shovelled through the relentless system.

The last time I went into hospital I left after 10 days. I am usually pretty level-headed about my illness. It doesn't control my life; it's an extension of it. I've learnt to deal with it to a certain degree. However, there are certain things my mind cannot deal with; lack of sleep is one of those. I left hospital a week early. I would like to tell the Taoiseach and Enda Kenny why.

They might not be aware that elderly, senile patients are forced to share rooms with CF patients in a way that poses a threat to us both. In this environment, I have to get used to being cursed at continually.

My crimes include opening windows, running taps and pulling my curtain to change in privacy. I have laughed nervously as psychiatric patients have sat on my bed trying to convince me that the world was going to explode. I have met people who have wandered into the six-bed room where I sleep and attempted to convince me they could heal me if I only let them touch my arm.

I've seen beautifully glamorous elderly ladies urinate on the floor through no fault of their own.

I've maintained my composure as other friends with CF are attacked by elderly people or family members for being too loud or for having the gall to have the window open.

Sleep is not possible at night and, with breakfast at 7am, cleaners at 8am and a barrage of doctors, blood-tests, physio and medical students to occupy, it's not possible in the day. iPods are a handy way to try and escape unless they go for a walk, like mine did the last time I was there. That theft, along with nine consecutive sleepless nights, instigated my decision to leave.

Checking myself out had fortuitous consequences – a much sicker friend, who had been in a different six-bed room, was moved into a cubicle. A week later I found out that my friend had passed away. I took a small comfort that her last few days were in the privacy of that room with her family, and not with five other people and theirs.

I have often observed old and young people dying in the room I sleep in. The unspoken rule is, if you can walk out, you leave or if you can't, you put on your headphones and pretend. You pretend you cannot see the silhouettes through the curtains, bending down to give one last kiss. You pretend that you do not feel guilty for being there, guilty about your hacking coughs which interrupt their final moments.

Going home, you pretend you have never seen the big blue body trolleys rush by. The old lady across from you, cursing ferociously when you open a window and praying out loud for hours on end at night, does not bother you. At least that's what you pretend.

There is a constant fear of infection when we come through A&E. My latest jaunt there was over two days, where I was exposed to infection and left coughing on a plastic chair. At 3pm I got a drug line inserted, whilst awake, into my arm. I watched it all on the big screen in fascination, then returned to my plastic chair in the waiting room.

I waited again before being transferred to the actual A&E bed area, where I waited on a larger plastic chair. I then spent the next 10 minutes waving furiously at a porter I recognised. Half an hour later he emerged with a trolley.

He worked hard to get it. When I returned from the bathroom the pillow he also worked hard to get was gone. With a respiratory disease and gloopy, mucus-filled lungs, lying flat is not acceptable. Without a pillow my trolley was useless as I had to sit up anyway.

This situation is unfathomable. People with CF are sick of hearing the statistics. We are sick repeating the same line: 'We have the highest instance of CF in the world, with Third World facilities.' We are sick of hearing that money is coming, that somebody somewhere just has to sign something. We are sick of waiting and I am sick of watching my friends die while we wait.

Recently a newspaper printed an article about another pal who passed away a month before the friend I mentioned earlier. This young woman came up with the slogan 'Sick Waiting' because she felt it encapsulated the mood of people with CF in Ireland. The general consensus is, she was dead right.

My friend wrote a letter, which was published in *The Irish Times*. She was left in A&E in agony for hours without an X-ray, painkillers or a chest drain. Her lung had collapsed and this agony was prolonged. To add insult and torture to an already appalling case, my dear friend had her chest drain lifted incorrectly which messed up the gravity and blew her lung out for the second time. She never recovered from that infection.

Outside of hospital, my friend worked selflessly editing a CF magazine and gathering extensive knowledge on treatments and funny anecdotes regarding the disease. She also completed an MA, fell madly in love and won the Young Scientist of the Year exhibition. Her team won the European Scientist of the year too. She fought every inch of the way for her life. Nobody wants to be a victim. This is something I personally loathe.

The idea that someone is poor, fragile, incapable and not in control of his/her destiny

Orla Tinsley. Photograph: Cyril Byrne.

terrifies me. Yet right here, in this shambles of a health system, the reality is that what we fight so hard not to become has become us, uncontrollably so.

When not in hospital we fight to stay alive. We also fight for our health care. Daily we take our drugs, nebulisers and 50 or so tablets. There are also, for some CF patients, enemas, needles, insulin, and bags of diluted feed fed through naso-gastric tubes.

We do it because we are lifers. We have the illness and we deal with it in different ways. Yet most of us work hard at keeping well because we are determined to have the best quality of life possible, because we, like everyone else, deserve it.

Every time we enter a hospital this idea is undermined. Our hard work to stay on this journey called life is destroyed by the broken promises, by the bloody politics of it all. The money was there for staffing but the number of staff was capped. The plans were there and six months later we still 'just need someone to sign off' on them. There is no more time for planning; the time for action is now.

I am 20. The average life expectancy for a person with cystic fibrosis in Ireland is 21. In Northern Ireland it's 33. In Britain, we live longer again, reaching up to late 40s in the US.

I am in first year in college, have missed 10 weeks of this school year but I intend to do my exams and do well. I will then go on to write, act and live my life the way I want, alongside CF, as I have always expected to. I am not ready to be stopped yet.

Waiting for the presentation to begin . . . From left: Philip Motyer from Rathfarnham, Co. Dublin; Emma Morris from Barntownin, Co. Wexford; Juliette Morrison from Dundalk, Co. Louth and Alastair Earley from Berrings, Co. Cork; all winners at the presentation of awards of the 53rd Texaco Children's Art Competition. Photographer: Dara Mac Dónaill.

Taoiseach, Enda Kenny, our lives are quite literally in your hands. We want an honest shot at it. Even if we have a few limitations the system should not accentuate them. It should work in favour of its long-term patients.

Allow us to recuperate with sufficient sleep and without fear of infection. Enable us to leave hospital without having to take two extra weeks off to sleep, or spend time weaning ourselves off the sleeping tablets.

Bertie, Enda, give us a chance at life and I assure you, as the youth of today who have truly experienced both the ugliness and the miracle of life, we will not let you, or ourselves, down.

SATURDAY, 26 MAY 2007

Long John Gormley Clings to Mast as Michael McDowell Walks Plank

Frank McNally

Michael McDowell was said to have spent election night at the cinema with his children, watching *Pirates of the Caribbean: At World's End*. Maybe he knew something. Twenty-four hours later, in the shark-infested waters of the RDS, he was locked in a grim struggle with his old seafaring nemesis, Long John Gormley. This time it was a fight to the death. One of them would walk the plank.

When the end came last night, it was for McDowell. Shortly after 8.30pm, he arrived at the count centre not merely to concede defeat, but to announce his departure from public life.

It was a dignified speech, despite his surroundings. As he left the RDS, it was not so much the sharks he had to worry about as the Shinners, who jeered him into retirement with a chorus of 'cheerio, cheerio, cheerio'.

Ultimately, it is the electorate who did for the Minister for Justice, answering the question he didn't ask them – 'Michael McDowell in government?' – with his favourite answer: 'No thanks!' But the instrument of his demise provoked strong feelings of déjà vu. This was not the first time he had been done down by his old buccaneering rival. The Johnny Depp and Geoffrey Rush of Irish politics have provided no shortage of excitement over the years, since fate and the constituency of Dublin South East first threw them together.

Who could forget The Long Recount (1997), that gripping drama in which Gormley took the seat from under McDowell's nose, despite having his chads examined by half the Law Library? Certainly not those of us who spent five days watching it, that's for sure.

Then there was the 2002 sequel, a romantic comedy by comparison, when the two men sailed in together on a fair wind. It was entertaining enough in its own way but the plot lacked something. The feeling was that when the two men met again, the action would return to the blood and guts of the original.

The darker theme was confirmed in last week's trailer – shot under a lamp-post in Ranelagh – when not even Lucinda Creighton's cameo could lighten the mood of menace between the old protagonists.

Such was the build-up to the latest Dublin South East epic that, when it came to the real thing yesterday, you couldn't help feeling something was missing. On closer inspection, it emerged that neither of the leading men was in the RDS all day. Once it emerged that the figures faced another grim struggle for the last seat, both absented themselves until their fate became clear. Nobody with a heart blamed them.

In their absence, campaigners from both sides predicted victory. Fianna Fáil's Eoin Ryan was adamant that transfers from his party's Jim O'Callaghan would elect the minister. But most of the predictions were just educated guesses. Only

Jimmy Verbergh, a judge at the Red Bull X-Fighters International Freestyle Motocross event taking place at Slane Castle in Co. Meath, putting himself and his machine through their paces prior to the event. Photograph: Dara Mac Dónaill.

Joe McCarthy, the man who exposed the flaws in the Government's e-voting machines, produced a figure. Ominously for McDowell, he had Gormley taking the seat by 189 votes (it was rather more than that in the end).

While we awaited the official verdict, we had to make do with subplots. Creighton duly won a seat, joining the poll-topper – Fianna Fáil's Chris Andrews – in providing the Dáil with an infusion of new blood. Then there was Sinn Féin, descending on the RDS en masse, the way they always do, as if they were the big story. And yet they too were only a subplot, a minor one at that.

The real drama was confirmed at about 8.30 pm, when the Minister for Justice and the final figures arrived almost simultaneously. If McDowell had a consolation, it was that in going down with his ship, he had inflicted severe damage on the Good Ship Gerry Adams and most of his left-wing adversaries.

Except for one, of course. Long John Gormley had bested him yet again. In this pirate drama, it was McDowell who didn't have a leg to stand on.

THURSDAY, 31 MAY 2007

Lack of Oranges Leaves Sinn Féin Sucking on a Lemon

Newton's Optic, by Newton Emerson

Sinn Féin has blamed 'a serious shortage of Protestants in the 26 counties' for its poor showing in last week's election.

'Sinn Féin draws its core support from people who can't be relied on to vote,' explained Dr Pat Answer, Professor of Advanced Shinnerology at Dublin Sunday Business College.

'They might be too drunk or hung-over on election day, or have a court appearance or a meeting with their parole officer.

'They might have injured themselves by climbing through a kitchen window while carrying a wide-screen television. Or they might simply have lost track of the date because they never go to work.

'Whatever the reason, Sinn Féin voters need to be provoked to the polls and there simply aren't enough Protestants in the Republic to cause the necessary level of antagonism.'

The situation is very different in Northern Ireland, where the daily sight of Protestants cutting their perfect hedges, driving their sensible cars and going to church in elaborate hats wedged tightly onto their pointy little heads ensures that Sinn Féin voters are always angry enough to cast a ballot. Attempts to widen the party's southern appeal beyond its traditional sectarian base may only have made matters worse.

'According to our research, many Sinn Féin voters thought that Mary Lou McDonald was a Protestant,' Dr Answer said. 'She certainly has that smug look about her. Or at least she certainly did.'

Dublin Sunday Business College has defended the wider sociological methodology behind its research, which overestimated Sinn Féin's final tally by a statistically acceptable 300 per cent.

'We were right about the number of people dumb enough to vote for Sinn Féin,' Dr Answer

Shaena Brandel with Nofit State Circus performing at the Spaceship Silver Big Top at George's Dock in the International Financial Services Centre in Dublin. Photograph: Alan Betson.

said. 'We just forgot that they were lazy as well.'

For party activists the question now is where they go from here. 'Well, we can't go back up North,' Sinn Féin community outreach negotiator Anne Phoblacht said. 'It's full of Protestants.'

Developing a separate southern strategy could also prove problematic. 'We warned people on the doorsteps to vote for us or the Protestants would get in,' Ms Phoblacht said. 'But everyone just laughed because they thought we meant Trevor Sargent.'

The Irish Times understands that senior party figures have already discussed the possibility of bringing more Protestants into the Republic. Martin Ferris has agreed to charter a boat and Aengus Ó Snodaigh has offered the use of a van.

'We're mainly interested in people from Nigeria,' Ms Phoblacht said. 'You can have any Protestants you like as long as they're black.'

Experts agree that this is Sinn Féin's only hope for an electoral breakthrough. 'There's no point being sectarian when there aren't any Protestants and no point pretending to be non-sectarian when there aren't any Protestants,' Dr Answer explained.

'There's also no point talking about equality when you've no Protestants to be equal to and no point talking about rights when you can't claim that Protestants are infringing your rights. So really it's all the Protestants' fault. No wonder people hate those hedge-cutting freaks.'

But it's not all bad news for Sinn Féin. The party polled quite well in Border counties due to Northern Ireland's provocative proximity. 'If there had still been some Protestant farmers in the area we might even have won a few seats,' Ms Phoblacht said. 'What a pity we killed them.'

SATURDAY, 2 JUNE 2007

Modern Moment

John Butler

When aliens land on earth, as they inevitably will, they'll have to interpret the sight of humans picking up the faecal matter of dogs as proof that cocker spaniels rule the planet and that we are indentured slaves in their regime.

It's absurd to note humans walking the pier holding plastic bags, comfortable with the knowl-

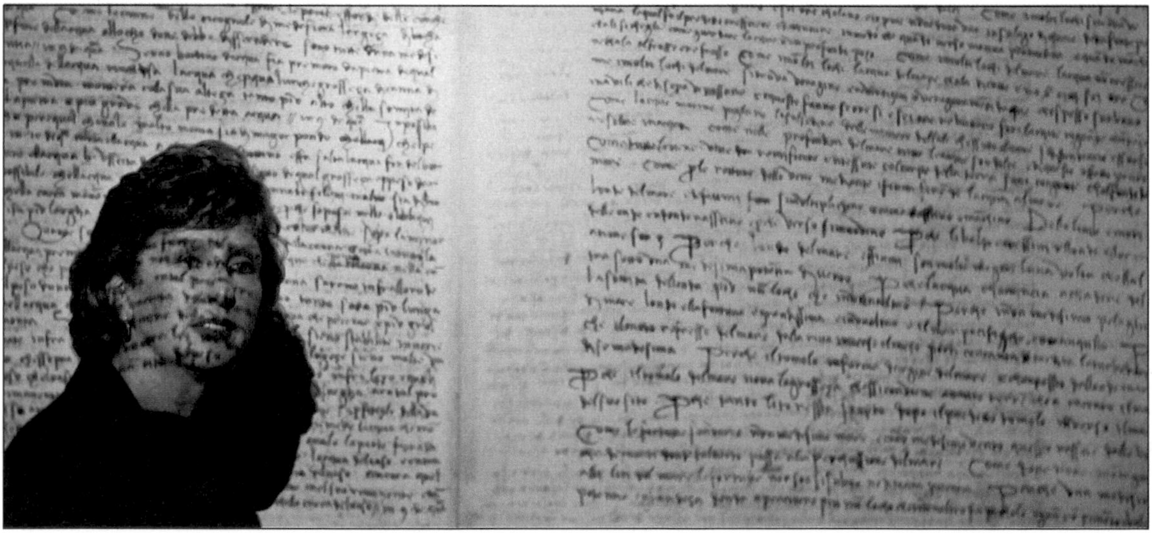

President Mary McAleese opening the exhibition 'Leonardo: The Codex Leicester – Reflections on Water and the Moon' at the Chester Beatty Library in Dublin. Photograph: Aidan Crawley.

edge that soon they will be lifting animals' turds in their hands. It's one of the many tiny insanities that we have fashioned in these times, because dogs are at the middle of many people's lives. In fact, dogs are some people's lives.

You don't need great powers of psychological insight to guess that, for many people, the dog takes the place of human affection, substituted in the heart for the love of a partner or a child. They are treated as humans, dressed, carried by their owners in papooses. There's something a little strange about all of it, and I have heard it said that it is wrong to waste all that love on a pet, but it doesn't seem like a waste to me.

A dog can teach you how to love. In fact, parents bring pets into the home to teach their children about love and about death. It makes sense, as the lifespan of the family pet is shorter, with luck, than that of any family member. If death is a lesson that must be taught at a young age, better that it comes with the death of an animal.

We had two in our family. The first was a King Charles spaniel called . . . Charlie. For a dog of such regal pedigree, Charlie was a hooligan. He would pick fights with Alsatians. He humped cushions. Once, when we came home, we found Charlie on the kitchen table, eating butter from the dish. I first learned about death when I was seven, and Charlie was replaced by a female beagle called . . . Seve. Like the boy named Sue in the Johnny Cash song, Seve overcame the difficulties of being assigned a name associated with the opposite gender, and she hung around for many years. Man, I loved that dog.

Recently, though, my relationship with dogs has become a little complicated. From them I have now learned more than I ever needed. I took a summer walk around Howth Head a few years ago. Two friends and I were walking, and these friends are both actors. This is an important detail, because it means that each of them is a great storyteller, and if you are walking and they are telling you a story, you can become so engrossed with the accents, the mimicry and the physical embellishments that you can find yourself walking off a cliff.

Actor number one was in the middle of a gargantuan tale when actor number two jumped over a fence with a 'no trespassing' sign fixed to it. Actor number one followed suit, and I, too, vaulted, engrossed. We started to walk across a field, with actor number two leading the way.

Fifty metres in, actor number one was nearly at the punchline when we heard actor number two, up ahead, say: 'Um, this doesn't look too good, guys.' Actor number one and I looked up, and it was true: it didn't look too good. It didn't look too good at all. A Rottweiler was hunched low in the grass, creeping towards us, teeth bared. From its throat issued a deep guttural growl: the sound of hell. From the dog's mouth hung a rope of thick saliva, his stomach priming itself to eat. I shall never forget those shoulder blades rising and dropping as the animal crept towards us, the machinery working beneath a glossy coat that barely disguised the brute power.

Actor number two was right in the firing line, yet when he spoke his voice was calm. He was an actor. At this point I was willing to do what he said. Except what he was saying to us was: 'Stand perfectly still. Don't move. The main thing to do here is not to show fear. Because if you show fear . . .' He was gone. Actor number two had bolted, mid-sentence, for the gate, the adjoining house and safety. Seeing this move, the Rottweiler began to sprint towards us, and we turned and ran.

We've all heard of the mother lifting a car with one hand to free her child from beneath it, and I can confirm that in times of great distress you acquire superhuman powers. Within five seconds I was past actor number one. Within six I had passed actor number two. Within 10 I had run through a thick wooden fence, exploding the planks as if they were made of balsa, and flinging myself into a deep ravine of gorse.

A few seconds later actor number one landed on top of me. We struggled to our feet, and from our home in the bushes we could see actor number two vaulting the fence farther down the field, the dog attached, viciously, to his back. The most terrifying sight was yet to come. As man and beast landed on the other side of the fence, and actor number two struggled on to his hands and knees, the Rottweiler primed itself to launch, jaws first, at his neck. It was curtains for actor number two.

Out of nowhere a human whistle sounded. The dog looked around and saw its owner, and we were saved. We were given bandages and tea with lots of sugar in it, and later we drank pints and muttered about litigation.

Nothing ever came of it, and, thankfully, the story ended with a whimper. We each had learned our lesson. But I didn't need to learn it, because Charlie had already taught me that one.

Oh, Sweet Mystery of Life

Aidan Dunne

Leonardo da Vinci fits any definition of the word genius. A Renaissance polymath, the breadth of his achievements is astonishing, and art was but one aspect of a crowded portfolio. But even if his activities had

Flamingos take to the air over Lake Elementieta in Kenya — a shot caught by Alan Betson, which earned him a Special Award in the Olympus Nature & the Environment Photographer of the Year section of the Picture Editor Awards in London's Guildhall.

been strictly confined to the sphere of fine art, his accomplishments would have been more than enough to secure his reputation. He had an unparalleled ability to turn out works, each of them distinct and exceptional, that engaged the imagination in a deep and persistent way.

The Mona Lisa, The Last Supper, his drawings of The Virgin and Child with St Anne and Vitruvian Man are all absolutely iconic images. You could add many more to that list, including his self-portrait, and drawings of plants and natural phenomena, as well as his engineering sketches. And The Battle of Anghiari and his monumental equestrian bronze are among the most famous lost works in the history of Western art, the source of much speculation. He believed painting to be the pre-eminent art, and after his death his thoughts on it were assembled and published in a text that is still relative and perceptive.

The surviving pages of his famous sketchbooks are crammed with beautifully made drawings, spontaneous and informal, comprising a kind of visual diary or autobiography, reflecting the observations, thoughts and activities of every level of his life (including a few dirty jokes, and shopping lists).

He regarded every aspect of the world with fascinated, analytical attention, and his vision is organised and articulated in his drawings. The key to his mind is his assumption of the role of independent observer.

His own perceptions superseded received opinions on any subject, from philosophy to anatomy. Rather than being satisfied with surfaces, he continually delved into the underlying reality, in everything from the human body to flowing water, leading to startling insights in several areas of exploration.

He was an obsessive perfectionist and when he set about making a commissioned painting you could guarantee that it would generate a huge amount of supplementary material. Before something found its way into a painting, he wanted to

know it inside-out. Hence masses of studies – of draperies, figures and animals, for example – inform eventual, single images, often very indirectly. A wealth of immediate, anecdotal observation is digested in the cause of devising an authoritative, idealised account of a subject. The result is the extraordinarily definitive feeling imparted by, say, his figure compositions.

Practically everything he did provided succeeding generations of artists with archetypal models that provided that basis for myriad variations. It is hard to think of more quoted works of art than the Mona Lisa or The Last Supper. They are so universally recognisable that they can be used as references in practically any context. As Dan Browne realised, an element of mystery is close to the heart of Leonardo's appeal. People are drawn to puzzles. The idea that a work of art harbours a secret makes it all the more interesting. Just what is the Mona Lisa smiling about?

Darian Leader's fascinating book Stealing the Mona Lisa recounts the story of the painting's theft from the Louvre in 1911. He points out that the picture's disappearance sealed its fame. Remarkably, more people turned up to look at the empty space where it had been than had come to see it when it was there. It is generally agreed that the most obvious mystery of the Mona Lisa, the identity of the sitter, has been solved. Yet the sitter's identity is not particularly interesting; it doesn't really explain the picture or dispel its underlying mystique.

One could point to another conundrum evident in the painting, one that has also generated much debate: the apparent visual disparity in the fragments of landscape we see beyond the sitter. Left and right don't seem to match up. But even if this issue were definitively resolved, the picture would still exert a curious fascination, still draw hordes of visitors to a room in the Louvre.

He left many projects unfinished, and his completed works are relatively few. But then, he embarked on so many ventures in so many areas

that it was never likely that they could all be completed. His numerous beginnings, his expressions

of intent to return to particular works and subjects
for extended attention, and his apparent reluctance

A young male giraffe born on 31 May 2007 was officially shown off to the public with his mother in June 2007 at Dublin zoo. Photograph: Robbie Reynolds.

to conclude any particular endeavour, led to an intriguing psychoanalytical diagnosis, the idea that he evidenced signs of a closure complex, linked to his sexuality.

There may well be some truth to the idea, though more orthodox art historians reasonably shy away from it. However, a single human being could hardly hope to see through the sheer volume of work he initiated. Late in his life he became depressed when he realised that even the task of organising his collections of notes and papers was so vast that he could not hope to complete it. He couldn't have done so even if he'd had another lifetime to devote to all this unfinished business.

Across the range of his endeavours, he was driven by curiosity and a sense of possibility. These were defining traits of his genius.

The idea that his work harbours an arcane secret, the basis of Dan Browne's bestseller, is surely a legitimate expression of what engages us about it, but doesn't reflect a literal truth. That is, it's not something hidden and arcane that makes Leonardo interesting, but the fact that he shows us how to look at the world around us, how to address its profound mysteries and possibilities with fresh eyes and an open mind.

THURSDAY, 14 JUNE 2007

Polish Dictionary Not Much Help on Business Language

Exam diary, by Miroslawa Gorecka

Now that my time in the Irish school system is coming to a close, I am getting some perspective on the whole experience.

The exam process over here really is horrible. It has not been possible to do my best under this kind of pressure. With three-hour exams every day, switching from one subject to another with only a restless night's sleep in between, I cannot say that I have been able to demonstrate all that I have learned.

The business exam yesterday was a good example. I'm not sure that I managed to improve on the B1 I got in my mocks. Also my little Polish/English dictionary is not much help when is comes to business language, I'm afraid.

The Leaving Cert has been a strange experience, and this diary has made it even stranger. Famous Miroslawa has crossed the Irish Sea and is now talking to journalists from the *London Times*. Meanwhile, I am trying to undo some of the damage she has caused over the last week. Here we go:

To Mr Kellet: I really do like business and you are a wonderful teacher.

To Drogheda Grammar School: I know I've done a lot of complaining but it was never about you. The teachers at my school are AMAZING and they worked so hard to help me.

To the Polish film industry: I'm sure there is a Polish film out there that is not about drinking and fighting and as soon as these exams are over I will try to watch it.

To any Irish person that I was impatient with in the last year: I know that we 'non-nationals' are not always so easy to understand. Being treated differently does not always mean being treated badly.

To all my future patients: If you have a problem with your Follicle Stimulating Hormone I may have to send you to another doctor (I couldn't answer that question on yesterday's biology paper).

To anyone whom the famous Miroslawa has offended: She has a mind of her own.

Now that I have made my apologies, I want to say a big thanks to everyone who helped me and to the Irish system for making room for me. I never wanted to come here, but after 18 months in Ireland I have learned so much more than I would have learned at home in my little Polish town.

I have found the real world, and that is a real gift.

Welcome to Planet Bertie

Fintan O'Toole

And so, the man they couldn't hang lopes amiably onwards, doing what he has always done, turning apparent weakness into strength. If the result of the general election was an equivocal triumph for Bertie Ahern, the formation of the Government made it unequivocal by turning the obvious on its head. Parties that lose seats in an election are not supposed to end up stronger than before. Coalitions made up of disparate parties are not supposed to be easy for a taoiseach to control.

Yet, on what his new friend John Gormley calls Planet Bertie, these immutable laws of the

Taoiseach Bertie Ahern leaves Leinster House for Áras an Uachtaráin after being elected Taoiseach by the Dáil for the third time in a row. Photograph: Frank Miller.

political universe do not apply. Having suffered a small loss of seats, Bertie Ahern has manoeuvred himself into a position of even greater strength.

From a coalition in which he had to keep the Progressive Democrats onside, he has created a coalition in which he has to keep no one onside. All he has to do is to stop the PDs and the Green Party – parties with sharply opposed perspectives – from being so unhappy with anything he does that both pull out of the Government at the same time. He has locked both of them in by making it possible for either of them to leave. He is now in the position of the parent faced with the stroppy adolescent who is always threatening to leave home. If the moaning becomes unbearable, he can use the most effective line of all: 'There's the door. Who's stopping you?'

There has been much talk of Bertie Ahern's achievement in matching the record of Fianna Fáil's founder, Éamon de Valera, by winning three elections in a row. What may matter more to him, however, is that he has now definitively surpassed his mentor and hero Charles Haughey in his domination of the political landscape. He learned a great deal from Haughey, and much of his populist political ideology derives directly from The Boss. But in one crucial respect he moved in an entirely different direction. Haughey dominated Irish politics by making his own personality the great dividing line, not just within Fianna Fáil, but within the nation. He understood that being hated was a form of power, so long as the hatred produced an equal and opposite reaction of love and loyalty.

That has never been Bertie Ahern's way. Where Charlie was a centrifugal force, Bertie is centripetal. Where Haughey carried a knife to cut the unfaithful away from the faithful, his protegé carries a magnet. It is significant that he has reiterated recently that his favourite politician is Bill Clinton, with whom he keeps in touch, and from whom he received a glowing endorsement for his party political broadcasts. Clinton's craving for love was extravagant and extraordinary. Bertie's has

Green Party TD John Gormley is presented with his seal of office at Áras an Uachtaráin by President Mary McAleese with Taoiseach Bertie Ahern. Photograph: Alan Betson.

been quiet and ordinary. But the impulse is the same: the desire to pull everything towards himself. His political method is to establish himself as the nucleus of pragmatic good sense, and attract disparate elements towards that centre.

Over the years, the force has been felt by the old anti-Haughey camp in Fianna Fáil, by the general public, by trade unionists and employers, by big businessmen and street traders, by Gerry Adams and Ian Paisley, by the PDs, and now by the Greens.

The real evidence of Bertie Ahern's power this week lay in his virtual invisibility. He had to do little but wait for the votes he needed to form a government to come to him. Planet Bertie spins serenely on its own axis, exercising its own silent gravity. Approaching objects, even those that once looked like potentially destructive meteors, fall into its orbit and take up their positions as compliant

satellites. Media allegations about his personal finances ease his path back to government by neutralising the Mahon tribunal hearings, which would otherwise have made things awkward. The Greens, for whom coalition with Fianna Fáil would be a pact with the devil, ask meekly, 'Where do we sign?'

For many Fianna Fáil backbenchers, the deal with the Greens was puzzling because it was unnecessary. But politics is not the art of the necessary, it is the art of the possible. Bertie Ahern did it because he could. Every atom of his political instinct is honed on the spotting and taking of opportunities. He is, for all his seeming caution, a brilliant opportunist. The Greens could be taken with relative ease. He knows from football – his one true passion outside of politics – that you win the game by taking the chance when it presents itself. If you're three-nil ahead (which, in political terms, Bertie Ahern was in the game of becoming taoiseach without the Greens), you don't spurn an open goal for a fourth.

And, paradoxical as it may seem, Bertie Ahern was never so Fianna Fáil as when he was bringing the Greens into his orbit. In the back of his mind (and sometimes at the front), he still thinks of Fianna Fáil, not as a political party, but as the national movement, the Irish people meeting in one giant cumann. He knows that such rhetoric doesn't wash in this more justly sceptical age of Irish politics. But he still believes it, and that belief shaped his impulse to bring this new, strange bit of Irish political culture, these youngish idealists with their own language and world view, into his fold. The attraction of the Greens was not that they are part of his world, but precisely that they're not. They bring him something he doesn't already have.

This matters because his Everyman persona is not, as it is often misunderstood to be, simply about being Joe Soap. The true Everyman is a complex creature, because he has elements of everyone else. Bertie Ahern's leadership has been all about this capacity to absorb everything except the one true untouchable, Fine Gael. Faced with Labour, the trade unions and Joe Higgins, he declares himself a socialist. Faced with the PDs, he adopts right-wing economics and privatisation. Faced with Sinn Féin, he revives Fianna Fáil's republican heritage by parading Kevin Barry through the streets of Dublin and restoring the commemoration of the 1916 Rising. Faced with the consistent, forensic criticism of Fr Seán Healy of CORI, he invites the turbulent priest to a party think-in and embraces him as a spiritual comrade.

And now, with no one else left to absorb, he goes Green. He sings along with Kermit the Frog's moving *Sesame Street* anthem, 'It's Not Easy Bein' Green': 'When green is all there is to be/ It could make you wonder why but/ . . . I am green and it'll do fine, it's beautiful!/ And I think it's what I want to be.'

Getting the Greens to sign up to a programme for government that is essentially the Fianna Fáil manifesto with a few aspirational twists is an especially brilliant stroke, but one that fits a pattern. One of his great political talents as Taoiseach has been his ability to present things he would have had to do anyway as gracious concessions. He has done this time and again in social partnership talks, giving trade unions, in return for wage moderation, commitments that Fianna Fáil would probably have had to make for political reasons anyway. He has done this with consummate, almost effortless, skill to the Greens. They get things that any Irish government would have to sign up to under international commitments. He gets their support as Taoiseach.

But he also gets more. The Greens ward off, at least for a while, the threat of political boredom. They allow him to present what is essentially an old Cabinet, with most of the same Ministers, as a new, exciting, youthful force. A deal with Labour would have cost a great deal in terms of policy concessions (on hospital co-location, for example) and cabinet seats. It would have had little novelty value, either in terms of the combination itself or of unfamiliar faces at the cabinet table. The Greens cost less and, at least for a taoiseach who has no political long-term to consider, offer more.

It matters little, of course, that the Taoiseach's own coat of green gloss will be a very thin veneer. No Irish political leader has ever been so openly contemptuous of environmental concerns. This is the Taoiseach, after all, who complained in 2003 that every big infrastructural project has to 'go through eight hoops, through all environmental, planning and blah blah blah, and every blah costs a few hundred million'. This is the Taoiseach who loftily dismissed all objections to motorway routes as being about 'swans, snails and people hanging out of trees', and who sighed with envy in Shanghai at the power of a Chinese mayor to bull-doze everything in his way: 'Naturally enough I would like to have the power of the mayor that when he decides he wants to do a highway and, if he wants to bypass an area, he just goes straight up and over.'

What he will be hearing in his own head when John Gormley and Eamon Ryan sound off at a Cabinet meeting is more 'blah, blah, blah' from people hanging out of trees. Their presence in his Government represents, on his part, not a conversion but a calculation.

This is the other side of Bertie Ahern's political genius. Just as the formation of the Government demonstrates his ability to turn a weakness into a strength, it also reminds us that much of his strength derives from a central weakness. His adaptability and opportunism, his talent for absorbing all sorts of forces within himself, have their source in a kind of emptiness. There is no great store of convictions or ideals to get in the way of his nimble manoeuvring. There is no hard core of moral passion to weigh him down as he shifts from friend of the rampant rich to sentimental socialist, from arch-developer to environmentalist.

The blankness has given him more than the ability to remain, for all the apparent permanence of his power, a moving target. His famous Teflon surface is really a blank screen onto which people can project an image they like. It is the image, not of a ruthless politician whose mentor was flagrantly corrupt, but of a character in a long-running soap opera. Such characters are meant to be people like us, except that an absurd number of dramatic things happen to them. Their marriages break down, they have complicated, drawn-out love affairs, their children marry pop stars and have twins, or become famous novelists overnight. Their careers follow strange paths, with incredibly

Four-year-old Oisín Hills from Sandyford, Co. Dublin, at the Bloom garden show in the Phoenix Park. Photograph: Gary O'Neill.

dramatic twists in which the job they want is suddenly snatched from them before, following further trials, they finally get it. But they themselves remain solid, reliable, familiar. The things that happen to them are functions not of their character, but of the plot.

This is the way Bertie Ahern is seen, and it is the reason for his legendary invulnerability to scandal. When he signed blank cheques for Charlie Haughey, it wasn't something he did but something that was done to him, as the innocent victim of an older man's wiles. When he brought Ray Burke back into cabinet, it wasn't a conscious decision, just an accidental twist in a complicated story of which he knew nothing. When he got money from businessmen, it was something they did to him, an event beyond his control. And when he had to explain it, he did so by shifting it back onto the soap opera territory of private life, in which he could no more help what happened than Ken Barlow in Coronation Street could help leaving Deirdre for Denise and then Denise for Deirdre.

This kind of Bertie is, for a man who looks set to have dominated the political landscape for the best part of 15 years by the time he is 60, a curiously powerless figure. He has one towering, genuinely historic achievement in his management of a peace process that he did not invent but that found in him the right man at the right time. It is, for the history books, more than enough to mark him as a figure of real significance. But, for the present day, his blankness has expressed itself in a strange lack of ambition. Big targets that he once set himself, like eliminating consistent poverty and creating 3,000 new acute hospital beds, have now been abandoned.

When he said, towards the end of his first term as taoiseach, that he wanted the legacy of the economic boom in Ireland to be his grandiose sports stadium, the odd thing was that he clearly meant it. When he came to imagine a historic achievement in the Republic, the Bertie Bowl was as far as his

vision could stretch. Beyond that, his goal was to keep the boom he inherited going, to hold things steady, to manage crises and stay in power.

Asked yesterday by RTÉ's Seán O'Rourke how he would change in his third term, he spoke of more efficient management, not of new horizons. Those are not the typical aspirations of a politician with a world-class electoral record. But perhaps the very reason he has been so supremely good at holding power is that he is so relatively unconcerned about what he does with it. Not worn out by pursuing high ambitions, he has preserved his political stamina. Not distracted by grand ideals, he has kept his eye on the prize. Now that he has gained power for the last time, he will take pride in handing it on intact, unworn by overuse, to his chosen successor, Brian Cowen.

SATURDAY, 16 JUNE 2007

My Kind of Hero

Róisín Ingle

My friend had a friend who, while growing up in Dublin, possessed a Madonna-like ability to reinvent himself. Let's call this friend of his Gerry Bloom.

Just because I like the name Gerry. And Bloom because it's Bloomsday. Gerry Bloom was a small boy with big obsessions who changed direction like the wind, and for this he made no apologies. Even though I've never met him, and even though he doesn't seem quite real, Gerry Bloom is something of a hero of mine.

This was Gerry. One day he would wake up and decide he was crazy, just crazy, about U2. He'd buy all the U2 records and memorabilia and head up to Bray, where at the time Bono lived in a Martello tower. Gerry camped outside the tower until, one day, Bono appeared and signed all his records. A few weeks later my friend would say to Gerry Bloom something like: 'What about this U2 thing, huh? You must be their biggest fan in Ireland.' And Gerry Bloom would look at him quizzically, head cocked, and say: 'Are you on drugs?' You see, Gerry Bloom had moved on.

To Japanese fighting fish. Overnight he decided they were the best thing since, well, Bono. Gerry Bloom bought a tank and filled it with fish and educated himself about their eating habits. He looked after them, never stopped talking about them and brought people home from school to see them. One day my friend asked about the health of the Japanese fighting fish, and Gerry Bloom denied all knowledge, seeming offended by the suggestion. My friend had seen them with his own eyes, but still Gerry Bloom maintained he had no knowledge of or interest in such creatures. He'd tell you what he did like, though. He was mad into American football.

One Friday at school, Gerry Bloom told his classmates that he had an American-football game on Monday but needed a helmet. Did anyone have an American-football helmet? To this day my friend doesn't know why he told Gerry Bloom: 'Yeah, I have one of them.' Gerry Bloom was suspicious. 'Are you sure you have an American-football helmet?' he asked my friend. 'Yes I do, course I do,' said my friend. 'If I find out you are lying,' said Gerry Bloom, 'I'll never speak to you again.'

My friend said nothing and just hoped an American-football helmet would somehow, miraculously, turn up over the weekend, the way you do when you're a teenager.

Yvonne McDonagh from Rathfarnham, Co. Dublin, enjoys the haymaking in Derrylea, Co. Sligo. Photograph: Brian Farrell.

On Sunday evening Gerry Bloom knocked on my friend's door in full American-football get-up. My friend opened the door long enough to hear Gerry ask for 'that American-football helmet'; then, in a panic, he closed the door in his face. He went out to his back garden, where over the fence he spotted his young neighbour's CHiPs toy motorcycle helmet. Knowing it was wrong but finding it perversely funny, my friend went out to the door and placed the CHiPs helmet on Gerry Bloom's head. Dribbles of muddy water ran down the side of his face. He didn't speak to my friend for six months.

In the years that followed, Gerry Bloom continued his random obsessions. He got into John Lennon. Worshipped Bruce Springsteen. Became Barry McGuigan's biggest fan, even bunking off school to try to meet the boxer. He shed skins like a snake, never looking back to the skin that had gone before. It was as if the past had never happened. He was a caterpillar, constantly emerging from a chrysalis, a multiple butterfly boy.

The next time my friend saw him, he had a job. 'I'm a carpenter,' said Gerry Bloom.

When I tell my friend what I'm up to these days, he likes to call me Gerry Bloom. I'll be evangelising about this new diet or that new form of meditation, or a new exercise regime, and he'll say: 'I never have to argue with you about your latest fad, because the fact that two weeks later you are not doing it any more is argument enough. You are just like Gerry Bloom.'

Last week I told him that I was now living a wheat-free, dairy-free, sugar-free, caffeine-free existence, and he laughed his head off. And when he laughed I thought of Gerry Bloom, always on the lookout for the next new thing. I should mention that when Gerry was in first year, going through an intense Michael Jackson phase, his mother died, so you could say he'd been looking for something else entirely during all those years.

The last time my friend saw Gerry Bloom he had just bought every record The Beatles ever made, but my friend could tell he still hadn't found what he was looking for. You are not the only one, Gerry Bloom.

FRIDAY, 22 JUNE 2007

An Irishman's Diary

Frank McNally

I don't seriously blame them for it, except on some subconscious, irrational level. But it has to be said that the weather has deteriorated disastrously since the Greens went into government. The promise of a long, hot summer – so persuasive only a few weeks ago – has suddenly vanished, as so many promises from election campaigns seem to do.

I accept that a guarantee of blue skies and balmy temperatures did not feature in any party manifesto. And yet all those sunny faces on posters during the hazy days of May seem, in retrospect, complicit. No sooner was a Government elected and the posters removed than it emerged that the weather was in for a serious downturn, with the Met Office issuing grim new figures, seasonally adjusted.

Rain can be a good thing, I know, and not just for farmers. One undisputed benefit of a wet summer is that it keeps the streets of Dublin clean – something the municipal authorities, apparently hamstrung by their fierce commitment to the environment, and the conservation of water in particular, cannot otherwise do.

During any dry spell, however short, the city becomes an embarrassment to live in. The detritus of hard nights is visible everywhere on streets and footpaths, in dribbles and spillages and bodily effluvia. The bottoms of rubbish bins ooze like sores until the sun forms scabs around them. It's a small mercy when the colours on the footpaths merge and fade, and you can no longer tell which leaks are which. Even so, when you see tourists tiptoeing through the squalor sometimes, it can be hard not to squirm.

Singer Peter Gabriel performing at Marlay Park in Dublin. Photograph: Alan Betson.

A lesser body than Dublin City Council might panic on such occasions and order wholesale street-washing of the kind that occurs daily in Paris. Not the hardened eco-warriors of City Hall, however. Like so many of Dublin's shopkeepers – who, if weak-minded, might be tempted to clean their own stretches of pavement and shame the neighbours – they hold their nerve. They know the rain is coming, sooner or later.

If only the rest of us could remember this vital information. Unfortunately it is part of the Irish condition to be eternally optimistic about the climate, given any encouragement. A few days without rain is always enough to convince us that this is the new norm. Which is why we have never quite learned to dress for the conditions we live in.

I'll speak for myself anyway. One evening this week, I cycled into the office for something,

having made a quick assessment that I could get there and back without waterproof clothing (not that I own any). There were specks of rain on the breeze, it's true. But a sniff of the air, informed by that deep well of intuition about the natural world that all Irish people inherit from our ancestors, assured me it would stay dry.

Half-an-hour later, I stood staring out the office window as an Atlantic depression deepened over Dublin, dumping biblical quantities of rain on to the streets below, where not even Green Party ministers could be seen cycling home. There was nothing for it, I realised, but to abandon the bike for the night and get the Luas instead.

A slight weakness in this plan was that, naturally, I had no umbrella. And by the time I was half-way to the Luas stop, it was clear that my tactic of dashing between doorways and covered

193

shop fronts was only partly successful. What you avoided in first-hand rain you absorbed in the torrents of second-hand stuff gushing from canopies and gutters. So having reached the River Liffey – which was still just about distinguishable from the streets – I opted to cut my losses and get a bus.

It had been a while since I did this. But it soon came back to me forcefully how waiting for a bus on a wet evening in Dublin can sap your will to live. When you're sodden, and huddled in a shop entrance, and having your space invaded back and front by wet strangers and an automatic door, the charm of watching the world go by wears very quickly.

In the entrance I chose, smoke from my neighbour's cigarette lingered around me, apparently reluctant to drift outwards and get wet. Since the smoker was also swigging from a beer bottle between drags, I thought better of complaining. Instead I did my best to appreciate the street scene, which included another drinker urinating, not in a doorway or alcove – a gesture that passes for politeness in Dublin – but against the general shop-front. With so much water around, maybe he thought no one would notice.

There was no street scene visible from the bus, because all the windows were steamed up. For entertainment, we had to make do with the small stream that had formed itself on one side of the upper deck, and was washing an empty Coke can to and fro. I watched it from the opposite bank, with grim fascination. When the bus climbed a hill, the can floated down to the back. When we descended, the tide turned and it floated forwards again.

There were four other passengers on the upper deck, all wet and on their mobile phones and speaking languages other than English. One laughed every so often – a little hysterically, I thought. Maybe he was talking to his family in the Caribbean and trying to describe the Irish summer.

I wiped the glass to see where we were and, peering out into the Stygian gloom, suddenly realised that the longest day of the year was almost

upon us. When the can floated past again, I felt like putting an SOS in it.

MONDAY, 25 JUNE 2007

Mighty Ending to Four-Hour Epic

Tom Humphries, at the Gaelic Grounds

That's all, folks. Even epics have endings and yesterday at the Gaelic Grounds, Limerick, driven by a desire which at times was ferocious enough to be frightening, finally slew Tipperary and rode off after many years of wandering to the high chaparral. A Munster final awaits. If the final reels of this blockbuster lacked the quality of what went before, well at least the drama was still there.

Time now for everyone to move on? Well not just yet. On their home turf a huge portion of the 30,608 attendance danced and sang long after the final whistle yesterday. In some counties All-Irelands have been greeted with less fervour.

Limerick winning their first Munster championship game in six years was a significant event in itself. The manner in which they did it has, however, annexed the imagination of their long-suffering public.

As for Tipperary? Old Oscar, who could hurl off both sides, noted that a person can survive anything except death and live down anything except a good reputation. Hmmm.

Hurling's system of resurrection through the back door means yesterday's demise of Tipperary is just a temporary setback. And Babs Keating's? His reputation as a golden well for sparkling quotes and a wand-wielding magician of a coach may well have been lived down too. Babs was silent after this game, and one wondered did he still want or need the stresses which come with managing Tipp.

Tipperary, not quite deservedly, stole the initiative with a goal in extra time yesterday and

Limerick's James O'Brien strains every sinew in trying to keep the sliotar *from going over the end line beside Tipperary's goal in the second replay of the Munster championship semi-final at the Gaelic Grounds, Limerick. Photograph: Brendan Moran/Sportsfile.*

underlined their good fortune with an Eoin Kelly free almost immediately after.

Limerick were faced with yet another hill to climb. Tipp just had to finish the ascent, plant the flag and enjoy the view. Yet again they got caught.

If there was a difference between these teams after 250 minutes of hurling it wasn't one which could be expressed in terms of hurling. If anything Tipperary enjoy a natural advantage in terms of access to skilled practitioners. The difference was hunger; Limerick were ravenous for success. Not winning seemed unthinkable to them.

Tipperary, who gave up leads in the series as if there was an amnesty on them, never seemed to need it as much as Limerick did.

'Mighty,' said Richie Bennis, Limerick's manager. 'Mighty for the supporters and mighty for the team. I never thought that the game was gone for us, not even when they scored the goal in extra time. The way things were going, anything was possible.'

Bennis spoke of the last six months and the effort involved in bringing Limerick to this height and then reflected that the next two weeks will be devoted to bringing everyone down to terra firma again. One hopes the descent from altitude will involve no compromise of the will which drove Limerick through this series.

What makes the forthcoming Munster final so attractive is the desperate need in Limerick and Waterford to win. Both will survive death and live to play in the quarter-finals but their sense of honour screams for a win.

Limerick's half-forward line, staffed in two of the three positions by the Moran brothers from Ahane, was the most visible difference between the sides yesterday and the purest reflection of Limerick's passion. Ollie Moran has hauled Limerick through two drawn games, and if yesterday his overall contribution was overshadowed by Niall's five points, the torture the pair of them inflicted on Tipperary was instrumental in deciding the outcome of this series.

Yesterday Niall scored Limerick's last point in normal time before Tipperary came back to drag the game to extra time again. Ollie scored Limerick's first point when extra time began.

Tipperary slugged them with a goal and a point before Limerick found themselves again. They had pushed back to a point ahead when Tipperary enjoyed a short period of residence in the Limerick half.

All precedent and Eoin Kelly suggested they would equalise and force a fourth game. Instead Niall Moran came bursting out of defence, hurtling through a thicket of Tipperary players to clear the ball.

We moved into injury time. Still a point dividing them. Bang, bang. Two scores. Ollie Moran, then Niall. All over. Back to the saloon.

Tipperary head off into destiny's waiting room, or the qualifying series, as it is known. They face Offaly next weekend. Limerick, without a Munster title since 1996 and without an All-Ireland since 1973, might not end either famine this summer but they have come a long way already. Mighty, as Richie Bennis said. Mighty.

WEDNESDAY, 27 JUNE 2007

We Need Vision of Who We Are and What We Want to Make Migration Work

Ruadhán Mac Cormaic

On the veranda of his modernist cube in a quiet, residential part of Anápolis city, the Brazilian listens to his own story, soaking up the comic, marvelling at every turn.

A lime-green parakeet chirps in its cage and a soft hiss rises from the lawn where the gardener is dousing the sun-singed palms. Outside, even the cars seem slowed by the heat.

His name is Bill O'Dwyer, great-grandson of an Irishman who came here to work in the lumber business at the turn of the last century. He settled in Goiás, in central Brazil, and never returned home.

Bill hasn't yet seen Ireland, but he is the country's honorary consul here and the coat of arms is a prized adornment in a house coming down with antiques and artwork.

These days, from his desk at the Mercedes dealership on the city's main boulevard, O'Dwyer takes pride in how the local economy – booming louder with every week – is being fed by a link that has made Ireland the destination of choice for the city's aspirant young.

'Once the dream was to go to the United States, but now they go to Ireland, and they can buy houses, they can buy cars,' he says. 'For many families, it was a gift from God. Now they have better life conditions: they're eating better, they're living better.'

Listening to O'Dwyer brings a few things home, but above all how the magnitude of the historical reversal that has made Ireland one of the rich world's magnet-states is such that sometimes it can best be appreciated from afar.

Vila Fabril, the Anápolis district where the dilapidated shacks are now outnumbered by new two-storey homes and cars bought with wages from the factories of Clonee and Naas, provides some of the simplest, most striking illustrations of Ireland's position in the globalised world.

This country's experience is global in another sense too. Last month I told someone I was writing a series on migration. 'Are you interested in birds?' he asked.

The truth is that, like him, most of us still think of the movement of people across borders as immigration, not migration. But Ireland's rehearsal of the immigration debate is being played out on the fringes of a larger, planetary drama that is, in the words of the UN's former special representative for migration, Peter Sutherland, 'the key international question for this century'.

Across the rich world, where migrants account for a large and rising share of the population, governments and citizens are grappling with the same questions that preoccupy Ireland: who to admit and how to incorporate them into society? Given that a country that was until recently seen as a serial exporter of youth has in less than two decades reached a position where it is admitting more immigrants per head than most other countries in the world, so far it has been a relatively smooth revolution.

An ever swelling economy finds jobs for most who want them, and there has been mutual gain in the government's decision in 2004 to open the labour market to those from eastern and central Europe. The exchange makes Ireland better off as well as the migrants, many of whom take the jobs that Irish people spurn.

The social space has become deeper and wider with the introduction of new languages, cultures, religions and experiences, and in general the price to be paid in racial tension has been low. Though there are pockets of loudly-expressed resentment towards immigrants, there is little evidence of widespread antipathy, and election results show consistently that overtly anti-immigrant politics meet little success.

Many institutions have responded briskly to the new demands: the Garda Síochána, for instance, has made it easier for immigrants to join

Councillor Rotimi Adebari, who came to Ireland from Nigeria as an asylum seeker in 2000 and was elected Mayor of Portlaoise by the local council on 28 June 2007. Although not yet an Irish citizen, he quipped: 'Ireland is not just the country of a thousand welcomes, but a country of equal opportunity.' Photograph: James Flynn/APX.

and has invested time and money in anti-racism projects and links with new communities.

But the real challenges remain. The recent appointment of a Minister of State for Integration points to a shift in focus from admission to incorporation, but as a report published by the Immigrant Council earlier this month suggests, the Minister faces a daunting in-tray.

There is no lead agency responsible for migration policy and co-ordination of migration-related activities in Ireland, it pointed out. And 'this is exacerbated by a general lack of vision or strategy in migration and integration policy. The lack of consistency has led to the piecemeal development of policy and legislation.'

This lack of a guiding vision is the master-theme for those working in the area. It explains the dearth of data on Ireland's immigrants as well as a plethora of problems that would not have arisen had government been thinking strategically about integration long before now. Problems in the country's classrooms – where the State has been strangely slow to appreciate the difficulties posed by the influx of large groups of non-English speakers – reflect a wider pattern. Across the State apparatus, the lack of standards in language and interpreting obstructs even the most basic communication between its institutions and many of those they serve.

Minority ethnic voices, in fact, are virtually unheard in many spheres of public life, from the arts and media to politics and the law. When the 30th Dáil convened for the first time recently, there was among the 166 TDs not one member of an immigrant or ethnic minority community that numbers over 10 per cent of the population. Political parties are among the most monocultural groups in society.

If there are signs that State services are not keeping pace with demographic changes, there are also indications that the mental leap that will be required to fully absorb immigrants has yet to take place.

The general tendency of politicians, for instance, is to speak of immigrants exclusively as members of the workforce, not of society, as though migrants were only actors in the global job market and not prospective members of the community.

In effect, the public is asked a variation on the question once posed by J.K. Galbraith: considering how migration so manifestly made all parties better off, he asked, what 'perversity of the human soul' would cause people to resist so obvious a good? If only it were that simple.

The reluctance to talk about the social and cultural shifts has two significant effects. First, while allowing myth and prejudice to circulate freely, it absolves people of the need to think about the deeper ramifications of these changes. What does migration mean for our notions of citizenship, of the welfare state and reciprocity, of culture, of nationhood? Or do we not trust ourselves to talk about it?

Speaking privately last month, a senior politician who is an enthusiastic public advocate of immigration hesitated when the conversation turned to cultural give-and-take. 'Anyone who feels passionately Irish, whether you like to admit it or not, you do feel an element of challenge about all of this,' said the politician.

Second, the silence obstructs the integration process itself by relegating newcomers ('non-nationals') to the role of economic automatons with no stake or future in society. One impression that has returned to me over the past four months is that huge numbers of immigrants are fully-fledged members of the economy but have no place in society, living their lives in parallel to (and unheeded by) the rest of the community.

Piotr from eastern Poland has been living in Dublin for almost two years. He works as a security guard at an office complex in the IFSC six nights a week, he told me. He sleeps in a hostel (where he shares a room with two strangers) for most of the day, then strolls around the city for a few hours in order to kill some time before work. He has no friends in Dublin and the farthest he has travelled from the city is Howth.

Window on a wider world: an Asian woman looks out of her shop window as a pedestrian walks along Moore Street, Dublin. Photograph: Kate Geraghty.

Asylum seekers, many of whom are forced to wait for years while their applications for leave to remain are processed, are consigned to poverty and effectively kept at a remove from the rest of the community by a ban on paid work and a punitive allowance of €19.10 a week.

If immigrants such as these are to be integrated, says Dr Jean-Pierre Eyanga Ekumeloko of Integrating Ireland, it will require reciprocal negotiation on the part of native and newcomer. There are practical challenges – how to make sure that immigrants can access services and compete for jobs on an equal footing, for example – but there are more searching questions too.

If what emerges will amount to a redefinition of society, as Ekumeloko puts it, then the greatest leap will be essentially an act of imagination, requiring us to reinvent the mental framework

through which we view such ideas as identity, citizenship, sovereignty and belonging.

The question is: are we ready? In one sense, Ireland should be better placed than others. The country has in ways been multicultural for centuries, and long experience of emigration has given Irishness a malleable, open quality. As Declan Kiberd points out, the recognition during Mary Robinson's presidency that the overseas Irish were also part of the national family suggested a corollary: that many immigrant peoples living on the island of Ireland might also have their own global communities over and above the immediate society to which they belong.

And in 1998, 94 per cent of the Republic's electorate endorsed the idea of hybridity when they voted for the Belfast Agreement.

Speaking recently to Zeljka Doljanin, a

Croatian woman writing her PhD on the stranger in current Irish fiction, I was struck by her view that in reading John McGahern and Brian Friel she found a more fully-formed sense of belonging and self-assurance than she sensed among those reaching maturity today. With self-confidence came a greater curiosity and openness to the outsider, she said, reminding me of a point made very often by recent immigrants: how Irish people seem to lack a clear sense of themselves and their own culture. As Ekumeloko puts it, 'the question you have to ask is, what are we integrating into?'

The paradox is this: if ambivalence towards the outsider is an extension of ambivalence towards ourselves, then not until we can explain what it is that makes us Irish will we be capable of dealing confidently with those who are sure of what sets them apart.

News or Piffle

Net Results, by Karlin Lillington

So which came first, the dumbing down of media or the internet? Anyone with a sense of media history can tell you that the movement away from hard news coverage and towards lifestyle and celebrity piffle started well before the net had anything like a significant presence. Many however would see a correlation between 'news lite' and the ever-growing role of the internet in the way media is consumed.

You really only have to look at the popularity of a site such as the Drudge Report (drudgereport.com) and the way it has made trash stories front-line news for its massive audience to see that more measured media sources might think: 'We'll offer a bit of that too.'

The defining moment for the Drudge Report, and perhaps for a certain kind of salacious story's ability to cross over now into serious news, was the

Bill Clinton/Monica Lewinsky saga that nearly became a presidential impeachment. Drudge reported it first and the rest was certainly history – though whether anyone really cared or ever should have cared is another thing.

In the current context of wars, terrorism, eco-fears and the massive burden of developing world debt, getting upset over the sexual peccadilloes of a public figure seems even sillier than it did to many of us at the time. And, one might argue, the Drudge Report is the Drudge Report – its entire purpose is gossip and dirt and that's what people go there for.

However, it isn't as if the media lost its silly head over a sexual scandal and then, post-9/11, set its nose back to the current events grindstone. Pick up a newspaper, watch the television news or listen to the radio broadcasts and there's no indication at all that a weightier current events agenda has superseded the silly trash celebrity stories. If anything, the trash is ever more prevalent. Two words: Paris Hilton.

The wall-to-wall coverage of this woman's tedious life has got to be the phenomenon of our times. I can see her place in between the covers of *Hello!*, but how did her release from a minuscule prison stint end up as the lead news story for so many supposedly credible and serious media outlets recently? She even made the top of the news on the hourly bulletins on RTÉ Radio One.

No wonder hundreds of thousands have flocked to see the YouTube video of American newscaster Mika Brzezinski refusing to read the item as her lead story on an MSNBC morning news programme despite her producer's attempt to keep handing it back to her as the lead.

On the day when a key Republican senator and Bush supporter indicated he would be unlikely to support further funding for the Iraq war – major news – Brzezinski out and out refused, on air, to lead with Hilton. She tries to burn the script, she tears it up and finally, the third time it is handed to her, she puts it through the

Mr Big, aka comedian and drag artist Gary MacSweeney, gives passers-by on Quay Street in Galway a taste of what to expect during the Macnas parade at the Galway Arts Festival. Mr Big will be the lead character in the parade. Photograph: Joe O'Shaughnessy.

shredder. View it here: http://tinyurl.com/2jmu6r. Magnificent.

In the wake of her lone act, some commentators were saying the Parisification of mainstream media was largely due to the internet – it has drained the audiences for print and broadcast media, which struggle to win back readers, viewers and listeners with tales of Wags, Paris and the latest celebrity to detox.

Is that true? I think it is a lot more complicated. First off, readership of newspapers was dropping before Matt Drudge ever considered paying for a URL. Reality television thrived on its own without much help from the internet (though, granted, plenty were happy to go watch hours of dullness on the *Big Brother* webcams. Personally, my dull webcam of choice is the very slowly aging wheel of cheese on CheddarVision (www.cheddarvision.tv).

Some, maybe much, of the shift to online news is to real news – witness the massive growth in the Guardian Unlimited's website from the start of the Iraq war, with most new traffic coming from a US wanting weightier coverage than was easily found in the States – or to discussion of issues on current events weblogs, among those with the biggest audiences.

If the internet arguably gave birth to the monster that is Paris Hilton (by making her ex-boyfriend's notorious sex video of the pair available to a global audience), the internet has also supplied a perfectly succinct critique of it in the Brzezinski clip, with just one of several versions posted watched over a million and a half times by last Monday.

Déise Like This Hard to Beat

Tom Humphries, at Semple Stadium

Some games grow to fit the occasion they are supposed to grace. Waterford and Limerick are unaccustomed to being asked to uphold the tradition of great Munster hurling finals, and yesterday through a dogged and tight first half it looked as if their honest endeavour just wouldn't be enough.

After the break, though, the game defied the rain and the sceptics and caught fire. Waterford duly won their eighth Munster title, their third since 2002, and if the margin of nine points flattered them slightly there were no complaints from the customers.

Limerick, whose road to this final was long and winding and involved three bruising meetings with Tipperary, were beaten on a day when they were never seriously favoured to win. Their own benchmarking will tell them, though, they have made progress, and only for a few fluffed chances early on yesterday the narrative might have been different. They live to fight on in the quarter-finals.

Two youths from the loyalist Ballycraigy estate in Antrim town stand on an unlit bonfire of pallets and tyres in expectation of tonight's celebrations to mark the Twelfth of July. Photograph: Charles McQuillan/Pacemaker.

This was a day of odd sights and bizarre visions. Those early birds among the 48,371 who paid in were treated to the sight of a minor final played out between the royal families of Munster: Tipperary and Cork.

The weather, as it has done all summer, refused to co-operate and the terraces were afforested with umbrellas for much of the game. Yet the tough honesty of Limerick's challenge and the persistent charm of Waterford's striving engaged us with increasing strength as the day went on.

As his colleague Paul Flynn had done a few years ago, Dan Shanahan scored 3-3 against Limerick. Dan's story and his ethic of work, work and more work are almost a parable of Waterford's search for a first All-Ireland since 1959. Derided in his early days as a big, slow player with a moderate

third touch, Shanahan has become a top-class forward whose legacy will be plain from the stats he leaves behind. Yesterday's splurge leaves him with 16 goals in his last 17 championship games going back to 2004.

Shanahan's goals, all three opportunist, snugly fitted the final margin between the two teams, but there was more to Waterford's excellence than one man, and more to Shanahan's own contribution. His three points were important and fine scores – the first came while he was under pressure out on the right sideline, the third while he was under similar duress out on the left sideline – and he gave the Limerick defence one of the more difficult afternoons they have endured. As Shanahan was quick to concede though, games like yesterday's aren't won by a single player.

Waterford's Eoin Kelly gathers the sliotar *and finds himself in open space as the pursuing Mike O'Brien of Limerick loses his hurley during the Munster hurling final in Semple Stadium, Thurles. Photograph: Dara Mac Dónaill.*

His first goal came at the end of a splendid move. Séamus Prendergast played the sweetest angled pass off the hurl to Stephen Molumphy, who handpassed to Paul Flynn. The mind's eye was already celebrating Flynn's goal when Limerick's goalkeeper, Brian Murray, pulled off an astonishing save. Shanahan was on hand though to pump the breaking ball into the net and put Waterford two points clear.

There were 19 minutes left but it seemed like a turning point. Shanahan's final two rapier thrusts came at the end of equally creative passages, a lovely ball from Michael Walsh setting up the second, a fine long pass from Prendergast again creating the third, a goal Shanahan noted with a grin he enjoyed because by then 'I was able to relax.'

'That', said his manager, Justin McCarthy, 'is Dan Shanahan. I've seen him nights in training matches when he might score seven goals. He has the secret around his wrist: Work. Work. Work.' That secret is apparently widely available in Waterford.

The addition of players like Stephen Molumphy and Aidan Kearney has hardened the puritan ethic McCarthy imbues his teams with, and yesterday, though they were required to produce the panache with which they have decorated many games in recent years, Waterford gave us something else: guts and 70-minute commitment.

What aches most in the Déise is the thought of becoming the best team of recent times not to win an All-Ireland final. Indeed all their excellence of the past few years has not brought even a big day out in September. 'It's all about getting to an All-Ireland final for us,' said Eoin Kelly, their mercurial forward. 'We'd never get tired of winning Munster titles, but the Waterford public deserves an All-Ireland. We'd fill Croke Park three times over on All-Ireland final day.'

To that end the draw for the quarter-finals was made yesterday, and all that became clear was that Waterford will have to continue playing Munster opposition in the short term; they meet the runners-up in the qualifier group currently headed by Cork and Tipperary, who play in Thurles next week. If form is any guide it would appear Tipperary will lose that one and face Waterford.

On the other side of the draw, Kilkenny, the All-Ireland champions and recently crowned Leinster winners, seem likely to play Galway, who were beaten by Clare on Saturday night in Ennis.

For Waterford, yesterday in Semple Stadium was a day of affirmation, and their progress and delirium were marked more than anything by 20 minutes either side of the final whistle. While the game was still on, they closed out business in ruthless fashion. When it was over, they accepted the trophy and got back to thinking about September without any trace of delirium or exultation.

TUESDAY, 10 JULY 2007

Meet Again in Sunlit Uplands

Heart Beat, by Maurice Neligan

In an appreciation I wrote about a recently departed colleague, I quoted from American poet Emily Dickinson's poem titled 'The bustle in a House':

The bustle in a house,
The morning after death
Is solemnest of industries,
Enacted upon Earth.

I know. As many of the readers will know a very bad thing has happened to our family. We have lost our middle child, our beloved daughter Sara, in tragic circumstances. For obvious reasons I am constrained from writing too much about this now.

Dear Sara, I do want to write to you and about you, but as now my heart is too heavy and my eyes too full of tears. Your passing leaves a void in our hearts, which the most loving memories can fill only inadequately.

A mother and her child sit at a feeding centre run by Action Contre la Faim (Action Against Hunger), with support from the UN World Food Programme, in Wajid, 340 km west of Somalia's capital, Mogadishu. The leaders of Somalia's national reconciliation conference opened up the talks to Islamists and insurgents. Photograph: Damien Guerchois.

Shelley wrote that 'grief itself be mortal'. It does not seem so now and we are very far from being so dispassionate. With God's help, the pain will lessen and we will be able to remember you as you were, a beautiful, caring, dignified and compassionate girl and woman who brought so much happiness into so many lives.

Our family has been strengthened and comforted by the truly enormous outpouring of sympathy and succour from friends of all the family, from colleagues, acquaintances, clubs and organisations and from people we never even knew but who reached out their hands to us in our distress.

It has been a constant theme in the many thousands of letters we have received that the writers acknowledge that they can but find inadequate words of comfort or indeed no words at all.

I would like to say to them all and to those who attended the services for Sara that you provided a strong bulwark for us in our time of sorrow and this family would like to say from our hearts to those who stood with them: God bless you all and thank you.

I am conscious in writing that we are a privileged family with wide-ranging contacts who have rallied to our support. I am aware also that there are many who undergo similar deprivation and indeed worse, who do not have similar support. How they can cope is beyond my comprehension.

Yet folk do move on, the strength coming for

some from the unquenchable human spirit. For others it comes from faith and the promise of resurrection. We unreservedly believe that we shall meet Sara again in the sunlit uplands.

Returning to contemporary Ireland; much has happened over the past few weeks. We've sort of got a new Government, with a different set of fall guys to replace the PDs who sank almost without trace. Otherwise, it seems, unfortunately, to be the mixture much as before.

I do note however that the Minister for Health, Mary Harney, to whom I offer sincere condolences on the death of her mother, has sat down with the consultants to explore the way forward. Hopefully this will issue in an era of consultation and co-operation, rather than antagonism and suspicion.

Col William Blacker (1727-1785), a man solidly of the unionist persuasion on this island, wrote a poem called 'Oliver's Advice'. It is a martial work full of fire and does not mince words:

> He comes the open rebel fierce
> He comes the Jesuit sly
> But put your trust in God my boys
> And keep your powder dry.

The last line attributed to the Lord Protector, Cromwell himself, is very sage advice indeed. It should be noted carefully by the doctors, nurses and paramedics as they wait to see if anything has really changed. It would be infinitely preferable with goodwill, mutual respect and endeavour to move everything forward together. It would be wearying indeed for our health professionals to mount the barricades once again.

In the past few weeks for obvious reasons I have talked to hundreds of those in the front line of the health service, and I must confess I am not too sanguine about ultimate outcomes. The experience of the past few years has left deep cynicism in its wake but also a powerful sense of solidarity. Having quoted from the Orange side of the Irish equation let me quote from the Green:

> That hour of weak delusions past
> The empty dream has flown
> Our hope and strength, we find at last
> Is in ourselves, alone
> (John O'Hagan – 1847)

In plain English, nobody can fix the health service without the willing participation of those working within.

I had alluded to the purchase of the Mater Private for the astronomical sum of €350 million. I read today that the money was advanced by one of our major banks. That is where the health service is headed; profit, not patients, being the motive. Co-location has nothing to do with patient welfare but is merely another prop from an overdeveloped and soon-to-be-troubled construction industry.

Sara, love, when I went through your papers and saw your miserable pay cheques as a fully qualified intensive care nurse, I made a promise to you that your old dad would fight this cynical inequality developing in our society. So I shall.

Back to Emily Dickinson and the lines I have quoted before: for us in family for us remains,

> The sweeping of the Heart
> And putting love away
> We shall not want to use again
> Until eternity.

MONDAY, 23 JULY 2007

Harrington Seizes Destiny

Philip Reid, at Carnoustie

Destiny doesn't make things easy. Yesterday, in the 136th British Open on the links of Carnoustie, it called two men; one a temperamental matador who had always seemed destined for major glory, the other an Irishman who started his

Pádraig Harrington celebrates on the 18th green after winning the British Open Championship tournament at Carnoustie in Scotland. He beat Spain's Sergio Garcia by one shot after a four-hole play-off and became the first Irishman to win a major since Fred Daly captured the same title 60 years ago. Photograph: Phil Noble/Reuters.

working life on tour content to be a mere journeyman.

That it was Pádraig Harrington who answered the call demonstrated how his goals changed since he first embarked on a career as a professional golfer back in 1995 just because all his peers in the amateur game had done so. Yesterday, Harrington, a 35-year-old Dubliner, achieved greatness, taming the famed links and out-duelling Sergio Garcia in a four-hole play-off to claim the Claret Jug.

This was a momentous day for Irish sport, and as the strains of 'Molly Malone' and 'The Fields of Athenry' and that ubiquitous anthem 'Ole, Ole, Ole' reverberated in turn around the 18th green and the sand dunes on Scotland's eastern shore, Harrington was allowed a tear or two at the presentation ceremony as his thoughts drifted for a moment to his late father, Paddy, who died two years ago and had been his golfing inspiration.

Harrington's victory – the first by an Irish player since Fred Daly's at Hoylake in 1947 – was the stuff of supreme sporting drama. It was a roller-coaster of emotions, with Garcia seemingly the champion in waiting as he started out with a three-shot lead over Steve Stricker. Harrington was one of seven players six shots adrift at the start of the day. He shot 67 to Garcia's final-round 73. In the four-hole play-off, Harrington went birdie-par-par-bogey (for 15) to Garcia's bogey-par-par-par (for 16).

Harrington's win ended the drought of eight years since Paul Lawrie became the last European to win a major. For a player who last year topped the European Tour order of merit, this victory

British Open Champion 2007 Pádraig Harrington with his son, Patrick, and wife, Caroline. Photograph: Martin Rickett/Press Association.

represented the pinnacle – so far – of a career that has seen him scale one height after another.

In typical Harrington fashion, this latest and greatest win was not achieved in a straightforward fashion. Just as he had done with the Irish Open in May and the Irish PGA last week, it came after a play-off. But this was more important, far more important, than the others. It was for a major title, taking the Claret Jug from Tiger Woods, who had won for the previous two years.

Despite being twice in the Barry Burn on the 72nd hole, and running up a double-bogey six, Harrington never believed his chance had gone. Instead, he locked himself into the recorder's hut behind the 18th green, turned down the sound on the television so he wouldn't have to listen to negative analysis of how he had finished, and waited for Garcia to play what is probably the toughest finishing hole in golf.

When Garcia, needing a par to win the title, put his approach into a greenside bunker and then missed his par putt, it put the two men – who had soldiered together in last year's Ryder Cup at The K Club – into head-to-head combat.

But Garcia hadn't been happy with the lengthy wait he had taken on the 18th tee, as the final groups backed up while Harrington's play of the hole in regulation saw him visit the Barry Burn on two occasions. 'Hitting a three-iron into a green where there's danger everywhere, having to wait at least 15 minutes to hit your shot doesn't help. It doesn't help at all. I wasn't very happy about that.'

Still, by the time the play-off started, Harrington was the one who got his head around matters best. He had spent a few minutes on the putting green with his sports psychologist, Bob Rotella, and he immediately birdied the first play-off hole while Garcia bogeyed. This time, he never let the initiative slip.

It was to be Harrington's moment and, when it was all over, and the crowds gave their acclaim on the 18th green, his wife, Caroline, who is expecting the couple's second child in December,

and three-year-old son Paddy had a family moment in the full glare of the world's media.

Of that time in the recorder's hut, not knowing if his title bid was over or still alive, and accompanied by his caddie, Ronan Flood, Harrington remarked: 'I never let myself feel like I'd lost the Open Championship as I sat watching. The one thing, I never, ever had in my head was that I'd lost.

'I sat there in that hut and I was as disciplined as I could be with my focus not to brood or not to, you know, have what ifs or buts, or to wonder "if I had done that". I never let it cross my mind that I'd just thrown away the Open. Obviously if I had just thrown away the Open, if it turned out like that, it would have been incredibly hard to take.'

The victory moved Harrington up to sixth in the world rankings, but its effect he feels will do wonders for Irish golf. 'Obviously, this hasn't sunk in yet. It is going to mean a lot to Irish golf, a lot to all the young lads that are competing as amateurs and who turn pro. Wow, we have an Open champion from Ireland! I'm very proud (of that).'

Harrington has been serenaded in the past to the strains of 'Molly Malone' in places such as Detroit and the Belfry and The K Club; but those had more to do with team wins in the Ryder Cup. This one was for him to savour, all alone. But he wanted to share it with all those who have helped him, his back room team of Rotella and Paul Hurrian and fitness trainer Liam Hennessy . . . but especially with his coach, Bob Torrance, who has been his swing guru for the past 12 years and changed him from a player who returned from the US Open at Congressional in 1997 believing he couldn't cope with major championships unless he altered his swing.

He did change, and yesterday's win – after a number of close calls, most notably at Winged Foot in last year's US Open – confirmed that he was right to lose the mindset of a journeyman to pursue a much tougher road that has led him to major glory.

'You know, the only reason I turned pro (in 1995) was that I went to college and I was 21 and the guys I was able to beat as an amateur were turning pro. It wasn't because I thought I was good enough. I thought I would have a great life and if I did well I'd make a comfortable living on the tour. I thought I'd have a couple of years to learn the ropes, but I started so well that I kept my head down and ran with it,' said Harrington.

'It's been a long road. I don't know if I ever believed I was going to do it, but I tried to convince myself, especially this week.'

MONDAY, 23 JULY 2007

O'Reilly Made a Calculated Effort to Sow Suspicion Among Rachel's Friends

Kathy Sheridan

The group of five women are standing around a bench, which was assembled by Rachel, in Jackie Connor's sunny back garden in north Co. Dublin. The air is scented with lemon geranium – the only plant Rachel could grow – and they are drinking Rachel's favourite tipple, red wine. There's an extra glass of red on the table, as always, for their dearly missed friend. Jackie Connor, Paula Carney, Celine Keogh, Helen Reddy and Bríd Horan weren't always so close. Some hardly knew each other; Rachel was the common denominator.

In the days after her death, each eyed the other warily, wondering 'what the hell she was doing here'. Each had been led to believe that the other had not been a true friend to Rachel. It was eight months later, over a weekend in Carney's Tipperary home, that they realised that all the tales – all lies – had a common source: Joe O'Reilly. He had calculatedly sown the seeds of division

between them, meanwhile isolating Rachel from her friends. He told her that he had met Paula Carney for lunch, for example, making it seem like a surreptitious act on Carney's part; in fact, it was four years since they had met for lunch. 'He was cutting off her escape routes,' says Carney.

These women believed him because they liked him, even loved him as a friend. 'Joe was my friend as much as Rachel was,' says Celine Keogh, a social worker, wistfully. 'He was very good to me. He did things like hire a van to help me to move house. He was very kind, very supportive, just a nice guy who would sit down for a chat and a cup of tea. I was able to confide very personal stuff in Joe. I really liked him. I knew he wasn't happy in his marriage. I just got on with it.'

At Keogh's karaoke and 'murder mystery' nights, he was the quick-witted 'hilarious' one. And he was kind. Bríd Horan, who knew him through softball, observed that if someone fell, he would be the first to run out with the first aid or to massage a tight muscle. 'And he'd always have this funny banter and innuendo going on,' she adds.

Women found him attractive then. He had two affairs – that we know of – in the last 18 months or so of Rachel's life; one with a sportswoman in the spring/summer of 2003, which fizzled out that same summer, and another, serious relationship with Nikki Pelley, begun following a work function in January 2004.

He was fitter and slimmer back then, says Horan, 'very tall and gently spoken, quite good on the softball field, a Kempo black belt, and very, very, very kind . . . If you saw him back in the early days with Adam [his and Rachel's youngest son], he'd be always laughing'.

He was also an achiever, working his way up from Arnott's stores, to senior management in Viacom Outdoor advertising at the age of 30, with responsibility for 26 workers. His family life as a child in Kilbarrack had been turbulent and difficult; his little sister, Martina, was born blind with Down's Syndrome; his parents separated. His mother Ann drove a minibus to make ends meet.

He was 20 and Rachel only 19 when they met in 1992. She was one of the five attractive, adopted children of Rose and Jim Callaly, a plumber, the centre of a vast, hospitable circle of extended family and friends. Five years later they were married, a couple of the Celtic Tiger, good-looking, vivacious, athletic, working hard, moving up, and moving out of Santry with their two little boys, to a home on its own grounds in the Naul in May 2003, with two cars in the yard.

But by then, six years into the marriage, with their sons, Luke and Adam, still only three and seven months, Joe O'Reilly was already into his affair with the sportswoman, already confiding to her − 18 months before Rachel's death − that anything less than full custody of the boys was not an option.

Paula Carney dates the deterioration in the marriage from the time he joined Viacom. Disappearances on overnight bus inspections, sometimes to Limerick and Cork, were routine. She had a friend working as a bill poster there who was often out putting up posters at 10 p.m. 'I'd say "but why would Joe be doing overnight inspections?" and [my friend] said, "he doesn't".'

For Rachel's 30th birthday in October 2003, Joe was on a softball trip to Florida, to which Rachel was not invited. Celine Keogh spent the birthday with her. That night, Rachel asked Keogh if she thought Joe was having an affair; Keogh said she didn't think so. Her friends knew that there was little love in Rachel's marital life. 'She'd say she couldn't remember the last time she kissed Joe, or the last time they had sex and that their beds were like musical chairs. One would get in and the other would get out,' says Carney. Meanwhile, Joe talked openly about 'not getting any' at home. 'He'd have you believe she was withholding sex,' says Bríd Horan, when they knew that the opposite was true.

The friends had concerns about the marriage. 'We could see that Joe didn't treat Rachel with respect,' says Keogh. 'As far back as 2001, I

Rachel O'Reilly with her son. Photograph: RTÉ

remember him roaring, "Are you f★★kin' stupid or what?" at her, and she cowered, with tears welling up in her eyes.'

In August 2004, the family holiday was in Blackwater, Co. Cork. 'He only went down for a day, said he couldn't get the time off. She was livid,' says Helen Reddy. He complained of a 'bad shoulder' and said the physiotherapist had told him not to wear his wedding ring. In September, rumours of an affair surfaced again. An O'Reilly relative heard Luke refer to 'Daddy's girlfriend Nikki' and told Joe to tell Rachel or she would be told by someone else. He told Rachel, in a jokey voice, that the relative 'thinks I'm having an affair and that I should tell you'.

Did the friends believe it then? 'We had no idea,' says Reddy. 'She laughed it off,' says Connor, 'and said "why would he have an affair when he isn't interested in sex?".' In a real sense, they had all lost touch with Joe in that last year. 'Rachel did everything in that house,' says Connor, 'from the DIY, to the accounts to the parenting. At her funeral, her DIY book was brought to the altar as one of the gifts. The only thing he did was burn the rubbish. I'd have seen Joe about five times in the last year. He was absent from the family, definitely from January 2004. She didn't have a family life.'

By May 2004, the once glowing, healthy young woman was 'very stressed, with psoriasis around her eyes, on her arms, between her fingers,' says Connor. 'She was practically a lone parent,' adds Horan, 'with two young kids – one at school and one in the crèche, a new house which she had found on her own and was trying to do up herself; selling her Avon and Tupperware and working part-time for a solicitor, and with a husband who was never there . . . and yet, she was always available, always, to her friends.'

It wasn't as if she was a perfectionist, they laugh. 'Rachel's house looked like it had been burgled. But lazy? Never. The complete opposite.' She was a force of nature, who gave 110 per cent in everything she tried; she loved nature, taught her boys to respect spiders and bugs, and how to do cartwheels; she was a 'Disney freak' who planned to get a Tinkerbell tattoo, screamed at her team on the hockey pitch, had no fashion sense, was never crude, came on like Madonna at the karaoke after a few glasses of red, and loved her 'sneaky' cigarettes.

Stories of Rachel's warmth, kindness, sense of fun and affirmation of her friends are legion. She insisted on Joe's sister Martina being included in family functions, cut her hair, and brought her gifts in her residential home in Ballymun. She never called without a gift of some kind. 'Yet she was always astonished if you ever bought her a gift or cooked her a meal,' says Keogh.

In June 2004, although none of them could know it, Joe was sending foul-mouthed, hate-filled e-mails to his sister, Ann, saying Rachel repulsed him and describing her as a 'lazy c★nt'.

The long diatribes reveal that his mother was the anonymous complainant to the social services about Rachel's parenting skills and that his greatest fear was of becoming 'Mr Weekend Custody' in a separation.

Ann responds that Rachel has organised Joe's mother to babysit the boys the following Friday and booked a meal out for herself and her husband.

'Where the hell did you hear I was going out with that c★nt?' he replies. 'A meal? I'd rather choke.'

Did the meal ever happen? Her friends remember Rachel's intense excitement that Joe, as she put it, 'was bringing her out to dinner', probably to Wong's in Clontarf. The outing was to finally mark her 30th birthday, 'a really rare, grown-up night out for her and she was making a big effort for her man,' Carney recalls. 'She said she was going to wear black trousers and a mauve top and her amethyst pendant and earrings and I was going, "make sure you wear lipstick, have your hair done".'

Carney rang her the following Monday to hear how she got on and found her 'terribly upset . . . She said Joe couldn't go for the meal because he got called to the office'.

Did she love Joe? 'Idolised him,' they agree. But she was wilting. During that last summer, Connor witnessed a 'huge argument' between them in the house, so explosive that she went outside. Afterwards, Rachel told Connor that she didn't love Joe any more but would try to make things work for the boys.

In the final months, says Connor, there was 'definite tension about an affair . . . There were rumours and she was questioning him a lot. She had laughed it off but I think she had a long, hard think. I was in Eddie Rocket's with her and the boys about nine days before October 4th [the day she was murdered], and she told me she did give him an ultimatum. He had gone to England and she'd spoken to him on the phone; there were to be no more late night inspections, he was to spend more time at home . . .' In court, however, Connor was only allowed to say that Rachel had said 'she wasn't happy in her marriage. She said family life was suffering because he was working a lot and she was on her own a lot.' It could have been a description of almost any Celtic Tiger marriage, not a dangerous spiral of hatred, betrayal and disaster.

On Friday, 1 October Rachel rang Carney. 'She was very upset, very depressed. She said she was putting on weight and that she needed to speak to me, that things weren't great at home.' Clearly, there was a sense of unease among them. On Saturday, 2 October Keogh mentioned a programme she had seen about men who murder their wives, which noted that they were often into martial arts and obsessions. They also dehumanise their wives by calling them names. 'I asked Brid and Helen, who does that remind you of?' She realised that Joe ticked the boxes: the Kempo black belt; the Star Wars obsession (he also collected knives); openly referring to Rachel as 'the Dragon' (they hadn't heard the worst, of course). And still, they now believe that Rachel was hiding much, even from her oldest friends. 'Rachel wanted to create a picture of a happy pixie family,' says

Horan, 'the house in the country, the nice lifestyle, the 2.4 children.' She was also a very private person, 'very dignified, very proper'.

This is why the loathsome e-mails between Joe and his sister were such a hammer blow in court for Rachel's friends and family. No one knew they were coming, not even her mother. 'Those e-mails are the voice of somebody who's already left,' says Horan. 'That's why he had no respect for her, because she still had expectations of him as a husband, so they became a burden to him and that's how the hate was breeding.'

'Rachel did not have a voice in that court,' says Connor. 'What was said in the e-mails was upsetting and devastating to us all, though she was living through it. The animosity that came through

The family of Rachel O'Reilly raise their hands in the air as they leave the court building after Joe O'Reilly, her husband, was convicted of murdering her. Photograph: Kate Geraghty.

from his family . . . we fear that the boys [Luke and Adam] will never know what their Mom was really like and the warmth she gave them.'

Far from the sadistic image of Rachel's mothering, painted by Joe and his sister, these women describe Adam as 'the Velcro child', always glued to his mother, and Luke as the one 'who idolised his Mammy and was the spitting image of her'.

Contact now between the Callaly family and Rachel's adored sons is intermittent at best. Nearly three years older, at seven and four, the boys no longer see any of the children or friends that were once their universe. It is believed that O'Reilly has since become a Jehovah's Witness.

Each of the five women admits that their sense of trust has been almost destroyed. 'I must have been the most gullible person,' says Helen Reddy, whose husband was one of Joe's closest acquaintances.

O'Reilly's extraordinary behaviour immediately after the killing should have alerted them. He took no part in her funeral arrangements. Rose and Jim Callaly paid for the funeral and the reception. He did not choose the coffin, and told the undertaker that he was not going to pay for a plot, as he was not going to be buried there. Eventually, his mother paid for it. It appears that while the Callalys own the grave in title, O'Reilly is legally next of kin and there remains a stand-off over a tombstone. On 'significant days', when the five friends take a bottle of red to share at Rachel's grave (as they did after the verdict), it is before a plain wooden cross marked with her name.

Joe O'Reilly leaving the Central Criminal Court during his trial for murdering his wife, Rachel, accompanied by his brother Derek and mother, Anne. Photograph: Cyril Byrne.

The bizarre behaviour extended to his demeanour – devouring sandwiches and laughing and joking with the media – before his appearance on *The Late Late Show* with the Callalys, appealing for help to find Rachel's killer. After the show, he left to spend the night with his lover, Nikki Pelley.

Nonetheless, Reddy managed to block out her suspicions for 10 months, until the day that Rose Callaly told her that she 'didn't know which side of Rachel's head she was holding', so mutilating were the injuries. 'And I thought oh my God, he [O'Reilly] told me where the cuts were on her head' – a reference to other evidence that never made it before the jury.

Within a week or two of the murder, he persuaded friends and loved ones to come to the house – having assured them that he felt Rachel was there and it was 'very peaceful' – while it was still spattered and soaked with her blood and gave them what he called 'the tour', during which he very calmly performed physical and graphic re-enactments of how, in his view, she was bludgeoned to death, how many blows were inflicted, how each pool and spatter of blood had landed where it had. The tour would end with him walking out of the bedroom to the bathroom whereupon he – as the killer – would hear her 'moaning' or 'gurgling' (choking on blood), and return to deliver several more blows to 'finish her off'.

Rachel's parents were among those forced to watch these performances, as well as her brother and his wife, and more than half a dozen close friends of his and Rachel's. Alan Boyle, a friend of Joe's for nearly 13 years, and who found him surprisingly calm when he made a sympathy call, wondered if she might have been having an affair. O'Reilly replied that he "'couldn't give a f*ck what Rachel got up to". He said that without a flinch,' added Boyle. 'That disturbed me.'

Defence counsel Patrick Gageby SC argued that Denis Vaughan Buckley SC, for the prosecution, 'was doing the Joe Duffy thing – "How did she feel?" – in an attempt to put into this case popular emotion'.

It was a tough case for the prosecution, relying almost entirely on circumstantial evidence. Joe O'Reilly's achievement was to commit a murder in which forensics could play no part to catch the killer, since the killer's DNA and prints were also those of the second adult occupant.

His first act when he arrived back to the house – after Rose Callaly, but before the police – was to fling items around the murder scene and to clasp his wife's body, thus ensuring that any DNA could have got there legitimately. It remains a mystery how he managed to commit such a bloody killing and to leave no marks outside the house. He may have had a shower – the bathroom, says Connor wryly, was 'spotless' – changed into another set of clothes and put the bloody clothes through a wash cycle. Asked where his gym clothes were, he said that his mother would have washed them. The kitchen tap was running strongly when Rose Callaly arrived, suggesting a calculated effort to wash away blood out of the system. Another piece of evidence not to make it before the jury was his left boot, on which was found a small bloodstain that, crucially, was 'airborne' when it hit the boot. This, however, had not been tested for DNA and dating it would have been impossible.

Nor was the murder weapon ever found. A decking spindle or hockey stick were considered. O'Reilly suggested to the Garda that it was one of his dumb-bells (one of which he reported missing, along with two bathroom towels). Almost farcically, certain items were left at the scene to suggest a burglary gone wrong – a black glove, a small necklace, as well as the careful placing of a 'stolen' camera bag and rucksack, in a culvert clearly visible from the road, with a tag 'O'Reilly Santry' on it. His willingness to divert suspicion on to innocents was notable: they included an NTL cable installer, Rachel's biological brother and mother; one worker whom he had sacked, and another who had run at him with a fire extinguisher when he sacked him and who, claimed O'Reilly, threatened to kill him and his family. Otherwise, he maintained his right to silence in hour after hour of questioning.

He outsmarted himself more than once. The Viacom van he claimed to see in Broadstone – the scene of his alibi – around the time of the murder, was in fact clamped that morning outside Pearse Street station.

And surprisingly, for such a calculated deed, he was clearly unaware of how powerful mobile phones are as tracers, although they had featured in several high-profile cases. When he claimed he was at Broadstone, a text from a friend placed O'Reilly's phone indisputably within half a mile of his home in the Naul.

Some mobile companies have systems where texts do not leave a trail; his downfall was that O2 Ireland's system does. He was also unlucky in

having such a determined judge on the bench.

For Rachel O'Reilly's family and friends, this is not the end. There are other battles to be fought. But perhaps the grieving can properly begin.

WEDNESDAY, 25 JULY 2007

'Every Day a Struggle' in Romania

Kitty Holland

Molodovar George, from a rural area near the city of Oradea in north-western Romania, says he 'borrowed money and sold all

Some of the Roma gypsies at the M50 campsites near Ballymun in Dublin. Around 30 remained at two makeshift camps following the departure earlier of about 70 others who had opted to return to Romania. The rest were eventually moved by Gardaí. Photograph: Matt Kavanagh.

possessions' to pay his €200 fare to Ireland. The middle-aged man came with his daughter and son-in-law and their four children. The Roma family has been living in teepee-type, plastic covered structures on a patch of mud off the M50 round-about near Ballymun for a month now.

About 30 Roma people remained between here and another makeshift camp across the road yesterday morning following the departure of about 70 others earlier who have opted to return to Romania.

'The police came and took many people this morning,' he says. 'The people who were inter-preting for the police told us we had to go, said we would get €40 if we went. But we can stay for another 15 days. I don't know what will happen then,' he says. Speaking through an interpreter he says he owes 'so much money at home' and has no prospect of work there. 'So I am not going back any time soon.'

Dressed in mud-slashed trousers, a mid-length jacket, sandals, socks and a woollen hat, he tells how he flew via Budapest to Dublin. 'At the airport the Hungarians asked us lots of questions. The Irish didn't ask any.' He and his family heard 'it was good living standard in Ireland'. People already living here told him he could get work in construction. 'I am a tiler. I build. I could build a whole house. But I know no one here who will give me a job.'

Asked about life in Romania, he says he had work 'all the time when there was communism. Now no one will give a job to Roma. Every day is struggle. Struggling to get food, worry about where to get food for your children, clothes for your children. So then you do things you don't like to do, to survive, like stealing.'

Their Irish home was yesterday reached down a wet, dirty path trampled into the mud, to the col-lection of about 10 small handmade shacks. Packaging, teabags and clothing sat deep in mud across the site; clothes hung on a makeshift line between two trees; the place smelt faintly of human waste and, probably, rotting food. Asked about the living condition here, Mr George shrugs his shoulders. 'It's not a good living standard but it's better than Romania.' At home he lived in a 'house made of horseshit and straw'.

Across the road, in the roundabout, is another muddy path down to where 31-year-old Marvara Rostas and her five-month-old son, Atei, remained living yesterday. 'They came this morning and sort of scooped them up,' she says of the others' depar-ture. 'I said "I don't want to go".' She is here with her aunt and uncle and says she is fleeing a violent, alcoholic husband as well as poverty. She shows a deep scar on her neck she says was inflicted by her husband.

She was told by a Roma family at home she 'would have a good life' in Ireland and her family raised money to send her here. Asked what she thinks now, she replies: 'I don't know what to believe anymore.'

THURSDAY, 26 JULY 2007

Sartorial, Soggy and Other Perils of the Sweltering Heat

Rome Letter: Paddy Agnew

It is time for a shameful confession. As regular readers of this letter will know, the Irish Times Rome correspondent would not dream of putting finger to keyboard without first putting on his Lord Reith-style dinner jacket. Decorum, after all, is decorum.

There have, however, been very hot times recently. (I realise that the mere mention of such climatic conditions is likely to prompt an unpleas-ant reaction among some of you. Even now I can hear the sound of Curragh season tickets being torn up as well as that of galoshes being dusted down.)

The point, however, is this. Such is the heat here that even your Rome correspondent has been

Diane Hayes from Enfield, Co. Meath, who was the winner of the Curragh Style Icon competition on Ladies Day. Photograph: Morgan Treacy/Inpho.

forced to suspend the dinner jacket in favour of more modest shorts and t-shirt. (Let us hope the editor is not reading this or I will be out the door, found guilty of failing to maintain traditional high *Irish Times* standards.)

There was a time when I used to measure the summer heat by its effect on the biro. In my first summer in Italy, many years ago, I left a biro on the dashboard of our little beat-up Fiat 127 when going off for a swim in the Gulf of Trieste. When I came back, the biro had melted into a splendid 'S' shape.

This startling discovery prompted weather analysts and forecasters worldwide to opt for the 'Agnew Biro Test' when assessing the impact of heat. Unfortunately, the net result for many

forecasters in northern Europe was that they found themselves with perfectly straight, totally soggy and unusable biros. Stationery expenses spiralled horrendously.

However, your fearless correspondent has just developed a new and perhaps more effective heat test, again one developed thanks to years of original research. It all came about when a chap was lazy about dumping the rubbish. Rather he took it out of the kitchen bin and then left it on the kitchen floor for dumping next morning.

It just so happened that one of the rubbish bags contained a half-consumed, half-chilled watermelon. Next morning, the kitchen floor was awash. Such was the heat of the night that the damned watermelon had melted into a huge and very sticky puddle. (Sorry, in these parts we have the heat at night too.)

Obviously, the watermelon lake in the kitchen prompted some harsh reprimands from the Baroness – indeed we experienced a rather 'mauvais quart d'heure'. (The Baroness, of course, is not always attuned with the niceties of scientific investigation, such as how chaps can discover all sorts of important things by merely getting into their baths.)

So, there you have it. Next time you are complaining about the Irish summer, or lack of, spare a thought for those of us who must manfully take up arms against a sea of melting watermelons and S-shaped biros.

For those of you back in the auld sod, however, the Rome correspondent does have some very good news. Your correspondent recently met Irish Foreign Minister Dermot Ahern in Rome. When he and his delegation finally sat up to the table (at first they were all bent over, wringing out their damp socks given that they had just arrived from Dublin), they gave me the good news.

Ireland is soon to have its long-desired roof. This will be called 'Bertie's Souwester' and will be a cross-Border, joint initiative that should cover most if not all of the 32 counties. Heat lamps and palm trees as well as comely maidens will be placed at all crossroads, dust will be imported from north Africa and town councils will be asked to lay in a supply of sombreros for heat-crazed council workers.

A word of advice, though, with regard to this forthcoming, technological miracle. In the new, 'covered' Ireland, be careful where you leave your watermelons and biros.

PS: The dinner jacket has just come back from the dry cleaner (note to the Editor – I promise I will be wearing it next week).

Yours in the Heat, Rome Correspondent.

MONDAY, 30 JULY 2007

Consumers Fight Back Against Rivalry and Planning Logjams

Paul Cullen

For years James O'Neill didn't get it. He went for the special offers, scrimped and saved, tried to make do, yet he always ended up short of money. Things just ended up costing more than he could afford.

A low-income single parent from Drogheda, O'Neill heard constantly from friends who travelled to Balbriggan and other towns in search of value. He could have joined them, or could have just complained; instead, he decided to bring the cheaper prices to his doorstep.

'We were being ripped off left, right and centre and we were letting it happen. The last straw was when I saw the town council block a plan by Lidl to open up a store here. I got five sheets of paper, started a petition and it quickly snowballed.' Over 17,000 signatures later, the council changed its stance and the Lidl store got the go-ahead. Now Drogheda has a Lidl and an Aldi and a second Lidl is opening shortly.

O'Neill's one-man campaign followed on one run by residents of Trim, who gathered 3,000 signatures in a successful bid to bring Lidl to the town. Last month, 7,000 residents of Kanturk joined this trend towards grassroots consumer activism with their call for the low-cost discounter to be allowed open in the Co. Cork town.

As least O'Neill has the new stores he fought for. Up in Donegal town, a series of battles between rival developers has stymied all retail development and the townspeople despair of ever getting a new supermarket. 'We're the meat in the sandwich in a fight between different interests. As a result, this part of the country is suffering drastically,' says Ernan McGettigan, the town's honorary mayor. 'We should be developing along with Letterkenny as the main hubs in the county, but instead we're 10 years behind.'

Last May, 400 people held a vigil to protest over the bickering between developers they say is killing the town. For the past seven years, a variety of schemes both in the town and outside it have been torpedoed, mostly by objections to An Bord Pleanála by commercial rivals. 'It has absolutely nothing to do with planning; it has to do with competitors trying to keep everyone else from going forward,' says McGettigan.

Donegal, which has a population of 4,000, has suffered 650 job losses in the past two years. McGettigan says new retail infrastructure to provide competition for the town's Supervalu store is urgently needed to attract fresh inward investment and stop the leakage of shoppers travelling to Sligo and Letterkenny.

As a butcher with a store in the town centre, McGettigan might be the first to feel the heat if large multiples were to arrive, but that hasn't influenced him. 'I would welcome Tesco or Dunnes Stores with open arms. If you're running a quality shop and providing reasonable service you should have no fear of competition.'

In the case of Donegal, commercial rivalry rather than planning considerations is at the heart

James O'Neill, outside the Lidl store he petitioned to have brought to Drogheda. Now he says some people see him as the 'biggest, baddest wolf in town'. Photograph: Alan Betson.

of the problem. However, the planning system, by facilitating objectors, has played a major part in the delays. Objections can add up to two years to the time it takes a retail development to come to fruition, according to Dermot Breen, corporate affairs manager with Tesco Ireland.

However, growth has been impeded by what Breen calls anti-competitive objections to new stores. In the decade since it came to Ireland, Tesco has opened almost 20 new stores – not bad perhaps, but less than half the rate it would like to have achieved were it not for serial objections.

In its home base in the UK, Tesco is often criticised as a monster, devouring all competition that comes in its path. Andrew Simms, policy director of the New Economics Foundation and author of a critical book called Tescopoly, claims the chain brings 'a level of aggression' to the market and, by dint of its size, competes unfairly with other retailers.

He says that if Ireland loosens restrictions on big out-of-town stores it risks creating a country full of 'ghost towns' with no local shops and 'clone towns' with little retail variety. 'You risk ending up like the dead zones in the US, with sprawling wildernesses in suburbia dependent on an inherently fragile, petrol-driven life of SUV drivers travelling to big box retailers. That is not a pretty future.'

Simms claims big retailers create fewer jobs than small shops; are often more expensive than markets for fresh goods; dissolve the glue that holds communities together; and cause money to leak out of the communities in contrast to small local shops which recirculate the money.

However, Breen says Tesco's position in Ireland and the UK is not comparable. 'We're not

Al Mennie, from Donegal, rides an Aileens wave off the Co. Clare coast. Aileens can rise to 60 feet between November and February. Photograph: Aaron Pierce.

as strong in Ireland as in the UK. Britain is a different market, with much higher population densities. If we're supposed to be so dominant, how come we're not the majority operators in most Irish towns?'

Chief among the objectors to Tesco's plans has been Rgdata, which is the grocers' federation but is actually dominated by the big distributors, especially Musgave (which owns Supervalu and Centra) and BWG (owners of Spar).

The battle between the large multiples – Tesco and sometimes Dunnes Stores – and Supervalu/Rgdata has been played out in large numbers of Irish provincial towns in recent years. 'In a lot of towns dominated by one retailer, their attitude is "keep the bastards out",' says one retailer of his commercial rivals. 'They throw the kitchen sink at you and then hope something might stick.'

Wexford, Carrick-on-Shannon, Youghal, Michelstown and Castlebar largely went Tesco's way, while in Loughrea, Cashel, Listowel, Tullow, Ballinrobe, Callan and Castleisland there have been delays or projects have been abandoned.

When asked about Tesco's experience of the planning system, Breen resorts to understatement: 'It's been a challenge certainly, but we've won most of the battles we fought.' The rules by which this war is fought are the retail planning guidelines introduced in 2001, which sought to limit the growth of out-of-town superstores by favouring town centres and limiting the size of food stores to 3,000sq m outside Dublin.

Rgdata says its objections to rivals' development plans are motivated solely by opposition to out-of-town centres. However, James O'Neill says it hasn't always stuck to the spirit of the guidelines itself; SuperValu's store in Clonmel, for example, is some distance out of town.

Tesco says it prefers to build in towns, provided a suitable site is available and the new stores do not add to traffic congestion – two mighty caveats in the circumstances. Breen also claims Irish towns are 'moving out' and development will soon arrive at the greenfield sites chosen for retail outlets.

Edel Clancy of Musgrave believes the guidelines are working well. 'They're doing what they are supposed to do – encouraging competition while maintaining the vibrancy of towns and villages.' She vehemently rejects Tesco's claims that her stores are serial objectors to rivals' plans, and points to towns such as Midleton, Glanmire and Carrigaline, where SuperValu stores live cheek by jowl with other retail outlets.

According to Henk van der Kamp, PRO of the Irish Planning Institute, the guidelines get the balance right between encouraging development in towns and not stifling growth outside.

A hierarchical approach to planning puts development in towns as the favoured option, but projects further out can get the go-ahead if it can be shown that no other sites are available. 'The competition issue lies completely outside the guidelines and that is the way it should be.' He says the cap on the size of retail units has worked well to prevent the rise of hypermarkets such as those seen in France.

The National Consumer Agency, whose acting chief executive Ann Fitzgerald believes 'the more competition the better', says local authorities should not be using the guidelines as a way of restricting competition.

There is, she says, a 'suspicion' that local retailers are using vested interests and the planning system to stifle competition.

The Consumers Association of Ireland is also calling for a review of the retail planning guidelines. Chief executive Dermot Jewell says consumer choice has improved significantly since discount retailers started opening stores around the country. Back in Drogheda, O'Neill has the cheaper shopping he craved but he still doesn't have full-time employment. 'For what I did, I'm the biggest, baddest wolf in town and people don't want to know when I go for job interviews.'

SATURDAY, 4 AUGUST 2007

'As He Lay Still on the Gurney, I Tried to Imagine His Last Moments of Consciousness. . .'

Denis Staunton

It was three hours before the state of Alabama was due to execute Darrell Grayson after 25 years on death row at Holman Correctional Facility, a maximum-security prison about two hours south of the state capital, Montgomery.

'It seems a little quieter on the exercise yard,' the guard said. 'This guy is more popular than most.' I was sipping coffee and nibbling a cookie from the prison bakery with two local reporters and a couple of prison guards as we waited in a low, brick building across the road. The guards expressed no pity for the condemned man but they showed no disrespect either as they spoke about him and the punishment he was about to receive.

Grayson was 19 years old when he confessed to one of the most brutal crimes committed in his home town of Montevallo, a few miles south of Birmingham. In the early morning hours of Christmas Eve 1980, two men broke into the home of Annie Laura Orr, an 86-year-old widow who stood just five feet and three inches. 'They entered Mrs Orr's bedroom, where she was apparently sleeping. They subdued and beat her, striking her in the head with a blunt instrument and breaking several of her ribs,' the court record said. 'Grayson then placed a pillowcase over her head and wrapped two relatively long lengths of masking tape very tightly around her head so that when they were finished her head appeared to be that of a mummy. They then proceeded to look for money and other valuables.

'During their assault, they raped Mrs Orr repeatedly. She lived through the assault of being raped, beaten, threatened, unable to see or adequately breathe, and begging her assailants not to hurt her but to take her money, for a considerable period of time. She then died.'

Police found a trail of playing cards leading from the crime scene to the home of 18-year-old Victor Kennedy, a petty criminal who had been drinking and playing cards with Grayson and two other men the previous evening. Grayson remembered nothing at first, because he had been so drunk after a drinking session that started at 5 p.m. He waived his right to have a lawyer present and, under questioning, admitted that he and Kennedy had decided to burgle Orr's house, where he had done odd jobs in the past. He said he put the pillowcase over Orr's face to prevent her from recognising him and admitted that he and Kennedy had raped her repeatedly. Kennedy tried to blame Grayson for both the rape and the murder, but both men were found guilty of murder during a burglary and sentenced to death at Holman Prison.

Grayson, an African-American, was tried before an all-white jury. His court-appointed attorney, who was given $500 to investigate the case, was a divorce lawyer who had never tried a capital case before. In the witness stand, Grayson again confessed to the crime but repeatedly said he was drunk at the time and couldn't independently recall the events. He also testified that he gave officers details of the crime that he didn't actually remember, based on what they said Kennedy had told them.

Passing sentence, the judge acknowledged mitigating circumstances, including the fact that Grayson had no prior history of violence or

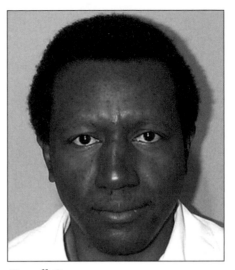

Darrell Grayson

criminal activity, that he came from a poor, single-parent family with 11 siblings, left school in the 10th grade, 'and had given his mother little trouble in growing up'. These factors were outweighed, however, by the aggravating factors of the rape and the brutality of the crime, which the court described as 'more characteristic of the actions of wild ravaging dogs of hell rather than even the lowest and most depraved level of humanity'.

Almost half of Alabama's 200 death row inmates are black, even though African-Americans make up only a quarter of the state's population. Although two out of three murder victims in the state are black, 80 per cent of the inmates on death row are there for killing whites. Death row inmates are overwhelmingly poor – 95 per cent of those at Holman are officially described as indigent. Alabama is almost alone among US states in having no state-wide public-defender system and does not guarantee appointed counsel for post-conviction appeals.

At Holman, death row inmates usually spend 23 hours a day in their cells, with an hour's exercise each day and a shower every other day. They can also leave their cells to attend church services and, on certain days, to visit the law library, which has mostly out-of-date books but functions as a day room where inmates play chess or draughts. Death row prisoners don't work, but friends and relatives outside can lodge money to PMOD (Prisoner Money on Deposit) accounts to pay for commissary items such as food and toiletries. They are allowed to own a TV if they can afford one.

When he arrived at Holman in 1982, Grayson 'wallowed for years in self-pity and ignorance until my mother's death became the catalyst for positive changes in my life', as he put it in an account of his case earlier this year in *Wings of Hope*, a journal written and edited by death row prisoners in Alabama.

He started to write poetry, which was published in magazines and chapbooks, and took educational courses that were then still available to Alabama death row inmates, receiving a GED (the US school-leaving certificate) and an associate science degree.

In 1994, he joined Project Hope to Abolish the Death Penalty (PHADP), a group run by death row inmates with the help of a handful of outside volunteers, becoming its chairman in 2000. 'During one of my quiet, lucid moments, I was shocked to realise the depth of loss and deprivation that is endured here on death row,' he wrote. 'I understood that each of us in our own way chooses to open the doors our own way, that can limit or increase the possibilities in our lives. Some doors open only onto the miseries of the world, overwhelm us and make us lose our focus . . . But there are other doors which we can choose that lead to spiritual growth and positive action.'

For 20 years, Grayson didn't question his own guilt, and Kennedy refused to talk to him about what happened the night of the murder. But on the night of Kennedy's execution in 1999, Grayson was taken from his cell to the captain's office. 'Victor had asked his personal preacher to tell me that he, Victor, asked for my forgiveness. I asked the preacher, "for what does he want my forgiveness?" The preacher told me, "that is not important",' Grayson said later.

In 2001, Esther Brown, a veteran Alabama activist against the death penalty, started to investigate the case and a witness came forward to say that Grayson could not have killed Orr because he was passed out elsewhere at the time of the crime.

Brown persuaded the Innocence Project, which has used DNA testing to exonerate more than 200 people convicted of serious crimes, to take up the case, calling for sperm taken from Orr's clothing to be matched against Grayson's DNA. If Grayson didn't rape Orr, the strongest plank in the prosecution's case linking him to the murder would collapse, leaving his own confession as the most compelling evidence against him. False confessions are not uncommon, even without evidence of police brutality, and DNA testing has cleared a number of people who claimed responsibility for high-profile murders they didn't commit.

In the weeks before Grayson's execution date, numerous groups and individuals including former taoiseach John Bruton, now EU ambassador to Washington, appealed to Alabama governor Bob Riley to stay the execution and order DNA testing.

The Innocence Project offered to pay for a test at a nationally accredited DNA laboratory, which could be completed within 30 days, but, with two hours to go before the execution hour, Riley said no, declaring that DNA testing would make no difference. 'DNA testing would neither prove nor disprove this killer's guilt. He was convicted of burglary and murder, not rape and murder, so legally DNA testing would not exonerate him even if there is no DNA evidence that he raped Mrs Orr,' the governor said. A few minutes later, the US Supreme Court rejected Grayson's appeal for a stay of execution with a two-line statement, closing off his last chance of avoiding death.

A guard came in with news of how Grayson had spent the day meeting friends and relatives, including his sister Betty, two nephews and a niece, as well as Brown and his attorney, Charlotte Norton. For his last meal, Grayson asked for a cheese omelette with fresh sliced tomatoes, and

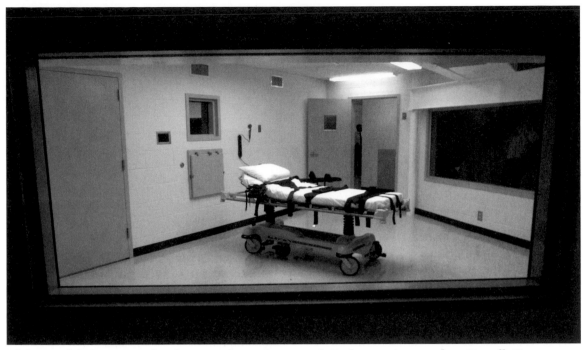

Alabama's lethal injection chamber at Holman Correctional Facility in Atmore where Darrell Grayson was executed. Photograph: Dave Martin/Associated Press.

during the afternoon he wrote his will: 'Inmate Mark Jenkins W/Z 527: 1 Sony radio, $100 from PMOD account. Inmate Jeffery Rieber W/Z 540: Assorted store items, $133 remaining money from PMOD account. Inmate Corey Grayson W/Z 598: 1 head phone set, 1 pair of shoes. Inmate Ronald Smith W/Z 586: 1 TV Sanyo. Esther Brown: 1 ring, assorted letters and books.'

At about 5.30pm, an officer patted me down, allowing me to keep a notebook and pen. Another told me that, if I changed my mind about witnessing the execution, I could back out. 'If you want to leave when you get in there because it's too much, or if you decide you don't want to see it, there's a small bathroom off the witness room and you can sit in there until it's over,' he said.

We piled into a white prison van and drove across the road to Holman, past the four-metre-high double-fencing topped with razor wire and through two gates to join a small procession of cars. In the exercise yard, a few prisoners stood in

silence, watching us pass a row of individual exercise cages on our way to the death house.

A heavy-set man in a short-sleeved shirt with a mobile phone strapped to his belt was chatting and joking with guards outside. The ears of a stethoscope stuck out of his back pocket – this was the county medical examiner, a qualified doctor who would pronounce Grayson dead.

We moved down a narrow corridor into a tiny room lit by a pink fluorescent bulb, with white, brick walls on three sides and a rectangular window taking up almost all the fourth wall. Sitting in the front row, our knees touching the ledge, were the three reporters, and Esther Brown, Grayson's sole witness.

Through a curtain, the shape of a hospital gurney was visible, with a few figures moving around it. Brown, a thin, grey-haired woman wearing a cotton print dress and a denim jacket, who had become Grayson's closest friend outside the prison, fidgeted and looked at her watch a couple of times.

A guard drew back the curtain and Grayson was lying just a few feet away, a lean, handsome man, dressed in a white prison uniform, draped in a white sheet and strapped to the gurney, his arms stretched out on black arm rests, almost in cruciform. Two drips attached to his right arm disappeared into a small square opening in the wall behind, next to a microphone hanging on a hook.

Grayson saw Brown and smiled and winked at her, flashing the peace sign with his fingers; he smiled at the chaplain, a thin, stern-faced man who was standing in the corner of the death chamber. Then Grayson looked through the glass on the other side of the chamber, where Lee Binion, Orr's granddaughter, was sitting. He smiled at her and she gave him a cold stare.

Holman's warden, Grantt Culliver, entered the chamber and approached the gurney. Culliver, an African-American, is obliged by Alabama law to carry out all executions at the prison himself. 'I look at it as part of the job,' he said in an interview two years ago. 'The people of the state of Alabama, because of the ways the laws are written, are as responsible as I am. I am the pawn or tool. The responsibility lies with the people of Alabama.'

As Culliver read the order of execution, Grayson's breathing quickened, his chest started to heave and, for the first time, a look of anguish crossed his face. When Culliver asked him if he wanted to make a statement, Grayson just said 'peace', and again formed the peace sign with the fingers of each hand.

Paul and Helen Cunningham from Fairhill in Cork city after collecting their cheque for €16 million, the largest Lotto win to date. Photograph: Eric Luke.

The warden left the chamber to start the process of execution in a small room next door, so Grayson was now alone except for the chaplain, who remained standing rigidly in his corner. Grayson was smiling again, looking over at Brown, who mouthed the words 'I love you'. He exchanged a few words with the minister, lay back and waited.

It was 6.04pm and the deadly chemicals must now have been coursing through the cannula into Grayson's vein but nothing seemed to be happening. 'What the hell are they doing here?' Brown said. A minute later, Grayson looked up, smiled one more time, turned to his right to look at Binion, and closed his eyes.

Alabama doesn't talk about the chemicals it uses in the lethal injection, but officials confirmed to me that the three drugs are similar to those used in other states. The first is sodium thiopental, a barbiturate to make the prisoner unconscious; the second is pancuronium bromide, which stops all muscle movement, except for the heart; the third, potassium chloride, stops the heart beating and causes death. A number of states have halted lethal injection executions after medical studies showed that inadequate dosing meant some prisoners may have died painful deaths by asphyxiation. Sodium thiopental is an ultra-short-acting barbiturate, the anaesthetic effect of which can wear off within minutes, so a prisoner could be conscious as the pancuronium bromide paralyses his muscles and asphyxiates him to death.

As the minutes crawled past and Grayson lay still on the gurney, I hoped he was feeling nothing now and tried to imagine his last moments of consciousness, the terror and the loneliness of dying in this empty chamber, surrounded by hostile faces.

I remembered my father's death long ago, how I held his hand and spoke to him as he drew his last breaths among those he loved. I pictured my own death and wondered if I would face it with the same grace shown by this poor convict.

I looked across at Binion, who had taken out a handkerchief and was dabbing her eyes. Suddenly, she was shaking violently as the tears rolled down her face.

It was 6.13pm and the medical officer, who had been sitting behind Binion all this time, stood up and took out his stethoscope, confident by now that it would register nothing. The curtains around the death chamber were drawn as the doctor approached Grayson and, three minutes later, declared him dead. 'Bloody murderers,' Brown said as she stood up.

Outside, in the prison van, the other reporters were filing their stories over the phone. Binion had issued a statement on behalf of Orr's family welcoming the execution. 'The family of Annie Laura Orr has seen the final chapter of this lengthy 27-year struggle come to an end. We are grateful that justice has finally been served,' she said.

As we drove away from Holman, a guard told me that just one protester had kept vigil outside the prison during Grayson's execution. 'Hell, even that's a lot,' he said.

WEDNESDAY, 8 AUGUST 2007

Wheeler Dealers

Kilian Doyle

Who among you remembers the lockhard men? Once as common on the streets of night-time Dublin as drunken teenagers, they're now thinner on the ground than lobsters in the Kalahari. Granted, the odd one or two still crawl out from under their rocks for big matches in Croker, donning their battered peaked hats, rolling up their *Heralds* and trying to cajole money out of hapless country folk unversed in the ways of the city.

But, the never-say-die culchie-vultures aside, the lockhards are an extinct breed, made obsolete by a combination of parking meters, multi-storey car parks, drink driving laws and, most importantly,

THE IRISH TIMES BOOK OF THE YEAR

Goatcatchers Frank and Francis Joy wrestling with a wild mountain goat in the shadow of Carrauntoohill. The goat was crowned King Puck at the annual Puck Fair in Killorglin, Co. Kerry. Photograph: Don MacMonagle.

people learning to tell them to get stuffed. They've been consigned to the dungheap of history like bus conductors and milkmen. Unlike bus conductors and milkmen, I'll shed not a tear for them. Useful as a chocolate fireguard, the whole shower.

I first came into contact with one of these vile specimens when venturing into the Big Smoke with my Dad. Trying to find a parking space off Nassau Street in which to squeeze his great boat of a Citroën DS, we were approached by a booze-sodden gouger sporting what he evidently imagined was an authority-endowing cap and a coat that looked and smelled like it was made of purest woven mildew.

'Howaya mister,' said he through a haze of Sweet Afton smoke, gesturing proprietorially over a vacant space. 'In here, bud. She'll be grand, boss,

I'll keep an eye on her.' My father stared contemptuously at him. The space was no wider than the crack of dawn. 'Arra, whatarye lookin' like dat fer? Ye could gerra bleedin' bus in dere, c'mon, back her up, back her up, lock hard, lock hard . . .'

'Dad, is he allowed do that?' I asked my father as we walked off after he'd grudgingly slipped a few coins into the blackmailer's grubby paw. 'Why didn't you just tell him to get lost?' My Dad sighed wearily. 'Because, son, we'd have no wing mirrors when we got back,' he explained.

'Why? Is it because he won't protect the car if you don't pay and then the bad boys will come and take them?' said I, with the wide-eyed naïvety of a mollycoddled eight-year-old. 'Sheesh, boy, your driveway doesn't quite reach the road, does it?'

Nine-month-old Thomas Loughney gets a lift with minder Rochelle Plank past Diarmuid Gavin's 'Pod' structure at the Electric Picnic at Stradbally in Co. Laois. Photograph: Brenda Fitzsimons.

Thus died my childhood innocence. I forevermore viewed the lockhards as deluded streetprowling sleeveens, thinking they were passing themselves off as harmless aul' Dublin characters, oblivious to the fact that everyone knew them for the extorting scoundrels they actually were.

Most were so stupid they'd lose an argument with a door handle. Still, even though their brains were only running on three cylinders, they had you by the bumpers. Everyone knew it was pay up or suffer the consequences.

The balance of payment was delicate. The amount you paid directly correlated with the amount of damage they'd do to your car. Underpay, and they'd accidentally scoop a hole out of your paintwork with a penknife or whip off your windscreen wipers with a theatrical flourish as

a warning to passing motorists. Overpay, they'd let the air out of your tyres to deflate your ego before retiring to the boozer. Get it just right and they'd simply stumble off, leaving your car to the mercy of the joyriders.

Gardaí turned a blind eye to their antics, left them to carve up their territories among themselves. Prime spots were guarded fiercely. I once had the singular joy of witnessing a fight between two lockhards near St Stephen's Green. A young usurper had evidently encroached on another's turf and fireworks flew.

The invadee grabbed the interloper by the neck, and started throttling him. 'Lock hard, lock hard,' taunted the swiftly-assembled gaggle of onlookers. The lockhards were not amused. I, on the other hand, was in stitches. I was about to offer

A replica Viking longboat, the Sea Stallion of Glendalough, *is lifted into the courtyard of the National Museum of Ireland at Collins Barracks in Dublin. The ship forms part of a Viking-themed exhibition that will run until June 2008. Photograph: Matt Kavanagh.*

to mind their caps for a quid a pop while they tussled when some wag beat me to it. Bad move. They turned on him as one and parked him in a dustbin. I imagine he's still got the scars.

SATURDAY, 11 AUGUST 2007

Unhappy Anniversary

DoubleTake, by Ann Marie Hourihane

It's been 100 days since Madeleine McCann went missing, and journalists are under pressure for a splash – but at what cost? Madeleine McCann disappeared 100 days ago today. If only we could say that she hadn't been seen since. But no child has been more visible, as carefully released photographs of her cute little face have been plastered over newspaper front pages, placards at the shrine at Fatima, and even the

windows of Irish homes. No parents have been more visible, either, than the McCanns, a photogenic couple who do not seem able to walk down a street without holding a cuddly toy belonging to their eldest daughter.

This media blitz has turned what is almost certainly a tragedy into a sort of freak show, and made gawkers of us all. The hysteria has been reminiscent of the death and funeral of the late Princess of Wales. It also seems to have been completely ineffective. Madeleine McCann is still missing. One hundred days is a long time for a four-year-old to be unaccounted for, and the Portuguese and British police do not appear to be any closer to finding the unfortunate child.

It is in the context of the 100-day anniversary that we must view the latest development in the McCann story. Because journalists covering the story will have been under pressure to come up with a big splash to mark it. The Portuguese police must know that the journalists are under the lash, and the McCann parents must know the same.

So the stories have started about blood stains being detected in the apartment from which Madeleine disappeared, giving us the Maddie-died-in-flat theory. The only suspect in the case, Robert Murat, has had the trees in his garden felled, as his home was searched again by Portuguese and British police. There has been an alleged sighting of Madeleine in Belgium (the DNA tests proved negative). In Switzerland, a convicted paedophile, Urs Hans Von Aesch, shot himself after being connected with the case. But, most significantly, the press looks as if it is turning on the McCann parents themselves.

To your average gawker, the behaviour of the McCanns has seemed strange from the start. They participated fully in media coverage of their daughter's disappearance. They always appear to be perfectly composed, and beautifully dressed. And gawking gets quite tiring. It is an uncomfortable moment when you are looking at television pictures of the mother of a child who has disappeared and the thing that strikes you most is that the mother's perfectly honed six-pack is visible under her tasteful vest; Kate McCann has been photographed jogging.

The McCanns have said that they made the decision on how they would participate in media coverage of their daughter's disappearance. They granted regular and constant access to the cameras – being photographed on their way to the shops, to Mass, to see the Pope, to the press conferences, frequently in the company of their younger twin children. The theory was that by allowing their photographs to be constantly taken, by giving strategic interviews when they so desired, they would keep their daughter's face on the front pages and so help her swift return.

As Madeleine fever swept across Europe – and children here are as familiar with Madeleine's face as they are with Avril Lavigne's – it never seems to have occurred to anyone that by maintaining such a high level of publicity the child's life may have been put in even more danger, by panicking her abductor.

It was noted quite early on that the Madeleine McCann tragedy is the perfect modern horror story: beautiful, professional parents (both Kate and Gerry McCann qualified as doctors), on holiday in paradise, undergo every parent's nightmare when their child is abducted by a faceless, monstrous intruder.

But this story can only run so long if both the monster and the little girl stay out of sight. At the beginning, little was made of the startling fact that the McCanns were dining some distance away at the time of their daughter's disappearance, leaving three children under the age of three completely unattended.

Back in England a local newspaper near the McCanns' hometown of Rothley closed down its website devoted to the case when this fact was repeatedly, and abusively, pointed out by local people – possibly the very same local people who were leaving pink teddy bears at the Madeleine McCann shrine in Rothley at the time.

Now the British press are turning on the Portuguese police, accusing them of incompetence, of turning on the McCanns and of leaking information to Portuguese newspapers such as *Diário de Notícias* and *24 Horas*. According to *24 Horas* this week, some of the friends who were holidaying with the McCanns at the time of Madeleine's disappearance – and there were seven of them – have been under police surveillance since their return to the UK.

So the story, having worn itself out over its first 100, is turning back towards home. There is now talk of a smear campaign against the McCanns, and Kate McCann is giving more interviews about how guilty she feels about having left the child unsupervised. Because gawking gets boring too, in the end. The child is still missing, and hope for her survival must be slim. Her parents' pact with the media is under severe strain.

TUESDAY, 14 AUGUST 2007

Fine Dublin Host Joins Ghosts of its Guests as Jurys Shuts

Patsy McGarry

It can now be revealed. Room 243 at Jurys Hotel in Ballsbridge, Dublin, was haunted. And, even more strange, there has been no sight of the ghost since the hotel and its two sisters, the Towers and the Berkeley Court, were sold to developer Seán Dunne in 2005. 'The ghost who upped and left' was followed yesterday by 608 staff. Head hall porter Vivion Sheehan spoke of it yesterday, sceptically. 'A shadow,' he said, 'could have been car lights.'

With Bach playing over the public address system and the last coach tour just departed, he was in melancholy mood. He spoke of other ghosts. Princess Grace, Dev, Yasser Arafat, Johnny Cash, the very much alive Mel Gibson, moonwalker Neil Armstrong, and The Rolling Stones, back in Ireland on Saturday to slay them at Slane. All stayed at Jurys on his watch.

It began 44 years ago in May 1963 when he saw an advert at the *Irish Independent* offices on Middle Abbey Street in Dublin. It was for a hall porter at the then Intercontinental Hotel, which was taken over by Jurys in 1972. He spoke of Jurys and its staff with an affection equal to that of

Vivion Sheehan, after 44 years working at the Jurys Ballsbridge Hotel, as the last customers prepare to depart, before it closed its doors for business in Dublin. Photographer: Dara Mac Dónaill.

Richie Bennis for his Limerick hurlers last Sunday. 'I really love this hotel,' he said. 'A landmark in Dublin. Wonderful, wonderful years. I'd love to do it all again.'

His feelings were echoed by general manager Glenn Valentine. There 20 years, yesterday was 'a sad and proud day'. His own association with the hotel has been a bit like that line from the Phil Coulter song 'The Town I Loved so Well'. He 'learned about life and I'd found me a wife...' His wife Diane worked at the Jurys Doyle group headquarters when they met.

Staff in Ballsbridge were 'like a family, a super bunch', he said. He was dreading his final address to them at 2 p.m. in Jurys ballroom. Upwards of 60 per cent of them had more than 20 years of service.

Seán Twohig recalled his days as night manager and how the lobby would be as busy at 3 a.m. as 3 p.m. each day with people queuing for the Coffee Dock, which was open 23 hours a day – it closed from 5 a.m. to 6 a.m. He remembered going along the queue at 4.30 a.m. to tell the likes of U2 or Daniel O'Donnell that it was unlikely they would get in. That was in the days when taxis were more rare and people would often stay on until 6 a.m. when the Coffee Dock reopened.

For Silvie Grossi from Italy and her Swiss boyfriend Charlie Ponti, it was something of a 'Last Breakfast Show', such was the attention showered on them over croissants and orange juice. They were the last to have breakfast there, it was their first time in Ireland and their first time to stay in a hotel which was closing. It struck them as 'a bit crazy', but they thought it 'a very nice hotel'.

Ester Schumpf from near Zurich was among the last guests to leave. She had been at the Dublin Horse Show and was a regular at the hotel. She was very surprised to hear it was closing. She believed there was no place in Switzerland where you would get such service. Then she was off to the airport in the last taxi.

The Oranges from Kent were regulars too. As they left for a last time, training supervisor PJ Ward

Model Rachel M wearing a handwoven cotton silk dress by Eilís Boyle and textured linen baubled scarf from Helen James as part of Dublin Fashion Week. Photograph: Brenda Fitzsimons.

waved after them. 'We'll meet again, don't know where, don't know when,' he chanted after them in a *Charity You're a Star* rendition of the Vera Lynn classic.

He spoke of how Yasser Arafat ate Rice Krispies with a teaspoon and how they broke the rules for Dana when she stayed there for three-and-a-half months during the 1997 presidential election by allowing her to eat breakfast in the lobby. Just the merest hint that more than a ghost has been kept hidden by staff at the three hotels over the years.

Identical twins Laura and Lisa Devane from Killarney, Co. Kerry, celebrating their Leaving Cert results, in which they got the same number of CAO points. The girls also got the same result in four subjects: art, biology, English and Irish. Photograph: Eamonn Keogh.

WEDNESDAY, 15 AUGUST 2007

Consumer Confidence at its Best

Quentin Fottrell

Sales of SUVs are up, consumer confidence is down and, in other news, my cleaning lady, Maria, went home to Romania for a few weeks and came back with a new set of porcelain teeth. She gritted them to show me. Clearly impressed, I said, 'Wow!' which encouraged her to open her mouth even wider. They are beautiful, and natural, too. Like Madonna, she cleverly kept the gap between the upper two she was born with.

I don't have middle-class guilt about having a cleaner. (On the contrary, it's bloody great!) I do have middle-class envy. She has a Hollywood smile; I still have my old teeth and painful whitening strips. But we understand each other. I started on £11,000 a year in London but, like a good little immigrant tourist, I was a regular in Harrods. I didn't have reason for consumer confidence, but that didn't stop me.

We have been indoctrinated to have the same aspirations, Maria and I, as we watch Dallas on UKTV Gold. 'Dallas? Very nice,' Maria said one day, as Sue-Ellen took another swig of bourbon. That was another thing we had in common. We both like a bit of glamour. She likes silk headscarves; I like cashmere sweaters. But we're not stupid: we both love Lidl.

'Lidl? Very nice. Cheap!' she says. And that's good enough for me. Unlike the dreaded Iceland, it has fresh produce, great parma ham, reasonable cheese selections and all kinds of everything. Everything except the brands we've been brought up with. This is what football teams and toothpastes have in common: they get you when you're young. Once your choice is made, you are hooked for life. I use Colgate. Always have.

Some brands are like mother's milk to us and, sure, not all Lidl's are successful. Its cheap razor blades were too good to be true. Unless we return to sharpening cutthroat razors like our grandfathers, Gillette will remain one of those recession-proof brands for men. But this is no reason why so many customers at my Lidl are foreign. This is partly because it's an urban area, but people have

SUVs to get there, don't they?

It is possible to debrand. Neil Boorman, author of *Bonfire of the Brands: How I Learnt To Live Without Labels* – published by Canongate in the UK next month – did just that. He lived without Gillette, advertising on TV and even made his own toothpaste. After years of being addicted to brands, he was free. He decided not to forego his mobile phone. He used a recycled handset, which he got for £20.

When the National Consumer Agency (NCA) published its first national comparison of grocery prices recently, it left Lidl off the list. It only compared Dunnes Stores, Superquinn and Tesco because they do the same brands. It says it will do another list with Lidl and Aldi, but it was still slavishly trying to compare like with like, and

Melanie Valanzoolo as Juanita in **The Taming of the Shrew** *in St Stephen's Green, Dublin. Photograph: Mark Stedman/Photocall Ireland.*

buying into the snob value of these brands by limiting its study. While the NCA said convenience stores are up to 20 per cent dearer than the big supermarkets, ValueIreland.com found the big three supermarkets are up to 25 per cent more expensive than the more taboo Lidl or Aldi.

We should be secure enough in our skins to embrace our inner yellow packer, not live in fear of it. Sarah Jessica Parker was reportedly seen in Lidl in Donegal. That should be enough for us lemmings to follow.

Even Eddie Hobbs, a walking, talking brand, is part of this sale of the century, though his Yoda-, sorry, Yeddie-like philosophy relies on gombeens who buy stuff on hire purchase and have multiple credit cards. His *You & Your Money* magazine has ads for furniture, timber floors and Scandinavian-style chalets with an orange glow, beckoning to be filled with your happiness.

Hang on. Wasn't he supposed to be saving us money? Yes, but . . . What could be better for mortgage brokers, estate agents, insurers, security firms, lighting showrooms, landscapers and – last but not least – building societies, banks and online spread betting companies than to hitch their sails to his trusty pole? It's not enough to keep up with the Joneses – we must keep up with the Dow Jones, too.

My cleaning lady may have the taste for the high life, but she is too wily to fall for stunts such as I'm Not a Plastic Bag, the limited edition 'green' accessory by Ana Hindmarch. It was like the fall of Saigon when it went on sale in Dublin and Cork. Hindmarch cancelled launches in Beijing, Shanghai and Jakarta, citing 'concerns for customer safety'. Like, what are we like, like? I want a bag all right. A sick bag.

I don't begrudge Maria her new chops. She could have saved for a Smeg oven or a Chevrolet, which advertise in Hobbs's magazine, though a new motor is a bad financial decision as it is a rapidly depreciating asset. (Sorry, Yeddie.) Let us hope that when Foxrock Fannies realise SUVs are really the preserve of the socially insecure, rather than giant baby tanks, they will go the way of Burberry check.

Still, I'm glad Maria didn't spend her money on a new kitchen. They say that you can't take it with you. But, at least in the case of porcelain teeth, you actually can.

TUESDAY, 21 AUGUST 2007

Lawful Way for O'Dea Is to Resign

Fintan O'Toole

Last May, members of the Opposition attempted to ask the Taoiseach questions about the cabinet subcommittee that was then deciding on the privatisation of Aer Lingus. Bertie Ahern refused to answer.

'Questions as to the business conducted at cabinet or cabinet committee meetings have never been allowed in the House on the grounds that they are internal to government. The reasons for this approach are founded on sound policy principles and the need to avoid infringing the constitutional protection of cabinet confidentiality.'

The 'sound policy principles' that were invoked by the Taoiseach are those to be found in Article 28.4.2 of the Constitution: 'The Government shall meet and act as a collective authority, and shall be collectively responsible for the Departments of State administered by the members of the Government.'

As Séamus Dolan of the law faculty at NUIG has explained with admirable succinctness: 'The concept of cabinet confidentiality flows from the notion of collective responsibility, as referred to in Article 28.4.2. Collective responsibility mandates that individual ministers present a united front to the public, and individual ministers must each offer public support for government decisions and policies, regardless of their own private or personal views on the topic. This, by implication, means the individual minister is not entitled to criticise

Michael Landers, Assistant General Secretary of Impact (left), and Capt Evan Cullen, President of the Irish Airline Pilots' Association (Ialpa), outside the Ialpa offices at Dublin airport, just before announcing the suspension of the proposed strike by Aer Lingus pilots. The picture amused some readers who spotted the chicken standing by the door. The bird was subsequently identified as 'Willie Walsh', a pet adopted by pilots who throw him scraps every now and then. Photograph: Kate Geraghty.

government policy or decisions if he wishes to retain his ministerial office.' Or, as the all-party committee on the Constitution put it even more succinctly, 'the only way to record dissent from a government decision is to resign.'

This is precisely what a number of honourable politicians did when they wanted to dissent from a policy position adopted by a government in which they served. Kevin Boland (and his parliamentary secretary Paudge Brennan) did so in 1970 over the arms crisis. Frank Cluskey did it in 1983 over the government policy on Dublin Gas.

In November 2003, Willie O'Dea's predecessor as minister for defence, Michael Smith, dissented

from the health policy of the government of which he was a part when he supported protests in his own constituency against the downgrading of Nenagh hospital. But he quickly apologised to the Taoiseach and issued a statement saying that it had not been his intention 'to breach the rules of collective cabinet responsibility or to undermine the efforts of his colleagues to implement government policy', and that 'he deeply regretted giving the appearance of being at variance with government policy.' The apology was the only alternative to resignation.

Four years ago, therefore, it was completely unacceptable for the minister for defence to play to the gallery in his own constituency by contradicting government policy and disowning the local consequences of decisions for which he himself was jointly responsible. Last week, in a statement issued through the Department of the Taoiseach – implying that she was in effect acting Taoiseach at the time – and explicitly 'speaking on behalf of the Government', Mary Hanafin issued a strong statement of its policy on the Aer Lingus decision to end its Shannon to Heathrow service.

She could not have been clearer about Government policy on the matter: 'As a listed plc, Aer Lingus has to take its own decisions. It is inappropriate for the Government to intervene in the decision making of a private company. To do so would ultimately be damaging to the company and its customers.'

Willie O'Dea is clearly and strongly opposed to this policy. He believes that the Government should support a Ryanair move to convene a shareholders' meeting to reverse the Aer Lingus decision. He believes that political pressure should be brought to bear: 'We will sit down and we will try and persuade them that they are wrong and we will try and persuade them to change their minds. If they don't change their minds, then there are other options.'

He told us Minister for Transport Noel Dempsey doesn't really understand the issue. He also strongly implied that the Cabinet is split on the issue: 'When the Cabinet meets, we will see if I was as totally isolated as I appear to be.'

Three things are absolutely clear here. Firstly, a Government decision not to interfere with the

Aer Lingus Chief Executive Dermot Mannion holds a model Aer Lingus aircraft after an engine fell off it during a photocall at Stormont with Northern Ireland First Minister Ian Paisley to mark the setting up of a regional hub at Belfast International Airport. Photograph: Paul Faith/Press Association.

Aer Lingus move was taken last week – otherwise Mary Hanafin could not have issued her statement. Secondly, Willie O'Dea profoundly disagrees with that decision. Thirdly, the only lawful and constitutional way for Willie O'Dea to express that dissent is to resign from the Government. Logic implies a fourth conclusion: Willie O'Dea's behaviour over the last week has been utterly unconstitutional.

The levels of hypocrisy involved in all of this are stratospheric. The man whose job it is to defend the State has been flouting its basic law. The principle that is so important that it justifies extraordinary levels of State secrecy means nothing at all when political expediency demands otherwise. It is unconstitutional to reveal even the agenda for a meeting of a Cabinet subcommittee, but fine for a Minister to dump collective responsibility when it becomes inconvenient.

The governmental chaos of the last week may look like anarchy, but it is really a form of autocracy: the Government owns the Constitution and can do with it what it likes.

WEDNESDAY, 22 AUGUST 2007

Kindly Tory Loyal to Craft of Journalism

Kieran Fagan

It was the voice I recognised. On a dreary November Sunday evening in Belfast, in the near-empty foyer of the Europa hotel, an old man tottered towards me. 'Do you know where the recepshun for the Shociety of Editorsh is being held, dear boy?' Bill Deedes inquired.

'Come on, I'll show you.' And so we stood at the pedestrian crossing on Great Victoria Street waiting for the lights to change. 'Not too shteady, dear boy, take your arm, if you don't mind.'

He asked where I was from. 'Dublin, yesh dear boy... Mother's people were from Dublin, Chevenix, sholicitors, Merrion Shquare . . . don't

make too much of that connection around here, shome of them don't go for it.' A huge security man stood in the door of a pub. 'Lord Deedes,' I announced grandly and we swept in.

I looked around for a seat for him in the small crowded room. He shook his head, and made for the bar. As I left an hour later, Bill was tête-à-tête with the prettiest woman in the place.

Next morning, Deedes showed up just as the first session of the conference began. He was out of breath. 'Very ugly shenes,' he said. He had been to Holy Cross school in the Ardoyne, where Catholic children had run the gauntlet of violent loyalist demonstrators to get to school, while the other hundred visiting hacks ate a posh breakfast. Deedes knew his duty – to bring those 'ugly shenes' to the notice of the wider world.

And in that brief tableau you have the whole man. The four careers in one. The young war correspondent in Abyssinia in 1935, where a version of him became the character William Boot in the Evelyn Waugh novel *Scoop*; the officer decorated for bravery in the second World War; the MP for Ashford in Kent in the 1950s, becoming a minister, who left politics to become editor of the *Daily Telegraph*, and then his last two decades as a roving reporter and much loved columnist.

Each could serve for a full life, but with Bill Deedes they are just pointers to the extraordinarily inquisitive yet respectful, diffident yet persistent, streak which took every opportunity life gave him.

When Max Hastings replaced him as *Telegraph* editor in 1986, Deedes went back to being a reporter. He recognised the opportunity offered by 'new technology'. The reporter with a laptop computer and later the 'satnav' phone, the electronic notebook, could travel the world, filing immediate copy from the scenes of great events and disasters.

The next two decades were the most fruitful. He went to Angola and Bosnia with Princess Diana, reporting on her anti-mine campaign. He criss-crossed the world in his late eighties – Angola,

Nargiza Yusupova of the Lyazgi troupe dancing with 'Rhythms of Uzbekistan' as part of the Festival of World Cultures in Dún Laoghaire, Co. Dublin. Photograph: Matt Kavanagh.

Kenya, Zimbabwe, India, where he suffered a slight stroke which he blamed on not being able to get whisky in a 'dry' state, but still wrote his reports and sent them back to London.

He reported from Darfur in his 90th year. His writings were clear, like letters home from a much travelled if slightly old-fashioned uncle. The facts first, then a slight change of pace as, metaphorically speaking, he folded his arms, and rocked back on his heels. 'If I might venture an observation . . .'

His manners, on and off the page, were impeccable. In person, he had the English habit of needing to address you by some handle, if not your name. 'My dear', 'old boy', 'Shquire' and even 'my lord' were deployed.

He was a High Tory, but recognised the responsibility for the less well off his party discarded in the Thatcher years. His army years formed him, but did not silence him on the evils of bullying in the military. A recent return to the battlefields unsettled him.

'In old age it is disquieting to be reminded how many young men on the threshold of life died in Normandy.' He lit a candle in memory of the German dead.

He had the countryman's eye for the 'harbingers of spring, the white candles of the horse chestnut blossom,' seen from the window of his Kent home, as a *Telegraph* reader reminded us this week. He liked cricket and rugby too, and was pained by the ban on hunting. My last note from him in 2003 quotes 'Mr Jorrocks of the Old Surrey and Burstow' hunt, a favourite reference.

The public persona, the figure of fun of the spoof Denis Thatcher correspondence in the satirical magazine *Private Eye*, his 'shome mishtake surely' understated response to yet another item of misinformation, amuses but tells us very little.

His celebrated reply to letters from incandescent readers lambasting the *Telegraph* for being mealy-mouthed about the restoration of hanging, or some other Tory article of faith — 'My dear Brigadier, I feel there is much good sense in all that you have to say to me' — has gone around the world.

His friend and fellow editor Charles Moore came closest to explaining Bill Deedes to us when he observed that conservatives must choose between being grumpy and bloody-minded about the modern world, or express the more kindly part of their culture, and that was the way Deedes chose.

For those lucky enough to work in journalism, the example is clear. Go and talk to people, listen to what they say. Then tell it in as straightforward and unvarnished way as you can.

And if as a reader you have a decent newspaper to read, like this one, you probably owe much of it to those who loved Bill Deedes and were inspired by the way he practised his craft.

Cheerio Shquire, we'll miss you.

Bill Deeds died on 19 August aged 94. His final article for The Daily Telegraph *— comparing the horrors of Darfur to those of Nazi Germany — was published on 3 August.*

FRIDAY, 24 AUGUST 2007

Rabbitte Staked All on Opposition to FF

Stephen Collins

The timing of Pat Rabbitte's resignation came as a surprise but the decision itself wasn't a complete shock. His six-year term as leader was due to expire in October of next year and he had to decide well in advance of that whether he wanted to stay on and lead his party into the next election or bow out before a divisive challenge.

Rabbitte pointed out yesterday that he went into the recent general election with the twin objectives of winning more Labour seats in the Dáil and forming an alternative government in alliance with Fine Gael. In the event, Labour won the same number of seats but, much more crucially, failed to get into power.

'As leader I take responsibility for that outcome,' he said, adding, 'I had my stint. I gave it my best shot.' However, he was not prepared to accept that he had made the wrong strategic decision to fight the election as part of an alternative alliance with Fine Gael.

'I remain absolutely convinced that it was correct at the time to offer the people the choice of an alternative, reforming government. It was not successful but unsuccessful only by a narrow margin.'

While the majority of his party members supported his strategy, a number of senior figures in the party and in the trade union movement disagreed profoundly with it. They wanted to keep open the option of going into power with Fianna Fáil after the election. There was no open revolt but it was hardly a secret that some were unhappy.

After the election, rumours of contact between some disaffected individuals in Labour and Fianna Fáil served to persuade the Greens that if they did not do a deal with Bertie Ahern, then Labour ultimately would. That influenced the dynamic within the Green Party and led to the overwhelming vote of party members in favour of coalition.

With the Fianna Fáil-Green-Progressive Democrat government securely in place by the beginning of the summer holidays, Rabbitte had to weigh up whether there was any point in staying on as leader until next year, when he would almost certainly face a challenge.

The chances are that he would easily have seen off any opponent, as his strategy had the support of the majority of party members, but a contest would not have helped his long-term chances of doing better in the next election.

More to the point, he had to ask himself whether he wanted to face the prospect of another hard five-year slog until the next election in the hope that the result might be different. Having rolled the stone all the way up the hill once, Rabbitte clearly decided he did not want to become a Labour Sisyphus, condemned to repeat the endeavour over and over again.

It was the timing of Rabbitte's departure before the end of the summer that was the real cause of surprise. There was a feeling in the party that he would wait to see how things developed in the autumn after the Taoiseach has given his evidence to the Mahon tribunal. There was also a view that he would wait and give his new TDs and Senators a chance to show their paces before deciding on his future.

Another reason for the surprise was that a national executive meeting was scheduled for September 1st, the parliamentary party is due to meet for a day-long session on 18 September and a national conference is scheduled for November in Wexford.

Nobody in the party was expecting Rabbitte

Eamon Gilmore at Leinster House after he announced his candidacy for the leadership of the Labour Party.
Photograph: Matt Kavanagh.

Monica Loughman, who performs in Cork City Ballet's Giselle, *the tragic story of a peasant girl who dies and returns from the dead to save her lover, at Jurys Hotel in Cork for the launch of the opera house's new season of events. Photograph: Michael Mac Sweeney/Provision.*

to go before the September 1st meeting. It seems, though, that after thinking things over during his holidays in Kerry, he decided to make a clean break so that a new leader could be in place early in the next Dáil session.

Liz McManus, the deputy leader, is now the acting leader of the party and will remain in the post until a new leader is elected. The procedure to be followed is that at the National Executive meeting on September 1st, a closing date will be set for the receipt of nominations for leader. The election must be held within 45 days of that and all members paid up for the past two years will be eligible to vote. The method of election will be by single transferable vote.

There was no immediate rush to join the contest, with McManus keeping her options open

when asked if she would be a candidate. The recently appointed Leas-Cheann Comhairle, Brendan Howlin, was also keeping his options open, saying he would take soundings and think about the issue before coming to a final decision.

Howlin was defeated for the leadership by Ruairí Quinn in 1997 and again by Pat Rabbitte in 2002. It could be third time lucky for him but he may be reluctant to take the risk. He will also have to decide what to do about his recent elevation to a post that carries the salary and perks of a Minister of State.

Eamon Gilmore, the other defeated candidate from 2002, has already been installed as the bookies' favourite. An effective performer inside and outside the Dáil, he would be a formidable candidate.

There are a number of other possible candidates. Róisín Shortall ran the last time around and may do so again as the representative of the left-wing TDs not enamoured of the Fine Gael alliance. Joan Burton, the party's finance spokeswoman, is a formidable intellect who has broadened her base in the party in recent years, while Willie Penrose, who represents the more traditional rural wing of the party, is another possible contender.

The last leadership election in 2002 generated a healthy debate within the party. Rabbitte emerged as the victor precisely because he convinced the members that he would not do a deal with Fianna Fáil.

He repeated his belief yesterday that to have gone into power with Fianna Fáil after the recent election would have done serious long-term damage to the Labour Party. It will be interesting to see if the views of the membership have changed on this issue following yet another Fianna Fáil election victory.

TUESDAY, 28 AUGUST 2007

Living Off the Soft Shoreline

Lorna Siggins

They call him 'Johnaí Dubh', and his nut-brown complexion reflects a life spent through all weathers and all seasons on the south Connemara shoreline. When we caught up with him on an early morning low tide in Carna, Co. Galway, he had already put in almost half a day's toil – on his own, and entirely by hand.

With his back to the sea and bent over double, Johnny Clochartaigh was sliding his knife over rocks as deftly as a barber trimming heads. 'I'm working on a climín,' he explains, a bale of seaweed. He is effortlessly gathering feamainn bhuí, a specific type of seaweed, to make several bales for the factory. Watching his technique, it seemed as if this might take for ever – in fact, he estimates that one climín takes 90 minutes to prepare.

Clochartaigh, who will be 50 next April, was born and bred in Mweenish as one of seven brothers in a family of 11. He's the only professional seaweed harvester among them, and one of a dwindling number on the Connemara coast. 'My grandfather did it, and my father did it, and my eldest, now 21, worked with me till he was 18. But you would never get rich on this, and it is such hard work that it is not something that the young people want to do.

'I don't blame them either,' he says, as he continues working his knife, transforming those first few clumps of Ascophyllum nodosum into a substantial mound. 'My son trained in film and now he is working on Ros na Rún for TG4. The girls are at college and school. My youngest, Katie, is 14 and she likes to come shrimp-fishing with me – she'd love to be down here now too. But there are other, easier ways to earn a living.'

Clochartaigh passes me the knife to show me how it's done, pulling the blade towards him with one neat stroke. Does he not use gloves? 'Never. You get a better grip of the weed with your fingers, but then you have to make sure you don't take the tops off your fingers too.'

Catching a clump, the first slice I make is a little too deep. 'You've got to make sure you don't take the holdfast,' he explains. 'That way, the feamainn bhuí grows back in the salt water and sunlight. It takes about five years for it to return to full harvestable length then. Any earlier and it isn't ripe enough for the factory.' Apart from the knife, his only equipment is a good pitchfork (previously used by his father), ropes, wellington boots – and his currach tied to the pier. 'I start with the low tide, and I don't stop till the sea is behind me,' he laughs.

In that six-hour cycle, he will have made several climíní which will be bound up and towed by his boat into shore. A lorry comes from the

Johnny Clochartaigh among the seaweed he harvests near Carna, Co. Galway. Photograph: Joe O'Shaughnessy.

factory in nearby Cill Chiaráin twice a week to collect his harvest, for which he says he is paid all of €38 a tonne.

The 'factory' is Arramara Teo, a State-sponsored body and one of the longest surviving manufacturing operations west of the Shannon, according to its manager, Donal Hickey. Arramara is marking its 60th anniversary this year as seaweed processor for the agriculture, horticulture, aquaculture and alginate industries.

This 2,700-mile coastline has 501 different species of seaweed, some 19 of which have commercial use worldwide and 16 of which are being exploited for substances such as alginates, which are used as gelling agents for ice cream, binding agents for tablets, wound dressing and dental impressions, and in textile and electrode production.

James Bond once had to risk his life for the formula, and various types of the weed – which the Japanese call sea vegetable because of its many valuable nutritional properties – are also used in fertiliser, as top dressing for soils, in biochemistry and biomedicine, for cosmetics and thalassotherapy and as tasty food snacks.

Clochartaigh hasn't been to Japan – he hasn't left Carna, he says, and sends his wife and kids on holidays: 'I like to stay here.' He keeps a few cattle, uses seaweed to fertilise potatoes in spring, and knows that there is nothing like carrageen moss for a chest infection. Yet the full significance of the resource around him seems almost ephemeral, as he moves alone, along a largely deserted shore.

'There used to be five or six around me,' he says. Now, the only sound is of the sea, a heron or two in the distance, scavenging rock pipits, and the incessant chattering of almost invisible brown crabs around him. 'Arramara is driving up to Belmullet, north Mayo, to get enough of the harvest. The thing is that there's plenty of crop, just not enough people to cut it.'

Donal Hickey of Arramara says that the company is well aware that hand harvesters are getting older. He estimates that about 300 work at it part-time in counties Galway and Mayo, and about 100 of those, including Clochartaigh, would harvest for most of the season. 'Our plant in Donegal closed in 2001, and there's a little bit of harvesting going on there now, but on a small scale,' he says.

'We are looking at ways of increasing the productivity of those harvesters we have, such as quicker techniques for collecting cut weed. In countries like Norway, harvesting is done mechanically by boat in inshore areas, but here the nature of the terrain is such that it is best done by hand. And there's a demand for what is perceived to be a wild, organic product, with export markets for our raw material in the US, in Asia, France, Germany and Italy.'

Even Japan buys in feamainn bhuí which has been dried and bagged and graded by Arramara. 'It is used there as an animal-feed supplement,' Hickey says. There is some processing of raw material here, by companies such as Brandon Products, for application in liquid-horticulture treatments, but adding value in Ireland is a concept that Arramara would like to translate into reality, Hickey says. Seven years ago, a report on the sector estimated that it was then worth €8.8 million to the economy. The national seaweed forum report forecast potential multiples of this figure with further research and development – and emphasised its considerable, inestimable, socio-economic value. But with demand always exceeding supply, the big challenge for companies such as Arramara is not only finding skilled harvesters, but also maintaining access to the shoreline.

In Johnny Clochartaigh's case, his family has worked Mweenish for generations, but there are other areas of the Connemara coast where he might not be so welcome. 'Spiteanna feamainne' is the local term for long-held seaweed rights, established at a much more difficult economic time, when the pickings from the shore sustained small farms and vegetable plots. Thus, even where the weed is not being cultivated, there are families who will fiercely defend their fiefdoms – a situation which a current updating of the State's foreshore legislation might seek to clarify.

And how would Clochartaigh feel if some of the new Irish from Galway were to join him on his patch of shoreline? 'I'd be delighted,' he says, without hesitation. 'There's way more than enough here for everyone.'

We come across some upturned broken bottles, and other debris. 'You have to be so careful, but it is a lot easier now that people are no longer dumping rubbish off the pier,' Clochartaigh says. 'Sure it is all so regulated now that we are wearing life-jackets just towing in the climíní.'

With that, he recalls how 18 years ago he almost lost his life in his currach when collecting pots. 'I do the shrimp fishing for two months of the summer – there's a truck comes all the way from Spain to buy from me, imagine,' he says. 'This day, I was out just off Mweenish when the currach went over and I had no jacket. I was lucky to get out of it – I remember climbing up on the boat.'

That coastal area, known as the Inner Passage, is replete with submerged rocks and shoals – a mirror image of the Twelve Pins mountain range which Clochartaigh can view to the north. Just 15 years later, in September 2004, the *St Oliver* fishing vessel was lost with all four crew on its way from Carna to Rossaveal. 'It went up on the very same rocks,' he says.

Clochartaigh takes his pitchfork, shakes up the cut weed, and lays out his ropes at right angles. He forks in the feamainn bhuí to make a neat, rectangular bale, and shows me how to tie it up with slip knots. 'I'll be back this evening now at full tide to tow it with the currach,' he says.

'The factory always needs the weed to be fresh, clean, and not too soft – which is why I am hoping it won't rain before the truck comes. When

I was working with my father, we had to fork it twice, as it was taken away on a donkey and cart.' He places the tied rope under a sturdy rock. It looks fairly tranquil now at low tide. However, just a year ago, a seaweed harvester preparing a climín further south was lost when he was washed into the sea. 'You're always watching that you don't slip,' Clochartaigh says. 'And then there are the days when the wind gets up before you have the climín tied, and it scatters the weed and breaks your heart. Best day is a good dry frosty day in winter. Then I wouldn't want to be anywhere else.'

SATURDAY, I SEPTEMBER 2007

Roysh Here, Roysh Now . . .

Ross O'Carroll-Kelly

'Have you seen her yet?' That's what he goes to me, over his shoulder, sitting in the bench in front of me.

I'm like, 'Who?' and he's there, 'Herself, Ross. Madam! No invite to the garden party this year. Understandable,' he goes, flicking his thumb in the direction of the judge, 'in the circumstances.'

I'm there, 'I've already told you – I only go in there to pick up my expenses. And you've a lot more to worry about than gorden porties. You're looking at a five-stretch here. How the fock could you do it – as in, like, plead guilty?'

He's like, 'Because I am guilty, Ross – according to the standards by which I'm being judged.'

I go, 'I thought you'd put up a fight. What about all that stuff you said to me about the gleaming new Ireland, with infrastructure and investment and full employment, and how that was always your vision of the future, and the vision of all those others currently being pilloried before the tribunals?'

He doesn't answer.

I'm there, 'You just want to be a mortyr – for all your mates out in Portmornck. I can't believe you settled with the Revenue . . .'

'And the Criminal Assets Bureau,' he goes, not ashamed of it or anything.

I'm like, 'You gave them everything, including my Z4. Have you any idea what an actual dickhead you are?'

The judge goes, 'I'm sure we're all very interested in your Z4, whatever that might be, but if you two are quite finished, we'll proceed with the case . . .'

******

She's, like, pretty surprised to see me, though not as surprised as I am to see her, standing there under a banner that says, Mount Anville Class of 1997. She looks amazing.

Straight away when she cops me, it's like, 'What are you doing here?' as in she's not a happy bunny to see me?

I'm like, 'Er, hello? It's, like, Ron Black's, Sorcha – in other words a public place,' and then – possibly a bit childish this – I let my eyes sweep the bor, then I go, 'A few familiar faces in here, it has to be said.'

'Hordly surprising,' she goes. 'You went through my year like a pathogen,' which is bang out of order, I'm pretty sure, even if I haven't got an Eliza Dushku what it means.

Did I mention that she looks amazing?

'I suppose you've heard the rumours,' I go. 'I'm thinking of going back playing rugby,' but she turns her head, roysh, refusing to meet my stare. Then she's there, 'Ross – don't do this.'

I'm like, 'As in Blackrock. Or maybe even Clontorf. Well, their thirds,' and she goes quiet for, like, 10, maybe 15 seconds, then she's like, 'That one's not going to work anymore, Ross. I've grown up. It's about time you did, too.'

So now I'm suddenly having one of my world-famous intellectual moments. 'Looking back,' I go,

'I'm like, "You gave them everything, including my Z4. Have you any idea what an actual dickhead you are?"' Ross O'Carroll-Kelly's Da goes down . . . as seen by Alan Clarke.

'our problem was we both wanted, like, different things out of life?' and, quick as a flash, she's there, 'Yeah, I wanted to abide by the vows we made on our wedding day, you wanted to have sex with our daughter's nanny.'

It's like, woah, of course it's going to sound bad if you put it like that.

I go to put my orm around her but she swats it away, roysh, with the force of a woman who's been playing tag rugby for most of the summer. 'Oh my God,' she goes, 'you actually need to get over yourself, you know that?' and she storms off, roysh, and of course every set of mince pies is suddenly looking at me, so I just, like, roll my eyes, as if to say, you can't talk to them when they're like that, can you?

I turn back to the bor, order another pint of the Dutch stuff and the next thing I hear is a bird's voice going, 'Hi, Ross.'

It's Ellie Banaher, as in Ellie who played the lyre in the joint production we did of *Annie Get Your Gun*. Or was it the bassoon?

I've had my sweaty way with her once or twice down through the years. She has a great boat race, it has to be said – a bit like Tea Leoni – but the bod wouldn't be the Rory Best; we're talking two breasts short of a dinner box.

I'm there, 'Ellie, how the hell are you?' which of course isn't a question, roysh, it's a figure of speech, but all of a sudden she's going, 'Aportment, job, cor . . .' and she's counting these things off on her fingers. When she reaches her fourth finger – her ring finger – she wiggles it at me, showing off a diamond that's probably visible from space, and she goes, 'Engaged – and we've been on three holidays this year . . .'

I'm thinking, that's the thing about these

school reunions – you ask a simple question and you end up getting a PowerPoint presentation.

Suddenly, Sorcha's stood on a high stool, with a microphone in her hand, going, 'Can everyone hear me?' and immediately there's, like, total silence in the bor.

'Thank you all so much for coming,' she goes. 'It's hord to believe that it's 16 years since we entered into Mount Anville, all young girls unsure of ourselves and our place in the world. Today, we gather as adults and it's great to see that every-one's looking so well and doing so well for themselves . . .' Everyone claps.

She goes, 'I, for instance, have a beautiful baby girl and I'm running my own fashion boutique in the Powerscourt Townhouse Centre, with exclusive Love Kylie, Chloe and Rock and Republic lines . . .'

Not a Charlie Bird about getting married to yours truly, of course. Probably doesn't want to have to go into the whole separation thing.

'Last year I met one of my all-time heroes – apart from obviously Aung San Suu Kyi and Ken Saro Wiwa – and that was Stella McCartney . . .' Another round of applause – you can see why she was head girl now. They lap this kind of stuff up.

'We were very lucky to have a year in which everyone got on so well and it's no surprise that so many of us have stayed in contact with each other. I really value my friendships from my time in school, as I'm sure all of you do.

'A couple of girls have e-mailed apologies, which I promised I'd read out. Bryana Kavanagh says, "Sorry, I can't be there tonight. But just to let you know, I'm doing really, really well in event

Excited and waiting for Björk in the audience at the Electric Picnic rock festival in Stradbally, Co. Laois.
Photograph: Kate Geraghty.

management and I'm going out with a really nice guy for three years." And Sarah Moore says, "Hi, everyone. Sorry I can't make it. I'm actually writing this e-mail sitting on a yacht in the Mediterranean, drinking a strawberry daiquiri. I've lost two stone since most of you saw me last . . .'" That gets another clap.

Then Sorcha's like, 'Oh, and just to remind everyone – we've booked Fitzers for nine, so we should all stort making our way there in, like, half an hour. Thank you.' When she's finished, roysh, she makes a beeline for me, presumably to ask me to leave. But she doesn't. What she actually says is sorry.

'I was way horsh,' she goes. 'Just because we've broken up doesn't mean we can't be civil to each other. And I know this is a majorly stressful time for you – how are you feeling about it?'

I'm like, 'Pretty confident actually – providing Drisco's fit for the Orgentina game . . .'

She's there, 'I meant your dad's trial, Ross. The sentencing is tomorrow, isn't it?'

I'm like, 'Oh – yeah,' and I'm about to tell her, roysh, that I hope they throw the key away, that he can, like, rot in prison for all I basically care, when out of the blue she goes, 'Dad said he saw you at the Berkeley Court auction. He said you bought your dad's favourite stool.'

I can feel my face suddenly redden and she kisses me on the cheek and tells me that that was, like, such a sweet thing to do.

★★★★★★

The end comes unbelievably quickly. His barrister – his new barrister, who actually doesn't look that much older than me – basically holds his hands up and goes, okay, my client admits basically everything, but please go easy on him and shit?

'Listen to that cloying sycophant,' Hennessy goes. He's sitting next to me in the public gallery. 'Oh, yes, he's going all the way to the top, that one – tongue up all the right holes in the Law

Library . . .' Hennessy would never have let the old man plead guilty, which is why the old man dropped him like honours physics.

At four o'clock on day two of the so-called trial, the judge tells the old man to stand up, which he does.

'Charles O'Carroll-Kelly,' he goes, 'whatever private beliefs you hold, the crimes of which you are guilty were not victimless crimes. As a property developer, you paid bribes in order to subvert the proper planning process and you did it in the name of greed. Most of your developments went ahead against the wishes and better advice of local authority planners, whose job it was to ensure a sensible and balanced growth for the city and county of Dublin. In doing so, you helped to create a legacy of social problems in many of the city's poorer areas . . .' Oh my God, if they're going to blame him for Ranelagh, he's going to end up getting life here.

'Your systematic evasion of tax was part of a general culture of avoidance, which deprived the Irish economy of billions of euros per annum, starving public services such as schools and hospitals of money . . .'

It goes without saying that Ronan's loving this. He's sat beside me, roysh, turned around in his seat, telling total strangers that that's his granddad up there in the dock, and that if he'd named names he'd be sleeping in his own bed tonight, but he didn't. 'He kept that shut,' he goes, pointing to his mouth. 'First rule of the underwurdled . . .'

'In sentencing you,' the judge goes, 'I must give due regard to your cooperation in this matter. Once some measure of corruption was discovered, you came clean, saving the Garda thousands of man-hours following the complex paper trail that constituted your personal finances for the best part of your life. I note, too, that you have been an exemplary remand prisoner and the Governor and staff of Mountjoy jail have been lavish in their praise of the leadership role you have assumed amongst your fellow prisoners. You have started, I understand, a prison rugby team, helping at least four long-term heroin addicts to achieve complete withdrawal from soccer.

'I hope that, upon your release, you will continue to work with those who have never enjoyed the same privileges as you and that this work will be part of your reparation to the community . . .

'However, given the scale of your dishonesty – and in particular your abuse of public office – I am going to impose a custodial sentence. And that sentence is two-and-a-half years' imprisonment. You look like you have something to say, Mr O'Carroll-Kelly,' and everyone, like, suddenly sits forward in their seats.

And all the old man goes – the only words he speaks in two days sitting there – 'With respect, Your Honour, it would be wrong to interpret my – inverted commas – co-operation with the Criminal Assets Bureau and the Revenue Commissioners as an indicator of remorse on my part. I feel none. Thank you . . .'

And then it's back to the can with him. As he's being led away, Ronan shouts, 'Don't worry about it, Charlie – we'll boorst you out of there,' and everyone in the courtroom just, like, cracks up laughing, obviously thinking it's a joke.

Outside, I notice the goys – we're talking Oisinn, JP and Fionn. Nice of them to turn up. And they're talking to someone. A bird. And I'd know that €2,000 Emilio Pucci kaftan anywhere. It's Sorcha. I tip over. It's like, a hug from my estranged wife and high-fives from the goys.

'Result, dude!' JP goes. 'With remission, and the time he's already served, the goy'll be out for Chrimbo.'

'And that stool,' Sorcha goes, 'will make – oh my God – such an amazing present.'

I'm there, 'Right now, I'm torn between giving it to him, to see the happiness on his face, and smashing it up with a hammer.'

Sorcha's like, 'That's, like, the perfect metaphor for your life, Ross.'

And of course I'm going to have to Google the word later on, but I still nod like I know what she means.

MONDAY, 3 SEPTEMBER 2007

Star-Struck Limerick Gone in 60 Seconds as Kilkenny Dictate the Script

Seán Moran, at Croke Park
Kilkenny 2-19 Limerick 1-15

For a few moments you could have been tempted to believe. In the match preliminaries the Limerick support made itself heard in a great, ravenous roar, baying for a performance to match their expectation and hunger.

But they were silenced by a powerful display from Kilkenny, whose quality and undimmed desire turned yesterday's Guinness All-Ireland hurling final into a rubber-stamping of the champions' status as the preeminent team in modern hurling.

Brian Cody's side now stand on the threshold of the century's first three-in-a-row and the supplanting of Cork at the top of the game's roll of honour.

It was almost as if they understood they had to defuse any sense of possibility and prevent the predominantly Limerick crowd from breathing further life into their county's challenge. Clinically and ruthlessly, the champions killed the match within 10 minutes and with it any hope the underdogs might have nurtured.

Goals from Eddie Brennan and Henry Shefflin in the space of a minute created a buffer between the teams, which was never significantly rolled back. Any time Limerick made inroads Kilkenny pushed them back to six points and frequently beyond. Hurler of the Year-elect Tommy Walsh had another rousing match, rounding off a typically dynamic defensive display with two points.

It was such an assured and commanding performance from the champions that, without their composure being ruffled, they could afford to lose first Noel Hickey, the full back aggravating a hamstring, and then captain Shefflin, who had to go off at half-time with a suspected cruciate injury.

The depth of the panel's strength was on full view as adjustments were made all the way through the spine of the team, centre back Brian Hogan reverting to full back and centrefielder Derek Lyng moving up to centre forward. They took it all in their stride and continued to absorb everything Limerick could devise and calmly keep the scoreboard ticking over, always that bit too far ahead of their battling but outgunned opponents.

For the match to ignite Limerick needed the good start but instead, just as in 2000 and 2002, it was Kilkenny who set about the underdogs in the opening minutes. As a statement of intent the team's top goal-scoring threats, Brennan and Shefflin, were positioned from the start in the full-forward line and with virtually immediate results.

In the ninth minute, with the champions already two ahead, James Fitzpatrick's lineball floated to Brennan, who rounded Séamus Hickey and stuck in the first goal. Within a minute Shefflin went up for a high ball, wrestled his way around Lucey and popped up the *sliotar* before somehow managing to get his hurl to it and bat home the second goal with all the finality of nailing the top onto a coffin.

Limerick had paid the price for lack of caution at the start. Instead of dropping back to limit space in the opening minutes and keep the match in the balance until they had settled – and certainly to prevent what happened happening so early – they hurled man on man and failed to impact up front while shipping 2-3 in the opening 11 minutes.

Kilkenny captain Henry Shefflin scores his team's second early goal against Limerick during the All-Ireland senior hurling final at Croke Park. Photograph: Dara Mac Dónaill.

And when Donie Ryan dropped back from corner forward the net effect was simply to leave Jackie Tyrrell looking like he was on a driving range, pumping ball all the way back down the field, as he held his position in splendid isolation.

Limerick's defence, like the team in general, battled hard but could not cope with the switching and work rate of the Kilkenny forwards. Lucey actually beat Shefflin to the first couple of balls but such was the pressure exerted on the backs that clearances were frequently fired out blindly only to be reclaimed by a striped shirt.

Mark Foley dug out ball, particularly in the second half, but in the difficult circumstances was rarely allowed much time to pick his shots. On the other wing Peter Lawlor was in so much bother with Eoin Larkin, who hit four points in the first half, that he certainly wasn't able to maintain his recent standard of supply into Limerick's danger man Andrew O'Shaughnessy.

Lawlor was more on top of things in the second half but by then the damage was done and O'Shaughnessy, whose afternoon began ominously with a free dropped short, had been switched out to the half forwards in an attempt to get him into the game and away from Tyrrell, who had marked him firmly the odd time anything got through.

It was Séamus Hickey who had the most torrid experience, Brennan giving the teenage defender a lesson in the harsh realities of life at this level and bringing to a chastening end what had been an impressive season for the young hurler, who also took much physical punishment, though his block on Brennan in the 24th minute turned a certain goal into a point.

Led by Ollie Moran, Limerick eventually got into the match but the two goals always stood there like reinforced gates shutting out realistic hopes of a comeback. After the goals had gone in, Limerick managed to get the deficit to dip inside six points for all of an accumulated three minutes.

Aside from the pressure at the back Limerick were in bother in too many other places. Centrefield struggled to limit the influence of Fitzpatrick, who provided intelligent service to the forwards. Brian Begley was well off his semi-final form and Limerick hardly got anything off his imposing presence on the edge of the square. Noel Hickey ruled him with an iron rod and by the time the Kilkenny full back had to leave the field, Begley had been moved out to the wing. He had no better luck with Brian Hogan, whose centre-back duties were taken by John Tennyson.

The half-time lead of eight, 2-10 to 0-8, was complemented by statistics showing that Kilkenny had shot 12 out of 14 chances and received – much to their at-times-justified disgruntlement – only two frees against 10 for Limerick. Shefflin didn't reappear after the break and the match had a loose quality throughout the second period. Early points from O'Shaughnessy, whose dead-ball striking was reliable after the early lapse, and replacement Niall Moran gave Limerick a good start but Richie Power – introduced for Willie O'Dwyer, whose failure to make more of an impact on Mark Foley resulted in summary replacement in less than half an hour – trumped that with three frees in the following seven minutes.

Ollie Moran's goal in the 47th minute capped a fine year and a hugely admirable display in difficult circumstances. Off a break from Begley, Moran rammed home the goal but it came at a stage when the deficit had stretched to nine.

A glimmer of hope shimmered in the last 10 minutes when Niall Moran had a chance to cut the margin to four and maybe ignite the crowd but blazed wide, and straight away Power popped one over at the other end to restore the all but inescapable six-point margin. Brennan exuberantly flashed an injury-time point for a seven-point win to break the bookies' handicap and a 1-5 personal tally. The whistle went shortly afterwards but the match had been over for a long time by then.

KILKENNY: 1. P.J. Ryan; 2. M. Kavanagh; 3. N. Hickey; 4. J. Tyrrell; 5. T. Walsh (0-2); 6. B. Hogan;

7. J.J. Delaney; 8. D. Lyng; 9. J. Fitzpatrick (0-1); 10. E. Brennan (1-5); 11. H. Shefflin (1-2, one free); 12. E. Larkin (0-4); 13. W. O'Dwyer; 14. M. Comerford; 15. A. Fogarty (0-1). Subs: 17. J. Tennyson for Hickey (23 mins); 23. M. Fennelly for Shefflin (half-time); 25. R. Power (0-4, three frees) for O'Dwyer (27). Yellow card: J. Fitzpatrick (36).

LIMERICK: 1. B. Murray; 2. D. Reale; 3. S. Lucey; 4. S. Hickey; 5. P. Lawlor; 6. B. Geary; 7. M. Foley; 8. D. O'Grady (0-2); 9. M. O'Brien; 10. M. Fitzgerald (0-1); 11. O'Moran (1-3); 12. S. O'Connor (0-1); 13. A. O'Shaughnessy (0-7, six frees, one 65); 14. B. Begley; 15. D. Ryan. Subs: 21. N. Moran (0-1) for O'Brien (half-time); 22. J. O'Brien for O'Connor (45 mins); 26. M. O'Riordan for Lawlor (68); 29. K. Tobin for Ryan (58); 30. P. Tobin for Fitzgerald (49). Yellow card: B. Geary (18).

Attendance: 82,127.

Referee: Diarmuid Kirwan (Cork).

TUESDAY, 4 SEPTEMBER 2007

The Only 'Wicked' One in the Family

Give Me a Break, by Kate Holmquist

While her husband and stepsons were playing their enduring roles in the sugary-pink Diana hagiography-fest last Friday, what was Camilla doing? Having a lie-in? Grooming her horses? Hiding away in pampered exile watching the coverage on Sky and asking herself why all the love she's poured into Charles, William and Harry still isn't enough to redeem her?

I doubt she was crying her eyes out, but still – it really is thankless being a stepmother. It's the only family title that comes with its own adjective: wicked. No matter how hard she tries, the step-mother is never going to make the grade. Her stepchildren are afraid to love her wholeheartedly because to do so is to betray their sainted mother, and the world sees her as a whore because – justifiably or not – she tore those vulnerable children from their mother's breast, what with access at weekends and so on. When the mother is dead, the stepmother seems to be usurping her role.

William and Harry wanted 'Milla' at the memorial service but with typical emotional unintelligence, Queen Elizabeth thought it best that Camilla decline the invitation. That wicked stepmother had to be shunned out of respect for the dead – a strange sort of respect that the queen had difficulty demonstrating when Diana was alive. It's unhealthy for any of us to keep seeing Diana as a wronged saint, when she was just another sinning human being, no better or worse than the rest of us.

The queen's advice struck me as particularly cruel because when I heard the news, I was in the throes of meeting my latest stepmother-in-waiting. We were on Cape Cod and I recall turning off CNN and getting all jolly about scooping out dishes of ice cream as a distraction. Those of us who have to deal with step-families in real life don't need people telling us that stepmothers are second-class family members.

Like other families, we have our own Diana, my mother who died 27 years ago. So we know what it's like to lose not just a mother, but also a grandmother who died too young to become one. Because there have been a few women in my dad's life since, my children and I know that a relationship with a stepmother/stepgrandmother is different to that with a mother/grandmother. It can be enriching and delightful – as well as confusing and painful.

We should really talk about it more, instead of pushing stepmothers onto the fringes of family life. Stepmothers in my peer group don't speak about their stepchildren very much – as though they're afraid of putting a foot wrong and upsetting whatever precarious balance they've achieved.

Ballsbridge resident Anne Collins in the Berkeley Court Hotel in Dublin when developer Seán Dunne displayed plans for his proposed redevelopment of the Jurys Ballsbridge/Berkeley Court site, including a 37-storey tower. Photograph: Brenda Fitzsimons.

Meanwhile, their efforts to forge healthy relationships with their stepchildren are unsung – maybe because stepmothers are buying into the shame around their wicked role and are afraid to boast.

Loving somebody else's kids – not to mention noisy grandkids – is hard. It's not the selfless, knee-jerk sort of love that comes from infant-mother bonding. When you're a stepmother, you really get to know your partner's kids and grandkids warts and all and decide to love them anyway. That's a strong sort of love. It grows out of action, rather than irrational fidelity.

My latest almost-stepmother (she and my dad are engaged but haven't set a date yet) made it clear from the beginning that she wanted to be a friend rather than a mother figure. The first thing she said

– after opening her arms for the first in a series of irresistible mother-bear hugs – was: 'I've been thinking about this. I want you all to call me Agnes.' So Agnes it is. And what a woman – 65 going on 25 and delighted to be blooming at her age after a lifetime of experience that she recounted with honesty and humour.

Agnes's approach was: 'Take me as I am.' We know what makes her happy (good food, great stories, sunshine and swimming) and we know what freaks her out (tantrums, wasting food). No hidden agendas there. She's an old-fashioned Lady and I reckon my kids could use a bit of that. And she adores my father, even though they had separate bedrooms – how cute is that?

Every family has its queen with the power to embrace or shun – even though others may resent it. This is probably why Agnes confessed that before meeting me she was terrified. I wondered what my father had been telling her, until I realised that Agnes was channelling the collective uncon- scious disapproval that we have of stepmothers. Or maybe my dad truly does think I'm a dreadful old harridan. I don't mind, really.

I hope there's a big wedding, because I'm looking forward to meeting my new stepsister (in addition to the previous steps and halves I wish I knew better). She's a nurse who lives near LA and has two kids the same ages as mine and is married to a cinematographer whose name I'll be looking out for in film credits from now on. That's the strange thing about newly reformed families, a lot of us have half-siblings and 'steps' we've scarcely met. But that's OK.

In step-families, the expectations are realistic. Biological families promise unconditional love even when they don't deliver. 'Steps' want to love you in their way even though they hardly know you, which is as good as it gets these days when so many of us are redefining what family means.

FRIDAY, 7 SEPTEMBER 2007

King of the High Cs Shared His Love of Singing and of Life

Michael Dervan

Luciano Pavarotti was in every sense a larger than life individual. There was that voice, unmistakable, ringingly clear, and with a command at the top of the range that fully warranted the moniker 'King of the high Cs'.

There was the Pavarotti bulk, so large in later life that he hardly moved in performance, and his con- certs were arranged so that he wouldn't even have to walk across the stage in front of the orchestra. There were the outrageous stories, about, for instance, his having the full staff of an Italian restaurant travel with

him to China for a performance in Beijing. There were his notorious tax problems in his native Italy, the last of which dragged on for years, leaving him with the threat of jail if he lost. There was the celebrity-style gossip about his private life, a snap on the beach with a former secretary, leading to divorce, remarriage and a second family. Wherever he went, whatever he did – whether he sang or whether he cancelled, whether he was on form or out of voice – Pavarotti was major news.

When I was young it was not really possible to move in musical circles in Ireland without hearing about the singer's important Irish connections. He sang for the Dublin Grand Opera Society (as Opera Ireland was then called) in 1963. And it was in *Rigoletto* in Dublin he was spotted and hired by Covent Garden's Joan Ingpen as a cover for an upcoming *La Bohème*. The Rodolfo for that bohème, Giuseppe di Stefano, cancelled, Pavarotti replaced him, and the rest, as they say, is history.

Most versions of this story have Pavarotti's Irish debut placed in Dublin. But, as John Allen wrote in *Music Ireland* magazine on the occasion of the singer's RDS concert in April 1990, the great tenor had preceded his Dublin debut with per- formances in *Madama Butterfly* in Belfast, and in Dundalk he sang in a concert with piano.

And the truth of his Irish debut may be even stranger than that. Legend has it that he first appeared on an Irish stage in Cork, at the choral festival of 1957, in his father's choir, the Corale Gioachino Rossini di Modena, which took the prize for male voice choirs that year.

When I was a music student, Pavarotti was a name frequently invoked to demonstrate the quality of casting that was to be found in the glory days of the Dublin Grand Opera Society. But that was the past, and the only way to hear his voice in Ireland was on record or on radio. Or, of course, you could travel to hear a performance abroad.

It didn't take Pavarotti long in the 1960s to become both a big name opera singer and a major recording star. He was a luminary of the Decca

Russian group Derevo's one-off performance in George's Dock in Dublin during the opening of the Fringe Festival. Photograph: Cyril Byrne.

stable, establishing famous partnerships with sopranos Joan Sutherland and Mirella Freni. But it took the use of his recording of *Nessun Dorma* for the 1990 World Cup, and the famous Three Tenors concert associated with that event, to launch him to megastardom.

I can remember a claim in the late 1980s that the early music band, the Academy of Ancient Music, had actually sold more records than the King of the High Cs. Within a year or two, that claim was history. The Essential Pavarotti became a top-selling album, not just in classical terms, but in pop terms. His personal success, and the success of the Three Tenors as a marketing tool, changed the face of classical music within the record industry.

His achievements were instrumental in turning executives' heads, and leading them to seek out ways of emulating the phenomenal sales he had

achieved. The scale of the Pavarotti fever can be gauged from the fact that his 1990 Dublin concert grossed more than €800,000, an amount for a single performance which at the time would have comfortably exceeded the annual box office takings of both the Abbey and Gate theatres.

Talk to the *aficionados* and you'll hear that he was not much of an actor on the operatic stage, that Plácido Domingo is a much more refined performer, a deeper and more profound musician, that the tenors of an earlier age had skills and insights that Pavarotti never mastered.

The truth, I think, is he had such a wealth of talent, a kind of natural ease and *savoir faire* that, combined with a voice of unique appeal, allowed people to take his achievements for granted, as if he had never had to work and train in order to sing so well.

He had the kind of personality that, for whatever reason, a mass audience simply related to without any difficulty whatsoever. His trademark gesture, a white hankie held aloft, was corny in the extreme. The thing about star quality is that it makes its own rules. In almost every way, Luciano Pavarotti did that, and his public loved him for it. He gave the impression of enjoying singing and enjoying life, and did it in a way that helped other people enjoy singing and enjoy life through him.

MONDAY, 10 SEPTEMBER 2007

'We Got Worse as the Game Went On'

Johnny Watterson, in Bordeaux

No doubt about it. Eddie O'Sullivan performed better in the media centre than his team did last night in a balmy Bordeaux night. The amateurs against the professionals fell the way of Ireland – the professionals – but the Namibian lap of honour was the most well received move of the evening. It was a *mea culpa*, or a collective version of it, from the Irish camp. There were no excuse, no ifs and no next times.

Then O'Sullivan put his metaphorical hands in the air and gave the most critical conference of his career to date. 'It was probably like watching a horror movie out there. It was our worst performance for a long time, very, very poor,' said the Irish coach. 'I expected us to be a little bit edgy in the first 20 minutes being the first game of the tournament but actually we got worse as the game went on. At half-time we talked about doing the basic things right and we didn't. We made an enormous number of unforced errors. All in all a very disappointing performance.'

Although the win arrived and Ireland scored their four bonus points to keep them in contact with the competition, the performance fell far from what the Irish side were expecting. For such a go-

forward coach, O'Sullivan found it difficult to see any positives.

'Winning the game, I suppose,' he said disconsolately. 'And getting the bonus point . . . At end of the day there is very little really. It's our worst performance that I can remember, for a long, long time. I certainly can't think of one as bad as that . . . We won the game and got the bonus point. I suppose its something but not much in the context of this World Cup.'

Just what he said at half-time when the sides went in was of some interest. But what was said was clearly not carried onto the pitch for the final 40 minutes as Ireland slid further into a hole.

'I asked them not to make the unforced errors they were making, to try and play some phases. I asked them to make some plays and stop allowing the mistakes creep in . . . But we didn't do that. We actually went on to make more errors in the second half. I think a bit of it is that maybe we forced things that were not on. That's down to the players making those decisions and we certainly didn't get that part of the game right tonight.

'I think our preparation is another day's work,' added the coach. 'We need to look at how we got to this level and up our performance. We've got to make sure our performance is a hell of a lot better next time. Georgia are a better side from what I've seen of them. We could come out on the wrong side of a result if we don't improve.'

Just how that will happen may be a mystery. Ireland have underperformed against Scotland and Italy and now Namibia. 'We can start by not making basic errors in losing the ball in contact or throwing it around loosely. I'm dreading looking at that. If you look at where we were in the Six Nations and now there is a big gap. It's getting refocused on the things we do well and get them right. We thought we had it right tonight but we didn't. We got it badly wrong.'

Hurt? Beat up? O'Sullivan was asked. 'Probably their egos were bruised more than their bodies,' he replied.

Ronan O'Gara and Brian O'Driscoll downcast after Ireland's stuttering World Cup Pool D win over Namibia in Bordeaux. Photograph: Inpho/PressSport.

WEDNESDAY, 12 SEPTEMBER 2007

Wall Joins 'Wads of Money' Roll of Honour

Miriam Lord

The planning tribunal has established an honourable tradition of key witnesses taking the stand to tell hilarious stories of how they happened to give large sums of money to politicians, while simultaneously failing to understand why ordinary people might not be inclined to believe them. Yesterday after-noon in Dublin Castle, the millionaire former owner of a Manchester bus company joined that dubious roll call of the Strangely Forgetful Financially Successful.

Michael Wall insists he is telling the truth when he explains how he took a notion to do a partial clear-out of the cash in his safe, stuck it in a briefcase, came over to Ireland, called to see the serving minister for finance, plonked a surprise £28,000 or so in used notes and different curren-cies on his desk and then walked away without as much as a receipt.

He stresses he is telling the truth when he says this serving minister for finance in a proud first world nation, days before he expects to be elevated to the position of prime minister, accepted without question the aforementioned wads of money, even though he had no prior notice that it was coming.

And he says he is telling the truth when he says he doesn't know the exact amount of cash he actually handed over to the serving minister for finance who expected to be taoiseach within four days. 'He didn't count it. I didn't count it.' As you do.

Bertie Ahern just said 'Okay' and took it away into a back room.

If ever there was a case for televising the Mahon tribunal, it was made yesterday. We were back to the halcyon days of the inquiry, when witnesses like the Bailey brothers and the Brennan and McGowan boys had the gallery in stitches with their wonderful yarns explaining how they selflessly disbursed money in the national interest to people like Ray Burke.

In the case of Michael Wall, it seems the urgency with which he rushed to financially assist Bertie was prompted, not by a love of the democratic process, but by the critical need to stick up a new conservatory on the back of a house that Ahern was about to rent from him.

Before we go any further, let us emphasise, as Wall did more than once, that he did not 'give' this lucky bag of mixed notes to Ahern. God, no. He 'made it available'.

Michael Wall first met Bertie Ahern in the late 1980s, when he was boss of a thriving coach hire business in Manchester and involved in promoting Irish tourism. The two men met regularly from then on. 'I would class him as a close friend,' said Wall. He also regarded the Taoiseach's then partner, Celia Larkin, as a close friend. While he says he is still a friend of Ms Larkin, they haven't spoken in two years – or since she split from the Taoiseach. The businessman remarked 'she's no longer in the circle' – otherwise known colloquially as 'The Drumcondra Mafia'.

Fast forward to the early 1990s, and Michael Wall is considering setting up a coach hire business in Dublin.

He discusses this with Bertie, and says he'll have to find a base in Dublin. Lo and behold, but isn't Bertie looking for 'accommodation' too.

They reach an agreement. Michael will buy a house. Bertie, struggling on his ministerial salary, will rent it from him with an option to eventually purchase, and his friend will be able to stay with him when he is in town. Michael leaves it to the minister and Celia to source a suitable property.

A nice house in Drumcondra comes on the market. Michael agrees to buy it. But Bertie, described last year by John O'Donoghue as 'a simple and frugal man' when the story of his unusual financial affairs hit the headlines, didn't want to rent any old luxury four-bedroom house on an exclusive estate in an upmarket part of Drumcondra.

Tribunal witness Wall explained: 'Mr Ahern mentioned a property that was suitable for him, but he mentioned a conservatory and other alterations which I expected a man in his position would want, and I said "no problem".'

Understandable, perhaps. He is the minister for finance, about to fulfil a lifelong dream and become taoiseach.

If he's learned anything from Charlie Haughey, he knows he has to acquire a conservatory and luxury drapes or risk becoming the laughing stock of Europe! Otherwise, what would Mrs Mitterrand say? Bertie had to get his priorities right.

On 29 November, Mr Wall's tender for the house – IR£138,000 is accepted. (Sale to include curtains, carpets and blinds.) This is a serendipitous turn of events, as the businessman is to attend Bertie's annual Christmas fundraiser just three days later. He tells the tribunal he had no idea when he attended that function that the entire country expected his close friend to become taoiseach four days later, on 6 December.

Nobody predicted the way events would turn out – Fine Gael's John Bruton became accidental

Michael Wall (centre, with beard) leaving the Mahon tribunal in Dublin Castle. Photograph: Cyril Byrne.

taoiseach when Bertie's hopes were cruelly dashed by Labour's Dick Spring.

Blissfully ignorant of the delicate political situation, but mindful of the pressing need for to get Bertie a conservatory, Michael Wall took 'a ballpoint pen figure' of around stg£30,000 sterling from his safe at home in Manchester and put it in a briefcase with the intention of giving it to the minister.

On the Friday night of the fundraiser, he stayed in the Ashling Hotel. He took IR£2,000 spending money from the briefcase for his evening out, and kept a bit more back for his return trip to Manchester. He left the briefcase in the wardrobe and went off for his 'Christmas treat'.

Whatever was left, something in the region of stg£28,000, he gave to Bertie, in the presence of Celia Larkin, the next day. And the minister for finance's and Celia's reaction when Michael opened his briefcase and took out the conservatory money?

'No particular reaction whatsoever.' Henry Murphy, counsel for the tribunal, was nonplussed. 'Were they surprised? Were they agog? Were they incredulous?' Mr Wall remained deadpan as he considered his answer. Then, through his bushy grey beard, which looks like a sporran transplanted onto his chin, he described their reactions.

'Normal.' Which, in the case of most men who are serving finance ministers and expecting to become prime minister in four days' time, would have been: 'Aaaargh! Get rid of that quick, for God's sake!'

Not so with Bertie.

And that's the truth.

FRIDAY, 14 SEPTEMBER 2007

Partners Taking Arnotts into New Territory

Barry O'Halloran

Arnotts chairman Richard Nesbitt is reportedly fond of telling how his great grandfather, Alexander, walked from the family farm in Co. Antrim to begin an apprenticeship at the Dublin department store. Hard work, and presumably good fortune, saw Alexander Nesbitt rise to the top at the company and ensured that his family didn't just run the business, it also became its longest-standing shareholder.

You get the feeling that Niall McFadden, executive chairman of Boundary Capital, which is soon to become Arnotts' newest shareholder, feels a degree of empathy with Alexander Nesbitt. While he didn't start out digging turnips in Antrim, he's still come a long way since he started doing business with Richard Nesbitt and Arnotts almost five years ago.

He's had a bit of good fortune too. The door opened for Boundary Capital just two weeks ago when Arnotts' other long-standing shareholder, the O'Connor family, sold their 24.57 per cent holding to Nesbitt for over €40 million in a move that ended an internal dispute.

This week, McFadden indicated that this gave Boundary the chance to come in, and both recapitalise the €40 million-plus spent by Richard Nesbitt – he personally paid for the O'Connor stake – and boost Arnotts' own coffers.

Boundary, in which McFadden is a 50 per cent shareholder with his partners, Declan Cassidy and Martin Cole, will have 28 per cent of Arnotts in return for €40 million. Anglo Irish Bank will hold 17 per cent in return for investing €25 million. The Nesbitt family, led by barrister and company chairman Richard, will hold 55 per cent.

McFadden made no secret of the fact that he was pleased with Boundary's good fortune. And it's unlikely that he expected things would turn out this way when he and Richard Nesbitt sat down for lunch one Saturday almost five years ago to discuss buying out the then Arnotts plc and converting it to a private company owned by the Nesbitts and the O'Connors.

At that point, McFadden's career had taken him from the Goodman meat processing empire to Tedcastles' fuels group and on to Hibernian Venture Capital. When he met Nesbitt, he was fresh from advising on the $376 million management buyout of another listed company, technology player Riverdeep. The Arnotts chairman, a practising barrister, was looking around for an adviser, and a mutual acquaintance recommended McFadden and Boundary to him.

They hit it off. Partly because McFadden was happy to do business on a Saturday, but largely because, as Nesbitt recalls, he was able to identify key issues facing the transaction before they had to be pointed out to him. It was the start of a beautiful business friendship. Once Arnotts went private, McFadden was appointed to its board. He took over as chair of its property committee and things started to motor, albeit in a direction that nobody expected.

Instead of offloading some assets, as most predicted, the department store group began buying them. First it purchased the old Independent Newspapers HQ, close to the flagship store on Dublin's Abbey Street. Then it plunged for a property portfolio belonging to Royal and Sun Alliance on Henry Street, also adjacent to Arnotts.

It was clear that McFadden was driving this, but very much with the support of his chairman. The O'Connors, and it emerged this week, some of the 800 workers, were beginning to worry that Arnotts was turning into a property developer instead of a retailer.

In some ways they weren't far off. McFadden and Nesbitt had a plan, which is now called the

Arnotts on Dublin's Henry Street . . . department store or second fiddle to property development scheme?
Photographs: Dara Mac Dónaill/Computer generated architectural drawing.

Northern Quarter. This calls for a wholesale re-development of an area bounded by O'Connell, Henry and Abbey streets into a 1.65 million square foot, mixed-used town centre with apartments, shops, a hotel, restaurants, cafés and bars.

It will cost €750 million to complete. Arnotts will own 80 per cent of it, and its development partner, British group Centros Miller, will hold 20 per cent. The concept hangs on two simple pegs: the area has the room to grow, which the competing Grafton Street shopping hub does not; and, most importantly, a lot of people go shopping around Henry Street.

And we mean a lot. Some 15,000 people an hour pass along O'Connell Street/Henry Street, which makes it the busiest in Europe, even busier than London's Oxford Street. Better still, this footfall, as it's known in the industry, has a high conversion rate. This means that a large proportion of passersby buy something. In other words, if you walk along Henry Street, that's footfall, if you drop into Arnotts and buy socks, that's conversion.

The project's official spokespeople do not have the actual rate, but Nesbitt indicated this week that it was over half, which is high by industry standards.

None of this has allayed fears expressed by some about Arnotts' future. This week, Linda Tanham, an official with retail union Mandate, which has 800 members in Arnotts, said many of them are worried that retailing is going to play second fiddle to property development. She is meeting management to put these concerns to them.

Arnotts says it is hiring Centros Miller precisely because it has expertise in managing the redevelopment of town centres, so thus, the department store group can focus on running its business (which will include an expanded flagship store). At the same time, it says Northern Quarter will be a separate company, so should the project fail, the core business will be protected. McFadden and Nesbitt are directors of Northern Quarter.

Not that either man is contemplating failure. With all shareholders now behind the project, and the planning permission falling into place, it's all systems go for construction to begin next year, and an opening set for 2012. It's from that point on that Nesbitt and McFadden will be proved right or wrong. Presumably, the acid test will be when someone walks from Antrim just to go shopping there.

Here Come the Brides

Mary Russell

By the time you read this, I will have a new daughter-in-law – Trace – and by tomorrow, she will have wed my daughter twice over.

It all goes back to last Christmas morning when Trace popped the question – for the fifth and absolutely the last time, she said firmly. The tactic worked: Freya accepted, the plans were set in motion and the wedding takes place this weekend in London.

Though it's nearly two years since the law in the UK made it possible for same-sex couples to legalise their relationship, the idea is still relatively new.

Take the language. Although we're all calling it a wedding, the legal term is 'civil partnership' and the whole event, spread over two days, takes place in two stages, with one part happening in the local registry office and the main part – the exchange of rings, the champagne, the speeches and the non-stop party bit – in the couple's garden. They'd have preferred to have the entire thing done there, but their garden is not a 'licensed civil partnership venue'.

And because they want some shape to the ceremony they've got a celebrant coming who will guide everyone through the whole thing. (The celebrant's other job is to do a Health and Safety check on the house and garden.) There's no aisle, but there's still the walk through the French windows across the grass and into the marquee – both dressed, of course, in all their finery. Each has confided in me as to what they are wearing and, although I'm not allowed to reveal details, suffice to say that both have, independently, chosen a colour not usually associated with weddings. And one at least will be wearing an outfit designed by someone whose name begins with the big A.

'Yes, I'm going to be the label queen,' announced Trace. Although there is one small problem: she's not looking forward to having to proceed down the aisle.

'That's what I can't bear,' she wailed. 'Everyone will be looking at me.' 'No they won't,' said Freya soothingly. 'They'll all be looking at me.' (That's my girl.) So, while Freya explained the running order to me, Trace sat out on the back doorstep, chain-smoking her roll-ups and feverishly working her palmtop game console.

'What's the matter out there?' I whispered. 'Nerves,' said Freya.

Nervous? Trace? Who whizzes round the kitchen in helmet, mouthguard and scarlet boxing gloves practising her hand chops and high kicks. 'I'm not nervous,' she said. 'But I thought we'd just do the business and then have a bit of a barbie in the back yard.' An Australian-Aboriginal, Trace believes that no party – wedding or otherwise – is complete without its barbie, and so, yes, they're having three. And a fire pit.

A lot of planning has gone into this. Trace took on the job of finding a celebrant, but the first website she contacted answered her phone call with a sort of drawn-out 'helloooo', which she found offensively English in some unexplained way, so she took her business elsewhere. Message: don't mess with Aussies if your accent doesn't fit.

Freya's job was to sort out the backroom team. In fact, the sisterhood has rowed in from all directions. One friend, who cooks for the House of Commons, is doing the food. Two others are

Mary Russell's daughter, Freya (left), and her partner, Trace, who cemented their relationship in a civil partnership ceremony. Photographs: Christian Sinibaldi.

doing the sound system and the lights. Others are providing spare beds. And not just the women. A former boyfriend of Freya's – from the old days – is running an unofficial taxi service.

But there's still the nitty-gritty. Can they get everyone into the marquee for a prompt 4 p.m. start? Freya's brother, arriving as a surprise from Australia, has already been given this task. But how will people know the plan of the day since few, if any, have been to a civil-partnership ceremony? Easy: on arrival, each guest will be given a welcoming card telling them exactly what's happening and when.

Will there be vows? Yes. Both Freya and Trace have written their own, and I know when they speak them to each other – that will be my damp tissue moment.

Choosing a reading required considerable research, since most on offer refer to heterosexual weddings. And they were all naff anyway, hetero or not, Freya reported.

Will there be music? Yes. When the celebrant gives me the nod, I have to pick up my sax and hit them with 'She Moved Through the Fair'.

No two weddings are the same, of course. In my own case, we met, fell in love, Ian proposed on the stroke of midnight one New Year's Eve and within six weeks we were married. He invested in a new shirt for the event but not a new suit – though he did splash out on a new one six months later when he was best man at someone else's wedding. Then, the night before the wedding, he lost the ring and the cheque I wrote for the celebratory drink bounced a week later.

My son's wedding in Australia was a red-carpet do with the couple's baby daughter as the guest of honour. My younger daughter, working as a sailor around the Caribbean, called one day to tell me she'd got married: 'Darling, married? Where?' I asked, thinking Barbados, Miami, New York maybe, 'Down by the railway station at Fort Lauderdale,' she replied.

Of course, the inevitable question is: why do it? Both Freya and Trace, independently, gave the same answer: 'Because now we can.' As simple as that, a celebration of equality.

But it's still worth recalling that gay and lesbian people have had to conceal their love for each other for centuries and have been marginalised and isolated as a result, as indeed many still are. As I write this, the press carries a story about a US Senator being hounded for his alleged homosexuality and another story which records the extent to which gay men in Zimbabwe are persecuted.

Here at least, the time has come and people are ready. 'Do I hear wedding bells ringing?' the florist asked Trace, and didn't bat an eye on learning yes but that there was no groom involved. Both workplaces have received the news with equanimity, and one is even giving a celebratory office party for the bride – and her bride.

Myself, I'm simply happy for the couple, recalling a vice-president of the World Bank who told me once: 'Love is like money – you take it wherever you can find it.' Except, being a banker, she said it the other way round.

And so the stage is set: the Aboriginal flag flies proudly over the House of Love, the barbies are firing up, the clothes are waiting to be put on and all I have to do is just stay off the champagne until I've performed my final duty, which is to make a speech – not more than five minutes long, I've been warned.

Then we have the wedding cake and the wedding song. No, I'm not allowed say what it is, but it's a mean number made famous by Dolly Parton and Kenny Rogers – and it's going to bring the marquee down.

FRIDAY, 14 SEPTEMBER 2007

Gloves off as Bertie is Dragged into Ring

Miriam Lord

'Hold me coat! Let me at 'em!' For the last couple of years, Bertie Ahern has been doing a passable imitation of the lion in The Wizard of Oz, dancing on the spot with his fists in the air, roaring 'Put 'em up! Put 'em up!' at his tormentors in Dublin Castle.

Very impressive it's been too. At every opportunity, the Taoiseach wailed about the Mahon tribunal tormenting him in private but refusing to enter the ring and take him on.

At every opportunity, he expressed his frustration at not being allowed to enter the witness box and tell everything. In letting matters drag on, and allowing rumour and innuendo against him gain currency, the tribunal was doing severe damage to his public and personal reputation, he complained.

Over the years, there was angry talk of witch-hunts and hidden agendas and smear campaigns and 'Lulus' waiting in the bushes to do him harm. As he put it himself yesterday while reading a statement at the start of his longed-for appearance in the witness box: 'it's the first opportunity in seven-and-a-half years of being tormented about these issues that I have had the chance to come before the justices.'

The tribunal, in the unwavering form of Senior Counsel Des O'Neill, spent the rest of the day framing its response. It was desperately tedious stuff, but legally necessary. That response can be summed up in six words: 'And whose fault is that, then?'

While the Taoiseach was winning headlines and sympathy with his cowardly lion routine, it turns out that the tribunal was gloved up and ready to go, but encountering severe difficulty enticing their witness out of his corner. It took them two-and-a-half years to do it, and enough correspondence from both sides to sink the Russian navy. In the end, they resorted to the legal equivalent of a block and tackle, hauling Bertie into the open with the threat of compelling him to attend a public hearing in order to get answers to specific questions.

The money in question, according to Bertie's explanations, related to the Drumcondra dig-out and Manchester whiparound, sensitively translated by the genteel souls in Dublin Castle as 'the good-will loans'. It also concerned money lodged in relation to the refurbishment of a house the Taoiseach intended to rent in 1994, with an option

A smiling and apparently relaxed Bertie Ahern leaving the Mahon tribunal. Photograph: Frank Miller.

to purchase, from Manchester businessman Michael Wall.

So far, so complicated. Although Bertie, a paid-up member of the Muddy Waters fan club, didn't seem to think so.

The chamber was packed, and in a state of high excitement, in advance of his appearance yesterday morning. The Taoiseach arrived about an hour ahead of time, smiling broadly and waving to the cameras. There was a large Garda presence, on the lookout for possible Lulus.

Very unusually, he was allowed read a statement before his cross-examination began. On familiar ground, Bertie read his 15-minute script, reiterating his innocence of any dodgy financial dealings during all his years of public life. He repeated the substance of press statements he issued in recent months, outlining details of his financial transactions. And he categorically denied ever dealing in dollars.

'It's a complete red herring,' said Bertie, who is already on the record deploring such tactics. 'People should stop throwing white elephants and red herrings at each other,' he once declared in the Dáil.

The tribunal hadn't expected him to make this statement, but allowed him to carry on with his successful pitch for the one o'clock news headlines. He threw some interesting new information into the mix, including the nugget that he engaged a banking expert, who has confirmed there is no evidence to substantiate a $45,000 transaction.

'My banking expert, chairman, is Paddy Strong, the former chief operating officer of Bank of Ireland Corporate Banking,' said Bertie, with no small hint of triumph. Move over Paddy the Plasterer, here comes Paddy the Banker.

He also clarified the confused story of the purchase of his home in Drumcondra. However, his addition of further, and hitherto unknown, detail only served to make the unorthodox story of how he got the house even more confusing.

Both Celia Larkin and Michael Wall said in evidence that Larkin sourced the house, Wall bought it, and rented it to Bertie with the intention he would eventually buy it from him. Which he did, two years later. The businessman only stayed there on about 20 nights in those two years.

As this was to be her home with her then 'life-partner', Celia wanted to build an extension to 44 Beresford. Bizarrely, Wall undertook to pay for it, giving Bertie £30,000 in cash for that purpose three months before purchase went through.

Ahern threw 50 grand of his own money into the refurbishment kitty for the relatively new four-bedroom semi-d. He transferred the sum into a new account opened by Larkin. All this happened on the weekend in December 1994 when he expected to become taoiseach. That's the big reason Bertie needed a proper house to live in.

In her evidence, Celia said she got stuck into 'administering the expenditure'. Then, in January, after things had gone pear-shaped for Bertie and he was leader of the opposition, he asked her to withdraw the £50,000 from the bank and give him the cash.

She was asked on Wednesday why he did that. 'Ask him,' was Celia's brusque reply. Chairman Alan Mahon asked her again. 'It was used on the house,' she said.

Yesterday, in Muddy Waters mode, her former partner said he had quickly changed his mind about buying the house. After suffering the disappointment of not being elected taoiseach, his need for suitable accommodation was no long pressing. He started looking actively at other houses.

Because he changed his mind, he decided to return Wall's £30,000, which is why he withdrew the £50,000 in January. In the end, he decided he didn't want to buy a new house at all.

Unfortunately, Michael Wall had an accident. Bertie and Celia went to visit him in Manchester, and it was decided to proceed with the original plan. Thus, Ahern wouldn't need to return the cash after all. This is all very strange. Neither Celia nor Michael mentioned Bertie's change of mind in their testimony.

And Bertie, having decided not to go ahead, and having withdrawn the payback money for his Manchester friend in January, didn't think to say anything to poor Michael, who was steaming ahead with the purchase of a house he didn't really need. And poor Celia was still consulting interior decorators and administering the expenditure. Bertie, as she said on Wednesday, never told her why he was withdrawing the fifty grand. She was under the impression it was to spend on the new decor.

Yet all the while, he had no intention of buying that dream house with his then life-partner.

Michael Wall exchanged contracts in February. Still no word from Bertie. The deal closed in late March. He now owns the house that Bertie doesn't want. Then he has his accident. It was around Easter, he confirmed on Tuesday.

Just as well that Bertie decided to stick with 44 Beresford after visiting his recuperating pal, because Michael was stuck with that house one way or the other.

This was the most exciting part of the day. The rest was spent putting the tribunal's tortuous correspondence with Ahern on the record. (Like when he tried to limit their trawl of his financial records to between 1989 and 1992, the period when the minister for finance didn't have any bank accounts.)

As the public gallery and press corps wilted, Deathly Des, unflappable as a concrete eagle on a gatepost, painstakingly went through the files. Bertie hardly opened his mouth for six hours.

But in the very last exchange of the day, he accepted that from October 2004 to April 2007, he never disclosed to the tribunal that the source of the lodgements in question came from foreign currency.

All the tribunal wanted from Bertie was a full reconciliation. They should have known it would be a tough task. Ask Celia Larkin.

Moira Cameron, the first woman to serve as a Yeoman Warder at the Tower of London, on show following her selection over five male candidates for a position as a Beefeater. Photograph: Cathal McNaughton/Press Association.

MONDAY, 17 SEPTEMBER 2007

Kerry Add Twists to Familiar Tale

Tom Humphries, at Croke Park

The house was full. It rained. The Gooch was sublime. Kerry won the All-Ireland football final. Suddenly yesterday the summer presented itself to us as just a sequence of glaring inevitabilities. Or if you are a Corkman, as a series of unfortunate events.

The game and Kerry's 35th title will be remembered less for the quality of the football than for the novelty of the goals Kerry scored. If that seems a harsh memorial for Kerry, who played brilliantly at times, and for Cork, who just deserve better, those are the breaks.

Kerry have so many All-Irelands that anything which distinguishes one title win from another must be pressed into play. This was their third title in four years, the first back-to-back win by any county since 1990, when Cork, led by Billy Morgan, did it. Kerry won by 10 clear points and have now won their last three All-Ireland titles by an aggregate of 31 points.

As a considered response to the revolution visited upon the game by Ulster counties in the earlier part of this decade that is quite a riposte. Football's leading franchise has re-established itself at the top of the game and Kerry now just compete with their own history when it comes to further motivation.

'We just started talking about the chance of three in a row in the dressing room next door,' said Paul Galvin, Kerry's extraordinary wing forward, within minutes of yesterday's game ending. 'That's what Kerry football is all about. Maybe it is time for a new dynasty in Kerry football. The greats are the greats but maybe we can create a new dynasty.'

Comparative assessments of Kerry's various dynastic eras will have to wait. This team, though buttressed by the experience and power of Darragh Ó Sé, whose eclipse of Nicholas Murphy was instrumental yesterday, are young and could take some satisfaction in winning yesterday with a brand new left wing to their defence.

They are young and have vacuum-packed so much experience into their lives it seems it would be harder to stop being dominant than to continue.

Colm Cooper is 24 and was playing in his fifth final yesterday. Kieran Donaghy is the same age and won his second successive medal. The third member of their full-forward line, Bryan Sheehan, is just 22. Frightening.

'There's still a lot in this Kerry team,' said captain Declan O'Sullivan, who at 23 years of age lifted the Sam Maguire for the second year in succession and won his third All-Ireland medal. 'There's still plenty to win.'

And how will it be won? O'Sullivan gave the answer when replying to a question about his feelings on creating his own little piece of history, the first man to lift the new Sam Maguire cup two years in succession.

'Yeah, a very proud moment,' he said, 'but it is all about the players one to 34, who have been training together to put back-to-back titles together. It comes down to work-rate and attitude and honesty.'

Work-rate. Attitude. Honesty. Everywhere in evidence yesterday. Probably it was all over midway through the first half when Cooper rose to contest a high ball with breathtaking bravery in front of the outrushing figure of Alan Quirke, the Cork goalkeeper. Quirke was bigger, taller and carrying more momentum and weight. The ball came off the Gooch's fist and flashed to the net. Cork looked winded, like men who had been sucker-punched.

It just got worse. That goal separated the teams at the break and Cork, whose every gamble seemed not to be working, went into the dressing room thanking the stars they still had enough chips left to play some more hands. Then Kerry came

Kerry's Kieran Donaghy signals his second goal as he celebrates with Colm Cooper during the All-Ireland senior football final at Croke Park. Photograph: Dara Mac Dónaill.

out and scored 1-4 without reply in the first seven minutes after the break. Gentlemen, please leave the casino.

The rout started with a goal of even more bizarre construction. Ger Spillane looked to have safe possession coming away from his goal. Quirke moved off his line and out to take a pass across the face of goal. Spillane had his pocket picked in what Kieran Donaghy, the thief, would later describe as a basic basketball steal. Donaghy looked up, saw the goal area evacuated of all life, practically paused to shake his head in disbelief, and deposited the ball for a goal.

Short of 36 minutes gone and people had a mind to head out and beat the traffic. Kerry, of course, had more work to be doing. Donaghy added a third goal when Quirke and his corner

back Michael Shields went for the same ball without consulting each other. Donaghy broke it, chased it down first and hit it on the turn into an empty net. Cork would lose by 10 points but at that moment it looked as if they would suffer a far greater humiliation.

They fought back briefly and perhaps hopelessly with a goal from substitute Daniel Goulding but had to endure a final quarter watching Kerry sending on a fleet of substitutes to testimonials of applause and cheering and Kerry players taking training-ground potshots, looking to add their names to the list of scorers.

It was an odd and slightly bizarre final, one which will haunt Cork for quite some time and will bear several retellings this winter in the heartlands of Kerry.

Index